Slavery and Race Relations in Latin America

Contributions in Afro-American and African Studies

Slavery and Race Relations in Latin America

Edited with an Introduction by
Robert Brent Toplin

Contributions in Afro-American and African Studies
Number 17

Greenwood Press
Westport, Connecticut • London, England

Library of Congress Cataloging in Publication Data

Toplin, Robert Brent, 1940-
  Slavery and race relations in Latin America.

(Contributions in Afro-American and African Studies,
no. 17)
  Includes bibliographical references.
  1. Slavery in Latin America—Addresses, essays,
lectures.   2.   Latin America—Race question—Addresses,
essays, lectures.   I.   Title.   II.   Series.
HT1052.5.T66   301.45'1'042098   74-286
ISBN 0-8371-7374-4

Library of Congress Catalog Card Number: 74-286
ISBN: 0-8371-7374-4

First published in 1974

Greenwood Press, a division of Williamhouse-Regency Inc.
51 Riverside Avenue, Westport, Connecticut 06880

Manufactured in the United States of America

Contents

Maps

Tables

Tables

Acknowledgments

This large-scale project could not have been completed without the academic leave time made possible through grants from the National Endowment for the Humanities, the American Philosophical Society, and Denison University. The generous assistance from these institutions is greatly appreciated. I also wish to thank the contributors to this volume who gave much time and labor to their own essays and to recommendations regarding the overall volume. Professor Frederick P. Bowser of Stanford University also gave very helpful recommendations and editorial suggestions. Finally, a note of appreciation is in order to Gail Lutsch, who offered valuable help in preparation of the maps.

Contributors

DAVID L. CHANDLER is a member of the Department of History at Brigham Young University. He was educated at Brigham Young University and Tulane University, where he completed a doctoral dissertation on the subject of health and slavery in New Granada. He is presently working on a demographic study of Colombian slaves.

ROBERT CONRAD teaches history at the University of Illinois, Chicago Circle. Educated at Columbia University, Professor Conrad has published articles on Brazilian slavery in the *Hispanic American Historical Review* and an essay on Brazilian historian João Capistano de Abreu in *Revista de Historia de América*. He is also author of *The Destruction of Brazilian Slavery, 1850-1888*.

ARTHUR F. CORWIN teaches history at the University of Connecticut. He studied at Trinity College, Dublin, the University of the Americas, and the University of Chicago. Professor Corwin's articles on poverty in Argentina, Mexican-American history, Spanish laws for the abolition of slavery, and Mexican emigration have appeared in the *Urban Affairs Quarterly*, the *Pacific Historical Review*, and Latin American journals. He is also the author of two books, *Contemporary Mexican Attitudes Toward Poverty, Population, and Public Opinion* and *Spain and the Abolition of Slavery in Cuba, 1817-1886*.

FLORESTAN FERNANDES taught at the University of São Paulo for many years as a member of the Department of Sociology. He also was visiting professor of sociology at the University of Toronto. Author of numerous books and arti-

xi

cles on slavery and race relations in Brazil, his major work, *The Negro in Brazilian Society*, has been translated and published in English by the Columbia University Press.

FRANKLIN W. KNIGHT teaches history at Johns Hopkins University. Educated at the University of the West Indies and the University of Wisconsin, he is the author of *Slave Society in Cuba During the Nineteenth Century* and a forthcoming work, *The African Dimension in Latin American Societies*.

JOHN V. LOMBARDI is associate professor of history and director of Latin American Studies at Indiana University. He completed his graduate education at Columbia University. Professor Lombardi's articles on slavery and manumission in Venezuela have been published in Latin American journals as well as the *Hispanic American Review* and *Agricultural History*. He also wrote *The Decline and Abolition of Negro Slavery in Venezuela, 1820-154*.

COLIN M. MACLACHLAN, a member of the Department of History at California State University, Long Beach, holds degrees from the University of the Americas, Long Island University, and UCLA. He has been a visiting lecturer at UCLA and a visiting professor at the University of California, Irvine. He has published wide-ranging studies on the Indian Directorate, Indian labor in the Amazon, and the "feminine mystique" in Brazil, and is the author of *Criminal Justice in Colonial Mexico*.

MARIANNE MASFERRER is executive director of Project HAND in New York City. She received her education at the College of New Rochelle and the University of Pittsburgh.

THOMAS G. MATHEWS is research professor at the Institute of Caribbean Studies, University of Puerto Rico. He holds degrees from Oberlin College and Columbia University. Specializing in Caribbean studies, Professor Mathews has written many articles about the region that appear in *The Hispanic American Historical Review*, *The Caribbean Historical Review*, *Current History*, and the *Encyclopedia Britannica*. He is also the author of *Puerto Rican Politics and the New Deal* and *Luiz Muñoz Marín, A Concise Biography*.

NORMAN A. MEIKLEJOHN is a member of the History Department at Assumption College. He was educated at S.T.L. Amgelicum, Rome, Georgetown University, and Columbia University. Professor Meiklejohn is presently working on a study of the legal profession in colonial Latin America.

CARMELO MESA-LAGO teaches economics at the University of Pittsburgh and is associate director of the university's Center for Latin American Studies. He holds degrees from the University of Havana, the University of Madrid, the University of Miami (Florida), and Cornell University. Professor Mesa-Lago is the author of numerous books and articles about Latin America, including *The Labor Sector and Socialist Distribution in Cuba* and an edited work, *Revolutionary Change in Cuba*. He is completing a study entitled, *Social Security Stratification and Inequality in Latin America*.

WILLIAM F. SATER is a member of the History Department at California State University, Long Beach. He was educated at Stanford University and UCLA. Professor Sater has published articles on Chilean education and the War of the Pacific in *The Journal of Developing Areas* and *The Journal of Latin American Studies* and is author of *The Heroic Image in Chile* (University of California Press).

WILLIAM F. SHARP is a member of the Department of History at Temple University. He studied at Stanford University and the University of North Carolina and served as a Peace Corps volunteer. Professor Sharp's essays on race relations have appeared in Colombian publications, and he is presently working on a larger study of manumission in western Colombia during the 1810 to 1855 period.

ROBERT BRENT TOPLIN is a member of the Department of History at Denison University and co-director of the university's Latin American Studies program. He was educated at the Pennsylvania State University and Rutgers University. Professor Toplin's articles on slavery, abolition, and race relations have appeared in *The Hispanic American Histori-cal Review, The Journal of Black Studies, The Luso-Brazilian Review, Black World, Civil War History* and *Harvard Studies of the African Diaspora*. He is also author of a book-length study, *The Abolition of Slavery in Brazil*.

WINTHROP R. WRIGHT is a member of the Department of History at the University of Maryland. He received his uni-versity education at Swarthmore College and the University of Pennsylvania and served as a Fulbright lecturer at the Universidad de Oriente in Venezuela. He is the author of articles on railways in Argentina, race relations in Venezuela, and university integration in Latin America, which have appeared in *The Business History Review, The Maryland Historian*, and *The Movement Toward Latin American Unity* (ed. Ronald Hilton). Professor Wright also wrote *British-Owned Railways in Argentina*, forthcoming from the University of Texas Press.

Slavery and Race
Relations in
Latin America

Introduction

Simón Bolívar, the "Liberator" of Latin America, once referred proudly to his native Venezuelans as members of "a family resulting from the fusion of three distinct ethnic elements."[1] A century later the Mexican educator José de Vasconcelos spoke of the "Cosmic Race," a new type of man appearing particularly in Latin America as a result of intermingling among Europeans, Africans, and Amerindians in the New World.[2] These and many similar glowing statements about social relations contribute to the impression that Latin America has become a racial paradise. Such observations suggest that miscegenation has been extensive throughout Latin American history, that there was little resistance to this development, and that, altogether, Latin American cultures have shown less evidence of bigotry and discrimination than have other cultures.

The present volume tests these assumptions by focusing on relationships between two groups in Latin America: Europeans and Africans. Through an examination of slavery in Latin America and the position of blacks after slavery's abolition, the studies raise many questions fundamental to Afro-Latin American history. For example: What is the relationship between slavery and prejudice? How were blacks treated under slavery? What were their opportunities to obtain manumission? How did abolition occur? What happened to liberated slaves? How do Latin Americans view the concept of "race"? How much racial tolerance exists in modern Latin America?

Before considering these questions in greater detail, we should point out that major terms used throughout the discussions must be defined very generally and flexibly. Words like "race" and

3

"blacks" and "whites" represent imprecise social categories, not exclusive groups or distinct biological types. There are no true "races" in the world, argue most modern-day anthropologists. Whether one speaks of Negroids and Caucasoids or blacks and whites, one should remember that these terms are only crude but popular man-made labels. The terms represent people's *perceptions* of differences, efforts to work out commonly accepted categories that identify groups according to skin pigmentation and physiognomic features as well as cultural characteristics. Thus race is a subjective concept, not an objective fact.

The social nature of the racial concept is well demonstrated by comparisons of its use in different cultures. Perceptions of what race means vary greatly in Latin American societies vis-à-vis the United States. For example, in the United States we commonly identify individuals as either black or white, whereas in Latin America people of mixed African and European ancestry are frequently identified by a different vocabulary. Someone viewed as a black in the United States may be considered a mulatto in Latin America. Whereas North Americans tend to use a two-category system of identification, Latin Americans employ a multitude of terms that show greater recognition of the tremendous variety of physical and cultural groupings. Latin American taxonomy even goes beyond matters of color and hair texture. A person's economic and social status may also affect the way others view him. Brazilians often say "money whitens," meaning that people tend to place a black man who becomes wealthy in a lighter-skinned "racial" category than the category he was in when poor. It is precisely this flexibility in Latin American racial thinking that points up the cultural bias built into terms like "race" and "racism" and "black" and "white." Latin American terminology has been far more sophisticated than North American terminology on the subject, because it has been less inclined grossly to simplify what is fundamentally a social rather than a scientific concept.

It is important to recognize these shortcomings in terminology before studying the chapters that follow. Throughout the volume authors frequently refer to "race" and "racism," "blacks" and "whites." Although it would be inappropriate to contrive a new vocabulary or place all such words in quotation marks, at least we can achieve greater sensitivity to the problem in this prefatory discussion. Readers should be aware that the authors employ these terms in the framework of popular North American usage but with full understanding that the words have very general meaning. References to blacks may imply inclusion of mulattoes along with Negroes; references to racism may connote class as well as color prejudice.

If racism is to be judged a social concept developing out of history, then it behooves students of the subject to scrutinize the black man's early experience in the Americas, namely, the record of slavery. Most blacks came to the New World as unwilling immigrants, a fact that complicates efforts to understand the origins of prejudice. Among the multiplicity of factors that influence modern-day racism, slavery certainly must rank among the most important. Because almost all blacks arrived in the Americas as slaves, the association between color and bondage became a cruel trap. Slavery, by legal definition, gave its victims a lowly status. In time, color came to symbolize lower status by stigmatizing dark-complexioned individuals with direct or ancestral ties to servility.

How much slavery contributed to racism remains a heated controversy. This subject has long been a point of debate among students of United States history. Oscar and Mary Handlin argued that bigotry developed out of the labor needs of colonists in the South. In order to maintain cheap and adequate plantation labor, they extended the servitude of Africans eventually to the point of identifying them as chattel workers. Prejudice served to justify perpetual exploitation.[3] On the other hand, Carl N. Degler contended that race prejudice caused slavery rather than the reverse. He found bigotry in force from the very early years of the black experience in America.[4] Finally, Winthrop Jordan has expanded on Degler's thesis to suggest that the process was circular: preexisting prejudices and the low status of blacks in the colonies reinforced prejudice among whites, making racism in North America especially virulent.[5] In recent years a similar controversy has been developing about cause-effect relationships in Latin American history.

The historical connection between slavery and color is fundamental in this debate. In antiquity—for example, such as during the periods of Greek and Roman hegemony—many slaves were white Mediterranean people. Often the slave population represented soldiers and civilians captured from neighboring lands during wars. In contrast, slavery in the Western Hemisphere in modern times became particularly associated with Africans. The Age of Exploration put new life in the old institution. When Portuguese sailors pushed down the coast of Africa in the fifteenth century, they brought African captives back to their homeland. For the next century, Iberian peoples made rapid new explorations and linked their growing settlements to African slavery. Spain laid claim to much of the Caribbean through Columbus' ventures; and later, conquistadores such as Hernán Cortes and Francisco Pizarro secured Central America and western South America for the Spanish crown. Portugal established control over the vast eastern region of South America, which it named Brazil.

Both the Spanish and Portuguese tried to enslave the native Indians of the Americas; but, for a variety of reasons, their governments decided to condemn Indian enslavement. In some cases the crown outlawed Indian enslavement to strengthen its control over colonial societies and check the leanings toward independence on the part of powerful settlers who controlled hundreds of Indian laborers. Eventually the colonies worked out other labor systems for the Indians that, although not formally called slavery, had many of the same effects. Moreover, most of the lowland Indians were unaccustomed to organized, group labor in agriculture. Many ran away or committed suicide. Faced with an unproductive and unreliable Indian population, colonists began looking for new sources of manpower. In both Spanish America and Brazil, the colonists turned to slaves imported from

Africa as the answer to their manpower needs. Spain outlawed Indian slavery early in the sixteenth century but permitted African enslavement. Although Brazil remained more ambivalent about Indian slavery for the next few centuries, Africans quickly filled most of the requests for servile laborers. By the late sixteenth century, a substantial number of Africans were laboring in the rich sugar plantation regions of northeast Brazil.

Thus, as slavery became limited largely to blacks, a popular association developed between color and bondage. Even freedmen carried the stigma of bondage, for they could not effectively hide the fact of their own or their family's former servility. Freedmen in slave societies faced many social and economic restrictions—evidence of some of the complex, intertwined relationships between slavery and race relations.

Quite understandably, the dominant social classes found it difficult to begin treating blacks equally after emancipation and abolition, in light of the very oppressive ways they had treated blacks under slavery. Their culpability in these deplorable conditions is more a consequence of the imperatives of slavery than an example of basic slaveholder depravity. Before the close of the Atlantic slave trade in the nineteenth century, slaveholders could easily purchase new manpower for relatively low prices, and often masters worked their bondsmen for long hours until sheer exhaustion brought on early death. In some regions African imports typically expired after about seven years of service. The work routine also became very oppressive because slavery usually did not offer incentives to the workers. Threats kept slaves toiling—negative reinforcement symbolized by the overseer's whip. Finally, the slavery regime contained built-in difficulties that could provoke greater repression. Many bondsmen refused to submit to continued injustices and tried to escape or rebel. Often they were captured and punished; sometimes they succeeded in establishing runaway slave communities in the backlands or in hiding within the free black population of urban centers. When slaves tried such resistance, slaveholders tended to clamp down on the servile community with new restrictions designed to discourage further challenges. As a consequence, efforts of slaves to find freedom frequently resulted in slaveholder reactions that made conditions more oppressive. Often this insecure situation created attitudes of distrust toward black people that had residual effects in the post-emancipation period.

It would, of course, be a mistake to assume that the history of slavery in Latin America is simply a long tale of exploitation and oppression. Slavery became a way of life. As in most human relationships, conditions for specific individuals varied greatly. Treatment of bondsmen depended considerably on the personality of masters and overseers. Latin American archives reveal great diversity in master-slave relationships. Some masters appear pathologically cruel; others viewed their workers as "members of a family" and demonstrated a truly paternalistic spirit within the institution. Economic conditions also affected treatment. In flush times, where opportunities to turn fast profits were great, masters often drove their slaves hard through long hours in the work gang. In areas of sagging economy, however, where masters felt less pressure to test the energies of bondsmen, slavery operated at a more relaxed pace; and in many instances, friendly relationships developed between manager and worker. Furthermore, conditions varied greatly according to the slave's occupation. Usually slaves working as artisans, day laborers, or household servants in the cities and inside the master's country estate fared better than slaves who worked as field hands or miners in rural areas. Finally, in some areas slaves were deliberately treated better as a means to reduce discontent and the prospects for rebellion and flight. These distinctions are generalizations, of course; it is easy to find many exceptions.

In several important studies of slavery in Latin America, historians have pointed to wide-ranging national, religious, and cultural differences as bases for various distinctions in the treatment of slaves. These scholars argue that, in general, slavery in Latin America was significantly milder than its counterpart in the United States. To a large extent, this assessment derives from travelers' accounts and books on the subject published in the early twentieth century, such as Sir Harry Johnston's *The Negro in the New World*.[6] Gilberto Freyre's famous study, *The Masters and the Slaves*, which concerns Brazil, contributed further evidence to theories about the mildness of Latin American slavery.[7] The late Frank Tannenbaum brought many of these ideas together with brilliance and compassion in an influential little book, *Slave and Citizen*.[8] The Tannenbaum thesis, which attracted persuasive advocates, holds that slaves in Latin America were recognized as "persons" with certain rights rather than simply as property, that they did not confront harsh racism, that opportunities for manumission were abundant, and that bondsmen generally were treated humanely. All this, he argues, stands in sharp contrast to the brutality and inflexibility of the "peculiar institution" in the United States.

The entire historical controversy over the treatment of slaves is a complex one with many ramifications. Although most of the essays in this volume lean toward the "revisionist" perspective on Latin American bondage, shedding light on many of its harsh aspects, these critical accounts do not attempt to create a monolithic picture of slavery. The authors recognize the many factors that can influence answers to questions about the treatment of slaves.

Several of the essays on the treatment of bondsmen refer also to the treatment of free blacks during the years of slavery, an issue that becomes more important under the rubric of race relations in the articles on abolition and its aftermath. Like the studies of slavery in this volume, many of these essays correspond to "revisionist" trends in historical interpretation. Their authors raise serious questions about the mildness of race relations in Latin America, an issue related to general questions about the mildness of slavery. Challenging traditional interpretations of Latin American cultures as racial melting pots or racial democracies, these studies reveal much evidence of prejudiced thought and discriminatory behavior in countries such as Brazil, Venezuela, Puerto Rico, and Cuba—nations that have been among the ones most acclaimed for achieving relatively egalitarian and tolerant racial attitudes. According to the authors, Afro-Latin Americans came out of slavery already the victims of bigotry. In the absence of institutional slavery, prejudice intensified as societies sought new ways to impose restrictions on blacks. Heightened attention to supposed racial distinctions helped to maintain disparities in status between groups and to protect economic advantages for the formerly dominant groups.

The studies also reveal that racism in Latin America increased during the period of abolition and its aftermath partly in response to changing intellectual currents in the Western world. Latin American leaders were keenly interested in the latest and most popular theories of Europe and the United States. Particularly during the late nineteenth century and early twentieth century, many important intellectuals of the Western Hemisphere expressed embarrassment about their cultures' mixed "racial" composition. They hoped to advertise their countries as attractive places for settlement by "pure" white immigrants from Europe.

Gradually a reaction against this form of self-hatred developed in Latin America. Many writers began to speak out in favor of their own cultures' long tradition of miscegenation, arguing that it produced a New Man who benefited from something akin to the vigor of cultural hybrids. Rather than condemning or apologizing for Latin America's multiracial past, they began to compare this history favorably with the record of intolerance, prejudice, and discrimination against dark-skinned peoples in other areas of the Western world. Advocates of this proud stance gained new respect from intellectuals around the globe when revulsion toward the racist doctrines of Nazi Germany and enthusiasm for the civil rights movement in the United States attracted considerable interest in Latin America's "different" history of race relations.

Although Latin America's racial thinking has come a long way from the imitative, intolerant attitudes of past years, it would be wrong to assume that racism is today a minor problem. In different degrees prejudice persists in all the Hispanic-American countries. This is hardly surprising, since no society, not even the relatively tolerant cultures of Latin America, can fully escape the pernicious social conditions that generate group stereotyping and bigotry.

Efforts to overcome these persistent problems of prejudice face formidable difficulties because of the very complexity of race relations in Latin America. In the most fundamental sense, advocates of full equality face two choices. They may seek change by stressing a need for greater racial consciousness, or they may stress the importance of general changes in Latin America's socioeconomic structure. If they choose to emphasize racial consciousness, they can attract attention to specific problems of color prejudice; but combating these problems may be difficult in societies where concepts of race are rather hazy and where many people do not clearly identify themselves with a particular racial grouping. If they choose to emphasize general changes in the socioeconomic structure, they can avoid the difficulty of trying to contrive attitudes about group solidarity, thus concentrating on the humanistic goal of uplifting the masses, regardless of color. Such a general approach, however, may leave specific prejudices toward blacks unchallenged, prejudices that can remain even when general economic conditions improve.

The inherent dilemmas in these two fundamental approaches to problems of racial inequality suggest that inordinant attention to one remedy at the expense of the other would probably not work. Perhaps a balanced approach, combining the two strategies, holds greater promise. By carefully examining the complex interrelationships between class and color bigotry that give racial prejudice its strength, we may develop a more sophisticated understanding of the problem in today's Latin America.

The following essays seek to understand the origins and developments of these relationships by examining the historical record from the period of slavery to modern times. Although the study topics are highly selective and the authors do not pretend to offer comprehensive treatment, these investigations should highlight some of the most important questions concerning slavery and race relations in Latin America. Scholars and students may never agree fully about the correct answers to the problems discussed here. Disagreements notwithstanding, the authors can contribute to the debate by trying to ask the right questions.

Notes

[1]Quoted in Winthrop R. Wright's essay in this volume.

[2]For a stimulating discussion of Vasconcelos' idea of the "Cosmic Race" as it related to larger issues of race relations, see Frank Tannenbaum, *Ten Keys to Latin America* (New York, 1964), pp. 112-118.

[3]Oscar and Mary Handlin, "The Origins of the Southern Labor System," *William and Mary Quarterly* 7 (April 1950): 199-122.

[4]Carl N. Degler, "Slavery and the Genesis of American Race Prejudice," *Comparative Studies in History and Society* 2 (October 1959): 49-66.

[5]Winthrop D. Jordan, *White Over Black: American Attitudes Toward the Negro, 1550-1812* (Chapel Hill, N.C., 1968).

[6]Sir Harry Johnston, *The Negro in the New World* (London, 1910).

[7]Gilberto Freyre, *The Masters and the Slaves: A Study in the Development of Brazilian Civilization* (New York, 1946).

[8]Frank Tannenbaum, *Slave and Citizen: The Negro in the Americas* (New York, 1946).

1

The Black Experience
in Chile

William F. Sater

William F. Sater's overview of the role of blacks in colonial Chile introduces many of the topics that are discussed in other studies in this volume. By examining diverse aspects of Afro-Latin American experiences in colonial Chile—the slave trade, economic activities of both slaves and free blacks, the treatment of bondsmen, opportunities for manumission, and the causes of abolition—Sater highlights major controversies that fuel important historical debates. Perhaps most significant, the author demonstrates that blacks did make meaningful contributions to early Chilean history.

Observers of modern-day Chile often comment on the virtual absence of black citizens and African traditions. From this situation they assume that only a few slaves went to the area in colonial times and most of those died off from disease or harsh working conditions. Consequently, many consider modern Chile one of the "white" countries of South America. Although admitting to marginal Indian influence in Chile, they tend to see almost no traces of African background. Professor Sater challenges this interpretation through an examination of the record of Afro-Chileans in colonial times. He points out that the influence of Chilean blacks is not generally recognized today because many generations of intermingling produced lighter and lighter mestizo groups—the result of miscegenation among blacks, whites, Indians, mestizos, and mulattoes.

Chile lends itself nicely to an overview of early Afro-Latin American history. In the colonial period the area of effective settlement in Chile

13

COLONIAL CHILE

- COPIAPÓ
- LA SERENA
- COQUIMBO
- VALPARAISO
- SANTIAGO
- RANCAGUA
- SAN FERNANDO
- CURICÓ
- CONSTITUCIÓN
- LINARES
- CONCEPCIÓN
- LOS ANGELES
- ANGOL
- IMPERIAL
- VALDIVIA
- OSORNO

was small, concentrated particularly in the region around Santiago. Moreover, the slave population remained small. These two factors make the subject of blacks in Chile a manageable topic for historical study. By focusing on a relatively compact population of whites and blacks, it is possible to touch on numerous issues relevant to a broader view of slavery and race relations in the colonial period.

R.B.T.

Chile is a distinctive nation. It is a land of rugged geography, of contrasting climates, and most uniquely, the home of *la raza chilena*. The latter term refers to the belief held by many Chileans that they are a special race, sired by the Gothic Spaniard and raised by the Araucanian Indian woman. One of the myth's most avid supporters was Nicolás Palacios, whose book, *La raza chilena*, profoundly influenced many, including one of Chile's foremost historians, Francisco Antonio Encina. Palacios and Encina both give a racist interpretation of Chile's history, ascribing the nation's virtues and flaws to its ancestors' supposedly innate characteristics. *La raza chilena*, however, does not exist, at least not as described by Palacios and Encina. The majority of Chile's Spaniards were not of Gothic extraction, and only a small portion of its Indians belonged to the Araucanian tribe.[1]

Yet there is an even more fundamental flaw in the theory, for never does it mention the role of the black man who, like the Spaniard, fought to wrest Chile from its savage inhabitants. Just as the Spanish deprived the black of the fruits of his labors, so the *raza chilena* theory denied him his place in Chile's history. This essay will attempt to describe the Negro's role in Chile's development. It is only a beginning, for the task is too great and the space too short for completion here. It will require the work of many before the black man and his role in Chilean history are recognized.

I.   The Beginning

The first blacks arrived in 1536, with Diego de Almagro, who claimed Chile for Spain. Subsequent expeditions to Chile also included blacks who acted as servants, and sometimes as concubines, for their *conquistador* masters. Many had been purchased in Spain or in one of the American colonies, and naturally they accompanied their masters when they began the conquest of Chile.[2]

Although they were slaves, the blacks seem to have occupied positions of some importance in the Spanish expeditions. Cristóbal Molina, one of Almagro's chaplains, noted that Negroes often acted as overseers in charge of Indian porters.[3] Many blacks were soldiers. A Negro named Felipe fought at Marihueni; Juan Fernandez soldiered at Cañete in 1569. One black soldier died at the battle of Chumumaguigi as did four others at Labapie. It was a black who killed the famous Indian *cacique*, Caupolicán.[4]

One of the most famous Negro warriors was Juan Valiente, a fugitive slave from Mexico. Valiente so distinguished himself that he was made a *capitán de infantería* and was granted an *encomienda* in 1550. Valiente tried to purchase his freedom from his owner, but the emissary entrusted with this task appears to have absconded with the money. Valiente's owner subsequently tried to seize the property of his slave as well as Valiente himself, but by the time he took this action, his former servant had died at the battle of Tucapel. Valiente's son later inherited his father's *encomienda*, although he had some legal difficulties.[5] Encina, one of the proponents of *la raza chilena*, somewhat patronizingly paid homage to the black soldier when he wrote that Valiente was worthy of praise ". . . because beneath his black skin throbbed the characteristics and virtues of the Spanish hidalgo."[6]

Another black soldier was Juan Beltrán, who fought so well at the battle of Villarica that the governor-general personally congratulated him, making him commanding officer of the local garrison. According to Antonio Vásquez de Espinosa, as long as

Beltrán lived the area remained pacified. After his death, however, Villarica once again became unsafe.[7] Blacks apparently played an important role in the conquest of Chile, for Rodrigo de Quiroga wrote the King that the Negroes ". . . often fulfill functions necessary to the war. . . ."[8] Despite this contribution, only three blacks, in addition to Valiente and Beltrán, won *encomiendas*: Cristóbal Varela, Leonor Galiano, the son of a Moorish slave, and Gomez de León.[9]

II.   The Slave Trade: Its Reasons and Routes

The Spaniards imported blacks primarily to supplement Chile's indigenous population, which was small, hostile, and less than enthusiastic about becoming vassals. Unlike the Aztec or Inca, the native Chilean did not live in a developed hierarchical society. Each tribe had its own leader or *cacique*, who achieved this status by merit and not through birth. The famous Caupolicán, for example, became a chief only after bettering his competitors in a three-day endurance test. As a result, when the Spanish arrived in the new country they did not encounter a native society already domesticated by some indigenous form of feudalism but a free, classless society that strenuously resisted the imposition of Spanish rule.[10]

Although estimates vary, Chile's pre-Columbian population was puny when compared with that of Mexico or Peru.[11] Thus when Pedro de Valdivia, a principal initiator of the conquest of Chile and, later, governor of the area, magnanimously granted 60 *encomiendas* to his comrades, he had to rescind 28 of these because there were not sufficient Indians to go around.[12] Although disease decimated the Indians, enough might have survived to work the *encomienda*, but what infection did not destroy, the Spaniard did. The *encomendero* often sent his vassals to work in mines where they were ill clothed, fed, and housed, beaten if unable to meet their quotas, and viciously mutilated for minor crimes. Indian women began to practice infanticide rather than raise their children to die in Spanish silver and gold mines.[13]

Those who could, fled to the safety of the south, which their
enemy had not conquered.

In Chile, as in the rest of Latin America, the crown and Church
fought to protect the Indian. The king, his counselors, and clergy
ordered the settlers to treat the Indians well, but local officials
were either unwilling or unable to implement these decrees
against the *encomenderos* on whose support they depended. To be
sure, Chile had its share of idealistic officials and clergymen who
tried to safeguard the Indians.[14] In general, however, neither the
threats of governmental punishment nor eternal damnation de-
terred the *encomendero* in his pursuit of wealth.

As a result, the *encomenderos* all but annihilated the indigenous
population of Chile's central valley.[15] Seeking new sources of
labor, the Spanish transported Indians from Peru and Argentina
to Chile. Eventually the settlers began to look avariciously toward
the free Indians in the south who had been able to resist the
foreign invaders. To tap this potential labor pool, the
encomenderos initiated a series of wars against the Araucanians,
enslaving those whom they did not kill, on the grounds that this
was a "just war" and that all prisoners became the property of
their captors.

The costly war not only accelerated the depopulation of Chile,
it drained the nation economically. Chile, a poor colony, could ill
afford the expensive fighting. The government, during the
seventeenth century, ordered a halt to offensive operations. The
Bio-Bio River in the south became the truce line across which
Spanish troops were not to cross, and the era of "defensive war"
began. The *encomenderos* often violated these injunctions and
attacked the Indians whenever they needed additional laborers.[16]

In order to provide the colony with a dependable supply of
labor, numerous Spaniards, beginning in the 1550s, requested
that the crown authorize the importation of black slaves.[17] Apparently some of these requests were rejected, because years later
Santiago's *cabildo* (municipal council) as well as certain colonial
officials were still begging the government for more slaves and

even sent representatives to Spain to argue their case before the crown.[18]

Some Chileans wanted the blacks for purely economic reasons. One individual, for example, wrote a short treatise extolling the virtues of the black as a laborer, claiming that he was more docile and a far more skilled worker than the Indian. Other Spaniards, however, argued that the only way to protect Chile's Indians was to replace them with Negroes.[19]

Although there was a heavy demand for black slaves, the Spanish crown refused to permit their duty-free importation, largely for financial reasons. Early in the sixteenth century, in an effort to increase revenues, the king began to charge what amounted to a head tax on each slave entering his domain. To permit slaves to enter Chile duty-free would have reduced the royal revenues needed for Spain's European ventures.[20] Thus, when Pedro de Valdivia sought the duty-free importation of blacks, the government rejected his petition. Occasionally the crown permitted certain royal officials to introduce small numbers of black slaves into Chile, without payment of duty and for use as personal servants, but this was as far as the government was prepared to go.[21] If the Chileans wanted slaves, they would have to pay. This policy, as we shall see, subsequently led to widespread smuggling.

Initially those slaves who reached Chile legally came by the Pacific route, a trip that originated in Cartagena or Panama, often with an intermediate stop at Callao, Peru. The voyage was long and arduous. Because of the poor diet and unsanitary conditions, the mortality rate among the slaves was high. Some scholars have estimated that as many as 50 percent perished, converting the slave ships into floating charnel houses. For some, death came no doubt as a blessing because there is evidence that certain blacks committed suicide, either because of the psychological shock resulting from their capture or because they were unwilling to endure a life of slavery.[22]

At its outset, slaving was a small-scale enterprise, conducted by a few individuals, although later some merchants pooled their resources to form companies. These legitimate endeavors often had illegal competition: many of the Spaniards who had been allowed to import slaves duty-free sold them. This unauthorized traffic reached such proportions that it even involved a governor of Chile and one of Peru's viceroys.[23]

It is extremely difficult to estimate the number of Negro slaves who arrived in Chile by the Pacific route. Rolando Mellafe used the Notorial Archives in Santiago to study this question, but unfortunately he only investigated these records at intervals of five years and then only for a limited period of time. Still it can be ascertained that 220 blacks, 141 men and 75 women, entered Chile between 1565 and 1615. Mellafe projected, on the basis of these figures, that approximately 3,000 slaves were transported to Santiago during this period. These calculations should be revised upward, since in 1630 and 1631 Santiago's *cabildo* estimated that the city's black population numbered between 2,000 and 2,500.[24] Given the prevailing high mortality rates, it would seem that many more than 3,000 slaves would have had to be imported between 1565 and 1615 to have a black population of over 2,000 in 1631.

The majority of the slaves introduced into Chile were young, most of them under thirty, which was quite logical since they had been purchased to be laborers. Although some were American born, the largest number were from Africa, and the price they commanded depended on their age, state of health, and skills.[25] At one time the crown established a price for which slaves entering Chile might be sold, but it later changed this policy and allowed prices to seek their natural level.[26]

Beginning in the late sixteenth century, the Pacific coast slave trade via Cartagena and Panama faced increasing competition from an overland traffic in blacks entering through the Atlantic port of Buenos Aires. This route had originally developed in response to demands by Argentine economic interests who wished to us the port as an outlet to exchange their agricultural and pastoral products for Brazilian sugar, African slaves, and

Spanish manufactured goods. Initially the Spanish government had been reluctant to grant these requests because Argentina was a relatively impoverished colony, and therefore not commercially significant; Spain also feared that opening up Buenos Aires to trade would result in widespread smuggling. Despite these factors, the king subsequently granted limited trade concessions, among which was the right to import a certain number of slaves under a monopoly contract (*asiento*) signed in 1595. Almost immediately the crown's fears about smuggling became an unhappy reality. The amount of contraband goods and slaves, "imported" primarily by Portuguese merchants based in Brazil, soon exceeded the legally permitted traffic.[27]

Official attempts to stop this illegal commerce were largely frustrated by the guile of Portuguese merchants and by the venality of the crown's own officials. In just one year, over a dozen ships docked in Buenos Aires laden with some four thousand blacks, of whom half remained in Argentina while the rest were shipped to Chile and Upper Peru.[28] Although infuriating to the Spanish crown, the contraband activities centering on Buenos Aires provided the Chileans with an alternative to the Pacific route. Initially this traffic was small, but as more ships docked in Buenos Aires the number of slaves reaching Chile increased substantially. Indeed, by 1616 Santiago's *cabildo* found it profitable enough to tax blacks entering from Argentina. A few years later the municipal government temporarily suspended the traffic because it suspected that the incoming slaves were bringing disease with them.[29]

After 1640 the pressure of foreign enemies forced Portugal to abandon her attempt to monopolize the African slave trade; and from the second half of the seventeenth century to the end of the colonial period, French, British, and Spanish merchants also used Buenos Aires to introduce slaves into Chile. This traffic became legal as a result of the various *asientos* concluded by the Spanish crown with private companies, and later by the development of a *de facto* free slave trade. Although the *asientos* permitted the French and British to import large quantities of blacks, these enterprises never fully exercised their rights. The French, for example, imported only 3,475 Negroes into Buenos Aires from 1702 to 1713, considerably less than the legal maximum. The English followed a similar pattern. Although the South Sea Company employed an agent in Chile and dispatched over 3,500 slaves to the colony from 1713 to 1743,[30] it appears to have used the slave trade as a means of smuggling manufactured goods into the colony. One American historian estimated that as much as 90 percent of the cargo of British slave ships was devoted to carrying contraband instead of blacks. Eventually the Spanish had to order that each company vessel transport a certain number of Africans in order to curtail the illegal trade.[31] Although Chileans were now legally permitted to import blacks, contraband slaving still existed. In 1764 the authorities in Santiago apprehended one Antonio Corrales for illicitly transporting slaves from Mendoza to Santiago, and they returned him to Argentina to stand trial.[32]

The Atlantic route was as unhealthy for the slaves as the Pacific. Shipboard life was ghastly: the slaves suffered from smallpox, scurvy, tuberculosis, and psychological shock. Some French and British slave ships lost more than 50 percent of their blacks before reaching Buenos Aires. The trip across the *pampa* and the *cordillera* was another trial. The captive blacks literally walked across a continent, spurred on by the lash, hunger, and thirst, and weakened by altitude sickness.[33] As more ships docked, the slave caravans became longer. In 1731 a group of 400 blacks was dispatched to Peru and Chile. Several decades later a Chilean, traveling between Santiago and Buenos Aires, passed one such party composed of 300 blacks,[34] walking, two by two, across the mountain passes. How many Negroes perished on the land portion of the trip is not known. Some blacks did not accept their fate so stoically. On one slaver, the *Prueba*, 72 Senegalese, en route to Callao from Valparaiso, seized the ship after killing most of its crew and passengers. It was only the timely intervention of an American merchantman, the *Perseverence*, that prevented the rebels from forcing their former master to return them to Africa.[35]

III.   The Black in Chile's Economic Life

The black's role in Chile's economic development will be discussed thematically, indicating the important part the Negro played in mineral exploitation, agriculture, and skilled labor. The Indians of Chile were already engaged in mining when the Spanish discovered them. Not unexpectedly, the new conquerors began to develop these resources to demonstrate that Chile was not a poor colony and, not incidentally, to enrich themselves. The principal source of gold was the placer mine of Marga-Marga, located near the present port of Valparaíso. Additional gold fields were those in the north at Limache, Quillota, and La Serena, as well as to the south, at Concepción, Imperial, Osorno, Angol, and Villarica.[36]

Perhaps more than any other factor, lack of manpower handicapped Spanish efforts to exploit Chile's natural resources. Local Indians could not be legally forced to work in the mines, and when they were, they did so without enthusiasm. Indians recruited from Peru and Argentina brought no improvement,[37] and therefore the Spaniards were forced to begin the importation of black laborers.

As previously noted, some of the earliest requests for Negroes were involved with work in the mines. There is evidence, however, to indicate that blacks were already being employed in this area of the economy before 1550. Valdivia's Ordenanza para minas, promulgated in 1545, attempted to regulate black labor, as did the Ordenanzas para las minas de plata of Antonio Nuñez in 1550. Nuñez' Ordenanzas suggest that Negro labor was highly prized, because he ordered that the mines be worked by teams of either four Yanaconas (Indians from Peru), five Indians, or one Negro and two Yanaconas.[38] Blacks were also employed in the mines to the south because Ferdinand Santillán included provisions for their control in his mining legislation of 1559.[39] There are other indications that Negroes became an integral part of the mining industry. The Ordenanzas of Francisco de Villagra stated that no black could force an Indian to work in the mines, and also prohibited any black or morisco slave from owning a mine.[40] The *cabildo* of Santiago, in 1553, forbade blacks, as well as Indians and Spaniards, to poach on the silver mine of one Gabriel Hernández, who was searching for silver near Santiago.[41]

Another indication of black involvement in mining can be found in the various proclamations regulating public conduct of the miners. Santiago's *cabildo*, for example, forbade blacks and Indians to gamble, to steal, or to use the second washings of a placer mine without the owner's permission. In 1550 the *cabildo* repeated its warning that no black or Indian could take gold out of any mine.[42] The penalty for such an offense was a hundred lashes for the first infraction, amputation of the ears for the second, and death for the third. Apparently these proclamations had little or no effect. In 1550 a commission was appointed to the mine at Marga-Marga to stop blacks and Indians from stealing. This committee appears to have been less than efficient, because a subsequent session of the *cabildo* noted that blacks and Indians were still purchasing merchandise with unmarked gold. Eventually the government appointed a special official, an *alcalde de minas*, as a law officer. In order to assure his complete honesty he was chosen from those who had no interest in or connection with the mining industry.[43] The Negro continued to be an important force in Chile's mining industry into the eighteenth century. Even when mining began to decline in importance, substantial numbers of blacks and mulattoes were to be found in Huasco, Combarbala, and Illapel, Chile's mining areas in the north.[44]

Although the Spanish crown did not permit the duty-free importation of blacks, it still encouraged their use, not only as miners but as agricultural workers, in preference to the forced resettlement of the Indians.[45] By 1641, 23.5 percent of Colchagua's and 14.1 percent of Maule's labor force were black. Slaves worked not only as tanners, cowboys, sheepherders, and domestic servants but as majordomos as well. In the *Norte Chico*, blacks also became more prominent on the *fundos* as the economic base of this area shifted to agriculture in the early eighteenth century. Eventually there were so many blacks employed in farm-

ing that various clergymen noted that a substantial portion of the rural labor force was either Negro, mulatto, or *mestizo de color*.[46]
   Some of the largest employers of black slaves were religious orders. In Santiago the Dominicans, Augustinians, and Jesuits utilized blacks on their farms and in their vineyards. One convent employed black millers. On the eve of its expulsion the Society of Jesus was the largest corporate owner of blacks in all of Chile, controlling between 1,200 and 2,000 slaves. Perhaps a typical example of a Jesuit *fundo* was Calera de Tango, located slightly south of Santiago. In 1742 the estate employed 101 black slaves, and when the government expelled the Society in 1767 the number had risen to 120. The majority of the slaves were married, with large numbers of children. When the estate was broken up, 34 of the slaves remained with the new owner; the remainder were sold in either Chile or Peru. The slaves occupied five rooms, although the priests later built two additional ones to separate the married and unmarried slaves. Judging from the plans of the buildings, these rooms were not spacious; it was perhaps for this reason that some blacks fled from their clerical masters.[47]
   Blacks and mulattoes remained in agriculture up to the Independence period. Vicente Carvallo Goyeneche noted their presence in Quillota.[48] Another observer, an Englishman named Davie, noted in 1810 that the "Spaniards and their black and Indian servants . . . are quite numerous . . . living on separate farms all along the country. . . ."[49] In Rancagua the largest *fundos* of Santo Domingo and Bucalemu had 30 blacks working in viticulture and livestock production. Further south, in the provincial capital of Cauquenes, there were more blacks. When the town of Peumo was founded in 1797, there were 211 black or mulatto inhabitants out of a total population of 3,682.[50] And as the census of 1778 demonstrates, blacks and mulattoes were found in large numbers in the agricultural areas of Rancagua, Maule, and Aconcagua.[51]
   The black was also important in the city as well. The decline of the Indian population, the migration of natives to the south, and the *encomienda* system created a critical labor shortage in the

urban centers, especially Santiago. The *asiento de trabajo* attempted to redress this problem. Although subject to certain individual conditions, the *asiento* was an agreement by which the worker contracted his labor for a specific time in return for which the employer was to provide either money, clothing, room and board, or training in a skilled profession. The specifics of each contract varied, depending on the wishes of the signatories. Generally, since specie was scarce, the majority of these agreements were barter arrangements in which the worker received food, clothing, and housing in return for his labor. There were, of course, some individuals who received a salary and even one or two who worked on a commission basis.[52]

The Chilean scholar Alvaro Jara made a detailed study of the *asiento de trabajo* as it functioned in Santiago from 1565 to 1585. It is worthwhile to examine his conclusions, because they reveal the important role that black labor played in the urban economy. Four hundred ninety-eight *asentados* were signed during this period. Of these, 59 or 11.8 percent were made with blacks or mulattoes, making the Negro the second most important component of the labor force after the Indian, far outdistancing the Spaniard or mestizo. Even more striking, Jara's work revealed that the black worker was highly prized; his salary was appreciably higher than that of any other racial bloc. Of the 59 *asentados* who received their salary in specie, 37 of these were blacks, far more than any other group. This did not include a mulatto woman who worked for 27.5 pesos a year, a sum applied toward the purchase of her freedom. Six black *asentados* were paid a combination of money and clothing; the remainder apparently received simply room and board. According to the statistics, blacks were among the most highly paid. One earned a salary of 50 pesos per year, the second-highest amount paid to an *asentado* during the period studied.[53] Another interesting fact is that 25 percent of the male blacks either had a skilled profession or were being trained in one: two were shoemakers, one a blacksmith, three were tailors, one a carpenter, and one a tanner. The women, it appears, were generally domestics.

Rolando Mellafe also studied the *asiento de trabajo*, although, unlike Jara, he only observed those signed every five years from 1565 to 1615. Still, Mellafe's study appears to confirm Jara's work. Of the 230 *asentados* signed, 10 or 4.3 percent were made with Negroes or mulattoes. Of the 230, 27 were to receive professional training. Of these 27, 5 *asentados* were black: a mason, 2 blacksmiths, a hatmaker, and a shoemaker. Only the whites, proportionately speaking, had a higher percentage of people employed in skilled trades. Apparently the importance of the black in urban labor continued for, according to Mellafe, "there was no *maestro*, of whatever profession, who did not have one or more black slaves to help him. Even the officers of these teachers had slaves and it was common that these black slaves might become in time officials and also masters in the offices of their owners."[54]

In addition to the *asiento de trabajo* there were also blacks employed as free laborers in other professions. One was a saddlemaker, another a sailor.[55] For some reason the majority of Santiago's town criers were also blacks, a tradition that persisted into the seventeenth century. One, named Francisco, served the *cabildo* so well that they honored him after his death.[56] Blacks seemed to dominate the professions of coachman and muleteer. Vicuña Mackenna commented on this, as did an English visitor during the war for independence. According to Jaime Eyzaguirre there were many black executioners, but unfortunately he gives no examples.[57]

Apparently the black occupied an important role in the urban labor force. It is interesting to note, for example, that the city government rarely called on the blacks to help in labor levies; these jobs were usually reserved for Indians, probably because the Negro was too valuable to be wasted in menial jobs.[58] Carvallo wrote late in the eighteenth century that "the Indian and Mestizo [are] in agriculture in two areas: selling fruit, vegetables and all kinds of foods, and providing provisions; the Negroes and free mulattoes carry on the burden of the mechanical trades in which also some Europeans are employed."[59]

As has been demonstrated, although the black initially came to Chile to work the mines, he rapidly spread into other areas of the economy. This had an important sociological effect on the Negro's development, for it meant that he was not confined to one geographical area or one profession. The importance of the black laborer cannot be overestimated. The Negro was a capable worker who aided in Chile's economic development. Furthermore, because of the almost uniform need for labor, the Chilean black, unlike his North American counterpart, eventually occupied a variety of positions throughout the country. In addition, the Negro apparently functioned as a highly skilled worker, especially in the economy's urban sector. The black's status as a skilled worker had enormous implications, because it permitted the black to enter the nation's economic mainstream, it provided him with an opportunity to purchase his freedom, it educated him or at least made him less provincial, and most important of all, it trained him so that he was technically able to compete with the rest of society.

IV.   *The Juridical Status of the Black*

Even though the Spanish apparently preferred the black to the Indian as a laborer, the Negro was not, legally speaking, the Indian equal, nor did he enjoy the protection of the various codes and decrees promulgated for the Indian's preservation. The first purely Chilean legislation dealing with slaves was the *Ordenanzas de policía de Santiago*, which perished along with other records of the *cabildo*.[60] Fortunately there are other examples of the early laws passed by Santiago's municipal government to regulate both the slave and the general citizenry. The *Actas* of 1545, for example, outlawed blasphemy, horse theft, the making of adobe without permission, and trespass on another's property. The *cabildo* ordered in 1549 that any Indian or black found tampering with an irrigation ditch would be punished with a hundred lashes.[61] Santiago must have been a relatively lawless city, for two years later the *cabildo* stated that no one, regardless of color, could be out after nightfall. This same decree also forbade Indians and blacks from playing games of chance or gambling and denied them the right to carry weapons. A few years later the municipality excluded blacks from trading in the public markets.[62]

One of the most complete laws regulating blacks was the *Ordenanzas de policía de la capital de Santiago de Chile*, promulgated in 1569. No Negro could be out after dark, a crime punishable with fifty lashes for the first offense and a hundred lashes for the second. A black could not employ Indians, nor could he carry weapons. If a Negro did carry a weapon and used it against a Spaniard, even if he did not wound him, he was to be lashed and his hand was to be amputated.[63]

It is difficult to determine how rigorously the government enforced the laws dealing with Negroes. Although many Spanish colonial administrators had the reputation for being notoriously lax, there are examples of blacks being castrated, mutilated, and hanged.[64] Furthermore there is no indication that the individual slave owner treated his blacks any better than the law. One of the most infamous examples of this was Catalina de los Rios y Lisperguer, who so abused her slaves, both black and Indian, that many died, including a nine-year-old Negro girl who succumbed to a beating.[65] To claim that all *encomenderos* were like Doña Catalina would be the equivalent of stating that Lucrezia Borgia was typical of Renaissance Italy. Unfortunately, however, there is no contrary evidence to suggest that maltreatment of the black was not uncommon. Certainly the standards of the time were quite brutal, and the Spanish were no exception: the Indians could attest to this. In addition Chile was a frontier society, on the fringes of civilization, where the *encomenderos* even mutilated and assaulted priests.[66] Given such a mentality and the prevailing mores, it is difficult, indeed impossible, to believe that the black did not suffer.

The large numbers of Negroes who fled from their masters tend to substantiate this theory. As early as 1551 Santiago's *cabildo* complained about fugitive slaves who either fled south or joined the *cimarrones*, outlaw bands that preyed on towns and Indian settlements. Gonzáles de Najera described one such group in 1605, claiming that mulattoes as well as Indians and even Spaniards were among its members.[67] Apparently *cimarrones* were active throughout Chile, for León Echaïz noted that they often robbed the isolated *fundos* in the Curicó region.[68] In 1593 the authorities apprehended Dionisio and Sebastián Castillo, two mulatto brothers who had been raiding Spanish settlements. As late as 1768 a band of blacks fled east to Mendoza and the government dispatched troops to apprehend them.[69]

The government attempted to stop fugitives by passing very stringent laws, the first of which was the *Ordenanzas para los negros*. Under the provisions of this law, a slave apprehended after more than four days' absence from his owner was to receive fifty lashes. If he had been gone no more than eight days and if he was captured within a league of his owner's home, he was punished with 100 lashes and was fettered for two months with iron shackles weighing 12 pounds. If a black fled no more than four months and did not join a group of *cimarrones*, he was lashed 100 times for the first offense and exiled for the second. If the fugitive joined the *cimarrones*, however, the law increased the penalty to 200 lashes. Any slave who deserted his owner for six months and had either committed a crime or had been captured with the *cimarrones* was to be hanged.[70]

Brutal as the law was, it did not seem to cure the blacks of the habit of fleeing. In the mid-1570s Melchor Calderón became governor of Chile. The archbishop of Santiago described him as a fierce man and his treatment of the black reflected this, for the law passed by Calderón in 1577 was more severe than earlier codes. Any slave who fled for less than three days was returned to his master and was not subject to any legal penalties. If a royal official, however, aided in his capture, he received a bounty of four pesos. A slave absent for more than three days but less than twenty was penalized with 100 lashes. The law punished the second offense with 200 lashes plus the loss of a foot. The third time, the slave was to be castrated, or have her breasts removed if a woman. Section Three of the law provided that a slave apprehended after an absence of between twenty days and two months would receive 200 lashes, and ordered both his feet amputated. If a slave managed to escape a second time, and remained at large for a similar amount of time, the penalty was castration. The law also authorized the automatic castration or the removal of a woman's breasts if the slave deserted an owner for more than two months. Any fugitive who committed an act of violence, either against a Spaniard or an Indian, regardless of the amount of time at large, could be killed on sight and his murderer would receive a reward of thirty pesos. A black who sheltered a fugitive incurred the same penalty as the one fleeing. Somewhat as an afterthought, the *Ordenanzas* also prohibited blacks from gambling and penalized them for being drunk in public.[71]

Apparently the law had little effect, for in 1605 the *cabildo* of Santiago again complained about the number of black fugitives and established a bounty system to reward those who apprehended them.[72] The next year the *cabildo* authorized the formation of a group of armed horsemen to apprehend any Indian, black, or mulatto, found either causing a public nuisance or violating the curfew. Despite the pressing need for labor, the *cabildo* later demanded that no blacks be imported from Peru unless the *Audiencia* of Lima certified that they were neither criminals nor troublemakers.[73]

In part, the government reacted so strongly to fugitives out of fear that such *cimarrones* might join the Indians in launching a rebellion. In 1630 the *cabildo* of Santiago feared that an Indian attack, in conjunction with an invasion by Dutch privateers, might spark an uprising among the city's 2,500 blacks.[74] A year later the *cabildo* stated that it did not have sufficient troops to "respond to the domestic enemies, of more than two thousand blacks and one thousand Indians who have been plotting lawlessness." These fears were not fantasies.[75] The year before, three thousand Indians had attacked Santiago, endangering the city. At the same time black and Indian agricultural workers poured into the capital; the situation became so tense that the government recalled the militia from the south and armed the monasteries for fear of an Indian-black uprising. Following an earthquake in 1647, many Spaniards believed that the Negroes and Indians would use this as an opportunity to pillage Santiago. The government apparently averted this possibility by executing a black and by imposing strict security measures.[76] As late as 1672, both the *cabildo* of Santiago and a Royal Cédula[77] denounced the damage caused by blacks, Indians, and mulattoes, ordered them off the streets after nightfall, and forbade them to carry weapons. Apparently the problem continued to plague Santiago; thirteen years later the municipal council again had to pass a similar ordinance.[78] Doubtless it was also the fear of potential trouble that induced the *cabildo* to try to restrict the sale of liquor to Indians and to blacks.[79]

As might be expected, the black was the stepchild of the Spaniard's laws. One Chilean historian wrote, "The Spaniard was the lord and ruled. He had the Indian beaten for a look, for a left handed remark, or on mere suspicion. The black, who politically was inferior to the Indian, was burned alive or was subjected to a more barbarous and incredible torture."[80] The laws governing Chile reflected this bias. When a Spaniard committed certain crimes, the government usually levied a fine. When an Indian or a black erred, he paid with his flesh. A Spaniard, for example, was punished with a fine of 6 pesos if caught trespassing. An Indian or Negro was to receive 100 lashes for the same offense.[81] If a Spaniard stole gold, he paid a penalty of 300 pesos; an Indian or black suffered 100 lashes for the same offense.[82] An Indian or black could be whipped for damaging an irrigation ditch; a Spaniard paid 5 pesos.[83] There are other examples of this legal discrimination, including prohibiting blacks and Indians from wearing certain types of apparel.[84] In a sense this prejudice was quite logical. A white man was presumed to have money, and therefore he could pay a fine when he broke the law. A Negro or Indian, however, who did not even own his body, therefore could pay in only one currency: pain.

Although Spanish law discriminated against both the Indian and the black, of the two, the Indian was the favored son. The king specifically ordered the *Real Audiencia* of Santiago to be especially vigilant in caring for the Indians and to be lenient with them should they err.[85] One of the best examples of this preferential treatment was the various provisions dealing with Indian fugitives. Unlike the black, the Indian could not be mutilated or executed for fleeing. Unless he joined a band of *cimarrones*, the government ordered that the Indian was to be punished with "moderation"; the severity of the penalty depended on the length of the absence. Although "moderate punishment" was not spelled out, it was not the automatic penalty incurred when the black fled. If a Negro sheltered another black fugitive, he was liable for the same penalty as the offender. If an Indian committed the same offense, he received two hundred lashes and had his hair cut off. The Indian became liable to the same penalty only if he harbored a fugitive black for a second time. Another example of judicial inequality was the law that authorized the castration of a black who raped an Indian woman. There does not seem to have been an equivalent penalty for the rape of a Negro woman by an Indian.[86]

The Indian enjoyed the protection of the government in other areas as well. Numerous laws regulated the hours and working conditions of the Indian, and officials were appointed to ensure that the *encomendero* or mine owner did not mistreat his laborers. The government extended this same protection to Indians captured in war.[87] Although it is well known that these provisions were often not enforced, they still gave the Indian a favored status that the black did not possess. The Spanish government also passed various laws to keep the black and brown races apart, which, according to Magnus Mörner, was a traditional colonial policy designed to shield the Indian from exploitation.[88] One of the first examples of racial segregation in Chile was a Royal Cédula in 1580 that prohibited blacks from living among the Indians. In 1593 Governor Martin Garcia Oñez de Loyola stated that no mestizo, Negro, or mulatto could live in an Indian settlement.[89] The mining ordinances of Pedro de Villagra barred blacks from working with the Indians on the ground that they might set a bad example and undermine their faith in the

Church. There were also laws that excluded blacks from trading at Indian fairs, for fear that the Negroes would exploit the Indians, as well as regulations that forbade blacks to employ Indian servants.[90] The Church joined the state in the effort to keep the two races apart. There were even special religious organizations for blacks, and mulattoes could not become priests.[91]

Despite these efforts, the blacks and Indians began to mingle. This is best demonstrated by the number of children born of Indian-Negro parents. A new phrase was coined—*mestizo de color*—to differentiate between a mestizo born of white-Indian parentage and one with a Negro father or mother.[92] The laws began to reflect the mingling of the races. Originally the Spanish forbade the selling of liquor only to Indians. By the seventeenth century, legislation was passed to curtail the establishment of bars selling to Indians and Negroes. By the eighteenth century the *cabildo* ceased to distinguish between Spaniards and Indians, and blacks began to differentiate instead between upper- and lower-class individuals.[93] A more subtle change came when Indians and blacks began to give their children upper-class names, thus effacing one of the more obvious social distinctions.[94]

Although one Spaniard declared black slaves "comparable to four legged animals and to be considered as merely physical possessions,"[95] colonial justiçe became somewhat gentler and fairer. The *Procurador de los pobres*, the Chilean equivalent to the public defender, even began to protect blacks. In one case the *Procurador* prevented a mulatto woman from being forced to accompany her new owner, saved a second from being sent to Lima against her will, and even aided a third black who wished to change masters.[96] The courts not only freed blacks and mulattoes illegally detained by people claiming to be their owners, but even sentenced one such individual to two-year exile for holding a free *zambo* (the offspring of a black and Indian) against his will.[97] In one case the *Procurador* secured the release of a slave from jail, where he was awaiting transfer pending his sale, because an outbreak of smallpox threatened his life.[98] Another court removed a *mulatilla* servant from her owners' control when both her master and mistress began beating her (the first for not yielding to his amorous advances; the second for having succumbed).[99]

Even the legal penalties for crimes became less onerous. When one mulatto was convicted of disrespect and of injuring another's horse, he was merely fined and sent to prison. There were no physical reprisals. When authorities apprehended a fugitive slave, after an absence of over a year, they simply returned him to his owners; no mention was made of the lash. Apparently society also believed that the blacks no longer constituted a threat to internal security; the existence of a company of mulatto militiamen in Quillota indicates that the former slaves could now be trusted with firearms.[100]

V. *Abolition and Obliteration*

Although there were some free blacks and mulattoes in early-nineteenth-century Chile, the majority were still slaves. This situation became repugnant to the nation's liberals who, led by Manuel de Salas, an educator, and José Miguel Carrera, a political leader, began to agitate for the abolition of slavery. In October 1811 Salas proposed a law banning the slave trade and declaring free all children henceforth born of slave parents. The proposed legislation was not too radical and won sufficient support to be accepted. Indeed, it even became somewhat fashionable to free one's slaves publicly. The Salas law, though moving in the right direction, was hardly definitive. It was like a terminal illness; it crippled slavery and eventually would kill it, but in the interim the sore still festered.[101] Carrera helped the abolition movement during the war for independence by promising freedom to any slave who joined a new unit made up only of blacks and mulattoes: *Los Ingenuous de la Patria*. Under the proposal the blacks who enlisted would be freed but would have to compensate their owners out of their salaries. To encourage slave owners to participate, the government threatened them with severe penalties.[102] Obviously neither the blacks nor their owners were as enthusiastic as the *cabildo* of Santiago, which had earlier endorsed the plan, for within a few days of its proclamation, Carrera increased the penalty on the slave owner and threatened harsh punishments for those slaves who did not join the regiment.[103] The unit was eventually formed, however, and performed brilliantly at the battle of Maipu. According to a British observer, the black soldiers were enthusiastic and extremely aggressive.[104]

The struggle for independence momentarily submerged the abolition question. After a few years, and under the proddings of José Miguel Infante, the abolitionists began to demand the complete end of slavery. The conservatives, who tended to be slave owners, resisted, claiming that they were entitled to some compensation. President Ramón Freire agreed, stating that the state had no right to intervene in the individual's property rights without offering some recompense for his loss. The abolitionists retorted that some rights were superior to those of personal property and, by 1823, were able to persuade a majority of legislators to agree with them. In June of that year, slavery was abolished. The victory was almost hollow, however, for the black in Chile was fast disappearing.[105]

As the appendix to this chapter indicates, although Chile's black and mulatto population grew during the sixteenth and seventeenth centuries, it began to level off thereafter. By the twentieth century, Alberto Cabero and Luis Thayer Ojeda calculated that less than 1 percent of Chile's population was of African extraction.[106] At the present time the Negro is almost nonexistent.[107] Occasionally one sees a black face, but it usually belongs to a visitor—an American or a Brazilian—or a recent immigrant. Since at one time the blacks outnumbered the whites, one is impelled to inquire: What happened to Chile's Negroes?

Francisco Encina, Vial Correa, and Thayer Ojeda have claimed that alcoholism, disease, or the climate destroyed the black.[108] These answers are too simplistic, sophistries, at best. True, alcoholism was a problem in Chile, but there is no proof that it was solely an affliction of the black. Disease did decimate the nation, but again it is questionable whether the Negro suffered more than the Indian or the white. According to Mörner the Spaniards imported the black because he was considered stronger than the Indian.[109] Had this not been the case, had the black succumbed to disease as quickly as the Indian, then doubtless the Spanish would have sharply curtailed the purchase of slaves. The issue of climate is also a straw man. Chile's climate is no more rigorous than that of the southern United States. If the Negro could not have adapted himself, the Spanish would have been quick to discontinue the slave trade.

It was not disease, drink, or climate but miscegenation that annihilated the black. Some of the earliest birth records show this. Of the 120 children born of African ancestry in Santiago between 1581 and 1596, less than 31 percent were pure, the remainder being either mulattoes (70) or *zambos* (13).[110] Chile's 1778 census offers additional proof that miscegenation is what destroyed the blacks, for it demonstrates that mulattoes outnumbered blacks by more than 6.4 to 1; by 1813 this ratio had increased to more than 19 to 1. This pattern holds true in various regional studies of Chile. In the *Norte Chico*, for instance, the number of blacks declined from 830 or 2.4 percent of the population, in 1778, to 320 or .008 percent in 1813. In the identical time period the number of mulattoes had increased from 3,958 or 11.4 percent to 6,528 or 15.1 percent. The same phenomenon occurred in the district of Rauquén, where the blacks declined from 16 to 0 while, during the same number of years, the mulattoes increased from 136 to 179.[111]

Various reasons account for the "whitening" of the black population. There is some evidence that twice as many black men as women were imported into Chile.[112] Thus the black reproductive structure was incomplete, forcing the Negro male to seek companionship outside his own race. The fact that blacks were not confined to one section of the country may also have contributed to the rate of interracial births. Regardless of the causes, however, miscegenation occurred, not only in cases of extralegal relationships, but in legally contracted marriages. In the Doctrina of Curepto, for example, there were thirty-three marriages involving blacks. Of these only two, or 6 percent, were between blacks. The remainder had spouses of different races, including one case of a Spanish woman who married a mulatto slave.[113]

Despite the numerical gains of the mulatto population, however, this segment of society was not increasing at the same rate as the rest of the community. For example, the percentage of mulattoes dropped from 9.6 to 7.6 percent between 1778 and 1813. During the same time, as Appendices II and III demonstrate, the whites, mestizos, and Indians were more prolific.[114] It appears that miscegenation occurred basically in two stages. First the black was diluted with the Indian, white, or mestizo, and then the resultant mulatto appears to have mixed with these same racial groups. Thus slowly, generation after generation, first the black and then his hybrid son were absorbed into the population.[115]

Although the black is no longer visible in Chile, he is nonetheless present. He is an integral part of the nation's gene pool, the ancestor to thousands, perhaps millions, of people. His most lasting monuments are the fields and cities of Chile, both of which he helped cultivate and build. The black is part of the *raza chilena*, not the romantic, pseudoscientific myth, but the real *raza*: those who lived, worked, and struggled to free and build Chile.

APPENDIX I

Racial Composition of Chile, 1540-1813

Year	Spanish	Indians	Mestizos	Negro-Mulatto		Total
1540	154	1,000,000		10		1,000,164[a]
1570	7,000	550,000	10,000	10,000		624,000[a]
1590	9,000	540,000	17,000	20,000		582,000[a]
1600	10,000	500,000	20,000	19,000		549,000[a]
1620	15,000	480,000	40,000	22,500		557,000[a]
				Negro	Mulatto	
1777	124,292	18,798	16,609	3,103	19,712	182,514[b]
1786	187,056	15,220	22,339	5,646	15,220	245,481[b]
1813	281,287	36,739	34,061	1,531	29,086	382,704[b]

a. Mellafe, p. 226.

b. Marcello Carmagnani, "Colonial Latin American Demography: Growth of Chilean Population, 1700-1830," *Journal of Social History*, I (1967), pp. 183, 185. The figures given are only for the Bishopric of Santiago. The population of the Bishopric of Concepción, where the largest concentration of Indians were to be found, was not tabulated by Carmagnani. (The figures given for the Bishopric of Santiago are only approximate. They were obtained by taking the percentages given by Carmagnani and then applying these to the total population.)

APPENDIX II

Comparison of Racial Components in the Bishopric of Santiago for the Years 1778 and 1813

	Spanish	Indian	Mestizo	Negro	Mulatto
1778	120,646	18,301	16,169	2,912	19,149[a]
1813	281,287	36,740	34,061	1,531	29,085[b]
	160,641	18,439	17,892	1,381	9,936
	133%	101%	111%	−47%	52%

APPENDIX III

Racial Composition of Births in Quillota, 1640-1800

Decade Ending in	Spanish	Indian	Mestizo	Negro	Mulatto	Total[c]
1650	16	111	1	23	0	151
1660	32	76	5	9	0	122
1670	87	108	26	5	8	234
1680	67	97	5	2	5	176
1690	92	85	13	4	11	205
1700	248	112	31	8	29	428
1710	261	77	74	14	16	442
1720	286	26	78	11	22	423
1730	314	35	69	14	18	450
1740	691	74	151	24	25	965
1750	757	60	93	18	33	961
1760	1,039	108	48	22	75	1,292
1770	851	75	101	13	96	1,136
1780	420	53	115	10	108	706
1790	1,878	71	51	7	73	2,080
1800	1,165	59	54	16	44	1,338

a. Klein and Carmagnani.

b. Marcello Carmagnani, "Colonial Latin American Demography: Growth of Chilean Population, 1700-1830," *The Journal of Social History,* Vol. 1, 1962.

c. Carlos Ponce de Leon Gotternarm, "Quillota y su etnologia durante la colonia," *BACH* 21 (1954); 136.

Notes

[1]*Raza chilena: libro escrito por un chileno i para los Chilenos* (Valparaíso, 1904); Francisco A. Encina, *Historia de Chile* (Santiago, 1949-1952), 3: 5-73; Luis Thayer Ojeda, *Elementos étnicos que han intervenido en la población de Chile* (Santiago, 1919), pp. 134-136.

[2]José Antonio Saco, *Historia de la esclavitud de la raza africana en el nuevo mundo* (Barcelona, 1879), p. 166; Domingo Amunátegui Solar, *Historia social de Chile* (Santiago, 1932), p. 173; Docs. 40, 41, *Colección de documentos inéditos para la historia de Chile*, ed. José Toribio Medina (Santiago, 1888-1902), 5: 219, 223, 229; Doc. 26, 8: 91; Doc. 2, 9: 9; Doc. 2, 23: 27; Doc. 15, 22: 267; Docs. 1, 4, 12: 26, 262 (hereafter cited as *CDIC*); "Will of Diego de Almagro," *Harkness Collection in the Library of Congress* (Washington, D.C., 1936), pp. 7, 35, 69, 115, 117, 121 (hereafter cited as *Harkness Collection*); "Algunos documentos relativos a Pedro de Valdivia," *Revista Chilena de Historia y Geografía*, 115 (1950): 20, 25-26 (hereafter cited as *RCHG*).

[3]L. Strude Erdman, "La ruta de D. Diego de Almagro a Chile," *Revista de Historia Americana* 55 (1963): 6 (hereafter cited as *RHA*).

[4]Tomás Thayer Ojeda, *Formación de la sociedad chilena* (Santiago, 1939), 1: 239; "Memoria de la gente que han muerto los indios en estas provincias de Chile después que gobierna Francisco de Villagra," in *Colección de historiadores de Chile y documentos relativos a la historia desde el viaje de Magallanes hasta la batalla de Maipú, 1518-1818*, ed. José Toribio Medina (Santiago, 1861-1953), 29: 505 (hereafter cited as *CHC*); Alonso de Ercilla, *La araucana* (Buenos Aires, 1944), 2: 224.

[5]Tomás Thayer Ojeda and Carlos Larrain, *Valdivia y sus compañeros* (Santiago, 1950), p. 58; Thayer Ojeda, *Formación*, 3: 20-23; Tomás Thayer Ojeda, *Las antiguas ciudades de Chile* (Santiago, 1911), p. 9; Tomás Thayer Ojeda, "Biografias de conquistadores de Chile: Don Martin de Avendaño y Velasco; Leonardo Cartés y Alonso Despero," *RCHG* 49 (1922): 372. An *encomienda*—an institution that entrusted a group of Indians to the custody of a Spaniard who, in return for providing for their spiritual and physical welfare, was permitted to exact a tribute in labor from his charges. See Charles Gibson, *Spain in America* (New York, 1966), pp. 49-50.

[6]Encina, 1: 421-422.

[7]Pedro Mariño de Lovera, "Crónica del reino de Chile," in *CHC*, 6: 375; Antonio Vásquez de Espinosa, *Compendium and Description of the*

West-Indies, trans. Charles Upson Clark (Washington, 1942), p. 743.

[8]"Cartas de Rodrigo de Quiroga al Rey de España," in Claudio Gay, *Historia física y política de Chile: Documentos sobre la historia, la estadística y la geografía* (Paris, 1852), 2: 118 (hereafter cited as *Documentos*).

[9]Gonzalo Vial Correa, "Teoria y práctica de la igualdad en Indias," *Historia* 3 (1964): 124. Thayer Ojeda questioned whether Varela was of African extraction. See his *Formación*, 2: 206; 3: 325.

[10]Alejandro Lipschutz, *El problema racial en la conquista de América y el mestizaje* (2d ed., Santiago, 1967), pp. 204, 206-207.

[11]Borah and Cook estimated Mexico's pre-Columbian population at 25.2 million: Woodrow W. Borah and Sherburne F. Cook, *The Aboriginal Population of Central Mexico on the Eve of the Spanish Conquest* (Berkeley, Cal., 1963), p. 89; Peru's population was between 3.5 million and 6.75 million: John L. Phelan, *The Kingdom of Quito in the Seventeenth Century: Bureaucratic Politics in the Spanish Empire* (Madison, Wis., 1967), p. 44. At approximately the same time, Chile's population was numbered between 500,000 and 1 million: Anjel Rosenblat, *La población indígena y el mestizaje en América* (Buenos Aires, 1954), 1: 318-319.

[12]Domingo Amunátegui Solar, *Las encomiendas de indígenas en Chile* (Santiago, 1909), 1: 60.

[13]Doc. 50, *CDIC*, 28: 284-297; Doc. 23 in Elias Lizana M., *Colección de documentos históricos recopilados del archivo del arzobispado de Santiago* (Santiago, 1919-1921), 1: 63-68. In a letter from Fray Juan Pérez de Espinosa to the king, he noted that "the unsubjugated Indians preferred to die rather than surrender, since if they capitulated, the Spanish would only work them to death." See also Doc. 25, Lizana, 1: 117-119.

[14]Doc. 50, *CDIC*, 28: 284-297; E. Pereira S., "Las Ordenanzas del Gobernador de Chile don Francisco de Villagrá," *RHA* 32 (1951): 207-225; "Tasa y ordenanzas sobre los tributos de los indios, hechas por el gobernador Martín Ruiz de Gamboa, 7 de mayo de 1580," *Colección de documentos inéditos para la historia de Chile*, 2d series (Santiago, 1956), 3: 58-68 (hereafter cited as *CDIC*, 2d ser.); "Instrucciones y ordenanzas para los administradores del pueblo de indios dictadas por el gobernador Martin Garcia Oñez de Loyola, 4 de febrero de 1593," *CDIC*, 2d ser., 4: 259-267; "Tasa y ordenanzas para el Reino de Chile, hecha por don Francisco de Borja, Principe de Esquilache, 28 de marzo de 1620," in Alvaro Jara, *Fuentes para la historia de trabajo en el Reino de Chile* (Santiago, 1965), pp. 71-89; Docs. 2, 12, 17, 122, in Lizana, 1: 3-4, 32-34, 41-43, 292-293; "Dictamen del Padre Diego de Rosales de la Compañía de

Jesús, sobre la esclavitud de los indíjenas chilenos, dirijido al majestad de Carlos II, en el año 1672," in Amunátegui Solar, *Las encomiendas*, 2: 184-272.

[15]Alonso de Góngora Marmolejo, *Historia de Chile desde su descubrimiento hasta el año de 1575*, in *CHC*, 2: 57; Rosenblat, 1: 260.

[16]Real Cédulas 201, 202, 206, 214, 217, in Lizana, 2: 407-408, 410-416, 424-425, 437-438, 442-443 (hereafter cited as RC); see also Eugene Korth, S.J., *Spanish Policy in Colonial Chile* (Stanford, Cal., 1967), pp. 117-138.

[17]Archivo Gay-Morla, vol. 95, cited by Rolando Mellafe, *La introducción de la esclavitud negra en Chile* (Santiago, 1959), p. 59; Doc. 50, 28: 291.

[18]Medina, manuscripts, Vol. 273, doc. 8028, in Mellafe, p. 147; Amunátegui Solar, *Historia social de Chile*, p. 177; RC 230, Lizana, 2: 471; Actas del Cabildo, 17 February 1626, in *CHC*, 28: 354; *Archivo de la Real Audiencia*, Vol. 1698 (hereafter cited as *RA*).

[19]Alonzo González de Najera, *Desengaño y reparo de la guerra de Chile*, in *CHC*, 16: 259-302; Doc. 50, *CDIC*, 28: 284-297; Doc. 46, Lizana, 1: 111; Korth, pp. 96-116. See also Roberto L. Brady, "The Role of Las Casas in the Emergence of Negro Slavery in the New World," *RHA* 61 (1966): 43-57.

[20]Saco, pp. 69, 81, 141. For additional material on this subject, see Georges Scelle, *La traite négrière aux Indes de Castille: Contrats et traités d'asiento* (Paris, 1906); Phillip D. Curtin, *The Atlantic Slave Trade: A Census* (Madison, Wis., 1969).

[21]Doc. 4, *CDIC*, 60: 109; Doc. 60, *CDIC*, 8: 180; Doc. 43, *CDIC*, 2d ser., 2: 79; Archivo Gay-Morla, Vol. 95, in Mellafe, p. 59; RC 26, 30, 42, 44 in Lizana, 2: 43-44, 49-50, 171, 174-175.

[22]Benjamin Vicuña Mackenna, *Historia de Valparaíso*, in *Obras Completas de Benjamin Vicuña Mackenna* (Santiago, 1936), 4: 429-431; Elena F. S. de Studer, *La trata de negros en el Rio de la Plata durante el siglo XVIII* (Buenos Aires, 1958). Cuadros 2, 5, 17.

[23]Thayer Ojeda, *Formación*, 2: 104; Mellafe, pp. 67-78; Doc. 8, *CDIC*, 30: 199; Doc. 192, *CDIC*, 2d ser., 2: 47-48.

[24]Mellafe, pp. 195-196; Actas del Cabildo, 9 August 1630, 17 November 1630, *CHC*, 30: 190, 300.

[25]Mellafe, pp. 198-201, 203-204.

[26]Amunátegui Solar, *Historia social de Chile*, p. 175.

[27]Studer, pp. 27-29; see also Alice P. Canabrava, *O comércio portugues no Rio da Prata, 1580-1640* (São Paulo, 1944); Diego Molinari, *La trata de*

negros: datos para su estudio en el Rio de la Plata (2d ed., Buenos Aires, 1944), pp. 58 ff.

[28]José Torre Revelo, "Un contrabandista del siglo XVII en el Rio de la Plata," *RHA*, 44 (1958): 123-128; Studer, p. 100.

[29]Mellafe, pp. 253-255, 257; Carlos Sempat Assadourian, *El tráfico de esclavos en Córdoba de Angola a Potosí, siglos XVI-XVII* (Córdoba, 1966); González de Najera, p. 270; Actas del Cabildo, 30 July 1616, 27 October 1622, *CHC*, 25: 149, 28: 84.

[30]Studer, pp. 126, 147-159, 237, provides a detailed analysis of the *asientos* during this period. Material on the changes in Spanish slave trade policy during the eighteenth and early nineteenth centuries can be found in James F. King, "The Evolution of the Free Slave Trade Principle in Spanish Colonial Administration," *Hispanic American Historical Review* 23 (1942): 34-56 (hereafter cited as *HAHR*).

[31]Curtis Nettles, "England and the Spanish American Trade, 1680-1715," *Journal of Modern History* 2 (1931): 3; Arthur S. Aiton, "The Asiento Treaty as Reflected in the Papers of Lord Shelbourne," *Hispanic American Historical Review* 8 (1928): 131. George Nelson, "Contraband Trade Under the Asiento," *American Historical Review* 51 (1945): 58-61, 63, 65.

[32]Studer, p. 238; Archivo de la Capitanía General, Vol. 906 (hereafter cited as ACG). For other examples of Chileans involved in this trade, see ACG, Vols. 131, 138, 148.

[33]Studer, pp. 112, 117, 235. For a more detailed study of the high morality rate aboard these ships, see Cuadros 2, 5, 17; Vicuña Mackenna, *Historia de Valparaíso*, 3: 153.

[34]Aiton, p. 171; Nicolás de la Cruz y Bahamonde, "Diario de viaje de Talca a Cádiz en 1783," *RCHG* 91 (1941): 149-150.

[35]Vicuña Mackenna, *Historia de Valparaíso*, 4: 431-438. See also ACG, Vol. 668. Gonzalo Vial Correa claimed that there was another slave rebellion on a vessel called the *San Nepomuceno*: Gonzalo Vial Correa, *El africano en el reino de Chile* (Santiago, 1957), p. 91.

[36]Vicuña Mackenna, *La edad del oro en Chile* (Santiago, 1932), 1: 35, 38-39, 59-60.

[37]Néstor Meza Villa, "La política indígena en el siglo XVI," *RCHG* 112 (1948): 36-37; Actas del Cabildo, 7 April 1622, 4 January 1627, *CHC*, 28: 14-18, 401; 4 May 1629, *CHC*, 30: 94-95.

[38]Actas del Cabildo, 9 December 1545, 9 August 1550, *CHC*, 1: 120, 252-255.

[39]Doc. 50, *CDIC*, 28: 299.

[40]E. Pereira S., pp. 221-222.

[41]Actas del Cabildo, 14 March 1553, *CHC*, 1: 341.

[42]Actas del Cabildo, 10 December 1548, 7 January 1550, 9 August 1550, *CHC*, 1: 161-162, 224, 254-255.

[43]Actas del Cabildo, 1 September 1550, 24 January 1551, 1 July 1553, *CHC*, 1: 258, 263, 352-352. The *alcalde de minas* was also supposed to protect the Indians and ensure their good treatment: Actas del Cabildo, 23 March 1579, *CHC*, 18: 103-104; 8 January 1627, *CHC*, 27: 401-402.

[44]Marcello Carmagnani and Herbert Klein, "Demografía histórica, La población del Obispado de Santiago, 1777-1778," *Boletin de la Academia Chilena de la Historia*, Vol. 32, 1965 (hereafter cited as *BACH*); Carlos Keller R., "El Norte Chico en la época de la formación de la República," *RCHG* 123 (1954-1955): 50-51.

[45]"Ordenanzas hechas para el servicio de los indios de las provincias de Chile y que sean relevados del servicio personal," Gay, *Documentos*, 2: 317-346.

[46](A *fundo* is the Chilean equivalent of the *hacienda*.) Amunátegui Solar, *Historia social*, p. 180; Mario Góngora, *Origen de los 'Inquilinos' de Chile central* (Santiago, 1960), pp. 130-133; Marcello Carmagnani, *El salariado mineros en Chile colonial* (Santiago, 1963), pp. 23-24; Docs. 77, 81, 98, Lizana, 1: 177, 188-189, 231-234.

[47]Vásquez de Espinosa, p. 728; Actas del Cabildo, 14 March 1656, *CHC*, 35: 170-171. See also Actas, 14, 27 June 1681, *CHC*, 41: 41, 50; Archivo de los Jesuítas, Vol. 62 (hereafter cited as AJ); See also AJ, Vols. 9, 23; ACG, Vol. 331; Korth, pp. 257-258; Amunátegui Solar, *Historia social*, p. 186; Horacio Aránguiz Donoso, "Notas para el estudio de la Hacienda de Calera de Tango, 1685-1783," *Historia* 6 (1967): 229-231. There were also cases, however, of blacks fleeing after the estates of the Jesuits were liquidated indicating that, at least for some, life was not all that bad with the blackrobes. See also ACG, Vols. 111, 326.

[48]Vicente Carvallo Goyeneche, *Descripción histórico-jeográfica del Reino de Chile*, in *CHC*, 8: 74.

[49](Davie) *Letters from Buenos Aires and Chili, with an Original History of the Latter Country* (London, 1819), pp. 124-125.

[50]Carvallo Goyeneche, p. 86; Lizardo Valenzuela, "Antecedentes de la fundación de Peumo," *RCHG* 55 (1927): 255.

[51]Carmagnani and Klein, Table III.

[52]Alvaro Jara, *Los asientos de trabajo y la provisión de mano de obra para los*

no-encomenderos en la ciudad de Santiago, 1586-1600 (Santiago, 1959), pp.
23, 25, 33, 57, 59, 71; Actas del Cabildo, 2 March 1611, *CHC*, 24:
240-241, prohibited the taking of gold outside Santiago because there
was not enough remaining for internal commerce.
    [53]Jara, *Asientos*, pp. 43-44, 56. The most highly paid were two
Indians—one a mason, the other a tailor.
    [54]Mellafe, pp. 141, 155.
    [55]Thayer Ojeda, *Formación*, 2: 120, 311.
    [56]Actas del Cabildo, 10 April 1541, *CHC*, 1: 72; 28 June 1567, *CHC*, 17:
164; 16 December 1580, *CHC*, 18: 263; 5 June 1628, *CHC*, 30: 20; 3
March 1685, *CHC*, 42: 27.
    [57]Benjamin Vicuña Mackenna, *Historia de Santiago*, in *Obras Completas*,
11: 390; Samuel Haigh, Esq., *Sketches of Buenos Ayres and Peru* (London,
1831), p. 149; Jaime Eyzaguirre, *Historia de Chile* (Santiago, 1956), p. 105.
    [58]Actas del Cabildo, 3 August 1629, *CHC*, 30: 116.
    [59]Carvallo Goyeneche, p. 55.
    [60]Mellafe, p. 76.
    [61]Actas del Cabildo, 5 January 1545, 25 October 1549, *CHC*, 1:
107-108, 211-212.
    [62]*Ibid.*, 31 July 1551, 19 December 1552, *CHC*, 1: 272, 321-322.
    [63]"Ordenanzas de policía de la capital de Santiago de Chile," Gay,
Documentos, 1: 201-202.
    [64]Mellafe, p. 90; Doc. 9, *CDIC*, 27: 501.
    [65]"Delitos cometidos por doña Catalina de los Ríos i Lisperguer, Es-
pocisión del oïdor Huerta Gutiérrez en 1660," Amunátegui Solar, *Las
encomiendas indíjenas*, 2: 159-179.
    [66]Doc. 122, Lizana, 1: 292-294.
    [67]Actas del Cabildo, 26 January, 27 November 1551, *CHC* 1: 266, 281;
6 August, 30 September 1630, *CHC*, 30: 188-189, 208; González de
Najera, pp. 36-37.
    [68]René León Echaíz, "Historia de Curicó," *RCHG* 50 (1950): 71.
    [69]Medina, Manuscritos, Vol. 95, doc. 1443, in Mellafe, pp. 101-102;
ACG, Vol. 111.
    [70]Book 7, titulo 20-21 in *Recopilación de las leyes de los reinos de las Indias*
(Madrid, 1943).
    [71]Doc. 4, Lizana, 1: 7; Doc. 129, *CDIC*, 2d ser., 2: 337-339. The *cabildo*
subsequently reissued these *Ordenanzas*, although without the name of
Calderón, in 1637: Actas, 3 March 1637, *CHC*, 31: 227-228.
    [72]Actas del Cabildo, 18 February 1605, *CHC*, 21: 191. If a slave was

absent for less than twenty days, his captor received five pesos; if gone more than twenty days, ten pesos; more than a year, twenty pesos. See also Actas, 22 October 1632, *CHC*, 30: 375; 21 January 1605, *CHC*, 21: 188.

[73] Actas, 19 December 1606, *CHC*, 21: 357; 13 December 1613, *CHC*, 24: 451; 17 February 1614, *CHC*, 25: 18; 10 October 1659, *CHC*, 35: 487-488.

[74] Actas, 9 August, 14 September 1630, *CHC*, 30: 188-189, 206-207.

[75] Actas, 17 November 1631, *CHC*, 30: 300.

[76] Miguel Luis Amunátegui, *Los precursores de la Independencia de Chile* (Santiago, 1910), 2: 217-219; "Carta de la real audiencia de Chile sobre el torremoto del 13 de mayo de 1647," in Gay, *Documentos*, 2: 459.

[77] Actas del Cabildo, 9 April 1672, *CHC*, 38: 217; RC 604, Lizana, 3: 614-616.

[78] Actas del Cabildo, 16 February 1685, *CHC*, 41: 21-23.

[79] Actas, 9 October 1608, 13 September 1611, 4 May 1612, *CHC*, 24: 102-103, 277-228, 318; 12 September 1614, *CHC*, 25: 56; 27 June 1625, *CHC*, 28: 279-280.

[80] Vicuña Mackenna, *Historia de Santiago*, 10: 85. Apparently the "torture" was castration.

[81] Actas del Cabildo, 31 December 1544, *CHC*, 1: 108.

[82] Actas, 10 December 1548, *CHC*, 1: 161.

[83] Actas, 25 October 1549, *CHC*, 1: 211.

[84] Actas, 23 October 1631, *CHC*, 30: 291. For other examples, see "Ordenanzas de policía," Gay, *Documentos*, 1: 196, 202-203; Actas, 20 February 1699, *CHC*, 44: 230-231.

[85] RC 190, Lizana, 2: 340, 348.

[86] Actas del Cabildo, 7 January 1550, 27 November 1551, *CHC*, 1: 227, 281. Subsequent legislation was altered to permit the branding of Indians captured in war: Actas, 27 August 1607, *CHC*, 24: 197; "Ordenanzas de Martín Garcia Oñez de Loyola," *CDIC*, 2d ser., 4: 265; Doc. 129, *CDIC*, 2d ser., 2: 377.

[87] Actas del Cabildo, 10 December 1548, 13 October 1549, 29 June 1550, *CHC*, 1: 161-162, 214-215, 218, 245; 3 July 1608, 17 July 1607, *CHC*, 24: 48, 91; 25 June 1629, 30: 103-104, 106; RC 12, 121, 235, Lizana, 2: 17-19, 191-193, 235, 480-516; RC 331, 356, Lizana, 3: 67-70, 116-118.

[88] Magnus Mörner, "The Theory and Practice of Racial Segregation in Colonial Latin America," *Proceedings of the Thirty-Second International*

Congress of Americanists (Copenhagen, 1958), pp. 709-710. The Real Cedula 655, published in 1702, prohibited Spaniards and mestizos from crossing the Bío Bío River, Lizana, 4: 55-57.

[89]"Real cédula al Gobierno de la provincia de Chile para que no permita que los negros vivan entre los indios, 23 de septiembre de 1580," in Jara, p. 197; Doc. 52, *CDIC*, 2d ser., 4: 267.

[90]Doc. 40, *CDIC*, 29: 295; "Ordenanzas de policia," Gay, *Documentos*, 1: 198, 202; Actas del Cabildo, 19 December 1552, *CHC*, 1: 322.

[91]Actas del Cabildo, 12 January 1617, *CHC*, 25: 171; José Toribio Medina, *Cosas de la Colonia* (Santiago, 1952), pp. 194-195; Docs. 155 and 235, Lizana, 1: 350-351, 502-503.

[92]José Armando de Ramón Folch, "La sociedad española de Santiago de Chile entre 1581 y 1596: Bautizos de indígenas según los libros del Sagrario de Santiago, correspondiente a los años 1581-1596," *Historia* 4 (1965): 230. Of the total of 1,943 children baptized, 120 or 7 percent were black, 13 or 1 percent were *zambos*, and 70 or 4 percent were mulattoes.

[93]Actas del Cabildo, 9 October 1608, *CHC*, 24: 102; 3 July 1700, *CHC*, 44: 347.

[94]Mario Góngora, "Sondeos en la antroponimia colonial de Chile," *Anuario de Estudios Americanos* 24 (1967): 1324-1355.

[95]ACG, Vol. 109.

[96]ACG, Vols. 29, 73, 87.

[97]ACG, Vols. 28, 30, 109, 697; *Archivo de la Real Audiencia*, Vols. 1765, 1779 (hereafter cited as *RA*).

[98]ACG, Vol. 17.

[99]Doc. 121, *Cosas de la colonia*, pp. 80-81.

[100]ACG, Vols. 28, 107, 805.

[101]Congreso Nacional, 11, 15, 16, 21, 22 October 1811, in *Sesiones de los Cuerpos Legislativos de la República de Chile, 1811 a 1843*, ed. Valentin Letelier (Santiago, 1887-1889), 1: 133-134, 150, 152, 370 (hereafter cited as *Cuerpos*); see also the comments of the English visitor Alexander Caldcleugh in *Viajeros en Chile 1817-1847* (Santiago, 1955), p. 162.

[102]If an owner refused to permit his slave to join the army, he was to suffer the loss of the purchase price of the slave, have one-half of his goods confiscated, and be exiled for two years: Bando, 29 August 1814, *El Monitor Araucano* in *Colección de historiadores y documentos relativos a la independencia de Chile* (Santiago, 1930), 27: 591-593 (hereafter cited as *CHD*).

[103]Actas del Cabildo, 10 April 1813, *CHC*, 29: 210. If the slave owner did not offer his slave, or could not justify his flight, he was to be fined a sum equal to twice the value of the slave. In addition, the slave would immediately be freed. Ironically, the penalty levied on a slave who did not volunteer his services was far more severe than that of a reluctant owner, indicating that judicial inequality between black and white still existed. "The slaves who prefer to hide like cowards or to flee their homes to avoid enlisting in the legions of the motherland . . . will be punished with 100 lashes, 3 years in jail, and condemned to perpetual slavery." *El Monitor Araucano*, 14 September 1814, in *CHD*, 27: 601-602.

[104]Haigh, pp. 213, 235.

[105]Congreso de Plenipotenciarios y Senado Conservador, 2, 9, 21 July 1823, in *Cuerpos*, 7: 252, 271, 297-298. For a definitive study of the abolition of slavery in Chile, see Guillermo Feliú Cruz, *La abolición de la esclavitud en Chile* (Santiago, 1942).

[106]Luis Thayer Ojeda, "La formación de la raza chilena," *RCHG* 26 (1918): 87; Alberto Cabero, *Chile y los chilenos* (Santiago, 1926), p. 86.

[107]In a recent article one scholar claimed that Chile's racial components were: Indians 3.17 percent; white 52.7 percent; mestizo 44 percent; Zambos, blacks and Negroes 0; various 0.13. Claudio Esteva Fabregat, "El mestizaje en Ibero-America," *Revista de Indias* 24 (1964): 336.

[108]Encina, 3: 55; Luis Thayer Ojeda, p. 87; Vial Correa, *El africano*, pp. 123-125.

[109]Magnus Mörner, *Race Mixture in the History of Latin America* (Boston, 1967), p. 19, claims that the blacks were more resistant to disease than the Indians as a consequence of the ordeals of the Atlantic crossing, which served to eliminate those blacks who were physically unfit.

[110]De Ramón Folch, p. 230.

[111]Carmagnani and Klein, Tables I, III; Keller, pp. 50-51; Archivo Nacional, *Censo de 1813 levantado por don Juan Egaña, de orden de la junta de gobierno formada por los señores Pérez, Infante, y Eyzaguirre* (Santiago, 1953); Marcello Carmagnani, "Colonial Latin American Demography: Growth of Chilean Population, 1700-1830," *The Journal of Social History* 1 (1967): 179-191. A word of warning must be given about these census figures. Because the determination of one's race was the decision of the local priest—the Church registered all births and deaths—this could, and often did, result in some rather curious results. In one case, of seven children born of a *zambo* mother and a "*cholo*," that is, a mestizo father, three were classified as *zambos*, three as mestizos, and one as Spanish. Of

the eight children born of a Spanish father and a *zambo* mother, four were classified as Spanish, one as a mestizo, one as a mulatto, one as a *zambo*, and the last was "unknown." Obviously one has to conclude that racial perception was not always accurate, and this limits the utility of the census figures. It is not only possible but probable that people who were either black or mulatto were inaccurately classified. The examples cited are to be found in the Parish records, *Doctrina de Curepto, 1750-1790*. The author wishes to acknowledge the assistance of Robert MaCaa, who very kindly allowed me to use the data he had collected for his doctoral dissertation.

[112]Studer indicates that of the slaves imported during the British *asiento*, there were approximately twice as many men as women. This appears to have been true for Chile as well.

[113]*Libros de matrimonios de Doctrina de Curepto, 1750-1785*. Of the thirty-three marriages involving blacks, twelve or 36 percent were with whites—eight Spanish women and four Spanish men; eleven or 33 percent were with Indians—six women and five men; eight or 24 percent were with mestizos—six women and two men; two or 6 percent were between blacks or mulattoes.

[114]Carlos Ponce de León Gutterbarm, "Quillota y su etnología durante la colonia," *BACH* 21 (1954): 136.

[115]Carl Stern, *Human Genetics* (San Francisco, 1960), p. 358, indicates that the absorption of the black population would indeed occur over a prolonged period of time.

2

Health Conditions
in the Slave Trade of
Colonial New Granada*

David L. Chandler

Of all the discomforting topics relating to slavery, perhaps the slave trade represents the most tragic episode of all. There is abundant documentation available on the seamy business of transporting human cargoes from Africa. Mortality rates soared on the crowded and unhealthy vessels; often ships arrived in America with less than one-half the number of Africans originally taken. Brazilians appropriately called the ships tumbeiros, *or floating tombs.*

The story of what happened to the millions of involuntary African immigrants after they first arrived in the New World needs greater attention. As David L. Chandler points out, safe arrival at a major slave depot like Cartagena (in present-day Colombia) was no indication that the bondsmen's confrontations with serious health hazards were over. Weakened by the rigors of their first voyage, Africans continued to contract diseases while waiting in crowded slave pens. Finally, the long trek over New Granada's rugged terrain and through varied climatic conditions raised mortality rates to still more staggering totals. The internal slave trade, an important element in colonial Latin American history,

*Research for this article was supported by the Tulane University International Center for Medical Research and Training, Grant TW-00143 from the Office of International Research, National Institutes of Health, U.S. Public Health Service.

51

deserves careful study, however grim the record may be. Yet, as Chandler notes, this historical record also contains some lessons that suggest hope. In time conditions improved for imported slaves—not only because of advances in science but also because of growing humanitarian sentiments.

R.B.T.

During the centuries of the slave trade, thousands of Africans were landed at the Caribbean port of Cartagena to meet the demand for labor in the mines and haciendas of the Viceroyalty of New Granada (modern Panama, Colombia, Ecuador, and Venezuela). Not only New Granada but the rest of the continent clamored for slaves, which Spanish commercial practice funneled through the Viceroyalty. Cartagena became the crossroads of the Spanish Empire in America, the principal city of the Spanish slave trade, and the supply depot for much of the rest of the continent.[1] The international slave trade that brought these blacks to New Granada, and the domestic trade that distributed them within her borders and beyond to other Spanish colonies, were marked at every stage by monumental suffering and staggering mortality. The transactions of this Spanish slave emporium give painful insights into the health conditions of the slave trade and the history of the Negro in Latin America.

The slaves and slaving vessels legally entering Cartagena and other Spanish ports during most of the colonial period underwent several standard inspections. There were at least five: the health inspection (*visita de sanidad*), the inventory inspection (*visita de reconocimiento e inventario*), the anchorage inspection (*visita de fondeo*), the entry inspection (*visita de entrada*), and the customs clearance (*visita de palmeo* or simply *palmeo*). Immediately after a slave ship anchored, the captain or supercargo registered the arrival of his ship and requested port officials to begin the inspections.

The health inspection was the most urgent, since it was deemed essential to prevent the spread of epidemics, and ships were required to lie at anchor in the harbor until they had received it.[2] When Negroes had to be kept on board for long periods after arrival in port, deaths among them often mounted so rapidly that importers faced financial ruin.[3] Most captains, therefore, urged port authorities to inspect their slaves as soon as possible, so that they could be put ashore. Since every slave ship was also a potential threat to public health, port officials acted promptly. The governor ordered the *protomedicato*, the royal health officer, to board slave ships and inspect the crews and cargoes of Negroes for evidence of epidemic, or "dangerous," disease. The purpose of the inspection was not a thorough medical inspection, but rather a hurried check to see if "pestilential" or "putrid" fevers or other "distempers" such as smallpox, measles, or yellow fever were aboard.[4] Medical men varied widely in the thoroughness of their inspections. Francisco Lasuriaga, *protomedicato* of Cartagena, was rather meticulous. He inspected 116 Negroes introduced by the Malhorti *Asiento* Company in 1742 and apparently examined each slave individually, for he informed the governor that "according to their appearance and their pulses they are completely healthy."[5] Most health officers, though, were less exacting. They tried to ascertain that there was no danger of epidemic disease, but were content with only a cursory inspection. Francisco Beltrán, acting *protomedicato* of Portobelo, Cartagena's sister city on the Isthmus of Panama, was typical. He hurriedly inspected 220 Negroes in 1778 and reported simply that they "seemed" well and were "without disease that might infect the citizenry, for which reason I contemplate no inconvenience in their disembarkation."[6]

If the *protomedicato*'s inspection revealed dangerous disease on board, the captain was required to land the Negroes several miles outside the city. This quarantine, until the mid-seventeenth century, applied only to the Negroes with actual symptoms of disease and not to the whole cargo, and captains usually divided their cargoes. Seemingly healthy slaves were sent to slave pens in the city, while the dangerously ill were quarantined outside the city. A third group was sometimes temporarily left on the ship. It consisted of slaves who were not dangerously ill, but who were physically unable to disembark—the invalids, the very weak, those with broken limbs. They remained on board until they were well enough to walk off the ship or until a cart could be secured to move them to the pens or occasionally to private homes for better care.[7]

Slave ships often arrived in port with their cargoes in terrible medical condition. The blacks harbored an inevitable assortment of physical defects, wounds, abscesses, bruises, and maimed and missing limbs as well as a variety of contagious and noncontagious diseases. A Jesuit in Cartegena, Father Alonzo de Sandoval, saw the arrival of many slave ships between 1607 and 1610. He calculated that the poor food and bad treatment of the Middle Passage killed one-third of the cargo before landing at Cartagena. He was little surprised that many of the remaining two-thirds were dying, or that all were but mere skeletons. He never failed to be scandalized by the stench and misery that he inevitably found in the holds of these "floating coffins" and remarked in disgust that "there is no Spaniard who dare put his face to the hatch without being nauseated, nor who can stay below deck one hour without risk of grave illness."[8] Sandoval's disciple and successor, Pedro Claver, later canonized for his work among the slaves, bore similar testimony of the health conditions of arriving slaves. He deplored the terrible stench always present among these Negroes and attributed it to "the many contagious diseases with which they came to these parts. . . ."[9]

The Negroes almost always brought scurvy, dysentery, and yaws, none of which concerned the health inspectors. Often, however, the ships brought slaves infected with typhus, measles, smallpox, typhoid, and yellow fever, which caused great concern to officials and public as well. In the case of these epidemic diseases the mortality rate could soar. Smallpox sometimes killed 70 percent of the Negroes it infected, and seldom less than 10 percent of whites. Measles, historically more virulent than it is today, often caused even more deaths than smallpox. Yellow fever was more lethal to whites than to Negroes, but both suffered in a general mortality that reportedly passed 60 percent.[10]

The arrival of ships with epidemics on board was frequent in the seventeenth century. In 1634 Viceroy Chinchón in Lima complained of the high incidence of smallpox and measles among Negroes arriving from Panama. He ordered that they be detained a league's distance from the city until a physician could certify that they were free from these two scourges that they "always" brought with them.[11] In Cartagena ship-borne epidemics were so frequent that every ship was suspect. Jesuits were urged routinely to meet every slave ship and inquire for the sick and the quarantined. Moreover, to the description of the terrible epidemic of 1651, Sandoval added cryptically, "I could cite many of these cases, being so continual as they are in shipments of Negroes. Each day there arrive some that are sick and bring contagious illnesses."[12]

The health inspection was intended to guard against the spread of these scourges, but given the inadequate quarantine restrictions of the day, the inspection usually failed to do that. As a result, epidemics were often generated by the arrival of a cargo of infected Negroes or by the arrival of the annual merchant fleet and convoy from Spain, which often brought Negroes. The fleet's arrival created a prime setting for the outbreak of an epidemic. It signaled the beginning of the celebrated Cartagena fair, which attracted thousands of merchants and buyers from inland provinces. The city was ill equipped to accommodate the hordes of visitors who in a crowded, medieval city like Cartagena became easy prey for disease.[13]

In some cases slave ships arrived in port to find the city already in the grip of an epidemic and lost many blacks as a result. Cartagena and other cities of the tropics, even until modern times, were proverbially unhealthy. Repeated epidemics of tropical fevers, dysenteries, and other illnesses sometimes killed thousands within a few days.[14] During the second quarter of the seventeenth century Cartagena was harried by four serious, though unidentified, epidemics.[15]

In some cases it was not clear whether the Negroes infected the town or whether contagion spread from the town to the Negroes. Such confusion was true of the devastating epidemic of 1651, which one contemporary thought was a lethal combination of smallpox, measles, typhoid, and dysentery.[16] The fleet had brought several thousand Negroes. Even though sick Negroes were set ashore far from the city, the epidemic struck. Overcrowding on the eve of the fair left no accommodations for the sick or for the well. Father Andrade, a Jesuit, described it:

> There began a most furious plague, which beginning among the visitors spread to the citizenry to such an extent that there was not a house nor a family that was not afflicted by the pestilential contagion. The hospitals contained 500 sick. All the houses of the city and even the ships themselves were made into hospitals. There was great need. The Negroes, as the people most forgotten and neglected, suffered most. They were full of sores and worms, with no beds nor shelter, and the pestilential odor that emanated from them was so vehement that it affected the head and paralyzed the senses of those that came near them. A monk tried to enter a place where some of them were, but upon merely arriving at the door, with its infected air, he lost consciousness and was so faint and nauseated that he was not himself for the next two days. Another priest went to administer the sacraments to a Negro, and from only the bad odor that he smelled, he became so nauseated that for two days he could not rid himself of headache, retain even a mouthful of food, nor attend to his duty.[17]

Father Sandoval confessed that on hearing of the arrival of a slave ship in the harbor he trembled in anticipation of his work

among the Negroes. In the epidemic of 1651 he visited the blacks
who had been quarantined outside the city. He found many of the
sick "swollen from the impact of the disease, and it would seem
very dangerous [contagious]." Three of the slaves he catechized
and baptized were ill with dysentery. Two died before morning,
and the other died in his presence later in the day.[18]

Fortunately the conditions of the slave trade to Spanish
America improved with the passage of time. Increased knowledge of disease and better methods of handling the sick caused
mortality to decline both at sea and in port. Quarantine regulations changed greatly by the middle of the next century to require
the whole cargo to be isolated if any were infected. This whole-
some change also played a part in dropping the mortality. The
most important factor in the decline of the mortality, however,
was the use of way stations in the passage from Africa. During the
last two decades of the seventeenth century, slave merchants
began supplying slaves to Spanish America from "refreshment"
centers in the Antilles such as Jamaica or Puerto Rico. There new
Negroes recuperated from the long, rigorous Middle Passage
and were generously fed with fresh food. Their ills were
treated—and camouflaged—and the very sick either died or were
left behind.

Even with these favorable factors in play, available records
from the eighteenth century indicate that fully 10 percent of the
slave ships that arrived in Portobelo were quarantined with some
epidemic on board.[19]

No health inspection records have been found for the seventeenth century, before the use of refreshment became general,
but health conditions must have been much worse, according to
contemporary accounts by Sandoval, Claver, and others. Conditions were bad enough in either century. With good reason the
city trembled when the fleet put into port or when a slaver
anchored in the harbor. It is easy to understand the eagerness of
city officials to conduct the health inspection. If the *visita* revealed
no epidemic disease, normal processing of the slaves began. The
captain was directed to disembark the Negroes on the wharf of

the royal counting house, where port officials took an inventory and compared it with the bill of lading issued at the port of embarkation. The captain had to account for any discrepancies. Deaths at sea, either of Negroes or of crewmen, were sworn to under oath both by the captain and by his men. After the slaves had been unloaded, officials conducted the anchorage inspection—a search of the ship for contraband—and then proceeded with the entry inspection, in which they required the captain to answer under oath a set of standard questions regarding the composition of his cargo, the behavior of his crew, the identity of his passengers, and the itinerary of his ship. When all these preliminaries were concluded, the cargo of blacks was released to the factor or owner, who made arrangements for their care during the minimum two-week waiting period before customs clearance could be effected.[20]

Occasionally the slaves were accommodated during that waiting period in yards adjacent to the counting house, but usually they went to barracoons or *casas negrerias* within the city itself. Sometimes these were compounds next to the city wall, which made use of archlike recessions in the walls for shelter. More often owners corralled the blacks in the patios of their own homes. One in Cartagena, belonging to Theadora de Rivera, was a high, elegant building located on Tezadello Street. Its large, walled backyard was evidently constructed as a barracoon or, at any rate, served that purpose well. Many merchants' homes had barracoons in their patios that could accommodate two to three hundred Negroes. Captain Francisco Caballero had one of these corrals in the rear of his large house on the main street of Cartagena. There was another in the house of Captain Granzo next to the convent of San Agustin. Gundisalvo Arias had another in his home next to the Plaza de los Gaguyes. Still another was situated on the main street not far from the cathedral. Cartagena had at least twenty-four of these slave houses in the first half of the seventeenth century. Other merchants whose houses would not accommodate the Negroes corralled them in barracoons elsewhere in the city, separated from, but usually near by, their houses.[21] The center of the black commerce and its slave pens was located in the city's Santo Domingo and Santa Clara districts just inside the wall adjacent to the wharf. The processions of newly arrived Negroes making their way to the pens were undoubtedly pitiful spectacles. Leaving the wharf, the gaunt, naked, sickly Negroes entered the city through the main gates and hobbled through the streets to reach the barracoons. The very sick and dying were piled into carts that accompanied the grim column.[22]

The world of the seventeenth century, with its meager knowledge of the nature and cause of disease, saw little harm in the quartering of new Negroes in towns, and the practice was common, at least until the eighteenth century. Not until 1735 did the important slave port of Jamaica, by then the chief supplier of Negroes to the Spanish mainland, propose its first quarantine act.[23] In seventeenth-century Cartagena even the most distant barracoons could not have been more than ten to fifteen blocks from the center of the city. Slave merchants of Lima, too, were accustomed to bringing freshly imported blacks into the heart of town, where, until 1630, they were lodged in crowded quarters, probably similar to those of Cartagena.[24] Spanish officials thought this practice to be free of hazard because the health inspection was expected to prevent dangerously ill slaves from landing in town.

Because the health inspection did not really serve its purpose, health conditions and mortality often became worse in the barracoons than on the ships. Epidemics in the pens were common and inevitably spread to the city. Dysentery and smallpox took the heaviest tolls, but pneumonia, fevers, typhoid, and measles claimed many victims as well.[25] Even when there were no epidemics in the pens, health conditions were so deplorable that Father Sandoval was astonished that any slaves survived their stay there. A common disease of the barracoons was what Sandoval called "incurable loanda" (probably scurvy), which swelled the body, rotted the gums, and caused sudden death.[26] Sores, wounds, and ulcers were extremely common, and complications caused by gangrene and flies were serious. On one occasion a fellow Jesuit accompanied Sandoval to the door of a room where the sick were confined. At first he could not bring himself to enter, for even from a distance he could see "their bodies, the sustenance of flies and maggots, so ulcerated and oozing pus and matter. . . ." Although Sandoval finally persuaded his companion to help administer the sacraments, the man's experience in the squalor, filth, and stench was so traumatic that he never returned to the slave pens. He was content from then on, as Sandoval observed, "to preach the glories of those who were engaged in this work."[27]

Nor were living conditions in the pens much better than on the ship. Each barracoon had two great cabinlike structures that served as sleeping quarters, one for men and one for women. These were damp, thick-walled structures, usually constructed of adobe, in which crude tiers of sleeping platforms had been erected of rough planks. The Negroes were herded into these for the night, after which the only entrance, a small door, was bolted. A small, high window provided the only ventilation, and sanitary facilities, if any, consisted simply of tubs. Hopelessly incurable slaves spent their remaining hours in these fetid cabins. Owners thought it was useless to waste effort, time, or medicine on them. The blacks were confined by their condition to the crude sleeping platforms "amist that misery and ill fortune and there . . . eaten by flies they finally die[d]." Sandoval understandably believed neglect to be a greater cause of death in the pens than illness.[28]

If a slave survived the disease and squalor of the pens and if his master's neglect did not kill him, ironically his owner's good intentions often did. Slave handlers hoped to fatten the slave for sale, but sometimes the very abundance of food after the privations and hardships of the voyage served only to sicken him—"as if it were a plague, so that in a short time the whole troop [was] inflamed." Negroes in barracoons owned by relatively poor men usually fared better than those belonging to wealthy merchants, since the personal attention of the poorer merchant, whose only concern was the Negroes, usually saved more of them. The wealthy merchant, on the other hand, was so involved in his many concerns that he left the blacks to the care of an employee, whose neglect often cost many lives. The problems caused by improper feeding and improper food, together with the general neglect of overseers, "convert[ed] the house and its contents into a hospital of sick men from which they people[d] the cemetery."[29]

The great mortality in the slave pens caused the Jesuit Provincial to order that all members of his order making visits to the pens had to carry with them at all times the holy oil and other essentials for administering last rites.[30] Except for this attention by the Church, however, dead and dying Negroes were of little worth or concern to most people of the time. Sandoval recalled having come to administer last rites to a slave, and upon arrival he found the slave already dead, lying in the middle of a patio, where many people were milling about. "He was naked, lying face down, swarming with flies. People took no more notice of him than if he had been a dog." On another occasion Sandoval came upon two dead blacks lying stark naked on the bare ground, "as if they were beasts." Nevertheless, by Sandoval's time, the care of the dead slaves had improved considerably. In former years merchants left bodies of Negroes in patios or corrals where they happened to fall, not even piling the dead in one place. By Sandoval's day it had become common among most slave merchants to wrap the bodies in reusable reed matting and throw them into a corner until they could be carted away for burial.[31]

The quartering of slaves in towns, with all its attendant problems and excessive mortality, was probably more common in the seventeenth century than the eighteenth. In Lima even before 1630 the city fathers recommended building a lodging for newly arrived Negroes out of town across the Rimac River near the slaughterhouse, a site well situated for the wind to carry the "corrupted air" away from the town.[32] Cartagena, at least as late as 1654, had not taken similar steps, but by the beginning of the next century, the practice of quartering slaves in Spanish American cities was modified if not discontinued. The *asiento* treaty of 1713 (see note 2), which granted the slave trade to England until nearly midcentury, authorized rental of "plantations" near port cities on which to grow food for "refreshing and preserving in Health the Negro Slaves which they shall import" (Article 35).

The British introduced Negroes in unprecedented numbers; and in order to obtain more ample facilities, as well as to prevent disease, they likely kept them on these outlying farms. Regardless of where the barracoons were located, however, slaves were retained in them for the two-week period stipulated by law before they could be evaluated for the payment of customs duties. The waiting period was designed primarily to protect the slave merchant, since he was exempt from paying duty on any slave who died during that time (Article 24). Perhaps the interim was also intended to protect the buyer and the general public as well, for it was expected that any latent disease would manifest itself by the end of two weeks. Such an interval also allowed an opportunity for the slaves to recover from the voyage, for their sores to heal, and for the sick to be nursed back to health so that buyers could better judge their value. It provided time to put on flesh and to gain strength for the inland trek that many of the slaves would make soon after purchase. This waiting period proved to be advantageous even for the king, since customs duties on a healthy slave could be several times as great as those on an unhealthy slave.

After two weeks had passed, the factor or owner notified the governor in writing and requested that he conduct the curious customs clearance called the *palmeo* (meaning to measure in *palmos*, a Spanish unit of length equivalent to 8-1/2 inches or a quarter of a *vara*).[33] The *palmeo* was an exacting medical examination on which customs duties for slaves were based. The governor notified the royal officials and the surgeon and fixed a date for the proceedings. On the appointed day these officials and the factor or owner met in the counting house, and in the presence of a scribe, who recorded the entire proceedings, took the royal brand (*coronilla*) from the strong box where it was securely locked, customarily under three locks with the keys being in possession of different officials. The brand was a capital R surmounted by a crown, both of which were fashioned from a single piece of heavy silver wire. The officials also took from its place in the counting house the official standard (*listón*) to be used in measuring the slaves. A wooden measuring stick slightly over six feet in length, it was divided by graduations into *palmos*.

Sometimes Negroes were brought to the counting house for the *palmeo*, as was common in Portobelo. At other times officials met in the counting house only to assure the presence of necessary officials and to obtain the *palmeo*. When slaves had been quarantined, the *palmeo* was usually conducted in the place of quarantine.

Slaves who were well enough to stand were divided into four groups according to size and approximate age: *piezas de indias*, adults measuring 7 palmos (5'0'') or more; *mulacones*, adolescents measuring about 6 *palmos* (4'3'') or more; *muleques*, older children measuring about 5 *palmos* (3'5'') or more; and *mulequitos*, young children measuring about 4 *palmos* (2'8'').[34] The slaves were then subdivided into male and female groups in each of these four categories. Children under 4 *palmos* were considered as babes in arms and apparently were not measured in the *palmeo* or considered as dutiable imports.

There was considerable flexibility in these groupings. A slave measuring less than 7 *palmos* but obviously an adult, was, of course, still grouped with the adults. Classification of children was especially flexible. Teenagers from thirteen to sixteen years of age, averaging in size from 6 to 7 *palmos* (4'3'' to the height of an adult) were classed as *mulecones*. Boys and girls from eight to twelve years of age and from 5 to 6 *palmos* in height (3'5'' to 4'2'') were classed as *muleques* or *mulecas*, whereas children under seven years of age but tall enough to measure from 4 to 5 *palmos* (2'8'' and 3'2'') were considered *mulequitos*. Physical development, of course, influenced the classification. If a boy measured 4-1/2 *palmos* but was frail and underdeveloped, he was classed as a *mulequito*, whereas a husky, well-developed boy of the same height and age was generally classed as a *muleque*.

Once this rough grouping had been completed, the surgeon went to each group with the standard and measured all the

Negroes in the group, tallying up the total number of *palmos* in each group. Thus a group of 20 girls (*mulecas*) might have as few as 91, or as many as 110, *palmos*. The surgeon went from group to group until the entire cargo had been measured. Then he revisited each group, examined each Negro for illnesses and defects, and figuratively docked each individual in stature according to the degree of damage caused by his defect. Most surgeons, however, probably with an eye to increasing the king's revenues, did not dock heavily even for serious and incurable ailments that almost totally disabled the slaves. For diseases such as advanced leprosy or mental illness surgeons usually docked only 1 to 2 *palmos*. For serious but curable diseases such as dysentery they usually deducted 1 *palmo*. Docking was correspondingly less severe for less serious defects. For a very bad hernia, slaves were docked as much as 1/2 *palmo* or more, whereas for minor hernias they were docked only 1/4 *palmo* or less. For skin diseases surgeons usually took off 1/4 to 1/2 *palmo*, and for minor defects such as the loss of a finger they reduced the stature only 1/8 *palmo*.[35] When the medical evaluation was finished, the surgeon calculated the total *palmos* docked for each group and subtracted it from each group's total measurement in *palmos* to leave the "effective stature" in *palmos*. After the total number of "effective *palmos*" had been determined for the whole cargo, it was divided by 7 to find the number of "pieces" (*piezas de indias*) or head of prime slaves. That figure was multiplied by the duty chargeable per "piece" to find the amount of duty the importer would pay. For example, in a shipment of 206 slaves introduced by the Ruíz *Asiento*, duty was paid on only 145 3/7 head (145 *piezas* and three *palmos*), the number of "effective head" the cargo was reduced to after the *palmeo* had taken into account children and the illnesses and defects of the cargo.[36] Slaves too sick to stand were reserved for a second *palmeo* and even a third if necessary. Subsequent *palmeos* were arranged by the factor as soon as the remaining group of slaves or a portion of it was well enough to undergo the examination.

Palmeo records reveal a wide variety of ailments among incoming Negroes.[37] Although a large number of slaves were vaguely classified by medical officers as being "sick," "old," "weak," or "dying," surgeons were more specific in their diagnosis in most cases. The most frequent complaint was hernia. It was noted nearly five times as often as other ailments. Dysentery and fevers ranked second. Complaints of permanent disability—such as paralysis, lameness, amputations—were very common too, as were temporary injuries. Impaired vision was surprisingly common among the slaves and was due almost entirely to cloudy lenses (*nubes*) and to a medical condition known as pterygium (*uñas en los ojos*) in which a patch of opaque tissue gradually extended over the clear cornea. Skin diseases, taken as a group, were among the most common complaints for which slaves were docked by port officials. Nearly one-third of these skin ailments were identified simply as "spots" (*manchas*) or "spots of ugly humor" (*manchas de humor feo*). In some cases colonial medical men identified these spots as symptoms of frush or as a disease called salty phlegm (*flema salada*). Probably, however, the symptoms were the purplish spots caused by scurvy, which were visible even on black and brown skins. Negroes having these spots had been introduced directly from Africa without being "refreshed" in the Antilles, and scurvy would certainly have been among them. These spots were never noted among Negroes introduced by later *asientos* after refreshment came into use.

Some common European diseases were absent among the slaves. The virtual absence of venereal and respiratory diseases could be expected, since both were relatively infrequent in Africa.[38] Cases of mental illness, however, were surprisingly rare, in view of the fact that despondency and madness were major health problems during the Middle Passage and in the guinea yards of the English slave trade a few decades later.[39] The scant mention of intestinal worms is also surprising, for this ailment was very common in Africa.

Palmeo records after 1750 reflect the improved conditions of the slave trade and the wisdom of refreshment. The seventeenth-century accounts by Sandoval and others testified to a frightening mortality among slaves at sea, which may have reached 33 percent and a mortality among slaves in the Cartagena guinea pens that probably was not less than 10 percent. *Palmeo* records a century and a half later, however, indicate that deaths at sea en route to the mainland from refreshment centers were negligible (0.4 percent) and that only one slave in a hundred died in the pens before *palmeo*. Under the improved conditions of the late-eighteenth-century trade, with its rising humanitarianism, enlightened regulations, and improved medical knowledge, even the English slave trade, which accounted for about half of the total international trade, showed a corresponding drop in slave mortality. Within a century mortality at sea fell from about 24 percent, where it had climbed by 1680, to perhaps as little as 5 percent in 1789, although another 5 percent still died in West Indian guinea yards.[40] Thus by 1750, thanks to improving conditions, mortality had almost vanished in the slave trade from refreshment centers to the Spanish mainland and in its guinea pens and had been sharply curtailed in the international slave trade as well.

Much of the mortality in either century was caused by conditions of the long Middle Passage from Africa to America. The voyage to seventeenth-century Cartagena in Claver's day, before refreshment came into practice, had been even longer and more disastrous for the slaves than was the voyage to the West Indies. The policy of refreshment after 1680 shortened the voyage by cutting off the last two or three weeks, the portion of the voyage in which illness and death were proportionally the highest. After 1860 the much shorter voyage to the mainland could be made later, after the slaves had overcome the worst effects of the Atlantic crossing. Of course, the trade to the mainland after 1680 became increasingly an extension of the English slave trade and shared its mortality. Consequently slaves who had formerly died in Cartagena and Portobelo now died in Jamaica, though in greatly reduced numbers. Nevertheless the improved conditions and the practice of refreshment resulted in gradual but significant decline in mortality after 1680 that within a century had drastically reduced the number of deaths. Better conditions and refreshment also benefited slave buyers in the Spanish colonies, who, as a result, bought generally healthier slaves and consequently faced considerably fewer risks to personal health and fortune (see note 33).

Even with the improved conditions and declining mortality of the second half of the eighteenth century, rarely did ships bring slaves in sufficiently good health that the entire cargo could be measured in the first *palmeo*. Even after two weeks some ships still had a quarter or more of their cargo too ill to submit to the first *palmeo*.[41] On the average, though, by the end of the two-week waiting period before the *palmeo*, only 4 percent of the Negroes were still too sick to be measured. For this small group a second *palmeo* was held two to three weeks later. Often a handful of slaves were too ill even to be included in the second *palmeo*. In such cases a third *palmeo* was arranged, usually about two weeks later.

After the *palmeo*, customs duties were calculated and paid. The royal brand was heated in a spirit flame and touched to the right breast of each Negro to indelibly mark him as legally entered. The slaves were then turned over to the owner or factor, who was now free to sell them. The crown usually did not allow representatives of *asiento* companies to reside in the interior, so the marketing and disrribution of slaves were left to another group of slavers—Spaniards and Creoles who bought slaves in the Cartagena slave mart and distributed them throughout New Granada and the other Spanish colonies. This royal policy became less rigid by the end of the seventeenth century, and some companies, especially the British *asiento* company (1713-1739), made sporadic attempts to maintain factors in principal cities of the Indies. They attempted to supply these agents from Cartagena either by shipping slaves to them by water or by having blacks driven inland from the port. This practice, however, was the exception rather than the rule, for most companies preferred to sell their cargoes wholesale soon after landing and to avoid the bother and expense of maintenance, as well as the risk of death before sale. Importers usually disposed of their slaves in a few large lots, ranging in size from twenty to two or three hundred blacks.[42] These sales, in fact, often took place even before the *palmeo*; in such cases the buyer was responsible for the *palmeo* and paid the customs duty.[43] These buyers usually sold smaller groups of slaves to lesser merchants as well as to the public, so that it was not uncommon for a newly imported slave in Cartagena to change hands three or four times in rapid succession.

Sometimes ranchers and miners bought slaves and took them inland either for resale or to work on their own haciendas or mines. Other times the buyers were merchants who took the blacks to their own slave pens for resale in Cartagena. These pens, usually the patios of their own homes, were similar to those described earlier. In any case, the blacks probably waited only a few days at most before they were sold. Probably the same cramped conditions prevailed in these retail pens, for even though slaves were often sold in smaller lots, the buyers were lesser merchants with smaller houses. Despite overcrowding, however, the general condition of the blacks was no doubt improved. The two weeks had allowed rest and recuperation; the very ill had died, and consequently a source of contagion and misery had been eliminated. The slaves were now in smaller lots and usually under the more judicial and attentive personal care of the owner rather than of overseers.[44]

Before the *palmeo* an importer had found little incentive to clean, clothe, and care for his blacks, since good appearance would only result in higher customs appraisal. After the *palmeo*, however, the situation changed radically. Every device was employed to trim and groom the slaves so they would bring high prices. The barracoon became a hive of activity. A contemporary observer described some of the preparations: "They fill them with drugs in order to make the skin lucid. They coat them with gun powder; they rub them with oil and lemon juice. To conceal the slave's age they shave his beard, for they know that the ideal slave is a boy of fifteen."[45]

These preparations completed, the day of sale was advertised either by printed notices posted throughout the city or simply by word of mouth. The slave market in Cartagena opened at daybreak. Business was conducted in the open air at the foot of the city wall in a space surrounded by temporary barracoons and caldrons of boiling water to be used in case of an uprising.[46] Each barracoon was divided by stockades into one or more pens in which slaves were corralled:

> Upon the arrival of buyers, the overseers cracked their whips—at those who were called *fouet* or *musinga* [interpreter?] in slave trade jargon—and they made the shaven, naked Negroes, rubbed with oil, trot, dance, sing, speak, and laugh. From a platform of planks, the overseer of the factories sounded a trumpet and cried the excellence of each piece of ebony which came near the prospective buyer. Among the buyers were monks, priests, and officials of uniform. At times there were ladies of rank and quality who had no scruples about scrutinizing the most private parts of those unhappy slaves as if they were examining cattle or horses. They parted with their pride and began to examine the Negroes minutely, feeling their muscles, touching to their tongue a finger moistened with sweat (for in the flavor of the sweat is known the health of the Negro). . . .[47]

Experienced buyers knew they could not be too careful in making their purchases. They were at least vaguely aware of the terrible condition of the ships and the pens. They knew that if blacks were not in good health, strenuous efforts had been made to cover up their illness and defects. Before purchasing any slave they carefully inspected eyes, ears, teeth, fingers, skin, breasts, and genitals and tried to assure themselves of the absence of chronic diseases and impediments to normal movement. Most buyers made the slaves cough in order to check for hernias and even devised ways to test for mental alertness. Veteran buyers, not to be deceived about the age of supposedly young Negroes, looked for cuts and felt the face for recently shaven whiskers. In suspicious cases they even passed their tongue over the slave's chin to be certain.[48]

When the buyer had selected his purchases he

> brought them to the center of the market for branding, where a man stood before hot coals. At his side, attached to a table standing vertically in the earth, was an alphabet in iron. Upon the arrival of the Negro, he took with some long pincers, the letter that the buyer selected and heated it. Meanwhile, he rubbed the Negro's left breast, just above the nipple, with tallow, covered the spot with an oiled paper, and gently applied the red iron. . . . The slave was marched away by the overseer, and another took his place . . .[49]

Whether the sale was transacted by slave companies at the port or by itinerant slave merchants in the interior, slaves were usually sold "with all their qualities bad and good, soul in mouth, and bag of bones, excepting only *gota coral*, otherwise called heart trouble."[50] This legal jargon was used in most sales, especially of *bozal* slaves (recent, unseasoned arrivals), although sometimes bills of sale for Creole slaves or slaves of long residence in the Indies were more specific concerning defects or expressly guaranteed their absence. The phrase was intended to mean that slaves were bought at the buyer's risk. Spanish law, however, did not honor such clauses and provided for redhibition (*redhibitoria*) in cases of fraud or bad faith. Simply stated, the law provided that "when the seller hides an evil that he knows about, and the buyer, if he knew of it, would not buy that which is sold, the contract is null and void. . . ."[51]

This law was not intended to protect a buyer who knowingly acquired a sick slave; but it did allow redress if he bought a sick slave who had been intentionally misrepresented as being in good health.[52] It was possible that a seller might not know of a slave's defects, and in the absence of malicious intent there were no grounds for redhibition. Thus a man who bought a slave who was later found to be mad lost his case for redhibition, since the seller knew nothing of the condition at time of sale and had acted in good faith.[53]

Occasionally suits arose over trivial defects. One buyer sued when he found his new slave to have the defect of wetting the bed, and surprisingly he won the case.[54] Generally, however, the law usually allowed redhibition only for incurable illness, such as heart trouble, leprosy, elephantiasis, or serious defects that impaired the use for which the slave had been purchased, unless the defects were self-evident or publicly known at the time of sale.[55]

Legal action ordinarily was limited to a six-month period following sale, but it was sometimes interpreted by local judges to mean six months after the defect became known to the new owner.[56] Consequently, some redhibition cases were begun as late as eleven years after sale.[57]

Those who sold slaves, whether slave companies or private individuals, tried to protect themselves from such legal action in a variety of ways. Bills of sale almost invariably included the standard phrase "sold with all their infirmities, hidden and manifest." The seller thereby advised the buyer that the slave had infirmities and consequently hoped he would be protected from redhibition on medical grounds except for epilepsy or heart disease, which the law specifically stated as sufficient cause. Slave merchants, especially factors of larger *asiento* companies, sometimes tried to protect themselves by stating clearly in the bill of sale that claims even for epilepsy or heart trouble would be allowed for only two months (instead of six) from date of sale.[58] Since the bill of sale was signed both by buyer and seller, slave merchants looked upon it as a binding contract. Many buyers probably believed such clauses were binding on them too. Consequently, if after purchase, slaves were found to have some chronic disease, the naive buyer could hardly complain, for he plainly had bought the slave with all his "infirmities, hidden and manifest." More sophisticated buyers, however, knew that none of these attempts on the part of sellers were valid before the law. The judiciary recognized that such phrases had become the "style" and "blind custom" in slave sales and therefore did not really serve to alert the buyers to defects.[59] Regardless of what the bill of sale said or did not say, any slave sale was subject to redhibitory action for six months and even longer for virtually any serious defect that had been intentionally hidden from the buyer. If a slave was sick or defective, the law expected the seller to inform the buyer and lower the price accordingly.

Despite the fraudulent marketing practices of the slave trade and the seeming utility of redhibitory law, redhibition suits seldom arose in the sale of *bozal* Negroes and were quite infrequent even in the sale of seasoned slaves. Lawsuits were costly and slow. Sometimes both litigants died before a decision was reached, and many buyers, even though they knew of the right of redhibition, perhaps chose not to bother with it.[60] The legal suits that were filed, however, always included medical testimony and diagnosis to establish grounds for redhibition and consequently reveal another dimension of the health condition in the slave trade of New Granada. Diseases of the genitourinary tract were the most frequent cause for legal action. Venereal disease, though virtually absent among freshly imported slaves, was apparently soon acquired after their arrival in the New World, for venereal disease, especially syphilis, was the single most common complaint, and "female trouble," especially prolapse of the uterus, was next. Slave owners were interested in expanding their slave gangs through natural increase. Females of "breeding age" brought top prices. Pregnant females in good health usually sold for even more money, for it was customary to add fifty pesos to her price for the child she was carrying.[61] Consequently, buyers sometimes brought suit when they bought female slaves and later found them to be barren or to have diseases of the female organs or venereal disease, all of which they thought robbed them of potential for natural increase of the slave gang. Diseases of the skin, especially ulcers, yaws, and leprosy, were also common causes for redhibition, as were dysentery, worms, and respiratory ailments, especially tuberculosis.[62]

After sale, most of the slaves were taken inland, since the greatest demand for slaves was in the mines and haciendas deep in the interior. Distribution to the interior, however, posed serious health problems. Slave owners in the West Indies found that

Negroes died in large numbers while being taken from guinea yards at the port to inland estates, especially if the estates were located in the mountainous interior. One Jamaican doctor cautioned slave handlers to send new Negroes inland by short and easy stages: "If they are conveyed to the plantation in a vehicle, either by land or water, so much the better." He particularly cautioned against forcing the sick to walk.[63] If health hazards to new Negroes on short inland treks in Jamaica were so serious, the danger was far greater on the longer treks through the sprawling mountainous terrain of New Granada.

The high, rugged Andes range extending northward from the southern tip of South America splits into three branches near the southern boundary of New Granada. These spur ranges continue northward for the full length of the Viceroyalty, creating an incredibly rough terrain of high mountains and deep valleys. Between the Eastern and Central Ranges flowed the Magdalena River, navigable for 600 miles inland. Between the Central and Western Ranges flowed the Cauca River. Travel over such terrain was extremely arduous. In order to traverse the colony from Santa Fé (modern Bogotá) in the east to the Pacific coast, for example, a traveler descended 7,000 feet from the Bogotá plateau to Honda on the Magdalena. He crossed the valley floor to Ibagué, where he climbed abruptly to cross the 11,000-foot Quindío pass of the Central Range, and descended again 8,000 feet to the Cauca valley on the other side. He then proceeded west to cross the 9,000-foot Western Range in order to descend to the Pacific coastal lowlands. This rough terrain gave New Granada the reputation of having the worst roads in the Spanish Indies.[64] Despite the inadvisability of forcing slaves to walk on the inland trek, there was no alternative. Consequently, the majority of the slaves sold in Cartagena faced a long, arduous journey of several hundred miles by foot over one, perhaps two mountain ranges.

Geographical problems were bad enough, but commercial policy made matters even worse. To maintain tighter commercial control, the crown prohibited the entry of slaves and other commerce to all but a few routes. Ironically, the forbidden routes were the ones that might have imposed the fewest hardships on the blacks. It was usually forbidden, for example, to supply the Pacific coast by shipment around Cape Horn or to supply the remote and inaccessible province of the Chocó through the A-trato River, which flowed to the Atlantic not far from Cartagena. Moreover, major commercial centers such as Popayán and Santa Fé, which served as interior slave markets, were located deep in the interior. The result was that slaves were often taken from Cartagena 900 miles south to Popayán, where mine owners from the Chocó bought them and marched them 300 miles north again to the Chocó. Although the Chocó lay not more than 350 miles by water from Cartagena, slaves taken there had to make a 1,200-mile elliptical trek through the interior to reach their destination. The same backtracking was true in the Pamplona region. Many slaves were taken from Cartagena 600 miles south to Santa Fé and then marched 250 miles north again to Pamplona, which lay only 400 miles from Cartagena.

Slaves were supplied to the interior by two routes. Many were shipped from Cartagena to Panama, crossed the fifty-mile isthmus on foot, and were loaded on ships that traded along the Pacific coast as far south as Chile. Most of these slaves were landed in Lima to supply the Viceroyalty of Peru, and even the distant port of Buenos Aires, lying 2,000 miles away on the Atlantic coast. A few of these, however, were sold en route to Peru in Buenaventura, Isquandé, Timbiquí, and Tumaco, settlements on the Pacific coast of New Granada. From these points they were transported inland to supply nearby mines. A few were also unloaded in Guayaquil (Ecuador) and driven inland to supply the surrounding coastal plain and the highlands near Quito. From Quito there was some movement of slaves northward into the mining areas of southern New Granada, especially to Pasto and Popayán (125 to 275 miles to the north). These towns in turn largely supplied the Pacific lowland mines around Barbacoas.

The main route of entry for slaves overland lay through New Granada. Slave caravans trekked seventy-five miles overland from Cartagena to the Magdalena, which they ascended to its

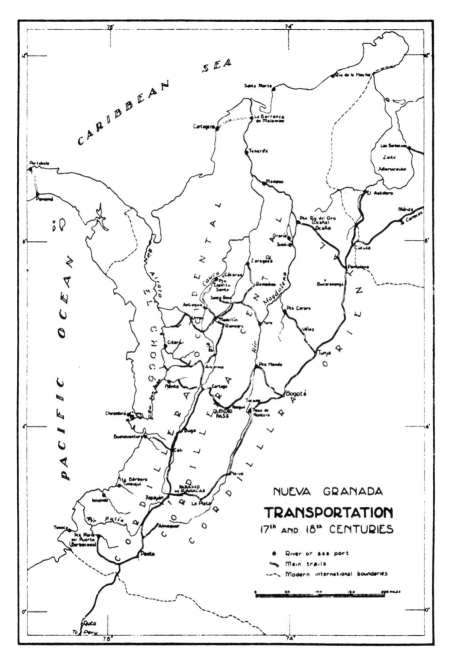

from: Robert C. West, *Colonial Placer Mining in Colombia* (Baton Rouge, 1952), p. 129. Courtesy of Louisiana State University Press.

confluence with the Cauca, where a branch led south through Antioquia and the Cauca valley. A parallel branch struck southward through the Magdalena valley. The Cauca route ascended the Cauca to the port of Espiritu Santo. Here a trail led south to Antioquia City and Medellin and connected with the western branch of the Camino Real (the principal road of Colony), leading south through the Cauca valley to the cities of Cali and Popayán, then on to Quito and Lima. The town of Zaragoza on the Nechí River, a tributary of the Cauca, also served as a port of entry for Antioquia. From Zaragoza a road led south to Remedios, Santa Rosa, and Medellín, where it joined the Camino Real. After 1700 the Nare Road further to the south became the main supply line of Antioquia. Slave drivers ascended the Magdalena for about 475 miles to Nare, where a road climbed the steep eastern escarpment of the Central Cordillera to intersect the Zaragoza Road and continue on to Medellín. The 125-mile trip from Nare to Zaragoza normally took 16 days. From Nare to Antioquia City via Medellín (150 miles) usually took 20 days. Slave caravans, however, traveled much slower than commercial caravans and took twice the normal time.

From Medellín, in Antioquia and from Anserma and Cartago in the Cauca valley, a number of transverse trails crossed the Western Range to supply the gold fields of the Chocó. Shorter and less arduous water transportation, via the Atrato and San Juan rivers, might have been used, but seldom was. The Atrato flowed north through the Chocó to the Atlantic and provided an easy water route for the entry of slaves, but despite repeated petitions by concerned residents to open it to legal traffic, it remained closed until the 1780s, after which few slaves entered the Chocó.[65] The San Juan flowed south from the heart of the Chocó to the Pacific and was open for the entry of slaves transshipped from Panama, but few entered that way, because of navigation hazards and the difficulty of securing food.

Slave caravans heading for Popayán and Cali in the upper Cauca valley, as well as those proceeding to the capital of Santa Fé, followed the Magdalena branch, which continued along the river to Honda, the terminus for river traffic, and an important junction on the Camino Real. From Honda a transverse branch of the Camino Real led eastward up the Eastern Cordillera to Santa Fé and westward to Ibagué. From Ibagué the road continued over the Quindio Pass of the Central Cordillera to Cartago and on to the Cauca River, where it intersected with the Cauca valley spur of the Camino Real. Slaves traveling west from Honda to Cartago were distributed northward to Anserma and Southern Antioquia, southward to Buga, Cali, and Popayán, and westward to the Chocó. Caravans traveling east from Honda arrived in Santa Fé to supply the capital. From there they were distributed northward to the highlands around Tunja and even farther north to the mines of Pamplona province. Pamplona received slaves brought overland due east from the lower Magdalena River ports of Rio del Oro (Ocaña) and Carare, and a few slaves also were supplied through the northern coastal port of Rio Hacha.

Slave caravans destined directly for Popayán continued south from Honda to La Plata, where the road climbed directly west to cross the Central Cordillera and descended to Popayán, the administrative, commercial, and culture center for all of western New Granada. It was the major supply center for slaves for the mines of the Almaguer district and northern Ecuador to the south, as well as for most of the slaves for Cali, Buga, and the rest of the Cauca valley to the north. Popayán was even considered the gateway to the Chocó, three hundred miles to the north. It was, in fact, the gateway to the entire Pacific lowlands.[66]

Arduous conditions of the inland trek were made even worse by security precautions. It was necessary to send dangerous blacks in "chains and handcuffs."[67] Most of the men, at least, probably made the inland journey chained by the neck or hand to one another in single file. Women, too, may have been chained, for overseers constantly had to watch their own step, and the rough terrain and dense vegetation afforded countless opportunities to escape with slim chance of recapture. Food on the trek consisted of hardtack, corn, meat, and salt, and perhaps plantains or other fruits purchased along the road. But food was often scarce in many areas, especially Antioquia and the lowlands, so caravans had to carry sufficient food or face starvation. Where road conditions permitted, a pack train of mules accompanied the caravan to carry food, blankets, medicine, chains, and other supplies, and peons were employed to help handle both slaves and mules. If mules were plentiful, slaves carried few provisions except a blanket and some yardage of water-repellent cloth as protection against rain. In rougher terrain Indian porters sometimes replaced the mules. In the absence of mules or porters, slaves themselves carried the provisions, a requirement that must have boosted the mortality among them.[68]

The internal slave trade, even under the best of conditions, caused considerable suffering and loss of life. If slaves were shipped to Panama, they experienced the horrors of another voyage. The passage to Portobelo lasted a week. The voyage to Lima lasted another two or three weeks. Shortages of provisions and shipwrecks were not uncommon.[69] Disease claimed some lives as well, for slaves seldom arrived in Lima free of contagious disease,[70] and few treks were made across the isthmus without the loss of at least some Negroes.[71] The experience of Sebastian Duarte, a Peruvian slave merchant, is illustrative. In the late 1620s Duarte bought 258 blacks in Portobelo. During the trek across the isthmus he fed the slaves with singular generosity on beef, pork, maize, plantains, barley, bread, salt fish, and eggs prepared with lard and vinegar. Special attention was paid to the sick. They were given special foods such as fowls, molasses, oranges, sugar, red wine, quinces, squashes, and cassava bread. Medical provisions included sugar for gargles, old shirts for bandages, syringes, bezoar stone, and yellow wax. On the trek Duarte purchased mustard and honey to make anti-tetanus compresses and hired a barber to give various bleedings and emetics. In spite of relatively good food and these elaborate medical precautions, however, thirteen of the blacks (5 percent) died while crossing the isthmus.[72]

Slaves supplied to the interior by river and overland routes faced even graver risks. Between Cartagena and the interior lay only "danger, trouble, and delays." The Magdalena lay seventy-five miles overland from Cartagena. In later years a merchant could make a trip by boat on the Dique Canal. But water transportation was only of slight advantage, for whether on canal or river, the "abominable" character and conduct of the boatmen of this "fatal navigation" made travel intolerable and losses certain.[73] A traveler in 1810 colorfully described the woes of river commerce:

The unhappy merchant embarks under the discretion of a pilot, without character, who obeys and fears the most depreciable of his crew; consequently the boat is left to the barbarous caprice of twenty-five or thirty men whose manners and feelings alienate them from human society. He is obliged to spend two or three months in a boat whose construction and the brush of the river put him in grave danger, where no superior is recognized, where all command and none obey, where never has discipline nor urbanity been seen, where libertinage is enthroned and insolence, theft, rapine, and as many iniquities as the relaxation of customs can suggest are so familiar among them and form a character so undisciplined that it sets them apart from the rest of the human species. . . . The merchant has to secure a boat in Cartagena, setting the price with the owner before leaving. He leaves when it is convenient to the boatmen. That same night perhaps he will be abandoned and will have to return by land. If that does not happen, he arrives near San Estanislao where disorders, drunkenness and desolation begin. Some crewmen flee the site, others hide in the mountains, living off what they have robbed from the merchant or the countryside until they can return to Cartagena and repeat the process again.

The same thing happens . . . in all of the towns through which they pass. If they take sixteen men in Cartagena and are due to arrive in Mompox in ten days (175 miles) they finally get there in a month and a half with four men left. . . . From Mompox to Honda vices only multiply.[74]

Once the slaves left the river, they were faced with another kind of danger posed by rough terrain and poor roads, many of which were mere trails that did not even admit mules. One sixteenth-century traveler believed that there were no worse roads in the entire world than those in the province of Popayán.[75] The royal road between La Plata and Popayán, over which probably more slaves passed than any other, was so steep, skirted so close to precipices, had so many obstructions, and was so weather-worn by gullies that even in the dry season there was serious danger to the life and property of those who traveled it.[76] Even the best roads through the rough, mountainous terrain of the Viceroyalty could have been little better.[77]

The number of slaves lost on the road was considerable. Bartolomé Guisir, a merchant of Cartagena in 1700, bought three slaves and headed inland for Santa Fé. When he arrived, two of the slaves were so near death that they died before he could sell them. The third was sold below market price because of a "lesion" in her arm, the result of an accident on the road.[78] A slave trader in Antioquia had slightly better luck, perhaps because he did not have so far to go. He bought twenty-seven slaves in Cartagena. Four died on the Magdalena, and two more died along the road from the river to the city of Antioquia. He lost only 22 percent of the slaves en route.[79]

The causes of death on these inland treks is seldom recorded, but dysentery probably headed the list. Epidemic disease and even natural disasters were blamed by contemporaries for many deaths.[80] Accidents, exposure, and exhaustion claimed many as well. Ulceration and damage caused by chains on these treks must have been extreme. Many owners and merchants were especially reluctant to send children on the road since they apparently suffered more than adults.[81]

A description of the health conditions of the slave trade to and within New Granada reveals deplorable conditions in the slave ships and slave pens, especially during the seventeenth century. Crowded confinement and harsh treatment made physical disability and injury extremely common. Deficient diet caused scurvy to be a certain plague of the trade. Overcrowding and lack of sanitation both at sea and in port allowed contagious disease to spread unchecked among the Negroes. In spite of meticulous official precautions, the trade ushered in countless epidemics from which both blacks and whites suffered and died. And finally, when a slave was eventually sold, he faced a grueling and sometimes fatal trek inland. Indeed, the suffering and loss of life in the slave trade to New Granada were so great during the seventeenth century that it is remarkable that the institution of slavery survived.

In a narrow sense the study of the health conditions of the slave trade is simply a narrative of the suffering and death of the captive black man, which illustrates the persistence of ignorance, greed, and inhumanity in history. Moral indignation is an understandable reaction in present-day students of slavery. The health conditions of the slave trade were an outrage against humanity that cannot be justified. Historical perspective, however, reminds one that health conditions during the seventeenth and eighteenth centuries were not good for people of any race. Living conditions were backward, and privation and hardship were a part of colonial life. Life expectancy, even for Europeans, was short. Mortality was especially high among Europeans in the tropics, and deaths among European sailors engaged in the slave trade were proportionally greater than among the slaves in which they trafficked. Nevertheless, the fact remains that the suffering and mortality in the slave trade to New Granada were painfully excessive.

In a broader sense, however, the study of the health conditions of the slave trade is also a narrative of improving conditions and changing attitudes. Indeed, one of the facts that stand out most clearly in the eighteenth century is the remarkable decline in mortality. During most of the seventeenth century one African out of three died in the passage from Africa to Cartagena. Within a hundred years the number of deaths fell to less than one per hundred. In the slave pens a mortality rate of 10 percent would probably be a very conservative estimate for the years before 1700. After that date loss of life began to decline rapidly, and fifty years later it had dropped below 2 percent. It is somewhat misleading to compare the mortality rates of the two centuries, since the slaves in the eighteenth century came to New Granada from the West Indies rather than directly from Africa. Consequently, these eighteenth-century figures do not reflect the mortality occurring in the passage from Africa to the West Indies or in the West Indian guinea yards. Even if mortality is adjusted to include these losses in the English slave trade that supplied most of the slaves to Cartagena during the eighteenth century, there is still a remarkable decline in mortality. Losses at sea between Africa and Cartagena via Jamaica probably fell to around 6 to 10 percent, and the combined losses in the English guinea yards and those of Cartagena did not exceed 6 percent. Mortality on the inland trek in New Granada may have reached 20 percent. Even that may have declined slightly over the decades as slaves began to arrive in better health and as roads improved slightly, bad as they still remained. Moreover, the population and the degree of civilization of the area increased and provided fewer hazards to travel and greater ease in acquiring food on the trek.

Moreover, the humanitarian ideas of the eighteenth century were hostile to slavery and would eventually abolish it in the Western world. These ideas inspired legislation that greatly improved conditions of the English slave trade after 1790 and found fertile soil in the Spanish colonies as well. In the last quarter of the eighteenth century, slavery would become an anachronism in Spanish America and within the next fifty years the independent nations that sprang from Spain's empire would lead the world in abolishing human bondage.

The declining mortality in all phases of the slave trade was due, then, not only to improved technology, growing medical knowledge, and more enlightened treatment and handling of slaves, but also to a growing acceptance of the black man as a human being and an increasing recognition that the inhuman conditions of the slave trade had to be ameliorated. Although it is true that the study of health conditions of slave trade reveals shocking ignorance, inhumanity, and misery, perhaps more importantly it also reveals improving conditions, advancing science, and growing humaneness.

Notes

[1] Angel Valtierra, *San Pedro Claver, el santo que libertó una raza*, 2nd ed. (Cartagena, 1964), pp. 315-316; Alberto Miramón, "Los negreros del Caribe," *Boletin de Historia y Antigüedades* 31, No. 351 (February 1944): 177 (hereafter cited as *BHA*).

[2] This requirement was often stipulated in the contract that granted the right to import Negroes. See *The Assiento; or Contract for Allowing the Subjects of Great Britain the Liberty of Importing Negroes into the Spanish America* (London, 1713), Article 21.

[3] Archivo Histórico Nacional de Colombia, Negros y esclavos de Panamá, 3: 610-611 (hereafter cited as AHNC).

[4] James F. King, "Descriptive Data on Negro Slaves in Spanish Importation Records and Bills of Sale," *Journal of Negro History* 28, No. 2 (April 1943): 208-209.

[5] Eduardo Posada, "La esclavitud en Colombia," *BHA*, 16, No. 189 (September 1927): 526.

[6] AHNC, Negros y esclavos de Panamá, 2: 629-630.

[7] Angel Valtierra, *Pedro Claver, S.J., el santo que libertó una raza: Su vida y su época*, 1st ed. (Bogotá, 1954), p. 205.

[8] Alonzo de Sandoval, *De Instauranda Aethiopum Salute: El mundo de la esclavitud negra en América* (Bogotá, 1956), pp. 105-108.

[9] Valtierra, 1st ed., p. 196.

[10] *Ibid.*, pp. 751-754; Edward Long, *The History of Jamaica. Or a General Survey of the Antient and Modern State of that Island with Reflections on its Situation, Settlement, Inhabitants, Climate, Products, Commerce, Laws and Government*, 3 vols. (London, 1774), 1: 434.

[11] Frederick Bowser, "Negro Slavery in Colonial Peru, 1528-1650" (Ph.D. diss., Dept. of History, University of California, Berkeley, 1967), p. 111.

[12] Valtierra, 1st ed., pp. 205, 234.

[13] *Ibid.*, pp. 751-754.

[14]Such disastrous mortality was graphically illustrated in the siege of Cartagena in 1697. Baron Dupontis reported that in barely six days 800 of his men became sick with a "fatal and contagious dysentery." The majority of them soon died. His attack force numbered 6,645 men, and his total losses were 3,200 or nearly half. The majority died from disease. Municipio de Cartagena, *Historial de Cartagena de las Indias* (Cartagena, 1943), p. 94. See also Valtierra, 2nd ed., p. 165; Frank W. Pittman, *The Development of the British West Indies, 1700-1763* (New Haven, 1917), p. 388, see also pp. 384-390; and Antonio de Ulloa, *Viaje a la América meridional*, 2 vols. (London, 1760), 1: 59 (Book 1, Chapter 5).

[15]In 1633-1634, 1636, 1639-1641, and 1651. See Valtierra, 1st ed., p. 233.

[16]*Ibid.*, p. 234.

[17]*Ibid.*, pp. 233-234.

[18]*Ibid.*, pp. 787-789.

[19]David L. Chandler, "Health and Slavery: A Study of Health Conditions among Negro Slaves in the Viceroyalty of New Granada, 1600-1810 (Ph.D. diss., Tulane University, 1972), pp. 73, 93.

[20]In the 1600s the importer and owner was usually the captain of the vessel that introduced the Negroes. From 1700 to 1789 the importer was usually a large slave company, whose factor or representative received the Negroes and made arrangement for their quartering, clearance, and sale.

[21]Valtierra, 1st ed., pp. 240-242; Valtierra, 2nd ed., pp. 133-135, 319.

[22]Valtierra, 2nd ed., pp. 131-135, 320-321.

[23]Jamaican Colonial Archive, Colonial Dispatches, Jamaica to England, Box 1, Major General Robert Hunter, Governor, to the Lords of Trade and Plantation.

[24]Bowser, p. 92.

[25]Valtierra, 1st ed., pp. 242, 240.

[26]Sandoval, pp. 108-109.

[27]Valtierra, 1st ed., p. 236.

[28]*Ibid.*, pp. 108-111; Valtierra, 2nd ed., p. 131.

[29]Sandoval, pp. 108-109.

[30]Valtierra, 1st ed., p. 237.

[31]Sandoval, pp. 108-110.

[32]Bowser, p. 92.

[33]Two series of *palmeo* records have been found. One consists of

records for seven ships of the Grillo Asiento at Cartagena between the years 1663 and 1674. The original documents of this series are in the Archive General de Indias in Seville, Spain, and copies were made for the private microfilm collection of Dr. José Maria Arboleda, Department of Anthropology, Universidad Pontificia Javeriana, Bogotá, Colombia. See Rolls 2 and 3. Used by permission. The second series consists of records randomly preserved for about forty vessels licensed under successive assientos held from 1754 to 1789 (Ruiz, Frier, Arechederreta, Valdehoyos, and Aguirre Asientos). Most of this series can be seen in AHNC, Negros y esclavos de Panamá, 2, 3 and 4. The reader who wishes more details and more precise documentation, where it has been impossible to include it here and elsewhere in this article, is referred to the author's Ph.D. dissertation. "Health and Slavery . . ." (Tulane University, 1972). The *vara* was a unit of measure equivalent to one yard. See Real Academic Española, *Diccionario de la lengua castellana*, 3d ed. (Madrid, 1791). Local practices, however, gave it varying equivalents ranging from 30.2 inches to 35.9 inches (0.768 meters to 0.912 meters). See *International Critical Tables of Numerical Data, Physics, Chemistry and Technology*, ed. Edward W. Washburn and others (New York, International Research Council, 1926), p. 12. In the measurement of slaves a *vara* of 34 inches was used and was divided into *palmos* or fourths of 8-1/2 inches each. See fold-out, schematic reproduction in AHNC, Negros y esclavos de Panamá, 2: 354 (1751).

[34]If these heights seem unusually low, it might be pointed out that the average European of the same day measured only 5'6''. C. D. Haagensen and E. B. Lloyd, *A Hundred Years of Medicine* (New York, 1943), p. 171.

[35]Arboleda Collection, Rolls 2 and 3.

[36]AHNC, Negros y esclavos de Panamá, 4: 480-483.

[37]Arboleda Collection, Rolls 2 and 3. See also note 33.

[38]Rudolph Hoeppli, *Parasitic Diseases in Africa and the Western Hemisphere: Early Documentation and Transmission by the Slave Trade* (Basel, 1969), pp. 98-105; Phillip Manson-Bahr, *Manson's Tropical Diseases*, 16th ed. (Baltimore, 1966), p. 531; Philip Curtin, "Epidemiology and the Slave Trade," *Political Science Quarterly* 83 (June 1968): 210.

[39]Great Britain, House of Commons, Select Committee on the Slave Trade, *An Abstract of the Evidence Delivered before a Select Committee of the House of Commons in the Years 1790 and 1791 on Part of the Petitioners for the Abolition of the Slave Trade* (London, 1791), p. 49.

[40]K. G. Davies, *The Royal African Company* (London, 1957), p. 292; H. Harold Scott, *A History of Tropical Medicine Based on the Fitzpatrick Lectures Delivered Before the Royal College of Physicians of London, 1937-38*, 2 vols. (London, 1939), 2: 993.

[41]AHNC, Negros y esclavos de Panamá, 4: 474-477.

[42]Rolando Mellafe, *La esclavitud en Hispanoamerica* (Buenos Aires, 1964), pp. 60, 66; Sandoval, p. 423.

[43]AHNC, Negros y esclavos de Magdalena, 4: 385-386.

[44]Sandoval, pp. 108-109; James F. King, "Slavery in New Granada," *Greater America: Essays in Honor of Herbert Eugene Bolton* (Berkeley, 1945), p. 308; Gustavo Arboleda, *Historia de Cali desde los orígenes de la ciudad hasta la expiración del periódo colonial*, 3 vols. (Cali, 1956), 2: 22.

[45]Valtierra, 1st ed., p. 6, citing Fernando Ortíz, *Los negros esclavos* (Havana, 1916).

[46]Miramón, (above note 1), pp. 180-182.

[47]*Ibid.*

[48]Valtierra, 1st ed., p. 6.

[49]Miramón, pp. 181-182.

[50]See any "*venta de esclavo*" in any colonial notary. A particularly good example is found in the Archivo Histórico del Departamento de Antioquia (Medellin, Colombia), Colonia 115 (Temporalidades), Doc. 3240 (hereafter cited as AHDA). Printed bills of sale can be found in Miramón, p. 183, and Arboleda, *Historia de Cali*, 2: 23-24. Actually *gota coral* was epilepsy rather than another name for heart trouble, although in earlier bills of sale such as this one (1733) the two terms are used interchangeably. By the last quarter of the century that is no longer the case and the phrase usually reads "excepting epilepsy [*gota coral*] and heart trouble." See Archivo Histórico del Cauca, Colonia, sig. 6222, f. 11v.

[51]Archivo Histórico Nacional del Ecuador, Esclavos, legajo 3, expediente 38, f. 1 (hereafter cited as AHNE).

[52]AHNC, Negros y esclavos de Bolivar, 4: 980.

[53]AHNE, Esclavos de Gran Colombia, only unnumbered legajo, expediente 2, f. 61v.

[54]AHDA, Colonia, 31 (Esclavos), Doc. 992.

[55]AHNE, Real Audiencia, Gobernación de Popayán, Caja 74, "Autos entre Francisco Cayetano Nieto Polo y Manuel Vicente Martinez sobre la recsindición del contrato de un negro," 1757.

[56]*Ibid.*

[57]AHNE, Esclavos, legajo 3, expediente 43.

[58]AHDA, Colonia, 115 (Temporalidades), Doc. 3240; Miramón, p. 183.

[59]AHNE, Esclavos, legajo 3, expediente 39, f. 3.

[60]AHNE, Colonia, Real Audiencia, Gobernación de Popayán, Caja 150, "Causa seguida entre Francisco Doneis y Juan Materón sobre la redhibitoria de una negra. . . , 1787, f. 62v.

[61]AHNE, Esclavos, legajo 3, expediente 30, f. 1.

[62]This medical information has been compiled from nearly 70 *redhibitoria* cases found in the AHNE, ramo de Esclavos.

[63](Dr. Collins), *Practical Rules for the Management and Medical Treatment of Negro slaves in the Sugar Colonies, by a Professional Planter* (London, 1803), p. 62.

[64]Robert C. West, *Colonial Placer Mining in Colombia* (Baton Rouge, 1953), p. 126.

[65]"Proyecto de hurtado sobre minas, 1783," *BHA* 13, No. 147 (May 1920): 182-183; *Relaciones de mando: memorias presentada por los gobernantes del Nuevo Reino de Granada*, ed. Eduardo Posada and Pedro María Ibáñez (Bogotá, 1910), pp. 340, 499.

[66]For the best discussion of roads, commerce, and supply, see West, pp. 126-130; Pedro Fermín de Vargas, *Pensamientos politicos y memoria sobre la población del Nuevo Reino de Granada* (Bogotá, 1953), pp. 27-35. See also James F. King, "Negro Slavery in the Viceroyalty of New Granada" (Ph.D. diss., University of California, Berkeley, 1939), pp. 213-214; AHNC, Negros y esclavos de Panamá, 3: 380.

[67]AHNC, Negros y esclavos del Cauca, 4: 636.

[68]AHNE, Real Audiencia, Gobernación de Popayán, legajo 1, expediente 3, 1769.

[69]Sandoval, pp. 569-570.

[70]Bowser, p. 93.

[71]AHNC, Negros y esclavos de Panamá, 3: 351-379, and 2: 933.

[72]Bowser, pp. 78-86.

[73]Redactor Americano del Nuevo Reino de Granada, 19 June 1807, pp. 108-110, and 4 July 1807, pp. 115-116.

[74]*Ibid*.

[75]West, p. 126.

[76]Fermín de Vargas, *Pensamientos*, p. 31.

[77]Viceroy Caballero y Góngora, "Relación," *Relaciones de mando* (Addenda), p. 744.

[78]Notaría Primera de Bogotá, year 1700, ff. 396v-398.

[79] AHDA, Colonia, 28 (Esclavos), Doc. 898.

[80] Juan de Velasco, *Historia moderna del Reino de Quito y crónica de la Compañía de Jésus del mismo reino*, 2 vols., Biblioteca Amazonas, No. 8 (Quito, 1941), 2: 457.

[81] AHNE, Esclavos, legajo 3, expediente 7, f. 1.

3

Manumission, *Libres*, and Black Resistance: The Colombian Chocó 1680-1810

William F. Sharp

William F. Sharp's study also provides an opportunity to focus on a particular slave society and to analyze the position of blacks in colonial Latin America. The theater for Sharp's investigation, Colombia's Chocó, provided a particularly harsh working environment for thousands of African slaves. In climatic terms the Chocó is extremely hot and humid. Its annual level of rainfall ranks among the highest for any area in the world. In human terms harsh working conditions in the gold fields added to the agony of laboring in the Chocó. Contemporary techniques of gold mining called for the formation of slave gangs or cuadrillas, *through which slaves panned for long hours under the watchful eyes of whip-carrying overseers. As in colonial Mexico, Bolivia, Peru, and Brazil, where man mined precious metals, slavery took on some of its most severe characteristics.*

Unfortunately for Chocoano laborers, there were few Spanish officials in the area to offer protection in accordance with written slave codes. Government bureaucrats did not wish to live in the humid and sparsely populated Chocó, and many of the slave owners became absentee proprietors, leaving responsibility in the hands of discipline-conscious managers. Understandably, some slaves in the Chocó refused to accept their lot.

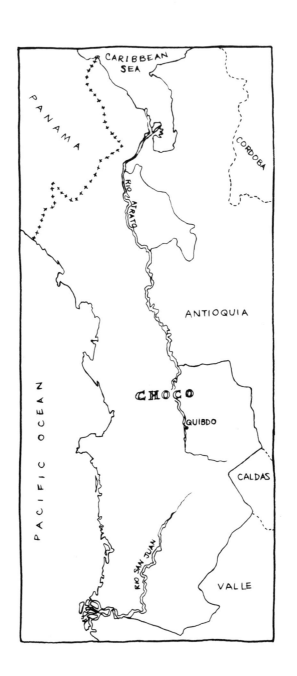

They opted for the extreme gamble of flight or rebellion even though chances of being caught and severely punished were great.

Despite the harsh conditions of slavery, in time a relatively large population of libres *(free blacks) appeared in Chocó society. Opportunities did exist to save money to purchase freedom. In other instances blacks received manumission as a consequence of their masters' benevolence, or they found liberty by escaping and settling in distant communities. Even in freedom, however, blacks could not easily escape the stigma of slavery. As in other places in the Americas, social restrictions and discrimination attended the lives of free blacks living in the midst of slave societies.*

R. B. T.

For almost a century and a half during the colonial period—1680-1810—the Colombian Chocó became an important source of gold in the Spanish empire. But guarded by towering mountains and dense tropical rain forests, the Chocó is an area of heat, humidity, jungle, rivers, and rainfall. Because of geography and climate the Spanish themselves rarely attempted colonization, although those who came succeeded in extracting millions of pesos' worth of precious yellow metal. These same Spanish officials and mine owners constituted a ruling elite exhibiting little interest in anything other than accumulating wealth. Laws were violated, Indians and blacks mistreated, and bullion was produced in large quantities.

Gold production in the Chocó necessitated thousands of slaves and hundreds of independent white and freed black prospectors who labored on small claims. Indians produced food for these miners and also served as transporters of goods. White merchants bought and sold various products, and the royal officials supposedly regulated commerce, prevented fraud, collected the king's duties, protected Indians and slaves from mistreatment, and oversaw the growth and development of placer mining. Hence virtually everyone depended in some way on the yield of the mines. Only escaped slaves and those Indians and free blacks who willfully separated themselves from society remained outside the gold-oriented economy, thereby contributing little to the Chocó's economic structure.

The profitable economic monoculture of mining, however, meant that Spaniards concentrated their efforts almost entirely on extracting gold from the placer mines. In doing so, they were at times almost impervious to the manner in which they exploited their surroundings. Indians died by the thousands and even slaves starved because their masters, intent on amassing fortunes, failed to establish proper supply lines or food sources. Often mistreated and limited in position, opportunity, and education, blacks had ample reason to rebel. That slaves resented their captivity is obvious from their numerous acts of resistance. But the Chocó's placer mines also presented an avenue of escape from slavery for many blacks. As Frank Tannenbaum noted so succinctly almost thirty years ago, manumission was an integral part of the Spanish slave system. Blacks could always buy their own freedom, provided they had the money to do so. In many regions of Latin America where slaves were employed in plantation agriculture, it was difficult for slaves to earn much extra cash, and they depended on the goodwill of their masters while seeking freedom. In the Chocó gold fields, however, an accessible cash crop existed that they were able to exploit during their own time, thereby accruing funds that could be used to purchase extra provisions and even freedom itself. The incidents of violence would perhaps have been much greater in the region had this safety valve of manumission not been present and effective. It is significant to note, however, that once freed, many *libres* rejected coexistence with the whites, instead seeking freedom from Spanish domination by moving to isolated jungle homes. The advantages of greater self-determination apparently outweighed all other considerations. Their chances of success by monetary or political standards were few as a result of this chosen seclusion, but in fact they were restricted in their opportunities for jobs, education, or authority even if they remained in the Spanish communities.

The Spanish knew that gold existed in the Chocó as early as 1511, when the conquistador Vasco Núñez de Balboa entered the area from the north,[1] but topography, climate, and irascible natives rebuffed attempts to enter this potential "El Dorado."[2] Conquest of the brooding jungle area the Spanish called the Chocó was a long and arduous task, but the precious yellow metal within its borders provided a powerful incentive and soothed all wounds for weary adventurers. Conquest, though slow, was never in doubt. From the time the Spanish gained a firm foothold in the Chocó in 1690,[3] until the end of the colonial period (1810), the Chocó placer mines yielded more than 75 million silver pesos (375,000 pounds) worth of gold.[4]

Human existence in the Chocó centered almost exclusively on gold production, and well over 90 percent of the metal mined came from the labor of blacks imported to work the gold fields. Whites arrived as masters and exploiters. So recklessly did they pursue their golden dreams that they frequently failed to establish supply lines or even food sources, and the grim specter of famine was a common companion in the Chocó. This was particularly true early in the eighteenth century when slave owners estimated that over three hundred slaves had perished from starvation.[5]

Whites who resided in the Chocó were generally small mine owners or overseers, crown officials, priests, or merchants. The wealthier mine owners and the *dueños* (owners) of the large *cuadrillas* (slave gangs) almost invariably lived outside the Chocó in the interior towns of New Granada (present-day Colombia)—especially in Buga, Cartago, Cali, and Popayán.[6] The hot, humid climate of the Chocó was not considered healthy for a white man, and few remained who could hire overseers to handle their affairs.[7] Whites arrived as exploiters, not settlers. In the year 1782, for example, when the central Chocó contained a total of

17,898 inhabitants, only 359 were Spaniards. The remaining population included 7,088 slaves, 6,552 Indians, and 3,899 free people of color (*libres de color*).[8] As a series of mining camps, or commercial warehouses, the Chocó did not really contain any large centers of population or any places that could be designated as cities during the colonial period. Not a single Spanish town—if that term may be used—was large enough to merit a *cabildo* (town council) or an *alcalde* (mayor).[9]

Spanish occupation during the eighteenth century seemingly did little to develop the Chocó. Late in the colonial period (1808), Chocó Governor Carlos de Ciaurriz reported that settlements were dirty and disorganized, and that there were few decent houses, official buildings, churches, or schools. The area was poorly supplied, prices were high, and, the governor concluded, there was scant evidence of any social refinement.[10] Despite the region's importance with regard to gold production, the population was always too small to justify the use and expense of the many minor administrators and military men who generally composed the broad lower base of Spanish bureaucracy. Governmental authority in the Chocó resided in the hands of relatively few individuals. The population was dispersed, slave gangs isolated, officials were few, and a profitable slave-dependent monoculture developed. Physical isolation because of mountains, rivers, and jungles, from other more populated Spanish regions, and within the Chocó itself, meant that each Spaniard—miner, merchant, or official—was very much his own master.

In at least one significant aspect Spanish societal mores with regard to slavery in the Chocó seem to have worked to the advantage of the slaves. Manumission in the Chocó was not only possible, but frequent. By the year 1782, over one-third of the black population (3,899 out of 10,987) was free.[11] Any Spaniard could free his slaves either during his lifetime, or in his will without restrictions, and a number doubtless did so.[12] The most common means of manumission in the Chocó, however, was the system whereby a slave purchased his own freedom. The value of a slave was legally established by one of the Spanish officials in the region (usually the lieutenant governor), and the owner had to accept this price. Slaves could work on their "free time," including religious holidays, and keep what they earned. Owners hoped slaves would use this money to buy extra food, tobacco, and liquor, which they sold to their slaves at high prices.[13] But with luck and hard work slaves working in the placer mines could save enough to buy their own freedom.[14] Because notary records no longer exist for the Chocó during the colonial period, it is impossible even to estimate the number of slaves who were able to purchase liberty, but the number was clearly substantial. Apparently many owners agreed to this "self-purchase," and at least by the nineteenth century some slaves had even made arrangements to pay for their manumission in installments. These slaves were freed from service to their masters once they had submitted a specified part of their value (the amount varied from 10 to 50 percent), but they were, of course, expected to continue payments.[15] Thus, following a down payment, some slaves were free to seek their own employment and work full-time on their own accounts.

Naturally some owners objected to slaves' rights to manumission. Occasionally a relative or heir contested a will freeing slaves, but to no avail.[16] In fact, verbal testimony was even accepted in place of written wills to prove that the deceased owner's intent had been to manumit a certain slave or slaves.[17] It is also clear that a few owners bitterly disputed their slaves' rights to purchase freedom because they feared that freeing slaves would lead to a drop in production in their gold mines. Slaveholders who challenged this type of manumission usually claimed the slave had either stolen the money (this had to be proved conclusively), or simply wished to cause trouble.[18] A typical example of this occurred in 1728 when Isidoro, a slave owned by Francisco Joseph de Arboleda, brought 600 pesos to the lieutenant governor of Nóvita and claimed his freedom. Arboleda contested the request, stating that Isidoro must have stolen the money—after all, the upset owner argued, everyone knew that slaves stole from the mines and then later pretended to have mined the gold during their free time. Testimony, however, supported the slave. Witnesses said that Isidoro worked efficiently, labored long and hard during his own time, had collected a considerable amount of gold (exact amount unknown); and finally, no witnesses offered any proof that the money had been stolen. Arboleda lost the suit and Isidoro gained his freedom, but the angry Spaniard direly predicted the ultimate ruination of the province, generalizing that slaves would now openly steal from their masters in order to buy their own freedom.[19]

Another bitter owner, forced to liberate a fifteen-year-old slave, argued that his private property rights were being violated. Since he did not have to sell furniture or other property against his wishes, surely he need not part with slaves simply because they had money! The judge (*fiscal*) reviewing the case for the *Audiencia* (Royal Tribunal) in Santa Fé de Bogotá ignored the dehumanizing aspects of the argument and openly sympathized with the distraught owner. However, the *fiscal* concluded that the law was quite clear and that he had no recourse but to declare the slave free.[20] It is quite likely that disgruntled slaveholders hoped to intimidate the slaves into forfeiting their legal rights to freedom, and they doubtless realized that many slaves able to buy their own liberty were the best-qualified or the hardest workers. Although the system was doubtless open to some injustice—at the very least in instances where owners did not agree to manumit a slave, the slave had to find an official willing to initiate an investigation —manumission laws clearly favored slaves. Thus an escape valve—manumission—did exist for the more aggressive slaves.

Freed blacks and mulattoes in the Chocó did acquire a greater degree of protection before the law than their slave brethren elsewhere, but very few *libres* seem to have taken advantage of this—probably because they did not know their legal rights or were too intimidated to use them. One of the only lawsuits this investigator discovered involving a free black versus a white occurred in 1747 when a *bozal* (black directly from Africa) *libre* complained that he had been jailed and his mine and several slaves impounded by the lieutenant governor of Quibdó. He admitted that he owed fifty dollars to a Spanish mine owner for some mining rights, but he refused to pay the outrageous interest rate on the debt that was being charged. The *Audiencia* of New Granada reviewed the case and agreed that the interest rate had been excessive. The lieutenant governor was reprimanded and the *bozal* was released from jail, his property restored, and he only paid the original sum of the debt.[21] Free blacks, like slaves, could win legal disputes with whites, but they suffered the obvious disadvantage of not knowing the law or not being able to hire lawyers who did.

Although black *libres* had a slightly higher legal and social standing than slaves, many of the regulations that applied to the slave also applied to them. Legally they could not bear arms or hold any political or military office without special crown approval; they could not live among the Indians or hold Indian servants;[22] nor could they use such prestige symbols as a walking cane.[23]

Unquestionably many *libres* were unemployed or underemployed, and the term *libre vagabundo* (shiftless individual, vagabond) frequently was used to describe them. In part this was due to the relatively simple economic structure of the Chocó, where, except for mining, there were few skilled or semiskilled jobs available. But free blacks even had difficulty attaining unskilled positions such as *bogas* (canoe men) or *cargeros* (cargo carriers) because the *corregidors* in the Chocó wished to retain monopolies on the carrying trade by utilizing only Indians from their *corregimientos*.[24]

Official positions in the Chocó were few in number and were reserved almost exclusively for whites. Most colonial documentation carefully recorded the race of an individual, especially if he was of Indian or African ancestry. This investigator discovered no archival source that mentioned a black, mulatto, or *zambo* (Indian-black offspring) ever being appointed *corregidor*, lieutenant governor, governor, or administrator of the major crown agencies in the Chocó. Nor were any of the major merchants of the region listed as being of African origin. Whites could easily have excluded blacks from most of the commercial business in the Chocó, since the contracts to carry supplies into the region were granted by Spanish officials,[25] doubtless exclusively to fellow whites.

Libres could and did own slaves and mines in the Chocó, but very few could be classified as major owners. Of the 72 individuals listed in 1755 and 1759 as owning more than 5 slaves, only 2, Miguel Ibo de Tovar with 5 slaves and Miguel Soliman with 20, were *libres*. By way of comparison, 10 Spanish slaveholders held more than 100 slaves, the largest owner being Sergeant Major Salvador Gómez de la Asprilla y Navoa with 567, and 44 Spaniards owned slave gangs numbering more than 30.[26]

Jobs were available in the mines and wages were often as much as a peso a day,[27] but few free blacks showed any desire to work in the mines of their former owners.[28] Although *libres* did do some mining, few qualified as *masamorreros* (independent prospectors). The term was usually used for those full-time prospectors who worked their own claims. In the province of Citará (one of the two Chocó provinces), which contained 814 *libre* males in 1782,[29] there were only 188 *masamorreros*[30] and some of these doubtless were Spaniards. Some *libres* attempted commercial agriculture, living near the mines and villages and selling their corn and plantains to the overseers of the large slave gangs.[31] Often, however, they were not welcomed near the Spanish communities and mines, because owners feared that the *libres* would be a corrupting influence on those who remained in bondage.[32] Many of the *libres*, joined by runaway slaves (*cimarrones*) both from the Chocó and neighboring regions like the Cauca valley and Antioquia, retired to hard-to-reach spots in the mountains near the headwaters of the numerous streams that meandered through the Chocó. There they produced their own food through primitive agriculture and mined just enough to supply themselves with basic necessities.[33]

Certainly one of the most serious handicaps faced by the *libres* was the virtual impossibility of receiving any formal education. This doubtless prevented them from holding many positions that required some degree of literacy (overseers, clerks, and so on). It was not necessarily a deliberate policy on the part of the Spanish to withhold education from blacks (although that conclusion seems justified), because schools throughout Latin America were few in number. In fact, no school of any kind existed in the Chocó until late in the eighteenth century, and that was a school created specifically for Indians.[34] Few blacks could afford the expense of sending a child to a school outside the province as did many of the whites. And finally, institutions of higher learning were exclusive, so the possibility of advanced training as a doctor, lawyer, or scribe was almost always denied blacks. Most university charters allowed entrance only to those of pure Spanish descent,[35] and the Spanish crown also frowned on black participation in universities. On 23 June 1765, for example, when reports reached Spain that some mulattoes and blacks had been matriculated in the University of Santo Tomás in Santa Fé de Bogotá, the king ordered the rector specifically to end such admissions.[36]

One of the few prestigious occupations open to a free mulatto or black involved a position in the colonial militia. Blacks could join the militia in the eighteenth century with crown approval, but except in times of dire emergency they formed segregated regiments. By the year 1761 a company of mulattoes *libres* existed in Nóvita (the capital of the Chocó)[37] and in 1774 the viceroy ordered the governor of the Chocó to form a company of mulattoes in Quibdó.[38] The crown did not always approve the formation of colored militia units in the Chocó, however. In 1779, for example, Governor Manuel de Entrena requested permission to establish several urban companies of militia that would include mulattoes; he cited the increased size of the slave gangs and the ever-present threat of Cuna Indian invasion as his reasons.[39] The viceroy of New Granada denied the request, stating that there was a dual problem involved in enlisting blacks into the militia in the Chocó. First, the viceroy explained, blacks were needed in the mines to ensure the continued production of gold; and second, although there was a need for militia units, blacks were not entirely trusted and some feared that arming them might actually lead to rebellion on their part.[40] Thus, although militia units containing *libres* existed in the Chocó, they were never very important.

Joining the militia did not depend on skin color, but color was a decisive factor in becoming a military officer. A male with black ancestry rarely advanced in rank, and then he did so only within the mulatto regiments. Even in these companies most of the officers were white.[41] However, a free mulatto, Juan Antonio de Lasprilla, was named captain and commander of the mulatto *libre* company of Nóvita in 1761. Governor Ponce de León, who made the appointment (pending approval from Santa Fé de Bogotá), assured the viceroy that Lasprilla was of honorable character and light complexion, and promised that the mulatto would derive no special privileges (*fueros*) from the commission, "nor any distinction other than carrying a cane, which here is much admired. . . ."[42]

Census reports listed the Chocó's large number of *libres*, but they did not include the considerable number of *cimarrones*. Blacks often took advantage of revolts to escape bondage and congregated in places that were inaccessible to Spaniards intent upon their recapture. These runaway slaves posed a real threat to the prosperity of the region, since they returned to the Spanish mines and villages on raiding parties, looting and burning, stealing women, and sometimes raping and killing the inhabitants.[43] Usually the *cimarrones* retreated before the forces sent to recapture them and were never really eliminated. In the beginning of the nineteenth century, for example, slaves from the Chocó, Barbacoas, and the Cauca valley formed a *palanque* (*cimarron* community) located just south of the Chocó. Expeditions sent against it found only deserted houses as the blacks slipped farther into the jungle. A foray led by the governor of Micay in 1819 finally succeeded in capturing a few of the *cimarrones* in this group and temporarily stopped raids on mines in the region. But the governor admitted that further problems would probably arise.[44]

The number of *cimarrones* in the Chocó is impossible to calculate because no one ever tried to compile statistics on runaways. It must have been a vexing and continual problem, however, because throughout the eighteenth century, property inventories, letters from overseers to owners, and documents written by Chocó officials enumerate expenses for the recapture of runaways or mention that slaves had escaped from the *cuadrillas*.[45]

Certainly, purchasing freedom or fleeing from the forced labor of the slave gang were forms of black resistance, and they could cost the owner capital investment or future profits in his mine —but these problems were not what the Spanish feared the most. The real threat was that of black aggression. Docility is not a word that can be used accurately to describe the blacks in Latin America, and the Spanish knew, from experience virtually everywhere in the Americas, to expect physical opposition from their African bondsmen. Therefore the slave insurrections that erupted periodically in the Chocó were to be expected, but it is especially significant that they occurred in this particular region of the Spanish empire. Blacks everywhere resisted slavery, but rarely did they have the legal opportunities to escape bondage that were available in the Chocó. Hatred of slavery could be relieved by following legal channels, and those blacks who were the strongest, most aggressive (and therefore potentially the most dangerous) slaves could gain liberty by working for it. Opportunities to amass savings in the gold fields were ever present, and the safety valve of manumission doubtless let off tension. There was a steady stream of young able-bodied blacks who purchased their own freedom. Armed revolt, on the other hand, was a serious crime known to all, and any large rebellion was inevitably doomed to ultimate failure and perhaps death. The Spanish wanted the Chocó gold, and no slave, or group of slaves, could prevent the continued exploitation of men and metals. But significantly, confrontations did occur again and again and clearly demonstrated the frustrations and impatience of blacks at their captivity.

As should be expected, many individual slaves reacted against mistreatment with minor acts of obstruction or sabotage, and sometimes their hatred exploded with extreme violence. In 1788, for example, a slave in the town of Bebará stunned his mistress with a club, ran to the house for an ax, and returned to hack his fallen victim to pieces. An investigation clearly proved that the slave had received unjustifiably cruel treatment from his mistress prior to her murder. She had overworked him in her mine and had whipped him so continuously that a doctor later described the slave's back as a festered open sore. But even worse, she had tortured her slave by placing hot oil and burning chili sauce on his genitals. Spanish officials agreed that even though the slave had not acted in defense of his life (the only possible legal justification for his actions), the mistress had behaved so as to provoke her own murder. Further discussion, however, convinced the officials that the death penalty had to be ordered, because anything less might encourage similar acts among the large slave population and endanger the lives of the white inhabitants of the region. Authorities had the murderer hanged, and his right arm severed and placed on a pole in the town square of Bebará as a lesson to other slaves who might strike their masters.[46]

When only one or two slaves rebelled and remained in the area, the Spanish easily captured them and inflicted harsh penalties —usually death by hanging.[47] But because so few Spaniards actually resided in the region, major insurrections were much more difficult to handle. Fortunately for the Chocó mine owners, such confrontations were few in number and when they occurred, help was always available from the neighboring Spanish provinces. The first such altercation took place in 1684 when slaves who joined rebellious Chocó Indians were finally defeated by troops sent from the Cauca valley.[48] The largest slave revolt to occur in the region took place in 1728 near the town of Tadó. Forty blacks who had been severely mistreated by a harsh overseer banded together and killed the offending Spaniard. Their hatred not satiated by this single act of vengeance, the blacks raided other isolated mines in the area, killing fourteen more Spaniards and enlisting other followers. The Spanish inhabitants of Tadó were terrified that the slaves would attack the town itself, and with only a handful of whites and a few weapons they thought themselves defenseless. But instead of making a direct assault on the town, the blacks scattered, attempting to get slaves from other *cuadrillas* in the Chocó to join them in a mass rebellion. The blacks, having few weapons, obviously believed that greater safety and effectiveness lay in numbers. But the tactic backfired as the savage initial outburst of the rebellion sputtered into inactivity, giving the Spaniards time to send reinforcements to the region. The governor of Popayán, afraid an organized slave revolt might spread into the Cauca valley, immediately sent an armed expedition to Tadó. Peace was restored to the area when the military commander of the Spanish expedition, Lieutenant Julian Tres Palacios Mier, tricked four of the rebel leaders into surrender and executed them. Lieutenant Tres Palacios had been correct in his solution to the rebellion. The remaining blacks, although a significant group, seemed lost and powerless without leadership, and the majority submissively returned to their owners. Some remained hidden as *cimarrones* along the jungle streams, but they posed no immediate threat to Spanish domination.[49]

The 1728 rebellion, however, did provide slaves with an example of violent resistance. A number of slaves had firsthand experience as participants in an open rebellion against their masters, and *cuadrillas* throughout the Chocó had knowledge of the revolt. Despite the effective countermeasures taken by Lieutenant Tres Palacios to end the uprising, tension remained high. In 1737 the governor of the Chocó concluded that the situation had once again reached an explosive stage, and he claimed that another mass slave revolt had been planned. As a result he ordered the lieutenant governor of Nóvita to forceably collect all weapons in the possession of slaves. The lieutenant governor complied with his instructions and even commanded slave owners in his district to gather all mining tools at the end of each working day on pain of a thousand-peso fine.[50] These measures would appear to be a combination of common sense and preventive medicine, but they imposed hardships on the slave owners and went against the customary procedures of the region.[51] The governor's orders clearly demonstrated the Chocó officials' continued apprehension about the growing slave population.

Disturbances continued in the region, and a number of small revolts on the fringes of the province involved blacks from the Chocó.[52] Chocó governors repeatedly warned the viceroy that uprisings could easily occur. In 1803 Governor Carlos de Ciaurriz wrote that although the Indians in the area were peaceful, numerous slaves in the province disregarded authority and needed constant surveillance. He requested all mine owners to report any disorders immediately to him.[53] Three years later Ciaurriz wrote that an explosive situation definitely existed. The Chocó slaves, he cautioned, knew of the horrible events that had recently occurred on the island of Santo Domingo (Haiti) and planned similar terrorism. The governor claimed that blacks throughout the Chocó were discussing the violent methods with which Haitian blacks had not only overthrown their white masters, but driven them from the island as well. Slaves openly refused to work and insulted their masters; even *libres* were increasingly insubordinate. Governor Ciaurriz asked that Spanish regulars be sent, for although violence had not yet erupted, signs of growing unrest were everywhere. Troops were sent from Cartagena,[54] and perhaps because of this an insurrection did not occur.

Black freedmen also initiated several serious incidents in the Chocó, and the threat of their involvement in seditious acts increased with their numbers. Limited in their opportunities and often resentful of Spanish authority, the *libres* constituted a large, potentially disruptive group. In 1766 free mulattoes in the town of Bebará, disgusted with high prices for *aguardiente* (a liquor —literally firewater) and food, and with the Spanish officials in the Chocó, broke into the royal *aguardiente* warehouse in the town and stole all the liquor on hand. After consuming large quantities of the firewater they drunkenly marched to the *corregidor*'s house. Armed with stones, sticks, and a few knives, they raised their own flags and openly insulted the *corregidor*. The unruly mob then presented a list of grievances that began "long live the King and down with bad government." Although the blacks took no physical action at the time, they controlled the town and the *corregidor* was powerless to prevent their continued defiance of authority.[55]

News of the incident reached both the black community and the Spanish officials in Quibdó (the largest town in the province of Citará). A number of citizens informed Governor Nicolás Díaz de Perea that the *libres* of Quibdó planned similar events. Blacks outnumbered the whites ten to one in the city, and the governor, believing he did not have sufficient forces to defeat a full-scale rebellion,[56] courageously bluffed the potential insurgents into submission. Favoring a policy of direct action over anxious waiting, the governor called for a meeting with all the town's blacks. Striding confidently before the large crowd that gathered, Díaz de Perea bluntly stated that he knew of the plot to break into the *aguardiente* warehouse and the royal treasury. Alone, unaided, and obviously unintimidated, the governor continued with a stern lecture concerning the king's policy toward those who violated his agencies or harmed his officials. Any who rebelled would be punished to the limit of the law. The only hope the would-be rebels retained was to quickly hand over all weapons and discard all ideas of subversion. The absurdity of the solitary official demanding surrender for a deed not yet committed, but one he was physically powerless to prevent, never had a chance to surface. Taken by surprise and perhaps aware that acts of rebellion would ultimately be avenged, most in the bewildered crowd submitted to the personally defenseless voice of traditional authority.[57] A strong man, confident in himself and the system he enforced, successfully rebuffed a challenge from dissatisfied but unorganized blacks.

However, the mulattoes in Bebará still remained to be dealt with. After organizing the "loyal vassals" of Quibdó, an expedition was sent to Bebará. The group was small in number, poorly armed, and the lieutenant governor who headed it, Juan Jiménez, expressed private doubts about some of the members because of their color. Despite these disadvantages the foray successfully restored the governor's authority in Bebará, and twenty-nine mulattoes were taken prisoner.[58] Some escaped and tried to flee to Antioquia. The leader of the rebels, Hipólito de

Viera, was later taken captive and sent for trial to Santa Fé de Bogotá. Viera had tried to initiate acts of atrocity against the Spanish, but it was too late.[59] Swift action, personal bravery, and good fortune had prevented the possible massacre of whites by blacks. But the crown was informed that great potential danger still existed, for if the *libres* actually did start killing whites, slaves and even Indians would probably join in the bloodbath. Lieutenant Governor Jiménez recommended that Spanish regulars be sent from Cartagena and permanently stationed in the Chocó, because the mulattoes, in the long run, would only respect force. The lieutenant governor also suggested that a strong fort be constructed by the Atrato River and that punishment be swift and severe for any black who committed a crime.[60]

The absence of a major revolt during the last decades of the colonial period did not mean that conditions improved or that blacks were satisfied. The insubordination and unruliness described by Governor Ciaurriz in 1803 and 1806 are clear indications that life in the Chocó depended on forced alliances and was filled with tension and fear. Revolts failed, or perhaps were not even initiated, because many slaves concentrated their efforts on purchasing freedom rather than rebellion. But also the blacks' lack of success in insurrection proved the efficacious nature of the Spanish slave system. The white minority maintained, through the use of regimented authority and threats of armed reprisals, an uneasy but effective dominance over the colored majority. The slaves, who were born or raised in bondage, were carefully taught the dictates of their masters, and lessons in submission were repeatedly driven home by the end of a lash. Blacks learned to obey or expect punishment. Rebellion had virtually no chance of continued success, because blacks relied on quick, isolated acts of violence rather than prolonged, systematically organized campaigns. Weapons, education, and authority were a Spanish monopoly. Trained leadership within the black community was not encouraged and rarely tolerated. For the slave, the only acceptable avenue for personal initiative was hard work. This might bring him increased personal comforts, food, liquor, clothing, or, if he was diligent and lucky, enough money to purchase freedom. But under the Spanish even the *libre* still knew who was master. It would be extremely naive to expect white masters to accept former slaves as equals. Positions and opportunities were never equal, and acts of self-assertion were not permitted.

But despite the attempts on the part of the Spanish to destroy black pride and limit initiative, despite the overwhelming odds against them, slaves did rebel and they continued to seek and work for their freedom—not just freedom from slavery (this was done in many parts of the Americas), but also freedom from Spanish authority, domination, and law. This is doubtless the real reason so many free blacks, desiring to be free in spirit as well as legal status, left the Spanish settlements and retreated to inaccessible locations in the jungle. Whether they failed or succeeded in their rebellions is in reality not nearly as important as the fact that they resisted, and resisted in many ways.

Notes

[1] Kathleen Romoli, *Balboa of Darién: Discoverer of the Pacific* (Garden City, N.Y., 1953), p. 154.

[2] Several excellent primary sources exist for this period of Chocó history, including *Documentos inéditos para la historia de Colombia*, 10 vols., edited and compiled by Juan Friede (Bogotá, 1955-1960); Juan de Castellanos, *Elegías de varones ilustres de Indias*, 3 vols. (Bogotá, 1955); and *Historia documental del Chocó*, ed. Enrique Ortega Ricaurte (Bogotá, 1954). For a more complete description of the conquest of the Chocó, see William F. Sharp, "Forsaken but for Gold: An Economic Study of Slavery and Mining in the Colombian Chocó, 1680-1810" (Ph.D. diss., University of North Carolina at Chapel Hill, 1970), pp. 45-62 (hereafter cited as Sharp, "Forsaken but for Gold").

[3] The Spaniards had defeated the Indians in a series of battles in the 1680s. By 1690 the Chocó was generally considered pacified. See Archivo Histórico Nacional de Colombia (AHNC), Bogotá, Colombia, Caciques e Indios 10, f. 605 (1695); AHNC, Empleados Publicos del

Cauca 22, f. 311 (1688); AHNC, Caciques e Indios, 23 ff. 849-853 (1685); AHNC, Reales Cédulas 4, f. 142 (1685).

[4]Sharp, "Forsaken but for Gold," pp. 338-341.

[5]Archivo Central del Cauca (ACC), Popayán, Colombia, signatura 8174, 1717. See also ÁHNC, Caciques e Indios 10, f. 509 (1691); AHNC, Caciques e Indios 23, f. 955 (1708).

[6]AHNC, Poblaciones del Cauca 2, f. 854 (1793), and f. 935 (1793).

[7]AHNC, Visitas del Cauca 5, f. 282 (1808).

[8]AHNC, Censos de Varios Departamentos 6, f. 377.

[9]AHNC, Poblaciones del Cauca 2, f. 937 (1793); AHNC, Estadistica 11 (Part 1), ff. 221-222 (1808).

[10]AHNC, Visitas del Cauca 5, ff. 273-285 (1808).

[11]AHNC, Censos de Varios Departamentos 6, f. 377 (1782). Unfortunately specific documents concerning manumission for the eighteenth century were located in Provincial archives and *notarías* (notary's office) in Quibdó and Nóvita that were destroyed by fire in the nineteenth century. Notary records extant in Quibdó for the years 1814 and 1817, however, list several dozen examples of manumission. See Notaria Publica de Quibdó, Quibdó, Chocó, Colombia, Años de 1814-1817 (hereafter cited as Notaria de Quibdó).

[12]If any problems arose concerning manumission, documents were often forwarded to the Audiencia of New Granada in Bogotá, and they have been preserved in the Archivo Nacional in Bogotá (AHNC). Hence, for a few examples of this type of manumission in the Chocó, see AHNC, Negros y Esclavos del Cauca 2, ff. 617-618 (1732); AHNC, Negros y Esclavos del Cauca 3, 822-826 (1780); AHNC, Miscelánea 2, ff. 390-391 (1797). Several of these cases involved masters freeing their own mulatto children.

[13]AHNC, Reales Cédulas 9, ff. 225-228 (1733).

[14]To work his owner's mine during fiesta days the slave had to have the express permission of the owner. But slaves could locate and work their own claims with no legal problems.

[15]Notaría de Quibdó, Años de 1814, 1817, 1818, 1819.

[16]AHNC, Negros y Esclavos del Cauca 3, f. 822 (1780); AHNC, Negros y Esclavos del Cauca 2, ff. 969-972 (1804).

[17]AHNC, Negros y Esclavos del Cauca 2, ff. 617-618 (1732).

[18]AHNC, Negros y Esclavos del Cauca 2, ff. 1-40 (1728); AHNC, Negros y Esclavos del Cauca 3, f. 913 (1790).

[19]AHNC, Negros y Esclavos del Cauca 2, ff. 1-40 (1728).

[20]AHNC, Real Hacienda 40, ff. 276-278 (1797).

[21]AHNC, Minas del Cauca 2, ff. 467-504 (1757).

[22]These restrictions were often repeated during the colonial period, a fact that shows both their continued importance and probable nonenforcement. For one early example, see Charles I to the President of the Audiencia Real de Nuevo Reyno de Granada, 27 February 1549, Valladolid, *Colección de documentos para la historia de la formación social de Hispanoamerica*, compiled and edited by Richard Konetzke, 3 vols. (Madrid, 1953), 1: 256.

[23]AHNC, Caciques e Indios 67, f. 766 (1761).

[24]The *corregimientos* in the Chocó were all originally *corregimientos de indios* (a district of Indians governed by a crown official called a *corregidor*). The Indians residing within these *corregimientos* had their own chiefs (*caciques*), governors, and mayors, but they were primarily responsible to and under the control of the crown's appointed official, the *corregidor*.

[25]AHNC, Visitas del Cauca 5, ff. 857-861 (1788).

[26]AHNC, Negros y Esclavos del Cauca 2, ff. 961-964 (1755); AHNC, Negros y Esclavos del Cauca 4, ff. 558-591 (1759).

[27]AHNC, Minas del Cauca 5, ff. 314-320 (1730); AHNC, Minas 1 (Part 2), f. 100 (1773).

[28]AHNC, Negros y Esclavos del Cauca 2, ff. 414-415 (1785); AHNC, Poblaciones del Cauca 2, ff. 116-118 (1803).

[29]AHNC, Censos de Varios Departamentos 6, f. 377 (1782).

[30]AHNC, Minas 3 (Part 1), ff. 38-39 (1780-1781).

[31]Balance sheet for the mine owned by Francisco de Rivas for the years 1752-1765, ACC, sig. 10362, ff. 55-90. The list of expenditures shows that corn and plantains were sometimes purchased from free blacks.

[32]AHNC, Minas del Cauca 5, 284-285 (1804).

[33]AHNC, Negros y Esclavos del Cauca 2, ff. 414-415 (1785); AHNC, Poblaciones del Cauca 2, ff. 116-118 (1803).

[34]AHNC, Visitas del Cauca 5, ff. 277-278 (1808).

[35]Regulations of the royal college and seminary of San Carlos in Cartagena, 29 December 1786, Konetzke (ed.), *Colección*, 3: 622-623; see also Juan B. Quiros, "El contenido laboral en los codigos negros Americanos," *Revista Mexicana de Sociologia* 5, No. 4 (1943): 475.

[36]Charles III to the rector of the University of Santo Tomás in Sante Fé de Bogotá, 23 June 1765, Madrid, Konetzke (ed.), *Colección*, 3: 331-332.

[37]AHNC, Virreyes 16, ff. 169-171 (1761).

[38]AHNC, Milicias y Marinas 30, ff. 633-634 (1777).

[39]AHNC, Virreyes 9, f. 40 (1779); AHNC, Milicias y Marinas 52, ff. 478-479 (1782).

[40]AHNC, Virreyes 9, ff. 4-6 (1782).

[41]AHNC, Virreyes 16, ff. 169-171, 173-175 (1761).

[42]AHNC, Caciques e Indios 67, f. 766 (1761).

[43]AHNC, Miscelánea 100, ff. 365-366 (1767); AHNC, Negros y Esclavos del Cauca 3, ff. 963-964 (1802-1803); AHNC, Juicios Criminales 134, ff. 195-223 (1802).

[44]AHNC, Minas 3 (Part 2), ff. 315-318 (1812), 439-441 (1819).

[45]See for example AHNC, Minas del Cauca 5, f. 298 (1726); AHNC, Miscelánea 130, f. 634 (1741); AHNC, Milicias y Marinas 116, ff. 253-254 (1788); AHNC, Esclavos 1, f. 500 (1789).

[46]AHNC, Negros y Esclavos del Cauca 1, ff. 511-561 (1788-1789).

[47]*Ibid.*; AHNC, Juicios Criminales 133, ff. 223-224 (1802); AHNC, Juicios Criminales 134, ff. 195-223 (1802).

[48]AHNC, Caciques e Indios 23, ff. 849-853 (1686); AHNC, Minas del Cauca 6, f. 649 (1702).

[49]AHNC, Reales Cédulas 9, ff. 225-228 (1733).

[50]Norman Meiklejohn, "The Observance of Negro Slave Legislation in Colonial Nueva Granada" (Ph.D. diss., Columbia University, 1969), p. 87.

[51]Although Spanish law clearly prohibited slaves from possessing weapons, enforcement of this proscription was usually quite lax (see Meiklejohn, "Negro Slave Legislation," pp. 82-87). In the Chocó, where food supply was always a major problem, it was common practice to designate several members of the *cuadrilla* as hunters, provide them with weapons, and assign them the task of supplying fresh game. The collection of mining tools at the end of each day was without precedent in the Chocó.

[52]AHNC, Negros y Esclavos del Cauca 2, ff. 196-197 (1781-1808).

[53]AHNC, Milicias y Marinas 126, f. 160 (1803).

[54]AHNC, Milicias y Marinas 124, ff. 1119-1121 (1806).

[55]AHNC, Milicias y Marinas 134, f. 254 (1767).

[56]At that time, Quibdó contained only twenty Spaniards and, according to Lieutenant Governor Juan Jiménez, "ten other citizens of some recommendation." *Ibid.*, f. 253. It should be noted that although the lieutenant governor was disturbed by the 10-to-1 ratio of blacks to whites in Quibdó the ratio for the entire Chocó was closer to 30 to 1 (10,987 to

359 in 1782). It is also significant that the Chocó's second-largest town, Quibdó, had only about 200 inhabitants.

[57] AHNC, Milicias y Marinas 126, ff. 185-186 (1766).

[58] AHNC, Milicias y Marinas 134, ff. 254-255 (1767).

[59] AHNC, Miscelánea 100, ff. 365-366 (1767).

[60] AHNC, Milicias y Marinas 134, ff. 258, 264 (1767).

4

African Slave Trade and Economic Development in Amazonia, 1700-1800

Colin M. MacLachlan

Brazil was a sleepy colony of secondary interest to Portugal until sugar turned the northeastern coastal strip into a rich plantation region in the second half of the sixteenth century. With significant development of a new commercial crop, Brazil's developers increasingly talked about ways to find reliable labor for expanding estates in the area of Pernambuco and Bahia. Settlers tried to put Amerindians to work, but these plans failed because of the sparse Indian population and the natives' lack of experience with organized, collective labor in agriculture. Since Europeans did not come to Brazil in sufficient numbers, and since many of those who did preferred to give orders to others rather than work themselves, a new source of labor had to be found. Africa quickly became a popular source of manpower. Settlers in Brazil found that Africans brought over by Portuguese traders made good workers and could be purchased as slaves for very low prices.

Since African labor came to represent an essential element in Brazil's sugar boom, the Portuguese regarded a plentiful supply of Africans as necessary for successful economic development. Gazing at their maps of the huge northern regions of the Amazon basin, bureaucrats in Lisbon deluded themselves into thinking that a second Pernambuco could arise in the jungle by mere manipulation of the slave trade. As MacLachlan observes, where these thoughts were accompanied by an awareness of the economic potentialities and limitations of the area (as in Maranhão, which became an important exporter of rice and cotton), success followed. Where they were accompanied by nothing more than a burning desire to emulate the success of a region with totally different prospects (as in the case of Pará), the importation of African labor was worse than useless. Development of the vast Amazon region would require more than just masses of laborers, as even modern-day economic planners in Brazil have discovered. To the present time, the Amazon remains an area of great potential but a region still far from delivering its long-celebrated promise. Now, several centuries after the grand experiment of Belém do Pará, man is making another attempt to conquer the Amazon, hoping that technology and social organization will help to overcome the long history of grandiose but largely abortive efforts.

R. B. T.

Successful establishment of a plantation economy in the sugar-producing regions of colonial Brazil created a pattern for colonial development. The combination of black slaves and land appears to have been responsible for the transformation of Brazil from a possession of limited utility into a profitable agricultural colony. Understandably, Portugal sought to duplicate the process in other parts of its American empire. A plantation system, supported by African slaves, became the "ideal" model that ensured wealth and prosperity.[1] When the Portuguese extended their authority northward, anchoring themselves at the mouth of the Amazon with the founding of Belém do Pará in 1616, colonial development was firmly identified with black labor and plantation crops.

Faith in the economic benefits of African slavery blinded the Portuguese to the limited agricultural potential of the Amazon. The wild profusion of jungle vegetation resembled a tropical garden that lacked only labor to bring it into a controlled and profitable flowering. When Portugal ousted the foreign interlop-

ers, it fell heir to the myth that Amazonia was an incredibly rich and fertile area.[2] Giving full range to their imagination, the Portuguese envisioned a vast plantation stretching from Maranhão to Pará, based on what almost had become a fixation—black slaves.

The existence of forest Indians in the Amazon basin strengthened Lisbon's faith in the benefits of introducing African labor, since previous experimentation with Indian labor in the south had not been successful. Brazil's seminomadic forest Indian had only a rudimentary grasp of agriculture and could not be adapted to the needs of a plantation economy. Lisbon was content to organize the Indian within a mission system to protect Portugal's claim to the region until European settlers with their black slaves arrived. The vast northern territory, embracing the captaincies of Maranhão, Piaui, and Pará, which then included the area of the future captaincy of Rio Negro (Amazonas), became the state of Maranhão. The huge state, formed in 1621, remained intact until 1772.[3] Inevitably, the political union of the Amazon basin obscured the fact that the economic potential of each captaincy differed in spite of its inclusion within the state of Maranhão. The crown assumed that the entire state could effectively utilize black plantation labor.

Initial Attempts to Introduce African Slaves

The Portuguese did not immediately begin the economic development of their newly secured northern territories. Seizure of Recife by the Dutch in 1630, and the struggle to evict them that lasted until 1654, diverted the attention of Portugal. In addition, the reestablishment of an independent Portuguese throne in 1640, after sixty years of union with the Spanish crown, required considerable diplomatic skill and energy; moreover, the limited resources of Portugal were habitually overcommitted. Such marginal areas of the empire as the Amazon basin understandably received little attention, and consequently the first serious attempt to establish a plantation economy was not made until 1682, when the crown instructed the Companhia de Commercio do Maranhão to import ten thousand African slaves over a twenty-year period.[4]

The company, however, suffering from mismanagement and the greed of its principals, failed to initiate the trade. Unmet labor demands resulted in constant petitions by the European settlers for a larger share of mission Indians. Acute labor shortages caused unrest, which eventually culminated in a sharp but ill-fated revolt in 1684 that forced the government to compromise and liberalize the settlers' access to indigenous labor.[5] This concession appeared in the new *Regimento das Missoes do Estado do Maranhão e Grão Pará* (1689), but in this same document Lisbon reaffirmed its determination to replace Amerindian labor with African slaves. One of its principal provisions called for the formation of a company to import black slaves; however, the lack of private capital made the formation of the projected company impossible.[6] The failure of private investors to initiate the slave trade forced the government to accept the responsibility, and in 1690 the crown financed the formation of the Companhia de Cacheu e Cabo Verde, setting a minimum goal of 145 slaves per year at a price to be officially determined. Additional government financing became available in 1692, when the crown ordered the governor of the state of Maranhão to reallocate 20,000 cruzados originally intended to buy forest products to the purchasing of slaves from the African company of Cacheu e Cabo Verde.[7]

The limited number and high price of black slaves introduced caused constant complaint. Both the municipal councils of São Luis do Maranhão and Belém do Pará believed that the crown set an excessive price. Such complaints appear justified by the rapid increase in the cost of slaves from 55$000 réis in March of 1695 to 130$000 réis in December of that year, reaching 300$000 réis by 1718.[8] Lisbon, however, noting that owners of sugar *engenhos* (sugar mills and surrounding plantation) continued to petition for even more slaves, impatiently dismissed such complaints. The small number of Africans entering the region became an object of competition between São Luis and Belém, and rivalry between the two provincial capitals continued throughout the eighteenth century. Since the port of São Luis do Maranhão was geographically closer to Africa than Belém, slave ships generally landed their cargoes in that settlement first. Quite naturally, the settlers of Maranhão selected the best physical specimens, leaving only the less desirable and the sick for sale in Belém. The inhabitants of Belém understandably believed that their labor needs were slighted. In response to their bitter protests, the crown ordered that each shipment of slaves be divided equally between the two settlements.[9] The unending criticism concerning the number and price of slaves must have angered the authorities. In 1708 the royal government unsuccessfully attempted to extricate itself from its uncomfortable position by urging wealthy settlers, in Maranhão and Pará, to send a ship directly to the slave coasts of Mina and Angola; however, as in the past, the limited capital of the region could not float such a venture.[10]

Unable to shift the burden of the trade to private initiative, Lisbon endeavored at least to control the use of servile labor. In order to obtain the most economically advantageous employment of African slaves, the crown decreed that all slaves must be devoted to sugar cultivation, a directive that ignored the fact that the Amazon basin was only marginally suitable for the cultivation of cane.[11] The poor quality of the region's sugar, coupled with transportation difficulties, had already prompted a switch from sugar production to the distilling of cane brandy.[12] *Cachaça* became the *bebida divina* (divine beverage) of the Amazon, serving as a medium of exchange as well as a stimulant.

In spite of seemingly obvious problems, the government continued to press for the development of the sugar industry. Since sugar depended on slaves, Lisbon continued its efforts to encourage the trade, but with little success. In addition, development of an intercoastal slave trade, linking the north with the sugar regions of the south, failed to materialize. The slave markets of Pernambuco and Bahia absorbed most of the slaves offered; consequently, traders did not turn to the more distant markets in the north.

Besides supply, the ability of the settlers to finance the regular purchase of slaves posed a problem. In 1749 the governor requested that the crown not only introduce black slaves, but that they also be sold to settlers on liberal credit terms; Lisbon apparently did not respond favorably to the proposal.[13] Subsequently, such suggestions would be reviewed by the future Marquês de Pombal and undoubtedly were taken into consideration when the crown decided to establish a monopolistic trading company. The number of African slaves introduced up to 1750 could not have exceeded a few thousand.[14]

African Slavery and Forced Development

The continued poverty of the Amazon state as well as the necessity of regular financial subsidies, which made the state of Maranhão an economic burden rather than an asset to the mother country, caused concern in Lisbon. The marked contrast between the north and the more favored areas of the south appeared to be explained by the lack of labor. It was observed that the sugar regions of Pernambuco and Bahia had only begun to flourish after the massive introduction of black slaves.[15] In response the crown urged increased efforts to stimulate interest in the slave trade. Subsequently, in 1751, several businessmen of Belém and São Luis petitioned for the privilege of forming a company to import two to four hundred slaves a year and suggested that the government grant them a ten-year monopoly as well as exemption from import taxes.[16] Lisbon rejected the monopoly proposal, but responded favorably to the idea of a tax-free slave trade, extending the exemption to include all slaves introduced into the state.[17] Although the proposed company never materialized, a number of private individuals took advantage of the new regulations to import black slaves.

The slave trade took on greater impetus under the influence of a more active government in Portugal. With the rise to power in 1750 of Sebastião José de Carvalho e Melo, the future Conde de Oeiras and Marquês de Pombal, the home government vigorously attempted to force the economic development of Amazonia. Carvalho e Melo viewed Belém do Pará as the northern anchor of imperial defenses, and he considered Mato Grosso, on the western frontier, as the keystone linking Pará with Rio de Janeiro in the south. A viable Paraense economy appeared vital to the grand design of empire that would be elaborated after 1750.[18] Since Lisbon did not question the basic value and potential of the land, attention focused on the means of production. When Francisco Xavier de Mendonça Furtado, the Marquês de Pombal's brother, assumed the direction of the state of Maranhão, one of his most important tasks was to facilitate the introduction of African slaves. The crown instructed the new governor to meet with the principal settlers to ascertain how many slaves could be effectively utilized and how the trade could be set up and financed.[19]

Governor Mendonça Furtado envisioned a Companhia Geral de Commercio Nacional dedicated to the African slave trade. Under official pressure, local capitalists contributed 32$000 réis, "in truth an insignificant sum" in the words of the governor.[20] Mendonça Furtado voiced the opinion, which by now had become an article of faith with the government, that the countryside would soon be dotted with sugar *engenhos* and plantations if black slaves could be introduced.

Responding to his brother's advice, Pombal concluded that only a well-capitalized company was capable of meeting the needs of such an undeveloped area. Quite obviously the limited capital of Belém or São Luis could not finance the African slave trade; consequently, the Marquês instituted the Companhia Geral do Grão Pará e Maranhão, capitalized with 1.2 million cruzados. Officially established in 1755, the company's charter specifically charged it with the introduction of African slaves as an essential part of its program to stimulate trade and general prosperity.[21] Recognizing the poverty of the inhabitants, the company's charter provided for the sale of slaves on credit, but to protect its interest, such slaves could not be seized to satisfy other creditors or any previous debts. The crown ordered the company to make every attempt to see that those engaged in economically productive tasks received preference. Only in the event of a surplus could slaves be sold to speculators, and such sales had to be strictly on a cash basis.[22] In order to head off the competition for servile labor, the government urged the company to introduce a sufficient number of slaves to meet the demand.[23] As originally envisioned, the company proposed to devote its efforts to stimulating the prosperity of both Maranhão and Pará without favoring one over the other.

Lisbon viewed the company's slaving operations as its most important obligation, assuming that once sufficient blacks had been imported the resultant surge in production would automatically increase profits. Essentially the crown considered the slave trade as pump-priming, the first step necessary to transform the Amazon basin into an economically viable part of the Portuguese empire. Because of the importance of the trade, the government gave the company broad administrative privileges in three African ports: Cacheu and Bissau in Guinea and Benguela on the Angolan coast. The Guinea privileges were in part illusory, Bissau and Cacheu were frequented as much by the English as by the Portuguese, and foreign slave traders frequently ignored the Portuguese presence, directly engaging in trade with African suppliers.[24] In order to take the traffic under firm control, as well as to eliminate foreign price competition, the crown authorized the repair and erection of fortifications and navigational aids. One of the company's major efforts, the fortress of Bissau, was completed in 1773 at a total cost of 147,690$763 réis.[25]

The African terminals, located in the deltas of extensive river networks with easy access to the interior of the continent, were ideally situated for collecting their unwilling cargoes. Their river location permitted the concentration of captives at spots convenient for both the African dealers and the European purchasers.[26] Tobacco, *cachaça* (cane brandy), cloth, hats, muskets, mats, and many other items of European manufacture served as the medium of exchange. To service the company's African complex, a fleet of at least eighteen ships crisscrossed the

Atlantic, bringing trade goods from Portugal and the Cape Verdes Islands in exchange for slaves to meet the needs of the Amazon's slave markets.[27] During the existence of the Companhia Geral do Grão Pará e Maranhão, approximately 75 percent of the slaves imported came from Bissau and Cacheu, and Angola accounted for the remainder.[28] The company thus linked the Amazon region directly with Africa's slave ports.

Although the labor problem had partially been solved, the other part of the economic equation—how to employ the black slaves imported by the new company—remained. Lisbon ordered a study of the region's products and their economic possibilities. Governor Mendonça Furtado investigated a total of thirty-nine different items of which sugar, cotton, rice, coffee, and cacao were reported to be the principal cultivated crops; however, most of the region's production was simply collected rather than cultivated.[29] Extension of the land under cultivation, as well as the adaptation of natural forest products to a plantation system, appeared possible, provided the necessary labor could be imported. Governor Mendonça Furtado recognized that certain areas seemed more suitable for certain types of crops, but failed to understand the agricultural limitation of the Amazon basin.[30]

The ability of the land to respond profitably to the application of African labor depended on its suitability for plantation crops. In spite of its size, however, the state possessed few areas capable of supporting intensive agriculture. In Pará only a small area around the city of Belém and across the delta in Macapá, given the limited technology then available, could support a plantation culture. In Maranhão, on the other hand, the delta formed by the Mearim and Itapecuru and the flood plains between the rivers provided a level and relatively fertile area suitable for plantations.[31]

Prior to the establishment of the company, rice and cotton had entered into the export market only in insignificant quantities. Although the native variety of rice grew profusely, it yielded little and its gains were small and brittle.[32] With the replacement of the *arroz da terra* by Carolina rice, introduced by the company in 1776, the crop became an important export commodity both in Maranhão and Pará. Low production, not poor quality, accounted for the failure of cotton to enter the export market; consequently, the importation of African slaves had a dramatic effect on production in the areas where cotton could be extensively cultivated. The degree of success of each of the major areas, Pará and Maranhão, in developing a plantation economy is revealed in their export statistics. Figures for the last five years of the company (1773-1777) indicate the trend that continued into the nineteenth century. During that period Maranhão exported 153,747 *arrobas* of cotton, compared to the relatively insignificant total of 3,013 *arrobas* shipped from Pará. Rice exports in the same period totaled 437,983 *arrobas* from São Luis and 95,796 from Belém.[33] Whereas rice and cotton became the principal Maranhense export crops, Pará's major export continued to be cacao, a natural forest product, dependent on Indian collectors.

Owing to the marginal economy of Pará, most complaints of high slave prices originated from that area.[34] In 1773, in response to the many pleas for relief, the crown ordered the company to sell slaves at cost, the price to be determined by the original cost in Africa plus the cost of transportation.[35] The regulation appears to have had little effect on the price of slaves; in 1773 the highest price paid for a prime slave was 129$000 réis; the following year, presumably sold at cost, the highest price obtained was 120$000 réis.[36] An embittered settler accused the company of padding the actual price paid for the slave on the coast of Africa to allow for a good profit margin. Allegedly the company purchased trade goods used in bartering for slaves on credit, immediately increasing the cost, and then overvalued the goods as much as 20 percent. Although the company actually paid 100$000 réis, their books indicated an inflated price of 120$000 réis. A steady decline from the high profit levels of the early 1760s may well have forced some shady accounting practices.[37] The company was also accused of indulging in the practice of selling second- and even third-grade slaves as prime specimens.[38] Complaints against the company probably owed more to the marginal financial resources of the settlers than to any other factor. Had the settlers enjoyed the profits of a successful plantation culture, their complaints would have been minimal.

Theoretically the company's charter obliged it to import black slaves into both regions, but economic realities modified the plan. Forest collecting, the economic standby of Pará, did not lend itself to the use of African slaves. A collecting expedition, dispatched into the interior following the extensive river system of the Amazon basin, lasted from six to eight months.[39] The impossibility of proper security to prevent escape was an obvious difficulty. Even the Indians who supplied the labor for the collecting expeditions often deserted even though they received a small salary. Desertion of an Indian, however, involved only a small loss for the settler who financed the expedition, whereas the escape of an African slave meant the loss of a sizable investment. In addition, forest collecting was one task where the native Indian proved superior to the African. Collecting to sustain the Amerindians' subsistence economy had been traditional long before the arrival of the Portuguese. Indians almost instinctively understood the complexities and dangers of river navigation, and settlers soon learned to cherish native river pilots.[40] The limited utility of African labor in the forest collecting industry, which unquestionably became the backbone of the Paraense economy, affected demand. Only those engaged in tasks other than collecting employed blacks; however, the marginal economy of the region barely financed the investment.

Black slaves introduced into Pará could only be purchased by individuals who were sufficiently affluent to pay for them outright or who were able to offer excellent security to underwrite the extension of credit.[41] The company understandably hesitated to tie up capital in such a profitless fashion, and as a result, avoided credit sales whenever possible. An official in Belém even proposed that slave imports be limited to a number sufficient to meet cash demand, in order to avoid the credit problem entirely.[42] Although the company would have preferred to follow such advice, it could not have escaped the wrath of labor-hungry settlers. Consequently, the company attempted to restrict credit sales to individuals obviously able to carry the debt; hence the settlers in Macapá, the prime rice-growing area of Pará, received two hundred slaves on credit.[43] The owner of two sugar *engenhos* situated on six or seven leagues of land, an excellent credit risk, purchased forty slaves on credit.[44] Less fortunate settlers, however, found it virtually impossible to conclude such transactions. Bishop João de São José Queiróz, during the course of his pastoral visit in the backlands, reported that many farms had been abandoned, allegedly because "the company won't sell slaves on credit."[45]

Reluctance to extend credit in Pará caused considerable bitterness. As previously noted, the company's administrator in Belém had advised restricting the number of slaves introduced, reasoning that the region already bore a heavy debt because of previous purchases. Such suggestions infuriated Governor Manoel Bernardo de Mello e Castro, who insisted that in order to satisfy its debts the region had to produce and in order to produce it needed more slave labor, not less. He complained that where a settler needed twenty or thirty slaves, he usually had to be satisfied with two or three—not enough to make a difference in production but just enough to establish a debt. Mello e Castro had absolutely no sympathy for the company's profits, and in fact accused the monopoly of making an excessive profit on cacao, paying 2$000 réis per *arroba* in Belém and selling for three times that in Lisbon.[46]

The government, both in Pará and in Portugal, refusing to accept the dominance of the forest collecting industry and the apparent willingness of the company to be satisfied with that line of trade, ignored the economic realities and continued to push the development of agriculture in Pará. Encouraged by initial success with rice culture in Macapá, officials urged the introduction of two thousand blacks for use in the rice fields.[47] Although the settlers of Macapá had no difficulty paying off their debts on the two hundred slaves previously purchased, the company showed no interest in the scheme.

Although the government in Belém constantly bemoaned the reluctance to remit slaves, implying that the company was responsible for the backward state of the economy, the slaves actually imported were often badly utilized.[48] The municipal council itself absorbed 207 slaves purchased on credit. Acquired ostensibly for municipal services, these slaves apparently were not indispensable, and the council found it profitable to rent them to the royal government for construction work on the fortress of Macapá.[49] The company itself employed a number of slaves in its own warehouses as well as in shipbuilding and logging operations and as a result was accused of hoarding slaves for its own use.[50] Perhaps a more serious drain on the supply of African slaves resulted from Pará's geographical position. Besides meeting the minimal needs of the subordinate state of Rio Negro (Amazonas), slaves landed at Belém do Pará became an item of trade with Mato Grosso. Traders came up to Belém through the river system, purchased European products as well as the number of black slaves necessary to conduct their heavily laden canoes back to Mato Grosso, and then profitably disposed of both goods and slaves.[51]

Ironically the very economic base of Pará encouraged the non-productive use of African labor. The forest collecting industry obviously could not utilize high-cost servile labor. Slaves not employed as field laborers to meet the needs of the limited agricultural production of the region could be utilized as servants or artisans, thus providing services but hardly adding to production. An interested observer would later note that the ladies of Belém went to church in hammocks carried by Indians and black slaves, with several more slaves trailing along for added effect, whereas the less fortunate attended early morning mass to avoid embarrassment.[52] Like the municipal council, settlers rented slaves to the government, which employed them in fortifying the Amazon basin in the face of menacing neighbors.[53] Government demands for labor apparently provided a constant market for rented slaves, which prompted the governor to propose that the state import black slaves for all royal needs in order to relieve the

Indian to concentrate on the forest collecting industry.[54] This extremely pragmatic proposal would have required an expansion of the slave trade, as well as a considerable royal investment; consequently, the crown showed little interest.

By 1770 economically viable Maranhão, in sharp contrast to Pará, could rely on its relatively strong economy to finance the importation of African slaves without assistance. The fall from power of the Marquês de Pombal (1777), coupled with other internal and international factors, led to the official dissolution of the company on 25 February 1778, ending the era of planned economic development in Amazonia.[55]

Success and Failure

The suppression of the company of Grão Pará e Maranhão caused initial uncertainty over the future of the slave trade. Governor João Pereira Caldas, a strong supporter of the monopoly, had observed the backward state of both Maranhão and Pará immediately before the creation of the company and was convinced that the continued economic activity of the region depended on the introduction of black slaves. Although Pereira Caldas willingly acknowledged that the results had been more successful in Maranhão, he ventured the opinion that Pará simply needed renewed emphasis on the importation of Africans and dismissed complaints against the monopoly, as well as demands for its abolition, as misguided self-interest on the part of those who hoped to gain from its suppression.[56] Scornfully he noted that when disgruntled settlers called for the importation of slaves on the same basis as in other parts of Portuguese America, they overlooked the fact that elsewhere slaves were purchased for cash, not credit. To seal the argument, the governor posed the rhetorical question, "Without the company who would introduce slaves?"[57] Pereira Caldas hastened to remind Lisbon that the reduced number of Indians that still existed in the region could not be expected to fill the gap should the slave trade come to a halt.[58]

The problem of the continued importation of black slaves concerned Pará more than Maranhão. As a result of increased demand for cotton, aggravated by the outbreak of armed rebellion in English North America (1776-1783), Maranhense cotton enjoyed a steady market and the resultant prosperity enabled plantation owners to finance the purchase of black slaves. Settlers in Pará, on the other hand, unable to participate in the cotton boom, had only limited financial resources to invest in slaves. Moreover, private slave traders, unlike the company, could not be forced to sell slaves on credit.

In an effort to compensate for the abolition of the monopoly, an imaginative plan was proposed that combined European with involuntary African immigration. The proposal advocated combining the initial capital investment of the company of Grão Pará e Maranhão with that of the company of Pernambuco e Paraiba to form a colonization company.[59] The capital of the proposed organization would then be applied to the purchase of carefully selected black slaves in the optimum age group of fifteen to twenty-five. In an effort to achieve a stable slave population, the plan envisioned the introduction of an equal number of both sexes. Concurrent with the importation of black slaves, the scheme called for the transporting of European emigrants, in an optimum age bracket between eighteen and thirty, from Portugal and the Azores. The colonization company would then supply each family with six slaves, three of each sex, while a bachelor would be entitled to an allotment of only three slaves, and a credit of 240$000 réis per family. In the unfortunate event more than one-third of the settler's slaves died before he had paid off his debt, they would be replaced on the same liberal terms. Rather than dilute the economic impact of the new arrivals by dispersing them throughout the Amazon basin, the proposal suggested they be settled around the city of Belém. This plan appears to have been the only attempt to institute a balanced immigration into Pará involving both Europeans and Africans.[60]

The crown, however, having acted against a monopolistic trading company, was not inclined to create a new one, preferring instead to trust free commerce to meet the demand for black labor. The switch to free trade resulted in little change in the number of slaves introduced into the Amazon region. Instead of a dramatic drop, the trade remained at approximately the same level as previously, a sign that the company had only met the market demand, especially in the last decade of its existence, without attempting to stimulate the economy by actively introducing a large number of surplus slaves. In Belém the company introduced an average of 581 slaves a year. From 1779 to 1790 the average number declined less than 10 percent, to 547. In Maranhão the upward trend begun by the company continued. From 1779 to 1790 the annual number was 1,605, a difference of three to one over the rate of importation into Pará, reflecting the continuing ability of Maranhão to finance African slaves.[61]

The suppression of the company of Grão Pará e Maranhão did not affect the operations of the African terminus of the slave trade. Nevertheless, the direct, one might say artificial, connection between the African slave ports and the Amazon was severed. Instead of a guaranteed and steady importation of slaves, settlers had to rely on private initiative. The company had necessarily accepted local products in exchange; however, with its abolition the settlers faced the problem of a market for their products in order to finance African slaves among other necessities. In Maranhão a steady demand for its crops presented little difficulty, but Pará, still dependent on the forest collecting industry, had no such advantage.

In spite of past failures Lisbon continued to encourage schemes to introduce black labor into the area, refusing to accept the relentless economic logic that explained the backward state of Pará. Aware of the government's interest, a group of Paraense businessmen proposed the formation of a privileged local slaving company to import slaves.[62] In exchange for a six-year tax exemption, they proposed to place four ships in the African trade. To facilitate purchases the government would guarantee that any slaves sold on credit could not be seized to satisfy previous creditors. As Governor Francisco de Sousa Coutinho observed, the government had very little to lose since theoretically any drop in customs revenue would be offset by the increased productivity of the area. The governor optimistically noted that if the company was exempted from taxes it would be more inclined to sell on credit; moreover, local merchants could judge more effectively the credit standing of their fellow countrymen. Although Sousa Coutinho backed the idea, he favored extending these privileges to any individual or group that agreed to bring slaves directly from Africa.[63]

Although the crown granted the requested privileges, the company failed to materialize; however, individual members of the group did engage in random voyages. In 1797 an obviously frustrated Sousa Coutinho analyzed the history of the slave trade and concluded that the lack of local capital posed the major obstacle. He suggested that the government lend individual businessmen capital, repayable within three or four years, to finance the African slave trade. The idea that Pará would eventually attract a substantial intercoastal slave trade with the sugar regions of the south was dismissed on the ground that the general poverty of the captaincy precluded cash sales. In fact, many settlers still owed the long-suppressed company of Grão Pará e Maranhão for slaves purchased as credit. The inability of the inhabitants to finance African slaves could only be overcome by government guarantees. Governor Sousa Countinho suggested that any slaves purchased as credit be protected from previous debts to eliminate uncertainty. More importantly, the governor urged the crown to authorize the government to buy slaves from traders for cash and to sell them to the settlers on credit.[64]

Lisbon, responding to the governor's pleas in a reasonably imaginative manner declared the reexportation of slaves, from Rio de Janeiro and Pernambuco to Belém do Pará, duty-free.[65] At the same time the crown dispatched a circular to the governors of Luanda and Benguela urging them to do everything in their power to encourage slave exports to Belém.[66] These tentative steps were soon followed by a more comprehensive tax incentive plan. A royal decree of 27 October 1798 exempted the loading of slaves in Africa and their introduction in Pará from all customs duties and in addition ordered that all products carried out of Pará up to the value of the slaves introduced were to be exempt from export taxes on leaving Belém as well as import taxes at Lisbon.[67] Such a measure was calculated to stimulate local production as well as to finance the trade.

In spite of these bold measures, the crown once again failed to consider the ability of the region's products to support the cost of African slaves. It remained for the governor of Luanda, from a position of objectivity on the coast of Africa, to point out the fatal flaw. The governor noted that although, on first consideration, the tax exemptions appeared to be all-embracing, in actual fact the only major change involved cotton exports since other products had previously been exempted. Moreover, Paraense cotton could not compare with the superior quality exported from Maranhão and Pernambuco; consequently, it was only in the total absence of better-quality cotton that Pará's product could be sold on the European market.[68] The governor observed that even intercoastal trading vessels refused to deal in local products, demanding payment in specie or coin so that they could purchase a load of hides or cotton in Ceará to carry back to their home ports. The desirability of exotic forest products was questioned with the observation that many, such as sarsaparilla, met an uncertain demand in Europe. Quite naturally these factors had an adverse effect in the slave traffic. A slave trader had only two alternatives if he chose to trade in the area: either sell on credit and tie up his working capital or accept a cargo of poor quality products for possible sale in Europe.[69] The governor of Luanda's analysis of the situation was one of the first official observations that recognized that the marginal economy of Pará could not sustain or finance African labor.

Besides the inability of the Paraense economy to sustain a regular triangular trade, its very geographical position discouraged links with Africa. The voyage from the Portuguese slaving ports in Africa to Belém was both hazardous and long. Many vessels survived the ocean crossing only to come to grief while attempting to enter the delta.[70]

Although Pará could not have utilized a massive influx of Africans, even the limited demand for slaves that existed could not be satisfied; as a result Belém made a good market for marginal slaves from the south. Each year three of four ships from Bahia, Pernambuco, and even São Luis do Maranhão arrived with small numbers of sick or recalcitrant slaves that could not be profitably disposed of in the more selective slave markets of Brazil.[71] Selling on a cash basis, but at attractive prices, these coastal traders quickly disposed of their cargoes. Such slaves proved a bad bargain at any price, since the sick soon perished and the "troublemakers" did little except sow dissension and violence among the more resigned slaves. The unwary buyer often found himself deprived not only of his new slave, but also of several others who had joined him in flight.[72] Although São Luis also fell prey to unscrupulous traders, Belém in particular made an easy target.

In addition to the individual loss suffered by the purchaser, the marginal intercoastal slave trade had a negative effect on commerce in both Pará and Maranhão. Such traders preferred cash and thus caused a drain of specie from the north. The governor of Maranhão estimated that each vessel removed from 20,000 to 25,000 cruzados from local circulation.[73]

Governor Francisco de Sousa Coutinho of Pará, in spite of the obvious negative effects of the trade on the economy, found the effect on public order to be of more concern. In an effort to control the introduction of "vicious slaves," the governor ordered customs officials to investigate such vessels entering port to ascertain the true origin of the slaves.[74] The governor's concern reflected the traditional problem of security and control in a mixed society of free and slave labor. The surrounding dense jungle offered the runaways the hope of concealment, and the myriad waterways that sluggishly penetrated the backlands permitted access to distant sanctuaries. Unfortunately, once the slave had successfully slipped into the jungle, his sanctuary offered little except loneliness and slow starvation. Without the Indian's knowledge of the jungle, survival became an uneven contest. A fugitive could not rely on making contact with forest Indians, since the Indians themselves frequently turned captured slaves over to the authorities and collected a reward for their diligence.[75] Unsympathetic Indians were not the only danger encountered by the runaway slave. Organized bounty hunters, under the leadership of a *capitão do mato* and composed of blacks, mulattoes, and Indians, scoured the jungles in search of fugitives.[76] Given the hazards and difficulties of sustaining themselves in the jungle for any extended period, many runaways attempted to integrate themselves into the free black population in an area where they were unknown. Fugitives from Maranhão often hoped to find a haven in Pará or, still better, to reach the French colony of Cayenne five hundred miles northwest of Belém. In Pará, Cayenne proved to be the biggest attraction, but runaways also headed for Maranhão and elsewhere.[77] The ease with which a slave could slip into the jungle proved a constant problem, especially in interior areas; one slaveholder in Macapá reportedly lost more than twenty slaves.[78]

Runaway slaves, who preferred not to risk integrating themselves into the free black population, banded together in *mucambos* or jungle encampments. These illegal settlements, by providing a definite destination that eliminated the uncertainty of attempting to flee to a vague sanctuary in an unknown area, attracted dissatisfied slaves from the surrounding areas. In Maranhão many small interior settlements such as Viana, Pinheiro, Alacantera, Guimaraes, and Maraacassume had a *mucambo* nearby that drained off discontented slaves in the district.[79] Such settlements, complete with abducted female slaves or Indian women, became shadowy societies mirroring the settlements of the Portuguese and often engaged in substance farming. Their desire for European goods could be met by raiding isolated settlements. Inevitably, success brought on a punitive Portuguese expedition, and few survived for long periods of time. One daring group terrorized the area around Belém, raising fears that they intended to attack the city and were allying themselves with another fugitive group for that purpose.[80] Soldiers dispatched to thwart these plans recaptured twelve blacks. Another African settlement, situated near the town of Santarém, three hundred miles from the mouth of the Amazon, held off a Portuguese expedition, which had to withdraw after killing one runaway and recapturing two. This expedition brought back word of several other groups of slaves, one rumored to be governed by a fugitive Jesuit priest who allegedly maintained contact with the French and the Dutch on the Caribbean coast.[81]

The existence of the French colony of Cayenne complicated the normal problems of controlling servile labor. Flight across international borders resulted in the convention of 1732, in which the French and the Portuguese agreed to exchange runaways.[82] It is more than probable that during the first half of the century most of the slaves exchanged were Indians, not Africans. In spite of the convention of 1732, Portuguese authorities proved less than zealous in returning runaways. For example, in 1756 the crown approved the distribution of fugitives to local settlers with the proviso that their disposal be officially recorded in case of a French inquiry.[83]

Portugal constantly suspected the French of plotting to seize its Amazon empire and viewed the flight of Indians and black slaves into French territory as a plot to weaken Portuguese control. The fear of suspected French attempts to encourage the desertion of slaves, present before 1789, became almost paranoid after the French Revolution. In 1795 the governor dispatched an expedition to the northern delta region to arrest all unauthorized individuals and put a stop to the loss of "our slaves" to the French.[84] When news reached the Portuguese that the French were freeing their slaves, the Portuguese almost despaired of being able to contain their own blacks.[85] The governor reported in horror that he had received word that the emancipated slaves of Cayenne refused to work; the result was extreme hunger in the colony.[86] The patrol boats posted in the mouth of the Amazon and along the northern coast were urged to make every effort to intercept runaways. War with France increased the fear of a foreign-instigated slave revolt, especially in Pará, whose proximity to the French colony was continually a source of regret. Suspicious gatherings of free blacks and slaves caused alarm; however, such apprehension proved needless since the resistance of the African to his imposed slave status continued to be the traditional one of desertion rather than rebellion.[87]

Although the importation of Africans into the Amazon basin was intended to increase the labor supply of the region, and hence its prosperity, it also had important effects on the native population. The success of the slave trade in Maranhão relieved the Indian of much of the burden of labor. Ironically, the availability of African labor made the constant subjugation of newly contacted Indian tribes unnecessary, and as a consequence, Maranhão would be plagued by hostile Indians into the nineteenth century.[88] In Pará the failure of the slave trade forced the Indian into the labor pool, and as a consequence by the early nineteenth century the depleted Indian population posed absolutely no threat to the state's security.[89] But if African slavery proved a blessing to the aborigines, it was a mixed one; epidemic diseases and slaves often arrived on the same ship.

After the creation of the company of Grão Pará e Maranhão and the start of systematic importation of African slaves, the frequency of smallpox epidemics increased markedly.[90] Scarcely a year passed without an outbreak of the dread disease, and often such outbreaks reached crisis proportions. The slaving operations of the company broke down the relative biological isolation of the Amazon basin. Before the arrival of regular shipments of slaves, the region had achieved a delicate balance. In the early years of the Portuguese presence in the basin, both measles and smallpox decimated the population. After initial havoc, these diseases seldom reached major epidemic proportion except in the late 1720s, early 1730s, and the middle 1740s, when thousands of Indians died from the smallpox.[91] Limited immigration and contact with the outside world offered some protection from fresh contamination; however, the company of Grão Pará e Maranhão, by breaking the isolation of Amazonia, exposed it to the horrors of frequent epidemics. The fact that the company generally sold part of each cargo of slaves in Maranhão and Pará almost guaranteed that disease would simultaneously be introduced into both areas. Once an epidemic had broken out, the authorities could do little to control it and primitive methods of fumigation had scarcely any effect. The sulphurous fumes of black powder fired by cannons in the districts most affected did more to disturb the ill than retard the spread of disease.[92]

The government recognized the importance of isolating infected slaves. São Luis' hospital of Bomfim served as a refuge for many unfortunate black victims.[93] In 1788 the municipal council of Belém proposed the establishment of a quarantine station on an island in the bay; subsequently, the island of Arapiranga and a location outside the city (Val de Caens) served such a purpose.[94] The municipal council of São Luis, noting that Lisbon routinely practiced quarantine measures, requested the governor to establish a quarantine station on the island of Mido.[95]

Unfortunately, quarantine regulations proved hard to enforce, especially since slave traders, after an outbreak of disease, did everything in their power to dispose of their property before more were stricken. When two infected ships arrived in Belém, one inappropriately named *Boa Fortuna* on which two hundred slaves died of smallpox during the voyage, authorities quickly isolated their cargoes; nevertheless, two slaves were surreptitiously sold, reportedly causing twenty cases of smallpox in the city.[96] In another case a smack from Pernambuco carrying diseased slaves arrived in Belém after a stop in São Luis. The captain, aware of the imminent loss of his human capital, evaded quarantine regulations, landed his slaves, and sold many of them before being apprehended. The remaining slaves were placed under three-month quarantine while those already sold were dispersed throughout the region.[97] Although all races and classes endured the ravages of these attacks, the Indian in particular suffered. Governor José Narciso de Magalhaes Menezes observed that even a slight case, in fact "one pox on an Indian," was almost a sure death sentence.[98]

Amazonia in 1800

At the end of the century the contrast between the two principal captaincies was reflected in the number of slaves. Maranhão had 36,880 black or mulatto slaves, who made up 46 percent of the population, as well as 13,613 free blacks, out of a total population of 78,860. Blacks and mulattoes constituted 64 percent of the population; the Amerindians, excluding unsubdued tribes, made up only 5 percent; and the remaining 31 percent were classified as white.[99] Pará, with a population placed at 80,000 in 1801, slightly more than Maranhão, presented an entirely different situation, with only 18,944 slaves or approximately 23 percent. Indians made up another 20 percent; the remaining 57 percent was made up of whites, mulattoes, and other mixtures as well as free blacks.[100] The figures demonstrate to what extent the cotton and rice economy of Maranhão depended on servile labor while Pará, territorially dwarfing the province of Maranhão, continued to depend on forest products and Indian labor to sustain its marginal economy. In 1800 Pará exported 127,181 *arrobas* of cacao, its traditional forest export, compared to 90,836 *arrobas* of rice and only 15,930 *arrobas* of cotton.[101]

Government attempts, especially after 1750, to encourage economic development and the introduction of African labor obviously succeeded in Maranhão, where the combination of suitable land and an international market for cotton provided the basis for a viable economy. In Pará, however, the effort failed. The crown's determination in the face of adverse economic factors stemmed from imperial considerations that viewed the north as vital to the future of Portuguese America. Political considerations motivated the drive to overcome the obstacles to development in Amazonia. In many respects Lisbon's approach is mirrored in modern Brazilian policy, which has recently been directed toward "national integration" of Amazonia. The artificial channeling of investment funds, the cutting of roads to the outer limits of the Brazilian Amazon, essentially are political actions designed to preserve an area viewed as vital to Brazil's future. The Marquês de Pombal certainly would have approved.

APPENDIX A
Number of African Slaves Landed at Belém do Pará, 1757-1800

Year	Number	Year	Number	Year	Number
1757	371	1772	341	1787	710
1758	1,103	1773	817	1788	631
1759	534	1774	307	1789	687
1760	209	1775	696	1790	473
1761	315	1776	870	1791	279
1762	1,637	1777	517	1792	204
1763	147	1778	765	1793	263
1764	885	1779	318	1794	522
1765	832	1780	845	1795	1,096
1766	138	1781	471	1796	—
1767	441	1782	329	1797	176
1768	268	1783	681	1798	400
1769	180	1784	470	1799	—
1770	704	1785	269	1800	514
1771	895			Total	23,884

Such figures must be used with caution. At best they indicate the trend rather than the exact number of slaves imported. The major difficulty lies in determining which figures represent the actual number of individual slaves and which indicate the number of *peça de India* (a standard unit measurement of slaves that could include one to three individual slaves). In addition, official statistics often are contradictory.

The above figures were collected from many different sources in the Arquivo Historico Ultramarino, Lisbon, and in the Arquivo

Nacional, Rio de Janeiro. However, one key document should be noted: "Mapa dos Escravos que a Companhia Geral do Grão Pará e Maranhão importou neste Estado do Pará . . . 1757 ate . . . 1772," AHU, caixa 32 (Pará). The figures listed here for Pará were erroneously used by Manuel Nunes Dias in his *Fomento e Mercantilismo* (see previous citation) to represent the total figure imported by the company in both Pará and Maranhão. That this is not the case is supported by the document cited above and the statistics contained in "Certidão do Juiz da Alfandiga (Pará) 1 March 1792," ANRJ, cod. 99, Vol. 13, f. 127, and "Os Administradores da Extincta Companhia, Reverdo os livros della . . . Numero de Escravos Introduzidos neste Porto . . . desde 1755 ate . . . 1766," ANRJ, cod. 99, Vol. 13, f. 125. Numbers for the years 1792, 1794, 1795, 1798, and 1800 have been taken from Davidson, Appendix V, pp. 477-481.

APPENDIX B
Number of African Slaves Landed at São Luís do Maranhão, 1757-1800

Year	Number	Year	Number
1757		1788	2,894
	10,616	1789	2,107
		1790	1,411
		1791	1,166
		1792	1,187
1778	—	1793	2,361
1779	1,474	1794	2,186
1780	926	1795	1,740
1781	944	1796	1,854
1782	752	1797	1,536
1783	1,602	1798	—
1784	1,375	1799	—
1785	1,345	1800	637[a]
1786	662		
1787	2,160	Total	40,935

These figures are also more indicative of a trend than exact statistics. The above figures were collected from AHU (Maranhão), caixas 47-49, 52, 55-68, and 70. Statistics for the period 1757-1777 were taken from "Recapitulacão dos escravos introduzidos pela Companhia do Grão Pará e Maranhão . . . de 1757 ate 1777," AHU, caixa 37 (Pará).

a. The small number of slaves introduced in 1800 probably resulted from the hostile action of French corsairs stationed at Cayenne. The following year (1801) the number was a more normal 1,328.

Notes

[1]The extent to which the Portuguese depended on the African and identified him with plantation labor, especially in the prime Brazilian sugar regions of Bahia and Pernambuco, was succinctly expressed by Antonio Vieira S.J.: "Without blacks there would not be a Pernambuco." Quoted in Alfonso de E. Taunay, "Subsidios para a historia do trafico Africano no Brasil," *Anais do Museu Paulista* 10 (1941): 8. See Vicente Salles, *O Negro no Pará sob o regime da escravidão* (Rio de Janeiro, 1971), for a general view of African slavery in the region.

[2]Ernesto Cruz, *Historia do Pará* (Belém, 1963), 1: 86. Some of the fragmentary details of foreign interest in the region have been drawn together in James A. Williamson, *English Colonies in Guiana and on the Amazon, 1604-1668* (Oxford, 1923).

[3]The state remained intact except for a brief two-year period from 1652 to 1654. Cruz, 1: 55.

[4]Roberto C. Simonsen, *Historia economica do Brasil*, 5th ed. (São Paulo, 1967), p. 318. In 1680 an earlier but less systematic attempt to meet the region's labor needs was undertaken when the crown financed the introduction of 350 slaves in Pará and 250 in Maranhão. See António Carreira, "As Companhias Pombalinas de navegação, comercio e trafico de escravos entre a costa africana e o nordeste brasileiro" (Part 1), *Boletim Cultural da Guiné Portuguesa*, January-April 1968, p. 20. This well-documented work appears in four parts, the other three being in May-August 1968, January 1969, and April 1969. The information supplied by Carreira deals mainly with the African end of the trade.

[5]Simonsen, p. 319.

[6]C. R. Boxer, *The Golden Age of Brazil, 1695-1750: Growing Pains of a Colonial Society* (Berkeley and Los Angeles, Cal., 1962), p. 270.

[7]Annaes da Biblioteca e Arquivo Publico do Para, 1: 104 (hereafter cited as ABAP).

[8]ABAP, 1: 106, and "Carta regia ao Senado da Camara," 6 February 1703. Biblioteca National, Rio de Janeiro (hereafter cited as BNRJ), 15, 4, 8 (Maranhão), and Carreira, Part 1, p. 29.

[9]ABAP, 1: 119. It is interesting to note that after official encouragement of the Madeira River trade with Mato Grosso, merchants from the far west in turn received the "pickings" from Pará. David M. Davidson, "Rivers and Empire: The Madeira Route and the Incorporation of the

Brazilian Far West, 1737-1808" (Ph.D. diss., Yale University, 1970), p. 150.

[10]ABAP, 1: 129.

[11]ABAP, 1: 114.

[12]The refusal of the crown to accept the manufacture of cane brandy in spite of many convincing arguments in its favor approached stubbornness. See Sue A. Gross, "Agricultural Promotion in the Amazon Basin, 1700-1750," *Agricultural History*, April 1969, pp. 269-276.

[13]Francisco Pedro de Mendonça Gorjao to the court, 26 April 1749. Arquivo Historico Ultramarino, Lisbon (hereafter cited as AHU), caixa 32 (Maranhão).

[14]Unfortunately no exact figures are known. The scattered references to African slavery only permit one to state with certainty that a number of blacks were imported into Amazonia before 1700 and during the first half of the eighteenth century. See ABAP, 1: 104, 106, 114, 119, 129; and BNRJ, 15, 4, 8 (Maranhão).

[15]Peracer, Conselho Ultramarino, 15 May 1750, AHU, caixa 32 (Maranhão).

[16]Consulta, 7 November 1752, AHU, caixa 35 (Maranhão).

[17]Carta régia, 22 November 1752, Biblioteca e Arquivo Publico, Belém (hereafter cited as BAP), cod. 884, doc. 29.

[18]Davidson, p. 157. The overall plan also envisioned transforming the Indian into a productive, profit-motivated "Portuguese" settler. See Colin M. MacLachlan, "The Indian Directorate: Forced Acculturation in Portuguese America (1757-1799)," *The Americas*, April 1972, pp. 357-387.

[19]Marcos Carneiro de Mendonça, *A Amazonia na era pombalina: Correspondencia inedita do . . . Francisco Xavier Mendonça Furtado* (São Paulo, 1963), 1: 29.

[20]Francisco Xavier Mendonça Furtado to Diogo de Mendonça Corte Real, 18 January 1754, BNRJ, 11, 2, 43 (Pará).

[21]*Instituição do Companhia Geral do Grão Pará e Maranhão* (Lisbon, 1755), art. 30.

[22]Carta régia, 13 June 1760, BAP, cod. 668, doc. 27.

[23]Carneiro de Mendonça, 3: 1052.

[24]José Mendes da Cunha Saraiva, *Companhias gerais de comercio e navegação para o Brasil* (Lisbon, 1938), pp. 32-34.

[25]José Mendes da Cunha Saraiva, *A Fortaleza de Bissau e a Companhia do Grão Pará e Maranhão* (Lisbon, 1947), p. 38.

142　　　Colin M. MacLachlan

[26]Manuel Nunes Dias, *Fomento e Mercantilismo: A Companhia Geral do Grão Pará e Maranhão, 1755-1778* (Belém, 1970), 1: 471.

[27]Nunes Dias, 1: 495. A substantial part of the company's trade was in Cape Verde textiles, which were highly prized on the coast of Africa. T. Bentley Duncan, *Atlantic Islands: Madeira, the Azores and Cape Verdes in Seventeenth-Century Commerce and Navigation* (Chicago, 1972), p. 221.

[28]"Recapitulação dos escravos introduzidos pela Companhia do Grão Pará e Maranhão . . . de 1757 ate 1777," AHU, caixa 37 (Pará).

[29]Carneiro de Mendonça, 1: 199.

[30]Carneiro de Mendonça, 1: 200.

[31]See Nunes Dias, 1: 159-162, for a concise geographical description.

[32]Jeronimo de Viveiros, *Historia do comercio do Maranhão, 1612-1895* (São Luis, 1954), 1: 76.

[33]Nunes Dias, 1: 430, and Manuel Barata, *A Antiga produccão e exportação do Pará* (Belém, 1915), p. 3.

[34]Such complaints were often petulant and almost invariably included a statement to the effect that Maranhão was favored over Pará. João Pereira Caldas to Martinho de Mello e Castro, 18 June 1777, AHU, caixa 36 (Pará); see also BNRJ, 11, 2, 43, docs. 121 and 189 (Pará).

[35]Edital, 1 December 1773, BAP, cod. 595, doc. 148.

[36]Mapa, AHU, caixa 34 (Pará) and caixa 43 (Maranhão).

[37]H. E. S. Fisher, *The Portugal Trade: A Study of Anglo Portuguese Commerce 1700-1770* (London, 1971), p. 46.

[38]"Minuta de um papel sobre a escravatura," AHU, caixa 35 (Pará).

[39]AHU, caixa 42 (Pará).

[40]João de Alburqueque to Francisco de Sousa Coutinho, 2 May 1791, Arquivo Nacional, Rio de Janeiro (hereafter cited as ANRJ), cod. 99, Vol. 13, f. 147.

[41]Nunes Dias, 1: 272.

[42]Manoel Bernardo de Mello e Castro to Francisco Xavier de Mendonça Furtado, 1 August 1759, BNRJ, 11, 2, 43 N 100 (Pará).

[43]João Pereira Caldas to Martinho de Mello e Castro, 18 June 1777, AHU, caixa 36 (Pará).

[44]João de São José Queiróz, *Visitas Pastorais: Memorias (1761 e 1762-1763)* (Rio de Janeiro, 1961), p. 176.

[45]*Ibid.*, p. 172.

[46]Manoel Bernardo de Mello e Castro to Francisco Xavier de Mendonça Furtado, 1 August 1759, BNRJ, 11, 2, 43 N 100 (Pará).

[47]João Pereira Caldas to Martinho de Mello e Castro, 18 June 1777, AHU, caixa 36 (Pará).

[48]João Pereira Caldas to Marquês de Pombal, 8 March 1774, BNRJ, 11, 2, 43 doc. 189.

[49]Portaria, 14 November 1771, BAP, cod. 592, doc. 914, and Carta régia, 11 May 1779.

[50]João Pereira Caldas to court, 8 November 1774, BAP, cod. 778, doc. 123.

[51]The trade between Pará and Mato Grosso, including goods and slaves, was estimated at 300,000 cruzados in 1775. João Pereira Caldas to Marquês de Pombal, 1 April 1775, BNRJ, 11, 2, 42, doc. 216.

[52]Alexandre Rodriques Ferreira, "Miscellanea historia para servir de explicação ao prospecto da cidade do Pará," ms. dated 19 September 1789, BNRJ, 21, 1, 1, N 2.

[53]Edital, 21 August 1771, BAP, cod. 858, n.p.

[54]João Pereira Caldas to Martinho de Mello de Castro, 7 April 1773, BNRJ, 11, 2, 43 doc. 176.

[55]Jeronimo de Viveiros, 1: 74.

[56]João Pereira Caldas to Martinho de Mello e Castro, 11 September 1777, BNRJ, 11, 2, 43 doc. 247.

[57]*Ibid.*

[58]João Pereira Caldas to Martinho de Mello e Castro, 1778, AHU, caixa 38 (Pará).

[59]António de Abreu Guimares, "Methodo facil, proprio e util para se animar e prover a importante povoação do Grao Para, suas lavouras, fabricas, navegação e comercio em ulitidade geral e do proprio estado," 1778(?), ms. in BNRJ, 1-28, 28, 32 A N-2 (Pará).

[60]*Ibid.*

[61]See Appendix A.

[62]Francisco de Sousa Coutinho to court, 25 April 1792, ANRJ, cod. 99, Vol. 13, f. 118.

[63]*Ibid.*

[64]Francisco de Sousa Coutinho to court, 21 August 1797, BAP, cod. 702, doc. 102.

[65]"Circular para Rio de Janeiro, Bahia, e Pernambuco," 16 April 1798, BAP, cod. 683, doc. 42.

[66]"Circular para Angola e Benguela," 16 April 1798, BAP, cod. 683, doc. 41.

[67]Edital, 19 October 1798, BAP, cod. 689, doc. S.

[68]São Paulo da Assumpção de Luanda to court, 12 October 1800, BAP, cod. 764, doc. 55.

[69]*Ibid*.

[70]To help avert maritime disasters, pilots were stationed at Salinas, close to the actual entrance to the river, with crews of Indians to board and direct ships to the port of Belém. José de Napoles Telo de Menezes to Conselho Ultramarino, 17 January 1781, BAP, cod. 714, doc. 81.

[71]Francisco de Sousa Coutinho to court, July 1790, ANRJ, cod. 99, Vol. 11, f. 72.

[72]Portaria, 22 June 1790, ANRJ, cod. 99, Vol. 11, f. 74.

[73]José Telles da Silva to Martinho de Mello e Castro, 31 December 1785, AHU, caixa 57 (Maranhão).

[74]Portaria, 22 June 1790, ANRJ, cod. 99, Vol. 11, f. 74.

[75]João Pereira Caldas to governor of Maranhão, 26 May 1774, BAP, cod. 589, doc. 81.

[76]Jeronimo de Viveiros, 1: 88. For more details, see C. R. Boxer, *Golden Age of Brazil*, p. 170.

[77]Governor José de Napoles Telo de Menezes noted that the Tocantin River was a virtual *"porta franca"* for fugitive slaves and others. José de Napoles Telo de Menezes to court 9 June 1780, BAP, cod. 714, doc. 71.

[78]João Vasco Braun to Francisco de Sousa Coutinho, 8 November 1790, *Instituto Historico e Geografico Brasileiro* (hereafter cited as IHGB), lata 278, ms. 14748 N 2.

[79]Jeronimo de Viveiros, 1: 88.

[80]Governor to court, 1771 or 1772, BNRJ, 1, 28, 27, 5 N 1-10.

[81]Francisco de Sousa Coutinho to court, 1 March 1793, ANRJ, cod. 99, Vol. 14, f. 96. A description of such a settlement in another region of Portuguese America is provided by Stuart B. Schwartz, "Buraco de Tatu: The Destruction of a Bahian Quilombo," *International Congress of Americanists* 3 (1968): 429-438.

[82]João Pereira Caldas to Martinho de Mello e Castro, 29 November 1773, AHU, caixa 34 (Pará).

[83]Carta régia, 26 May 1756, BAP, cod. 667, doc. 19.

[84]"Portaria para Alferes José . . . Rodgrigues Camello," 2 February 1795, BAP, cod. 567, doc. 15.

[85]Francisco de Sousa Coutinho to court 10 September 1795, BAP, cod. 682, doc. 54.

[86]*Ibid*.

[87]Francisco de Sousa Coutinho to court, 21 June 1795, BAP, cod. 682, doc. 41, and Luis Pinto de Sousa to governor, 23 March 1796, BAP, cod. 682, doc. 87.

[88]The Alto-Mearim was effectively blocked to advancing civilization until 1835. Jeronimo de Viveiros, 1: 291. Further references to hostile Indians in early-nineteenth-century Maranhão may be found in BNRJ, 7, 4, 74, docs. 4, 7, 19 (Maranhão) and 3, 4, 24 (Maranhão).

[89]The dependence of Pará on forest products collected by Indian laborers helped deplete the Indian population. In 1800 the governor aptly characterized the state as one of great territorial extension (*extenção*) and small intensity (*intenção*). Francisco de Sousa Coutinho to Rodigo de Sousa Coutinho, 25 September 1800, IHBG, lata 281, ms. 14769.

[90]Arthur Vianna, *As Epidemias no Pará* (Belém, 1906), p. 11. Archival research documents four major smallpox epidemics before 1755. After that date, smallpox outbreaks occurred on at least thirteen different occasions.

[91]*ABAP*, 5: 29.

[92]Vianna, p. 15.

[93]Juiz de Fora to Manoel e Pinto de Almdo e Lima, 17 August 1792, AHU, caixa 64 (Maranhão).

[94]José Narciso de Magalhaes Menezes to court, 29 August 1806, BAP, cod. 706, doc. 41.

[95]Senado da Câmara to governor, 23 April 1788, ANRJ, cod. 99, Vol. 9, f. 72.

[96]José Narciso de Magalhaes Menezes to court, 29 August 1806, BAP, cod. 706, doc. 41.

[97]Francisco de Sousa Coutinho to court, 22 July 1793, ANRJ, cod. 99, Vol. 14, f. 212.

[98]José Narciso de Magalhaes Menezes to court, 29 August 1806, BAP, cod. 706, doc. 41.

[99]"Conta das habitantes, novidades annuaes . . . de toda a Capitania do Maranhão anno de 1798," AHU, caixa 37 (Maranhão).

[100]Vianna, p. 11.

[101]Manuel Barata, p. 7.

5

Nineteenth-Century Brazilian Slavery

Robert Conrad

Many traditional historical studies that emphasize the mildness of slavery in Latin America give particular stress to the case of Brazil. According to these interpretations, slaves in Brazil were usually protected from abuse by specific legislation, the intervention of the Church, and paternalistic traditions. In recent years revisionist historians have taken a more critical look at life under Brazil's servile institution. The evidence they have uncovered creates a much less sanguine picture of Brazilian slavery than the depiction popularly accepted in the past. Pioneering works by C. R. Boxer, Stanley J. Stein, and Emilia Viotti da Costa demonstrated serious weaknesses in assumptions about the mild and humane conditions of slavery in Brazil. According to them, legislation was more a matter of theory than practice, the clergy sought mainly to please slaveholding interests, and paternalism often faded under economic pressure. In the following essay, Robert Conrad sums up many of these major points of criticism, basing his analysis on abundant primary documents from the Brazilian archives. In many respects Conrad's revisionist approach resembles that of Kenneth M. Stampp, whose well-known work, The Peculiar Institution, *critically reexamined slavery in the antebellum United States.*

It is important to preface Conrad's study with a reminder that conditions under slavery often depended on factors of time and place. Indeed, paternalistic traditions may have been particularly strong in the Brazilian northeast during the period of a decline in sugar profits when there was no great need for plantation managers to drive their workers hard. Professor Conrad's investigation concentrates on slavery in the coffee regions of nineteenth-century Brazil—in short, an environment of economic expansion and great pressure to maximize profits from the toil of bondsmen.

R. B. T.

In recent years various scholars have contrasted the institution of slavery in Brazil (and in Spanish America) with its United States counterpart. Their conclusions have been far from unanimous, but it is fair to say that two viewpoints have emerged. The older school of thought has held that the Latin American slave in general, and the Brazilian slave in particular, were introduced into a relatively humane slave system, that they were well protected by legal, ecclesiastical, and patriarchal traditions and institutions, and that freedom was a goal that they might reasonably have been expected to achieve. Books by members of this school, particularly Frank Tannenbaum's *Slave and Citizen*, have convinced a wide public that slaves in Brazil and Spanish America were granted advantages that made their conditions and prospects much more hopeful than those of slaves in the United States.[1]

More recently, however, other scholars have challenged this point of view. Confronting the question of Latin American slavery directly—not as an adjunct of United States history but as a subject worthy of consideration in its own right—and basing their studies on a far greater range of historical evidence, they have provided what I believe to be a much more realistic picture of Latin American slavery.[2] The aim of this article is to contribute to this reexamination of the institution in Latin America by elucidating a few aspects of slavery in nineteenth-century Brazil, specifically the aims and attitudes of the master class, slave mortality and population decline, manumission and illicit enslavement, the legal status of bondsmen, their punishments, marriage, and the integrity of the slave family.

The attitudes of the master class are fundamental to an understanding of the situation of the slaves. The Brazilian planters, whether their lands produced sugar, coffee, or other crops, were consistently impelled to the acquisition of labor at the lowest possible cost. The African or Brazilian-born slave was looked upon primarily as an expendable instrument of production, a tool to be acquired, maintained, and replaced at the lowest possible expense. For a significant number of planters, whose power on their own land was often nearly absolute, the economic motive was much stronger than humanitarian or religious drives, and during much of the nineteenth century the great waste of human life that was characteristic of the slave trade and the Brazilian plantation system hardly seemed to require justification.

Both opponents and defenders of slavery testified to the high mortality rate among slaves in Brazil during most of the nineteenth century. In 1823 José Bonifacio de Andrada e Silva claimed that forty thousand slaves had entered the country during the previous five or six years with no significant increase in the slave population.[3] A quarter of a century later a British subject, testifying before a Select Committee of the House of Lords, backed this observation when he said, "In Brazil the slaves are continually brought in and die off. The mortality rate in the first two or three years after importation, for some reason or other is immense." Those entering Brazil "do little more than fill up the generations that pass away."[4]

The reasons for this high mortality rate are not hard to find. How masters treated their slaves was closely related to their price, their availability, and their productive capacity. As long as the slave trade from Africa to Brazil continued to supply cheap adult workers, the masters' interest in the health, comfort, and lives of their property and its natural reproduction was minimized by the ease and cheapness of acquiring replacements.

Most observers agreed that the extraordinary loss of life among the slave population could be attributed to excessive labor, malnutrition, poor clothing, inadequate housing, epidemics and disease, severe punishment, and an absence of economic interest in the survival of children.[5] Senator Cristiano Otôni told the Brazilian upper chamber in 1883 that while the slave trade lasted slave owners had been "careless as to the duration of the life [*sic*] of their slaves." The masters believed that the "proceeds of the first year's labor of a slave were at least enough to cover his cost; that the second and following years were clear profit. Why then, said they, should we bother ourselves about them, when we can so easily get fresh ones at such a low price?"[6]

Writing in 1823, José Bonifacio claimed that an end to the slave trade would enrich the masters because it would increase the value of the slaves they owned, cause them to promote better care and living conditions, and to encourage marriage and a consequent growth of the slave population.[7] Subsequent testimony seems to bear out this conclusion. An abolitionist lawyer, writing in 1883, claimed that during the first half of the century slave mortality had been immense, but had decreased considerably after 1850, "when the lack of workers began to be felt, and diminishing even more after the epidemic of *cholera morbus* which victimized the slave population."[8] In short, as the slave population dwindled, masters took greater care of their human property.

Much the same conclusion was reached by a special committee of the Brazilian Chamber of Deputies in 1871:

When the importation of African laborers was legal, abundant, and at a low price, the well-being of those cheap machines, whose existence was equivalent to that of a domestic animal, was neglected. Every kind of labor was assigned to those workers, and dull laziness was reserved for the whites. With the slaves beginning to grow scarce, and increasing ten-fold in price, they represented considerable capital; from which cause originated much improved care for the conservation of elevated values and of instruments of labor irreplaceable in the same form.[9]

The loss of life was particularly heavy among the children born of slave women. In 1849 a Rio journalist pointed out that one advantage of free workers was their ability to produce children. Slaves, it was claimed, "give us almost no children, because the mortality rate among them is frightful in the first years, owing to a thousand circumstances which are not strange to us."[10] In 1871 opponents of the liberation of infants born into slavery affirmed that the death rate among children had been immense. Deputy Capanema of Minas Gerais testified in the Chamber that until the suppression of the slave trade in the 1850s 95 percent of the slave children born in Brazil, unwanted and neglected, had died before reaching the age of eight.[11] Barros Cobra of the same province asserted that the masters' material interest in children born into slavery was insufficient to prevent "a prodigious mortality."[12] A planter critic of the Free Birth Law[13] predicted, in fact, that this reformist legislation would not grant a life of freedom to the children of slave women because disgusted masters, calculating the loss of labor during and after pregnancy and the cost of rearing useless children, would not provide sufficient care. Half or more of the children would be sacrificed, he predicted, in order that a few might be free.[14] Otôni told the Senate in 1883 that until the end of the slave trade the mortality among slave children was at least 80 percent and that labor in the southern provinces was "so cheap that no one cared what became of the offspring."[15]

Statistics on Brazilian slavery support the abundant contemporary reports of the inability of the Brazilian slaves to expand their numbers through natural means during the first half of the nineteenth century.[16] The number of slaves in Brazil in 1798 is said to have been about 1,582,000.[17] Between 1800 and 1850 probably 1,600,000 were imported into that country.[18] If, therefore, the population had been maintained through natural reproduction (which of course was difficult owing to a low ratio of females to males), the slaves of Brazil should have numbered close to 3 million in 1871, the year of the Free Birth Law. Yet only 1,541,819 slaves were registered under the provisions of that legislation.[19] In contrast, the slave population of the United States, also afflicted by a high, though less shocking, mortality rate, grew from about 700,000 to nearly 4 million between 1790 and 1860, whereas the free colored population of the United States also expanded during the same period from 60,000 to nearly half a million.[20] These statistics are even more revealing if we compare estimated total slave imports for the two countries. The total importation of slaves into British North America has recently been put at 399,000 (between 1701 and 1870), whereas the number said to have been transported to Brazil is 3,646,000.[21]

Despite the greater care and improved living conditions resulting from the effective abolition of the African traffic about 1851, the slaves of Brazil were unable, even during the second half of the nineteenth century, to maintain their numbers through procreation. In 1855 the scion of a wealthy planter family of Rio de Janeiro observed in a small study of immigration and population that the ease with which Brazil had received slaves from Africa had "constituted an impediment to the propagation of the African race among us." Yet Brazil, he believed, might emulate the United States, successfully breeding slaves and increasing its existing slave population, if planters gave "more attention to pregnancy, rendered more zeal and care to babies and small children." The planters, he thought, should promote the increase of slaves by every means compatible with morality and religion. Better clothing, improved housing and nutrition, more care for the sick, "and other measures which are generally scorned among us" would result, he believed, in the saving of many lives "which today are sacrificed by indifference and carelessness. . . ."[22] A contemporary writer from Maranhão doubted, however, that Brazilian masters would take the trouble to provide the nourishment, clothing, housing, care of the young, and communication between the sexes that had made the natural reproduction of the slaves profitable in the United States.[23]

As late as 1870, in an era when the treatment of slaves had almost certainly improved and lives were being lengthened, Joaquim Nabuco wrote: "The Negro population, we confess, does not reproduce like the white; a long series of causes depresses it, debases it, suffocates it too much for it to increase through its descendants."[24] In 1871 a national deputy from Bahia asserted that an estimated 5 percent annual decrease of the Brazilian slave population was an abnormal condition with its roots in the precarious social and hygienic conditions of the Brazilian slave population. Observing that the free black population was expanding through natural means, he denied that the decline of the slave population was a consequence of race, upholding the view that the cause of the decline was slavery itself.[25]

It might be concluded that the decline of the slave population and the presence of a large free colored population were the result of frequent manumissions, a shift from a slave population to a free population that resulted largely from the benevolent acts of the master class. It is true that in Brazil no laws prohibited the liberation of a slave, and that in fact the master who granted freedom was likely to gain the approval of society. Provisions for the liberation of slaves (with perhaps a preference for the light-skinned) were often contained in wills.[26] Infants born into slavery were often freed at the baptismal font or left to the care of orphanages or foundling homes—probably a constant and major source of the free colored population.[27] Slaves, moreover, were often able to buy their freedom. Groups of bondsmen sometimes organized liberation societies for the cooperative and methodical emancipation of their members.[28] *Negros de ganho*, slaves permitted to wander freely in the cities and to sell a product or a service, could accumulate a fund with which to ransom themselves from servitude.[29] As a result of these and other factors, the free colored population of Brazil was larger than that of the United States while slavery was legal in both countries. Near the end of the eighteenth century, slaves in the United States outnumbered the free colored by more than eleven to one, whereas in Brazil the ratio was close to four to one.[30]

There is little doubt, however, that manumission affected only a small percentage of Brazilian slaves and that a majority of the free colored persons living in Brazil during the nineteenth century were born free and did not attain that status through emancipation.[31] In Brazil slavery was older by at least a hundred years than the institution in the United States, and the free colored population had been developing and multiplying for a longer time. Yet at the end of the eighteenth century, after nearly three hundred years of slavery in the Portuguese colony, only about one in every five blacks and mulattoes was free, despite the greater opportunities of free persons to live normal productive lives, to acquire families, and to increase their numbers.

Though the Brazilian-born slave was more likely to gain the sympathy of his master than the African, even the Creole captives, sometimes the children of their masters, had little hope of attaining freedom.[32] The existence of light-skinned slaves, presumably the descendants of the master class, was often attested to.[33] Slavery was "a taint in the blood," in the words of a British observer, "which no length of time, no change of relationship, no alteration of colour can obliterate."[34] Frederico Burlamaque wrote in the 1830s:

A slave master almost never liberates the children he has with his slave women, and he demands from them all the labor and submission which he requires of the others: he sells them, trades them, or transmits them to his heirs. If one of his legitimate heirs receives them as an inheritance, he makes no distinction between them and his other slaves. Thus a brother can become owner of his brothers; over them he exercises the same tyranny, and satiates the same desires.[35]

Even during the 1870s, when slavery was already doomed by the free-birth provision of the Rio Branco Law, masters were reluctant to release their human property. Of the more than 1.5 million slaves registered in Brazil in the years just after 1871, only slightly more than 35,000 had been freed voluntarily (with or without compensation to their masters) by May 1880, an average of about 4,000 per year—slightly more than 2 percent of the total in about 8-1/2 years.[36] The rate of liberations greatly increased with the growth of the abolitionist movement, particularly in such provinces as Ceará and Rio Grande do Sul.[37] Yet it was not until 1887 and 1888, when slavery was tottering nationwide, that individual manumissions were so common that freedmen (as distinguished from the freeborn colored) made up a large portion of the Brazilian population, and even during those final months freedom was usually granted in exchange for a pledge of continuing service for a stated length of time. Ironically, the mass liberation of slaves by the coffee planters of São Paulo, which won the public approval of the most dedicated abolitionists during the final chaotic months of slavery, had the calculated purpose of keeping a vanishing labor force on the *fazendas* for the duration of the labor crisis.[38] Prior to this great emergency, however, the bulk of the slaves in Brazil had always died in captivity, and the freedman had always constituted the exception.[39]

It is sometimes alleged, nevertheless, that the Brazilian slave had the right to demand his freedom when he had amassed an amount of money equal to his "value." Professor Tannenbaum wrote in *Slave and Citizen* that the Brazilian slave had possessed this privilege from the sixteenth to the nineteenth century,[40] and the claim has since been echoed.[41] Yet until 1871 there was no law in Brazil that guaranteed to the slave his *peculio*, as his personal savings were called, and nothing that forced a master to accept a cash payment from his slave in exchange for his freedom, though the practice undoubtedly conformed with custom. During the nineteenth century legalization of these privileges was sometimes proposed. Before his exile in 1823, José Bonifacio had planned to ask the Constituent Assembly to legalize the *peculio* and the slave's right to purchase his freedom.[42] In 1850 a deputy from Ceará urged passage of a bill to free the newborn, to ban the separation of married slaves, and to make compulsory the manumission of slaves offering their price, but his proposals were judged unsuitable for discussion.[43] In 1855, in fact, the Emperor's Council of State ruled that, since the Constitution guaranteed the right of property and since no exception had been made in the case of the slave who offered his value in exchange for his freedom, "the faculty of the slave to obtain his liberty by indemnifying his master has been denied, if the [master] refuses this act of justice, humanity and religion."[44] Even in 1869, when judges were given permission by law to grant freedom to slaves included in legacies who could offer an amount of money equal to their judicial evaluations, the slave could take advantage of this privilege only when there was no prior claim of heirs or debtors.[45]

In 1871 the Rio Branco Law finally granted the slave the legal right to possess gifts and inheritances, but even then he could keep the money acquired *through his own labor* only when he gained his master's consent. With his savings thus guaranteed in part, the bondsman was also assured the right to purchase his freedom when he had acquired a sum equal to his "value."[46] These rights, which the Brazilian slave possessed under law for less than seventeen years, were circumscribed by the theory that the product of his labor belonged entirely to his master and could not be transferred to him without his master's approval. It is easy to believe the claim of Joaquim Nabuco, moreover, that the effects of these benefits were felt almost exclusively in the cities, where slaves had greater access to income, information, and legal justice than had their rural counterparts.[47]

When considering the question of emancipation, it should not be forgotten that a multitude of persons—a number far exceeding those buying or receiving the gift of freedom—were held *illegally* as slaves during the nineteenth century. At times during that period certainly more than a third (and perhaps as many as half) of the persons regarded and treated as slaves in Brazil were legally free, though few possessed the practical means of claiming that freedom. This was true of hundreds of thousands of Africans imported after the law of 7 November 1831 had declared the freedom of all slaves entering the country from that day forward.[48] It was true of their children and grandchildren. It was true of thousands of Africans confiscated from slave ships at sea, freed by British-Brazilian Mixed Commissions, apprenticed to public or private establishments, and subsequently absorbed into the slave population, despite Article 179 of the Criminal Code of

1830 providing for prison sentences of three to nine years for reducing a free person to slavery.[49] In 1862 the British minister in Rio, William Christie, judged the number of persons held illegally in slavery in Brazil at 1 million, but warned his government that the Brazilian regime "would probably receive any representation of Her Majesty's Government [on the matter] with strong repugnance and opposition."[50] In 1869 Rui Barbosa estimated that more than a third of the persons held in servitude in Brazil were illegally enslaved.[51] The following year Joaquim Nabuco argued that if the law concerning illegally imported Africans were ever enforced, the slave population would be reduced by half.[52] In a great speech delivered to the Brazilian Senate in 1871 the dynamic mulatto statesman Francisco de Sales Torres-Homem reminded the nation's planters "that the greater part of the slaves who work their lands are the descendants of those whom an inhuman traffic criminally introduced into this country with an affront to laws and treaties." The planters had forgotten, he said, "that during the period from 1830 to 1850 more than a million were delivered in this way to the plantations, and that in order to obtain that quantity of human cattle it was necessary to double and triple the number of victims, strewing their blood and their bodies over the surface of the seas which separate us from the land of their birth." And yet, added Sales Torres-Homem, the slave masters were still trying to fetter the children and the grandchildren of the victims of that illegal traffic.[53]

Despite this considerable disregard for law, the possession of illegally imported Africans was only rarely questioned by the press, the government, the courts, or other powerful groups or individuals, though the ages and African origins of countless slaves were together convincing proof of their legal right to freedom. Though the law of 7 November 1831 was never revoked by the General Assembly or rejected by the courts, no government ever seriously tried to enforce its provisions affecting the status of imported Africans. A member of the Emperor's Council of State contended in 1874, in fact, that Africans imported after 7 November 1831 had lost their freedom to the benefit of their masters who were "sufficiently skillful in evading the vigilance of the naval auditor's office. . . ."[54] Slave masters, in fact, were convinced of their right to keep their illegal property, even flaunting their violation of the law before the public. Aware of the extralegal powers of their class and their virtual immunity from prosecution in matters concerning slaves, they righteously advertised in the press for the return of runaway Africans too young to have entered Brazil or even to have been alive before 7 November 1831. An advertisement in a Rio newspaper of 4 April 1880 concerned the runaway "slave" João Francisco, aged forty-eight and of the Angola nation, obviously imported some time after 1832.[55] A similar notice published in 1878 offered a reward of 100 mil réis for the capture of a forty-year-old African of the Mina nation named Luiz—presumably born across the Atlantic in 1838.[56] In the early 1880s Africans too young to have been imported before 1831, and the descendants of their kind born free in accordance with the Rio Branco Law of 28 September 1871, were openly placed on sale together in the province of Rio de Janeiro and advertised in newspapers of the imperial capital. The staid *Jornal do Commercio* ran notices of government-sponsored slave sales in the interior town of Valenca, listing the names and ages of free children whose "services" could be purchased for a few mil réis and of Africans whose ages, certified by public notaries, proved the illegality of their *de facto* slave status.[57] Though the abolitionist press protested against these practices, they continued as late as May 1884, four years before the end of slavery.[58]

Illegally imported Africans were not the only persons whose right to freedom was disregarded. The free status of men of color was generally tenuous while slavery remained legal in Brazil. Indians, for example, were free by the terms of a law of 27 October 1831, and yet reports of the enslavement of Indians were frequent in the following decades and have persisted until our own times.[59] In the province of Pará free Indians, mestizos, and blacks were pressed into provincial labor gangs as early as 1835 on the basis of their "perpetual intellectual minority." In 1858 many of the inhabitants of the runaway-slave camps of that province were free men who had fled into the forests to avoid forced labor.[60] In Ceará government authorities forced free persons to work gratuitously on cotton and sugar plantations, while slave owners were shipping their human property to the slave markets of Rio de Janeiro.[61] Just after the abolition of the African slave trade Brazilian raiding parties frequently invaded neighboring Uruguay to kidnap persons of color for delivery to Brazilian slave markets. Whole Uruguayan families, according to the British consul in Rio Grande do Sul, were seized, separated, and sold in Brazil with an ease that was strong evidence of the ineffectiveness of Brazilian law as a guardian of personal freedom.[62]

At times during the years when the labor shortage was most severe, to be nonwhite and without documents could be grounds for the presumption of slave status. In Pernambuco vagrant blacks unable to give a good account of themselves could be legally enslaved. In July 1852 the president of that province decreed regulations for the public auctioning of so-called contingency goods (*bens do evento*), defined as "slaves, cattle, or beasts" whose owners were unknown. Officials in charge of such auctions were ordered to register data concerning persons and animals found, including their names, origins, ages, colors, and markings. If owners could not be located immediately, the property in question was to be evaluated and pertinent information published in the local press. If after sixty days the human "property" was unclaimed, public auctions were to take place before the "collector of slaves and cattle" on a date and hour previously announced by placards affixed in public places. There was no provision whatever in this decree for the possible emancipation of unclaimed persons, though an imperial decree of 1859 that established similar regulations for the disposal of *bens do evento* nationwide gave human contingency goods the privilege of purchasing their freedom if they offered an amount of money equal to their official evaluations, even if other bidders offered more.[63]

These and similar national and local regulations upheld the interests of the masters, whereas slaves were protected by few laws. As Viscount Rio Branco observed in 1871, Brazil lacked the elaborate slave codes of the French and Spanish, placing instead greater confidence in the discretion of the master.[64] Brazilian slavery was based theoretically on Roman law, on custom, and on specific regulations and statutes that had grown out of the Brazilian experience, some of which were intended to protect the slaves.[65] Yet most of the legal and customary practices followed in Brazil were fashioned to ensure the owner's control over his property. According to the Brazilian Criminal Code the grievances of an offended slave came under the jurisdiction of his owner. Slaves could not legally denounce their masters, nor act as witnesses in courts of law or before magistrates.[66] On large rural plantations, moreover, the will of the master was above the law. The Archduke Maximilian, who was in Brazil in 1860, described the regime of a Bahian plantation as "an unlimited despotism." The master can punish when and whom he will," wrote Maximilian; "the only limit is found in his conscience; the only restraint consideration of his own interest."[67] Though the Imperial Constitution of 1824 prohibited whipping, torture, branding, and all cruel punishment, this did not apply to slaves. A section of the Criminal Code, in fact, prescribed whipping of slaves as punishment for minor offenses, the number of lashes to be fixed by sentence but not to exceed fifty per day.[68]

This ruling merely recognized the existence of a practice that had long been customary: the inflicting of corporal punishment over a period of days or weeks interspersed with periods of rest and recuperation. In 1827, before the punishment of slaves was regulated, Father Diogo Antônio Feijó introduced a bill into the Chamber of Deputies that was aimed at *improving* the lives of bondsmen. Article 3 of this bill would have limited the punishment of slaves to five hundred lashes, not to exceed fifty per day, "on alternated or successive [days] as the condition of the patient requires."[69] In rural areas masters often applied punishment in a manner cynically based on religious practice, ordering that their slaves be whipped for either nine or thirteen successive days, just as the Catholic Church was accustomed to hold religious devotions called *novenas* or *trezenas* for nine or thirteen successive days. This was done, says one informant, "to remain in harmony with religious practice."[70] If the slave sinned on the day of St. Anthony, said another of the many reports of the practice, he was given a *trezena* of whippings, sometimes including the dripping of hot tallow on the slave's skin at the end of each day. If he sinned on some other saint's day, he received a *novena*.[71]

The indispensable key to the slave system, in fact, was the whip and the threat of its use. The lash, "lying close at hand in the principal apartment of every Brazilian home,"[72] was used in both public and private establishments. On a large plantation visited by Maximilian, the slave to be whipped was tied to a ladder that was tilted against a wall. Severe punishment for rebellious conduct or insubordination amounted to a hundred lashes, which "generally costs a man his life. . . ."[73] In Rio de Janeiro slave masters could delegate the punishment of slaves to the local police at the Campo de Sant'Anna, a large public plaza, paying 160 réis for each 100 lashes. During 1826 a total of 1,660 slaves, both men and women, underwent this public punishment, for which, according to the police clerk in charge of accounting, their masters paid a total of 530$560. At the current price, this represented payment for a total of 331,600 lashes, an average of about 200 per slave and almost 1,000 per day, delivered in one year at one jail in the capital of the empire. The maximum number of strokes suffered by any one slave was 300, and this number was common.[74]

The number of strokes to be received by slaves who had participated in revolts was not established in legislation, but such slaves were at times severely punished. After the well-known insurrection of slaves in Bahia in 1835, alleged participants received as many as 1,000 lashes applied at the rate of 50 per day, Sundays excluded, with frequent respites of a week or less. The punishment of a slave named Pacifico began on 10 April and ended at last on 12 June. A slave named Belchior received 800 strokes for his alleged part in the revolt, his master paying 35 mil réis to the treasury of the Santa Casa da Misericordia for 35 days of confinement and cure in the hospital of that institution.[75]

Three years later Minister of Empire Bernardo Pereira de Vasconcelos ordered that every slave who had taken part in the
Farrapos revolt in Rio Grande do Sul was to be punished with 200
to 1,000 lashes in the nearest possible place and without trial,
though slaves who surrendered to the commanding general or
the legal authorities were to be amnestied and freed.[76]
Lesser forms of punishment existed, of course, for lesser offenses, including the confinement of slaves in shackles and stocks,
the use of the *palmatoria*, a rod for rapping the knuckles or
extended palms of offending slaves, and the assignment of work
on Sundays and holidays, times when slaves were normally allowed to rest or to look to their own needs. More severe was the
application of thumb screws, a device with implications of complex premeditation in a society little given to mechanical equip-
ment. For recaptured runaways there was a humiliating con-
trivance that was placed about the neck, "consisting of an iron
ring with a tongue on whose extremities was a large bell."[77] A
particularly devilish form of punishment, consisting simply of the
dripping of melted tallow, was so common that the term *pingar um
escravo*, "to drip a slave," has found its way into a modern
Portuguese-English dictionary.[78] Finally, the death penalty, re-
luctantly used by masters, was specifically prescribed by the law of
10 June 1835 for slaves who killed, gravely wounded, or committed any serious physical offense against masters, overseers, and
members of their families.[79]
The life of the slave in rural areas was particularly difficult.
Senator Otôni described the daily routine of the slaves in the
southern coffee regions in a speech recorded in the Senate in
1884. Slaves worked twelve or fourteen hours "in sun and rain,"
said Otôni, "still 2 hours at night in preparing cereals for their
own food and that of the domestic animals; . . . still 1 hour at
daybreak in cleaning up the drying ground ready for the coffee;
. . . in short, 15 or 16 hours of grinding toil, . . . which no constitution can stand; and to this must be added insufficient or inadequate food, and for clothing something just short of absolute
nudity."[80] Similarly, in an undated essay that survives in manu-

script form in the Imperial Archive a writer claimed that slaves worked fourteen or fifteen hours per day, ate "very bad, defective, and unwholesome food," went about almost naked, slept "without the necessary comfort for the prolongation of life, often in the open air and always in pig sties, exposed to the irregularities of the temperature."[81]

A Bahian planter spoke freely to a foreign visitor about the life of the slaves in rural areas a few years before the abolition of the slave trade:

> In the interior, he remarked, the slaves are badly fed, worse clothed, and worked so hard that the average duration of their lives does not exceed six years. In some districts it reaches to eight, while the number that see ten years after leaving Africa is small indeed.... On large estates [continued the foreign visitor] a few days rest are given them every three or four weeks during the sugar season, but on smaller ones, where owners commonly have difficulty to keep out of debt, they fare badly and are worked to death.... I would rather, a thousand times, be a sheep, pig, or ox, have freedom, food, and rest for a season, and then be knocked on the head, than be a serf on some plantation. I say *some*, because there are in Brazil, as in other lands, humane planters.[82]

The marriage of slaves was legal in Brazil and sanctioned and fostered by the Church, but despite the claims of some modern historians, most slaves never experienced marriage.[83] Concubinage was surely condemned in Brazil as licentious, adulterous, and immoral, as Stanley Elkins has written, but this did not prevent it. Laws against promiscuity may have existed, but they were not enforced with any amount of regularity, even among the Catholic clergy.[84] For moral and religious reasons masters were obliged to encourage marriage among their slaves, but they seldom complied. The unequal ratio between males and females —the result of the preponderance of males in the cargoes of slave ships—naturally prohibited marriage for many men, but the sexual life of even the women was not normally regularized by marriage. José Bonifacio, seeing the need in 1823 to promote normal family life among Brazilian bondsmen if the slave trade was to end, hoped to force masters to maintain a high percentage of married slaves on their plantations and to refrain from establishing obstacles to matrimony.[85] Yet travelers in Brazil in subsequent years found legal marriage among slaves to be rare,[86] and only a small minority of adult slaves were classified as married or widowed when reasonably reliable statistics were at last collected in the final years of slavery. Of the 13,020 slaves registered in the province of Rio Grande do Norte in 1874, only 723—a little more than 5 percent—were married or widowed.[87] Of the 723,419 slaves registered in Brazil in 1888—all of marriageable age—only 91,209, less than 13 percent of the total, were recorded as married or widowed (see table). Most of these, moreover, were located in the wealthier coffee provinces of the south, notably São Paulo and Minas Gerais, despite a comparatively low ratio of females to males in that region, whereas the number of married slaves in several northern, western, and extreme southern provinces and in the city of Rio de Janeiro made up an almost insignificant part of the whole. Of the 7,488 slaves registered in the Municipio Neutro, which included the city of Rio de Janeiro, only 56, or less than 1 percent, were recorded as widowed or married. This was true despite the nonexistence of children of premarital age among them (owing to the Free Birth Law of 1871, all slaves were adults by 1888), and despite the near parity of males and females.

Various explanations have been put forward for the failure of masters to encourage marriage. Normal wedlock was not suitable to brutish slaves, masters were said to have argued even before the nineteenth century, because they could not be faithful.[88] The propagation of slaves in Brazil, others declared, would create a "Western Guinea" and a threat to the established society.[89] The high cost of marriages was undoubtedly another factor, but

Sex and Marital Status of Slaves in Brazil (Sixteen or Older), May 1888

Province	Sex			Marital Status			Approximate Percentage Married or Widowed
	Male	Female	Total	Single	Married	Widowed	
Far North							
Pará	5,196	5,339	10,535	10,415	104	16	1.1
Maranhão	15,991	17,455	33,446	32,052	1,131	263	4.1
	21,187	22,794	43,981	42,467	1,235	279	3.4
Northeast							
Piauí	4,317	4,653	8,970	8,447	500	23	5.8
Ceará	54	54	108	81	22	5	25.0
Rio Grande do Norte	1,584	1,583	3,167	2,938	211	18	7.2
Paraíba	4,210	5,238	9,448	8,697	587	164	7.9
Pernambuco	20,531	20,591	41,122	36,734	3,480	908	10.7
Alagôas	7,449	7,820	15,269	13,700	1,322	247	10.0
Sergipe	8,147	8,728	16,875	14,541	1,872	462	13.8
Bahia	37,966	38,872	76,838	72,856	3,477	505	5.2
	84,258	87,539	171,797	157,994	11,471	2,332	8.0
West and South							
Mato Grosso	1,642	1,591	3,233	3,011	166	56	6.9
Goiás	2,430	2,525	4,955	4,582	307	66	7.6
Paraná	1,770	1,743	3,513	3,320	162	31	5.5
S. Catarina	2,769	2,158	4,927	4,875	46	6	1.1
Rio Grande do Sul	4,591	3,851	8,442	8,344	91	7	1.2
	13,202	11,868	25,070	24,132	772	166	3.7
South-Central							
Min. Ger.	104,748	87,204	191,952	158,983	27,713	5,256	17.2
Esp. Santo	7,112	6,269	13,381	12,232	953	196	8.6
Rio de Jan.	87,767	74,654	162,421	149,677	10,604	2,140	7.8
Mun. Neutro	3,653	3,835	7,488	7,432	38	18	0.8
São Paulo	62,688	44,641	107,329	79,293	24,018	4,018	26.1
	265,968	216,603	482,571	407,617	63,326	11,628	15.5
Totals	384,615	338,804	723,419	632,210	76,804	14,405	10.4

SOURCE: Reproduced from Conrad, *Brazilian Slavery*, p. 298.

perhaps the most important was the moral and religious obstacle to the free disposal of slaves that marriage theoretically erected in a Catholic society.[90]

To claim that marriage prevented the separation of slaves in Brazil, moreover, is to reveal a misunderstanding of the character of slavery in that country. Yet this too has been alleged.[91] Until prohibited in 1869, in fact, masters could dispose of married slaves by sale to different masters or sell a mother's children without committing any violation of law or custom. Prior to that date, moreover, the interprovincial slave trade, which carried thousands of slaves each year from the northeast to the wealthier coffee zones, separated many families.[92] In 1852 the British consul in Pernambuco characterized the slave trade at Recife as no less horrible than the former African trade: "the same forced transportation . . . without even the poor excuse of ameliorating the condition of the negro . . . the same disruption of natural ties of parent, child, brother or sister, the same eternal separation from these and from friends: indeed . . . most painful scenes are witnessed at the departure of almost every steamer. . . ."[93] In 1854 the British minister in Rio described the thriving slave business at Bahia: "All at once a slave-trader comes into the market from Rio de Janeiro, buys up from the needy or avaricious masters all those slaves he can obtain, and in most cases is the cause of the separation of a father from his wife and children. . . ."[94] In 1856 the British consul in Pernambuco wondered in a dispatch to London why a law could not be passed to protect the Brazilian slave from the hardship of a forced migration to the south. "Could not the law forbid the separation of man and wife, parent and child," he asked, "at least beyond the precincts of the province in which they reside?"[95] Such a law was enacted—thirteen years later—but the legislation of 15 September 1869 did not provide an absolute guarantee against the separation of kin. It merely prohibited separation *by sale*, and provided as the sole penalty for its violation the nullification of the sales agreement. The law, moreover, permitted the master to sell a child separately from his mother when he reached the age of fifteen, and this age was lowered to twelve two years later by the Rio Branco Law.[96]

It is undoubtedly true that Brazilian slavery varied in character with natural and economic conditions. The circumstances of the few hundred slaves of the province of Amazonas concentrated in scattered towns like Manaus were obviously different from those of slaves on the coffee plantations of Rio de Janeiro province. Many slaves in Brazilian coastal towns possessed great personal liberty and enjoyed access to pleasure and profit. The household slave was granted advantages unknown to most field hands. The mulatto or Creole slave with a superior knowledge of his master's world could ease his burden, and some slaves did enjoy normal family relationships sanctioned by the Catholic Church. In all likelihood, too, there were plantations in the Brazilian northeast and in other parts of Brazil where intelligent, humane, and Christian owners ruled over patriarchal establishments of the kind portrayed by Gilberto Freyre.[97]

There exists, nonetheless, abundant and persuasive evidence that the reputation for mildness of Brazilian slavery, which was propagated even during the nineteenth century, is undeserved. In the 1830s Frederico Burlamaque, protesting the dissemination of false opinions about Brazilian slaveholders, wrote: "If we be the most merciful what must others be! On the sugar plantations of the north, it would horrify any humane person to witness the misery of the slaves."[98] In 1882 a responsible American journalist in Rio editorialized on the alleged mildness of Brazilian slavery: "When . . . the European public is informed . . . that [the Brazilian slave] is well treated, enjoys comparative liberty, and is granted many privileges, we are inclined to believe that this wretched 'propaganda' has gone just a little too far." Those who made such claims were "either grossly ignorant or else . . . guilty of deliberate falsehood—and the evidence is in favor of the latter supposition." The *Uncle Tom's Cabin* of Brazil had not yet been written, wrote A. J. Lamoureux of *The Rio News*, but when it was there would be "no incidents lacking to fill it with horrors of which Mrs. Harriet Beecher Stowe never dreamed."[99]

Notes

[1]An earlier version of this paper was read at the Southern Historical Association meeting in Washington, D.C., in 1969.

In addition to Tannenbaum's work, first published in 1946, see particularly Stanley Elkins, *Slavery: A Problem in American Institutional and Intellectual Life* (Chicago, 1962 [first published in 1959]), pp. 63-80. Though Professor Tannenbaum drew on a wide range of sources, Professor Elkins' impressions of Brazilian slavery were derived primarily from Gilberto Freyre's *The Masters and the Slaves* (New York, 1946), Sir Harry Johnston's *The Negro in the New World* (London, 1910), and the Tannenbaum study. More recently Herbert S. Klein reached conclusions quite similar to those of Tannenbaum and Elkins in his *Slavery in the Americas: A Comparative Study of Virginia and Cuba* (Chicago, 1957).

[2]Listed in their order of publication are some recent statements on Brazilian slavery that seem incompatible with the views of Professors Tannenbaum and Elkins: Stanley J. Stein, *Vassouras, A Brazilian Coffee County, 1850-1900* (Cambridge, Mass., 1957), pp. 132-195; Roger Bastide and Florestan Fernandes, *Brancos e Negros em São Paulo* (São Paulo, 1959), pp. 1-68; Octavio Ianni, *As metamorfoses do escravo* (São Paulo, 1962), pp. 131-183; Fernando Henrique Cardoso, *Capitalismo e escravidão* (São Paulo, 1962), pp. 133-167; C. R. Boxer, *The Golden Age of Brazil, 1695-1750* (Berkeley, Cal., 1964), pp. 170-178; Marvin Harris, *Patterns of Race in the Americas* (New York, 1964); David Brion Davis, *The Problem of Slavery in Western Culture* (Ithaca, N.Y., 1966), pp. 223-243; Emilia Viotti da Costa, *Da senzala à colônia* (São Paulo, 1966), pp. 227-229; Leslie Bethell, *The Abolition of the Brazilian Slave Trade* (Cambridge, England, 1970), p. 4; Carl N. Degler, *Neither Black Nor White* (New York, 1971), pp. 25-92; Robert Brent Toplin, *The Abolition of Slavery in Brazil* (New York, 1972). See also my book, *The Destruction of Brazilian Slavery, 1850-1888* (Berkeley, Cal., 1972).

[3]Octavio Tarquinio de Souza (ed.), *O pensamento vivo de José Bonifacio* (São Paulo, 1944), pp. 48-50.

[4]*Report from the Select Committee of the House of Lords Appointed to Consider the Best Means which Great Britain Can Adopt for the Final Extinction of the African Slave Trade* (London, 1849), pp. 22-23.

[5]One foreign traveler ascribed the decrease in the captive population to "the ill-treatment of the slaves, their immorality, the necessity laid upon the expectant mother to continue her work as long as possible, and

the excessive use of cachaça [raw cane alcohol]." The same writer told of "the fearful instances of slave women committing child-murder in order to revenge themselves on their cruel masters and to rob him [*sic*] of valuable capital." See Maximilian I, *Recollections of My Life* (London, 1868), 3: 175.

⁶Quoted by *The Rio News*, Rio de Janeiro, 24 June 1884.

⁷Tarquinio de Souza, *O pensamento vivo*, pp. 48-50.

⁸Antônio Joaquim Macedo Soares, *Companha juridica pela libertação dos escravos (1867-1888)* (Rio de Janeiro, 1938), pp. 40-41.

⁹Quoted by Joaquim Floriano de Godoy, *O elemento servil e as câmaras municipaes da provincia de São Paulo* (Rio de Janeiro, 1887), p. 500. The nineteenth-century historian and lawyer Dr. Perdigão Malheiro gave four reasons for the inability of the Brazilian slave population to increase like the free: "1. because in general the importation was of men, and very few women; what was wanted mainly was workers, and not families; 2. because marriages were not promoted; the family did not exist for the slaves; 3. because little or no care was given to the children; 4. because sickness, ill-treatment, and excessive labor and service disabled, exhausted, and killed a large number in a short time." See Dr. Agostinho Marques Perdigão Malheiro, *A escravidão no Brasil. Ensaio histórico-juridico-social*, 2nd ed. (São Paulo, 1944), 2: 65.

¹⁰*O Philantropo*, Rio de Janeiro, 13 April 1849.

¹¹*Annaes da Câmara dos Senhores Deputados* 3 (1871): 173.

¹²*Ibid*.

¹³This was the well-known *Lei do Ventre Livre* or Rio Branco Law, which was sanctioned on 28 September 1871. Its most important provision freed the children of slave women born from that date forward, though with the responsibility after the age of eight to serve their mothers' masters without pay until reaching the age of twenty-one.

¹⁴*Reflexões sobre a emancipação em relação á lavoura patria e sobre a mesma lavoura* (Bahia, 1871), p. 27.

¹⁵Quoted by *The Rio News*, 24 July 1883.

¹⁶For the phenomenon of a "naturally decreasing slave population" in parts of Brazil and in the British Caribbean sugar colonies, see Philip D. Curtin, *The Atlantic Slave Trade: A Census* (Madison, Wis., 1969), pp. 28-29.

¹⁷Perdigão Malheiro, *A escravidão*, 2: 26.

¹⁸Alfonso d'Escragnolle Taunay, *Subsidios para a historia do trafico africano no Brasil colonial* (Rio de Janeiro, 1941), p. 305.

[19]*Relatorio apresentado á Assembléa Geral Legislativa* . . . *pelo Ministro e Secretario de Estado dos Negocios da Agricultura* . . . (Rio de Janeiro, 1884), pp. 187-191. This figure is probably nearly accurate, because the law provided that slaves not registered would be considered free.

[20]Joseph C. G. Kennedy, *Preliminary Report on the Eighth Census, 1860* (Washington, 1862), p. 7.

[21]Curtin, *The Atlantic Slave Trade*, p. 268.

[22]Luis Peixoto de Lacerda Werneck, *Ideas sobre colonisação precedidas de uma succinta exposição dos principios geraes que regem a população* (Rio de Janeiro, 1855), pp. 22-27.

[23]Fabio de Carvalho Reis, *Breves considerações sobre a nossa lavoura* (São Luiz de Maranhão, 1856), p. 6. For a discussion of the high mortality rate among Brazilian slaves, both infant and adult, see Viotti da Costa, *Da senzala à colônia*, pp. 255-261.

[24]Joaquim Nabuco, "A escravidão," *Revista do Instituto Histórico e Geográfico Brasileiro* 204 (July-September 1949): 105.

[25]*Discussão da reforma do estado servil na Câmara dos Deputados e no Senado* (Rio de Janeiro, 1871), 2: 193-194.

[26]Pierre Verger, *Flux et reflux de la traite des nègres entre le Golfe de Bénin et Bahia do Todos os Santos du dix-septième au dix-neuvième siècle* (Paris, 1968), pp. 515-518. Verger cites many instances of philanthropic emancipation but concludes that these represented very little when compared to the immense Brazilian slave population. In Bahia, he believes, it was mainly through their own efforts that slaves acquired their freedom (p. 518).

[27]The *roda dos engeitados* or rejection wheel, an enclosed turnstile set into the outer wall of an orphanage, foundling house, or Misericordia Hospital, provided a convenient way for mothers or slave owners to make anonymous deposits of unwanted children at places where they would presumably receive some care. Often described by fascinated travelers, these devices worked on the same principle as the nuns' wheels still in use in Brazilian convents.

[28]Verger, *Flux et reflux*, pp. 518-519.

[29]*Ibid.*, p. 515.

[30]The free colored population of Brazil, excluding Indians, was put at 406,000 in 1798, whereas the slave population was said to have been 1,582,000. See Perdigão Malheiro, *A escravidão*, 2: 26. According to Roberto G. Simonsen, *Historia economica do Brasil, 1500-1820* (São Paulo, 1937), 2: 56, in 1810 the Brazilian population included 628,000 free colored, excluding Indians, and 1,887,500 slaves, almost precisely one

free nonwhite person for every three slaves.

[31]The following statistics on the colored population of Rio de Janeiro provinces in 1840-1841, derived from an official provincial source, suggest that most of the free were Brazilian born. Most persons regarded as blacks, at any rate, were slaves, whereas most mulattoes were free.

Free				Slave			
Mulattoes		Blacks		Mulattoes		Blacks	
Males	Females	Males	Females	Males	Females	Males	Females
24,678	26,527	6,181	7,206	6,759	6,368	131,114	79,771

SOURCE: *Relatorio do presidente da provincia do Rio de Janeiro . . . para o ano de 1840 a 1841* (Niterói, 1851).

According to an 1848 census relative to the city of Rio de Janeiro, on the other hand, there were 8,449 free Africans (many of whom must have been *emancipados* freed by the Mixed Commissions and still at work in government establishments), 5,012 colored Creoles, and 110,512 slaves. See Verger, *Flux et reflux,.* p. 537.

[32]In 1860 the British consul in Pôrto Alegre estimated the annual manumissions in Rio Grande do Sul at 150 persons in a slave population of about 75,000. See *Class B. Correspondence with Foreign Powers Relating to the Slave Trade, From April 1, 1860, to December 31, 1860* (London, 1861), p. 46.

[33]See, for example, Henry Koster, *Travels in Brazil* (London, 1817), 2: 190-191; *Annaes da Câmara dos Senhores Deputados* 3 (1827): 41; *South American Journal and Brazil and River Plate Mail*, London, 16 October 1886.

[34]Robert Walsh, *Notices of Brazil in 1828 and 1829* (London, 1830), 2: 352.

[35]Frederico L. C. Burlamaque, *Analytica acerca do commercio d'escravos e acerca dos malles da escravidão domestica* (Rio de Janeiro, 1837), p. 31.

[36]*Relatorio apresentado á Assembléa Geral Legislativa . . . pelo Ministro e Secretario de Estado dos Negocios da Agricultura . . .* (Rio de Janeiro, 1880), p. 20. In 1871 Perdigão Malheiro set the rate of annual voluntary manumissions at 1 percent of the slave population. *Discussão da reforma do estado servil*, 2: 223.

[37]*Relatorio apresentado á Assembléa Geral Legislativa . . . pelo Ministro e Secretario de Estado dos Negocios da Agricultura . . .* (Rio de Janeiro, 1885), p. 372.

[38]See Conrad, *Brazilian Slavery*, pp. 239-260; Toplin, *The Abolition*, pp. 203-224; the Senate speech of Antônio Prado, 13 September 1887, *Annaes do Senado* 5 (1887): 229; *Correio Paulistano*, São Paulo, 11 November 1887; "Reunião dos proprietarios de escravos em S. Paulo para tratar da libertação dos mesmos em 15 de Dezembro de 1887," in Godoy, *O elemento servil*, p. 622.

[39]Joaquim Nabuco, *O Abolicionismo* (London, 1883), pp. 34-35.

[40]Frank Tannenbaum, *Slave and Citizen: The Negro in the Americas* (New York, 1947), p. 54.

[41]See Verger, *Flux et reflux*, p. 515; Elkins, *Slavery*, p. 75.

[42]Tarquinio de Souza, *O pensamento vivo de José Bonifacio*, p. 57.

[43]The bill of Pedro Pereira de Silva Guimarães of Ceará, his speeches, and the vituperative responses they aroused are recorded in "Pedro Pereira da Silva Guimarães (Documentos históricos)," in *Revista Trimensal do Instituto do Ceará*, Vol. 20. See also Raimundo Girão, *A abolição no Ceará* (Fortaleza, Ceará, 1956), pp. 17-27.

[44]Joaquim Nabuco, *Um estadista do Imperio* (São Paulo, 1947), 1: 249-250; *Colecção das leis do Imperio do Brasil*, 1855, pp. 454-455.

[45]Decree No. 1685 of 15 September 1869, *ibid.*, 29, Part 1 (1869): 129-130.

[46]Luiz Francisco da Veiga (ed.), *Livro do estado servil e respectiva libertação contendo a lei de 28 de Setembro de 1871* (Rio de Janeiro, 1876), pp. 27-28. Before the passage of this law, wrote Evaristo de Moraes, it was generally agreed that the slave had a right neither to his *peculio* nor to demand the purchase of his freedom. See Macedo Soares, *Campanha juridica*, p. 7.

[47]Nabuco, *O Abolicionismo*, p. 35. Percy Alvin Martin, who is among those historians who have attested to the kindness of Brazilian slave masters, has admitted that, with the exception of the Mina Negroes, "comparatively few of the slaves availed themselves of this privilege." See "Slavery and Abolition in Brazil," *Hispanic American Historical Review* 13, No. 2 (May 1933): 170.

172   *Robert Conrad*

⁴⁸Veiga, *Livro do estado servil*, p. 3.

⁴⁹*Colecção das leis do Imperio do Brasil* 1 (1830): 177. For contemporary accounts of the conditions of the free Africans, see Johann Jakob von Tschudi, *Reisen durch Südamerika* (Leipzig, 1866), 1: 178-183; Perdigão Malheiro, *A escravidão*, 2: 70-72; A. C. Tavares Bastos, *Cartas do Solitario* (São Paulo, 1938), pp. 123-146, 461-465; William Dougal Christie, *Notes on Brazilian Questions* (London, 1865), pp. xxxiv-xxxv. For a recent account of the *emancipados*, see my "Neither Slave Nor Free: The *Emancipados* of Brazil, 1818-1868," *Hispanic American Historical Review* 53, No. 1 (February 1973): 50-70.

⁵⁰Christie to Earl Russell, Rio de Janeiro, 3 May 1862, *British and Foreign State Papers* 53 (1862-1863): 1312.

⁵¹"Conferencia radical em 12 de Setembro de 1869," *Obras Completas de Rui Barbosa* (Rio de Janeiro, 1951), 1, Part 1: 172-173.

⁵²"A escravidão," pp. 83-85.

⁵³*Discussão da reforma do estado servil*, 2: 289.

⁵⁴See Macedo Soares, "O Concelho d'Estado e a lei de 7 de Novembro de 1831," *Companha juridica*, pp. 83-84.

⁵⁵*Gazeta de Noticias*, Rio de Janeiro, 4 April 1880.

⁵⁶*O Cruzeiro*, Rio de Janeiro, 13 April 1878.

⁵⁷*The Rio News*, 5 February 1881, 24 December 1882, 24 May 1884; *Gazeta da Tarde*, Rio de Janeiro, 9 May 1881, 23 February 1883; Nabuco, *O Abolicionismo*, p. 121. As Richard Graham suggests, the success of the abolitionist campaign of the 1880s resulted in many court decisions in favor of the freedom of Africans imported into Brazil after 7 November 1831. See *Britain and the Onset of Modernization in Brazil, 1850-1914* (Cambridge, England, 1968), pp. 181-182.

⁵⁸*The Rio News*, 24 May 1884.

⁵⁹Daniel P. Kidder, *Sketches of Residence and Travels in Brazil* (Philadelphia, 1845), 2: 267-268; Thomas Ewbank, *Life in Brazil* (New York, 1856), pp. 278-279, 323; *The Rio News*, 15 November 1880, 15 February 1881; Charles Wagley, *Amazon Town* (New York, 1953), p. 129. For a more recent report of the continuing use of slave labor in Amazonia and other parts of Brazil, see the editorial entitled "Lei Aurea," in the *Jornal do Brasil*, Rio de Janeiro, 13 April 1972.

⁶⁰*Discurso da abertura da sessão extraordinaria da Assembléa Provincial do Pará. Em 7 de Abril de 1858* (Pará, 1858), pp. 32-34.

[61]*Annaes da Câmara dos Senhores Deputados* 2 (1866): 41.

[62]British Consul to Earl of Clarendon, Rio Grande do Sul, 30 June 1856, *Class B. Correspondence . . . From April 1, 1855, to March 31, 1856*, pp. 251-252.

[63]Pernambuco, *Leis, decretos, etc.* (Pernambuco, 1855). See also Perdigão Malheiro, *A escravidão*, 1: 73-74. The imperial decree of 1859 defined *bens do evento* as "slaves, cattle, or beasts found without knowledge as to their owners. . . ." Such men and animals were to be evaluated and auctioned off if their owners did not respond to public notices. See Decree No. 2433 of 15 June 1859, *Colecção das leis do Imperio do Brasil*, 1859, pp. 452-453.

[64]*Discussão da reforma do estado servil*, 2: 398-399.

[65]See Nabuco, "A escravidão," pp. 93-94. Only those Roman laws that corresponded with Brazilian custom, wrote Nabuco, were honored in practice.

[66]See Luis Alves, "A questão do elemento servil. A extincção do trafico e a lei de repressão de 1850. Liberdade dos nascituros," *Primeiro Congresso de Historia Nacional*, Rio de Janeiro, 1916, Part 4, p. 254.

[67]Maximilian, *Recollections*, 3: 359.

[68]*Colecção das leis do Imperio do Brasil*, 1830, p. 153.

[69]The first article of this bill would have required masters to feed, clothe, and educate their slaves and to treat them.humanely, and Article 10 would have given the slaves the right to buy their freedom. Like so many other "humanitarian" bills presented to the Assembly during the nineteenth century, it was not considered. *Annaes da Câmara dos Senhores Deputados* 3 (1827): 49.

[70]Luiz Anselmo da Fonseca, *A escravidão, o clero e o abolicionismo* (Bahia, 1887), pp. 43-44.

[71]Luis Antonio de Oliveira Mendes, *Discurso academico ao programa: Determinar com todos os seus symptomas as doenças agudas, e chronicas que mais frequentemente accomettem os pretos recem tirados da Africa* (Lisbon, 1812), p. 36.

[72]Maximilian, *Recollections*, 3: 237.

[73]*Ibid.*, 3: 359.

[74]Receita dos bilhetes de correção de escravos (Policia), 1826, Arquivo Nacional, Rio de Janeiro, 385.

[75]Insurreição de escravos, 1835, Arquivo Publico do Estado da Bahia, pp. 26 ff.

[76]Cited by Nestor Ericksen, *O negro no Rio Grande do Sul* (Pôrto Alegre, 1941), pp. 25-26.

[77]*The Rio News*, 24 July 1882.

[78]*Novo dicionario da lingua portuguesa e inglesa* (New York, 1955), 1: 562.

[79]*Colecção das leis do Imperio do Brasil* 1 (1835): 5.

[80]Cited by *The Rio News*, 24 June 1884.

[81]"Ensaio sobre a emancipação do elemento servil," Arquivo do Museo Imperial, Petrópolis, 148-7179. For outstanding modern descriptions of slave life in the coffee-producing south, see Stein, *Vassouras*, pp. 132 ff., and Viotti da Costa, *Da senzala à colônia*, pp. 227-279.

[82]Ewbank, *Life in Brazil*, pp. 439-440.

[83]See Perdigão Malheiro, *A escravidão*, 1: 56.

[84]See Elkins, *Slavery*, p. 73.

[85]Tarquinio de Souza, *O pensamento vivo de José Bonifacio*, p. 60.

[86]See Viotti da Costa, *Da senzala à colônia*, p. 268.

[87]*Falla com que o Exm. Sr. Dr. João Capistrano de Mello Filho abrio a 1 sessão da vigesima legislatura provincial do Rio Grande do Norte, Julho de 1874*, p. 34. As Stanley Stein points out, free union (*amazia*) was prevalent among all classes. See *Vassouras*, pp. 155-156.

[88]Jorge Benci, S.J., *Economia Christã dos Senhores no governo dos escravos* (Porto, 1954), p. 83.

[89]*Discurso historico-refutatorio-politico sobre a carta do leitor effectivo que reprova a abolição da escravatura no Brasil* (Rio de Janeiro, 1825), pp. 38-39.

[90]See Conrad, *Brazilian Slavery*, pp. 32-33; Viotti da Costa, *Da senzala à colônia*, pp. 269-271.

[91]See Elkins, *Slavery*, p. 73; Tannenbaum, *Slave and Citizen*, p. 64.

[92]For two differing accounts of the interprovincial slave trade and its importance, see Conrad, *Brazilian Slavery*, pp. 47-69, and Herbert S. Klein, "The Internal Slave Trade in Nineteenth-Century Brazil, *Hispanic American Historical Review*, Vol. 51, No. 4, November 1971.

[93]Cowper to the Earl of Malmesbury, Pernambuco, 6 May 1852, *Class B. Correspondence . . . From April 1, 1852, to March 31, 1853*, pp. 278-279.

[94]Howard to Limpo de Abreu, Rio de Janeiro, 8 April 1854, *Class B. Correspondence . . . From April 1, 1854, to March 31, 1855*, pp. 90-91.

[95]Cowper to the Earl of Clarendon, Pernambuco, 17 October 1856, *Class B. Correspondence . . . From April 1, 1856, to March 31, 1857*, p. 246.

[96]Decree No. 1695 of 15 September 1869, *Colecção das leis do Imperio do Brasil* 29, Part 1 (1869): 129-130; Veiga, *Livro do estado servil*, p. 28.

[60]*Discurso da abertura da sessão extraordinaria da Assembiea Provincial do Pará. Em 7 de Abril de 1858* (Pará, 1858), pp. 32-34.

[97]See *The Masters and the Slaves*.

[98]Cited by G. W. Alexander, *Letters on the Slave Trade, Slavery, and Emancipation, etc.*, 1842, p. 114.

[99]*The Rio News*, 15 December 1882.

6

The Implementation of Slave Legislation in Eighteenth-Century New Granada[1]

Norman A. Meiklejohn

Norman A. Meiklejohn warns of the dangers of making broad generalizations about slavery throughout Latin America. Through an examination of legal cases involving bondsmen, he illustrates the importance of considering time and place when interpreting the condition of slaves in Latin America. Meiklejohn demonstrates that in New Granada, Spanish slave legislation was far from a pious recitation of good intentions, that slaves did have access to the law and to legal assistance, and that, indeed, many dedicated Spanish lawyers attempted to widen and strengthen the rights of the slave under the law. Although Meiklejohn acknowledges that many slaves were terribly mistreated, his evidence shows that in several representative cases Spanish slave legislation was living law. He suggests that these legal decisions be viewed in the economic context of New Granada society, since the pace of economic development in New Granada was sluggish throughout the colonial period. To be sure, there were short-lived periods of economic boom as new placer mines were discovered, but New Granada never experienced the frenzied cultivation of an exportable cash crop on a large scale. This fact does much to explain the relative mildness of conditions of slavery in parts of New Granada, and particularly for bondsmen who lived near the cities and centers of legal activity.

R. B. T.

There is considerable divergence of opinion regarding African slavery in colonial Latin America. Gilberto Freyre, Frank Tannenbaum, and Stanley Elkins have claimed that Latin American culture and institutions made for a relatively mild slave system. For example, the Roman Catholic Church welcomed the black slaves; it preached their equality with their masters before God, and it exhorted the masters to treat their slaves with Christian kindness. Medieval Iberian legislation, with its Roman, canon, and Visigothic elements, recognized the unnaturalness of slavery, fostered the kind treatment of slaves, and favored the recovery by slaves of their natural freedom.[2]

Charles Boxer, Stanley Stein, and Marvin Harris incline toward the opinion that the reputed mildness of African slavery in Latin America is a myth. They argue that the presence of supposedly humane legislation is no guarantee of its observance. In the absence of any proof, it is probable that this legislation, like all other legislation, was more often ignored than observed. Furthermore, judging by the evidence so far uncovered, Iberian culture and institutions did a rather poor job of protecting African slaves from cruel exploitation in areas like Cuba and Brazil.[3]

Actually, there are valid elements in both opinions. The disagreement stems, I believe, from a tendency to generalize from one region or country to the entire area, and from insufficient information on the slave institution at different times in different parts of Latin America. Indeed, there has been too little awareness that lack of uniformity in the practice of slavery must have been widespread because of the variety in performance by the Church, in the implementation of slave legislation by the courts,

and in the economic development of such different areas as Peru, New Granada, Argentina, Mexico, Cuba, and Brazil. Given the diversity of situations in different parts of Latin America, we must expect that the institution of slavery assumed diverse forms and practices during its long history there.

Certainly the institution of black slavery in New Granada was different in many ways from its counterpart in Cuba or Brazil. It was probably different from its counterpart in the other colonies of continental Spanish America. Numerous circumstances account for these variations. They include geographical location and topography, patterns of settlement and population density, natural resources and economic development, and the role played by certain churchmen, magistrates, and attorneys. A brief examination of these circumstances will help the reader to understand what made the slave institution in New Granada different. It will also furnish him with a context for the subsequent discussion on the implementation of slave legislation. That discussion in turn will serve to focus onto one country the general claims of the two opposing groups mentioned above and will help to move the debate away from the much questioned comparative mildness of Latin American slavery to the more measurable performance of a key institution. The discussion will show, I hope, that the legislation was not a dead letter, but rather that many judges and attorneys made remarkable efforts to protect the slave.

A final word on sources. The bulk of the information contained in this essay has been derived from the judicial records of the Audiencia of New Granada, which are located in the Archivo Nacional in Bogotá, Colombia. Most of the cases referred to in the text were submitted to the Royal Audiencia for adjudication on appeal from judgments given in provincial and municipal courts throughout the Viceroyalty.

In colonial times, as today, the greater part of the inhabitants of New Granada were settled in the western third of the country, despite its more rugged character. Three parallel extensions of the Andes fracture the greater part of western Colombia; they in turn are separated and drained by two large river systems, the

Magdalena and the Cauca. A large plain that is alternately arid and swampy lies between the northern foothills of these ranges and the Caribbean Sea.

New Granada enjoyed a variety of climates, flora, and fauna, and a wealth of natural resources. The most precious of these were the gold deposits in and adjacent to the Central and Western Cordilleras, specifically in the provinces of Antioquia, the Chocó, and Popayán. Another important resource was the fertile valleys and alluvial plains that lent themselves to the cultivation of sugar, cacao, and indigo and to the raising of cattle. In the exploitation of both types of resources the labor of African slave gangs was employed.

Notwithstanding the presence of these natural resources, the economic development of New Granada was very slow. It was hampered by natural obstacles to transportation and communications that were practically insurmountable until the advent of modern highways and airways. It was also hampered by uninspired and ineffective government. Fiscal policies were too rigid to fit the precise needs, at any given time, of the highly diversified economies of the coast, and of the mining, agricultural, and cattle-raising areas of the interior. Few royal representatives were able to see what really ailed the colony. And those few who did were neither able to persuade the crown to make the adequate reforms nor powerful enough to oblige the local magnates to sacrifice their personal gain for the long-range benefit of regions and the entire kingdom. For example, during most of the colonial period the Antioquia and the Chocó mining areas were little more than colonies of Popayán. All the activity in those areas was directed to the extraction of gold; nothing was put into the areas to favor their development. On the contrary, Antioquia and the Chocó continued to depend for their supplies and provisions on mule trains and canoes coming from Cartagena, Popayán, and Bogotá. Small miners were always on the verge of bankruptcy. They bought slaves and provisions on credit, counting on the slaves' paying for themselves. If, because of a bad season or bad luck, they were unable to meet their payments, their creditors sought to put their slaves in receivership and even sold them out of the mining area, disregarding laws prohibiting this practice.[4]

In 1739 New Granada was organized as a viceroyalty, and subsequent viceroys made some headway in revitalizing the economy. But this burst of development was short-lived. The disruption caused by the wars of independence undid the results of the Bourbon reforms, and the development of the New Granada economy had to await more propitious times.

Throughout the colonial period the population of New Granada had remained quite small.[5] The largest concentrations of Indians, and eventually of mestizos, were in the Eastern Cordillera around, and north of, Bogotá. Most whites resided in cities and towns, principally Bogotá, Cartagena, and Popayán; others were scattered in small villages and in the plantation and mining areas, surrounded by Amerindian or African populations. It was the misfortune of New Granada that its most profitable economic activities—commerce, mining, and plantations—developed in areas where native populations had been sparse or nonexistent. As a result, entrepreneurs of all kinds had to rely almost entirely on laborers imported from Africa. And these were never plentiful.[6] Requests by various New Granada interests for larger consignments of slaves were a constant refrain until 1791, when the *asiento* (contract) system was ended and the trade in slaves was liberalized. But then, although the demand persisted, the supply continued to be inadequate. Throughout the eighteenth century recurring conflicts with England, and in the first decade of the nineteenth century the Napoleonic Wars, had serious repercussions on the legitimate slave trade to New Granada.[7]

The slave institution in New Granada was greatly affected by these circumstances. The natural obstacles to economic development served to hinder the development of communication and cohesion among the widely dispersed slave gangs, making widespread slave revolts rather unlikely. The generally low degree of economic development precluded the type of excesses in the exploitation of slave labor that usually accompanied intense competition for markets and profits. The short supply of slave hands, and the difficulty and cost of replacing them, discouraged all but the most foolish masters from wearing out healthy young slaves within a few years. Stated differently, the New Granada circumstances that we have described helped to fashion a colony and a culture in which medieval Iberian attitudes and practices regarding slaves were able to survive and even to evolve.[8]

Finally, New Granada slavery, especially in the eighteenth century, felt the impact of attorneys and magistrates who strove to implement legislation favorable to the slaves. This is not to say that they always succeeded. Nonetheless, a remarkable, and heretofore unsuspected, effort was made by the courts to protect the slave. It is to the study of this effort that we now turn our attention.

The legislation governing slaves in New Granada, as in the rest of Spanish America, was of two kinds: one Castilian and the other American. The Castilian legislation, nearly all of which can be found in the *Siete Partidas* of Alfonso the Wise (completed in 1265 but promulgated only in 1348)[9] contained repressive as well as protective elements. But with the passage of time, the evolution of Castilian servitude and the institution's transfer to the Indies, some of the repressive elements seem to have fallen into disuse —for instance, the invalidity of slave testimony in courts of law, the inability of slaves to own property, and the liability of freedmen to reenslavement for improper behavior toward their former master.[10] Many of the protective elements, however, survived, very probably because of the universal character of the principles that they expressed. According to these principles, slavery was evil, a necessary evil that did not alter or diminish the human nature of the slave. Liberty was pictured as one of the greatest of human possessions.[11] Freedom remained a legitimate goal for the slave, and his attainment of it was facilitated by a variety of means such as manumission, liberation by a third person, and self-purchase with gift money.[12] Claims to freedom were privileged cases in royal courts of law. The slave, furthermore, had the right to be treated as a human being. Masters who treated their slaves cruelly were liable to punishment, and their victims could demand that they be sold to someone who would exercise his authority more benevolently.[13]

The American legislation, contained principally in the *Recopilación de Leyes de Indias*,[14] was enacted to cope with the particular problems arising from the Negro slave situation in the Indies. The protective provisions of this legislation were largely echoes of the older legislation adopted to colonial needs. Masters were ordered to Christianize and to Hispanicize their slaves.[15] They were reminded to feed and clothe them adequately,[16] and not to abuse them. Indeed, masters were berated for punishing their slaves more cruelly than the gravity of their offenses warranted. Most important of all, slaves were told that they should report cases of abuse to the officials charged with the protection of slaves for possible legal redress.[17] However, as we shall see later in this essay, colonial or American legislation regarding African slaves was predominantly repressive.

The Royal Cédula of 1789[18] (the Spanish Black Code) was an enlightened attempt to combine the better elements of both the Castilian and the American compilations. The objective was to protect slaves while strengthening slavery. The Cédula prescribed in paternalistic detail such matters as education, food, clothing, work, holidays, recreation, housing, health care, morality, duties, discipline, and punishment. Nevertheless, in a discreet move away from traditional practices, the decree indirectly discouraged the practice of manumission by omitting any mention of it.[19] In spite of efforts by colonial planters to have the decree rescinded, the Cédula of 1789 remained in force,[20] and although efforts to implement many of its provisions were not particularly successful in New Granada, the very existence of the decree added weight to the arguments of the slave defense attorneys.

As has been noted, the slave in Spanish America had certain basic rights and he was encouraged to report his master to judicial authorities when those rights were flaunted. In New Granada the lawsuits that followed such complaints reveal not only the evil but also, indirectly, the good done to black slaves by their masters. They also reveal in what way and to what extent men of law protected slave plaintiffs.

Slaves had recourse to the law in all sorts of instances. Principal among these were the vindication of freedom unjustly denied them, the resistance of masters to self-purchase by slaves, and the denunciation of cruel treatment. The easiest and most common way for a slave to acquire freedom was through manumission. The custom was generally accepted as a meritorious act of corporal mercy, and evidence shows that in New Granada it was practiced rather frequently.[21] Often masters freed their slaves while they themselves still lived, but more usually they did so in their will. As might be expected, manumissions by will were sometimes challenged in the courts by frustrated or outraged heirs. However, if a slave could prove authentic and legitimate manumission, his freedom was assured against those who would keep him in servitude.

More controversial and less easy of solution were cases of informal manumissions that had never been notarized, masters who left more than one will or who were thought to have made a will while of unsound mind, heirs who forgot about the manumission or "lent" the slaves to friends and forgot to reclaim them, and slaves who simply lost their writ of manumission. A striking example of manumission contests is the one provoked by Javiera Londoño, of Antioquia. In her second and last will she manumitted almost a hundred slaves and gave them the right to pan for gold in a section of her mine. The executor of the first will contested the validity of the second will and convinced the ecclesiastical court (for he was a cleric) that the testator had been senile when she had drawn it up. Another argument in favor of the first will (and another reason for its presentation in an ecclesiastical tribunal) had been its lavish provisions for the souls of Purgatory. Weighing the benefits to the holy souls that would be derived from the first will, and the benefits to the slaves included in the second will, the court did not hesitate to give preference to the first. However, as a result of slow and lengthy procedures, the second will had already been implemented before it was declared invalid. Thus the law officials and the executor of the first will found themselves in the very awkward position of having to rescind the manumission of a hundred slaves and the sale of the mine. Further complicating the situation was the lack of sympathy of some local officials for the executor, and for the court's decision regarding the validity of the first will. Nevertheless the validity of the first will was upheld. There is no record of how it was carried out. Besides illustrating the emancipatory sentiment of one slave owner, the case suggests the kind of obstacle that legally manumitted slaves sometimes had to overcome before enjoying freedom.[22]

The possibility of a slave's purchasing his freedom, with gift money destined to that purpose, was foreseen by the *Siete Partidas* and occasionally practiced in New Granada. More common, however, was self-purchase with money earned by the slave himself.[23] Now it should be noted that the *Siete Partidas* had not preserved the Roman tradition of the slave *peculium* (allowance or pocket money). On the contrary, it forbade ownership by slaves.[24] Yet the opposite custom had become rather widely practiced in New Granada. Because of the underdeveloped condition of the areas where many slaves labored, and the large investment that providing food for them represented, masters often left the procurement of staples up to the slaves themselves. Under this arrangement slaves worked for their own sustenance on Sundays and holy days and other free days, and they used tools, seed, and plots of land lent them by their masters. They were even allowed to work the master's mine for their own benefit on their free days. Consequently, some slaves were able to accumulate small items of property, sums of money, even animals and plots of land.

Another practice that led to similar results was that of allowing slaves to earn wages by serving people other than their masters. They were required to remit a certain stipend daily to their master, and when this was not done they were punished. When, however, they earned more than the required stipend, they were allowed to retain the rest for themselves.

Originally it had not been anticipated that many slaves might eventually earn and save enough money to purchase their freedom. But in practice, especially in the mines, slaves were able to assemble considerable sums of money that they then offered to the master for a writ of manumission.[25] When this happened some masters complied graciously enough. Other slave owners, instead, sought to have the law against slave ownership enforced. Their attorneys argued that it was illegal for slaves to own anything. Tolerating ownership by slaves amounted to a capitulation on a matter of principle; it meant condoning the erosion of the very core of the institution. To prevent this, they maintained, certain minimal rules should be clearly established and enforced. When a master wanted to allow a slave to earn, he must say so explicitly. When he wanted to revoke the permission, he might do so at any time, and if the slave had acquired any property in the meanwhile, that property reverted to the master.[26] Lawyers defending slaves contended, to the contrary, that ownership by slaves was an ancient Iberian practice; that permission for the slave to own need not be explicit, it could be implicit; and that once given, the permission was irrevocable. Furthermore, they said, property acquired by a slave, with proper authorization, was inalienable. And indeed, in the great majority of cases the decisions handed down recognized the right of slaves to own property.[27]

Another tactic of the promaster attorneys was to charge that even with the permission to own property, a slave could not honestly earn enough money to purchase his freedom. He had to steal it, and the burden of proving the contrary rested with the slave himself. Proslave lawyers rejected the blanket charge of dishonesty and denounced the idea of putting the burden of proof on the slave. To do so would be counter to the spirit of the law that intended to facilitate the slaves' emancipation. Rather, the burden of proof of dishonest gain should lie with the accusing master.[28] In most of the cases encountered, magistrates recognized the slave's money as being truly his own. Indeed, on a number of occasions, slaves were assisted in obtaining restitution of belongings that their masters had confiscated.[29] As a result of this recognition of slave ownership, a slave with the necessary funds could nearly always effect his self-redemption. Protesting against this last conclusion, promaster attorneys argued that the law forbade the forcible alienation of property. Even granting the slave's honesty and his right to earn money, a master could not legally be forced to part with his property. Proslave attorneys countered: the law's intent was to prevent the forcible sale of brute and inanimate property, not the sale of human beings. Refusing to accept a slave's purchase price was clearly against the spirit of the law.[30] In most cases, attorneys representing slaves who wanted to purchase their freedom won their cases. The sample case that we present below is a good illustration, not of self-purchase, but of the masters' resistance to the forcible sale of their slaves.

José Ibarrondo, a freedman, had given 300 pesos to Miguel Izquierdo for the redemption of his son, Juan Pedro Ibarrondo. Izquierdo accepted the money but refused to grant a writ of manumission. He argued that it was forbidden by the *Siete Partidas* to compel a master to part with his slaves, except in very specific cases that did not apply in the present instance. Furthermore, important jurists had denied the right of the courts to make exceptions to the laws. Izquierdo went on to recall the case of Barthola Arboleda. In 1776 she had complained to the Royal Audiencia that competitors were doing her and other citizens harm by conniving to redeem their slaves, thus depriving them of their much needed services. In response to the complaint, Joaquin de Mosquera, *oidor* of the Royal Audiencia, had issued an order restraining magistrates from compelling the redemptive sale of slaves, unless the redemption money had been acquired without fraud or deception, and unless there were other good reasons for releasing the slave. Using this decision as a precedent, Izquierdo contended that José and Juan Pedro had stolen the money and that there was no good reason why he should be compelled to free Juan Pedro. After due investigation, Prieto Dávila, the lieutenant governor of Popayán, adjudged that the money had been honestly acquired, thereby conforming with the order of Joaquin de Mosquera. He ignored the order's repressive measure against freeing slaves if, in spite of honest money, there was no other good reason for freeing them. Dávila ordered Izquierdo to cooperate in the redemption of Juan Pedro, stating that in many recent cases of similar nature handled by the Royal Audiencia, the decisions had been in favor of the slaves. Furthermore, he reminded Izquierdo, the laws did not prohibit the redemption of slaves with honest money. The law forbidding the compulsory sale of possessions by masters should not be applied indiscriminately to slaves and jewels. Rather, the spirit of the law clearly indicated that the slaves must be favored. Izquierdo of course appealed Dávila's decision to the Royal Audiencia. Unfortunately, the archives contain nothing further on the case.[31]

The practice of manumission among slaveholders in Latin America is rather common knowledge, and that of self-redemption only less so. Much less well known is the practice of denouncing masters for extreme cruelty.[32] The official in charge of receiving and examining these complaints was the *síndico procurador*, a court-appointed attorney who included among his duties giving legal aid to the indigent and to the slave. (After 1789 the attorney assigned to defend slaves was given the title *protector de esclavos*.) This kind of official existed on the local, regional, and the Royal Audiencia levels. They were the ones called upon to defend slaves' ownership of property, to obtain recognition of their manumission, to help them to effect their manumission, or to help them to effect their self-purchase. Above all they were called upon to protect slaves from cruel masters and even to deliver slaves from bondage to such masters. Once a denunciation had been made and its validity had been ascertained by a preliminary investigation, the *síndico procurador* initiated a suit against the master. If he won his case and the master was found guilty, the court ordered that a new master be found for the slave. Not infrequently masters and slaves appealed unfavorable decisions to the regional court and even to the Royal Audiencia.

Naturally, the prosecution of such offenses set the stage for vehement legal battles between attorneys defending masters and those protecting the slaves. Since promaster attorneys could not deny that the law encouraged such denunciations, they had recourse to two types of defense. First of all, the right of the master to punish his slaves was absolutely necessary. How else could he educate his slaves, correct them, get them to work and work well? Even a father, they said, had the right and the duty to inflict punishment on his disobedient sons. Besides, the slaves were brutes, and brutality was the only language they understood. Furthermore, restricting the master to twenty-five lashes (as did the Black Code of 1789), reprimanding him, and even penalizing him, seriously weakened discipline among his slaves. Indeed, it encouraged his charges to disobey and to neglect their work, for they knew that if the master punished them they could run to the law for protection and have him punished in turn. The second type of promaster defense was to quibble over what constituted cruel treatment, to deny that the treatment meted out to the slave had been really cruel, or to claim that the punishment had been richly deserved. Certainly twenty-five lashes were far too few to produce any worthwhile results, whereas a few hundred lashes were much more effective. These hundred or more lashes had always been allowed along with stocks, chains, and imprisonment. Treatment that some considered cruel, such as rubbing urine and salt in wounds and on welts after a lashing, was merely medicinal. Slave deaths following punishment were obviously accidental. After all, who would be so foolish as to destroy his own property? Unknown to their master, such slaves had been suffering from some disease or they had become infected with some illness after punishment had been inflicted. These deaths were entirely unpremeditated and should not be imputed to a master's cruelty.[33]

Proslave attorneys conceded the necessity of punishment, but denied that slaves were such brutes that cruel punishment was the only language they could understand. They contended, to the contrary, that if masters were to give their slaves better treatment, if they were to punish them only when necessary and with greater moderation, then there would be fewer slaves running away or joining up with the outlaw maroons. On the subject of deterioration of slave discipline they were silent. In general, however, proslave attorneys did not have to argue very much if they had concrete evidence to prove extreme cruelty. The testimony of other slaves, and often the wounds and scars on a slave's body, or the condition of his health, were eloquent proof of extreme cruelty.

But prosecuting masters for mistreatment was not an easy assignment. Slave masters were sensitive to having their reputation stained by such an accusation, and worse, by a possible conviction. Hence they fought these cases with every means at their disposal, causing the proceedings to drag on indefinitely and sometimes making life even more difficult for the slaves involved.[34] Furthermore, masters convicted of mistreatment were seldom punished to the extent that proslave attorneys considered just. Indeed, the most common penalty was the compulsory sale of the slave in question and occasionally the payment of the costs of the case. Consequently, proslave lawyers had recourse to another approach. It consisted in avoiding direct confrontation with the master and in persuading him that it would be to his advantage to sell the slave on his own initiative or to allow the slave himself to seek another master. Thus the slave would escape from a despotic master while the latter would save face and be rid of a troublesome slave. Nonetheless, whether reliance was placed on persuasion or on the coercive power of the courts, a number of masters still offered considerable resistance. They protested that such forcible sales deprived them of well-trained and consequently very valuable slaves. Moreover, a matter of principle was involved: the right of a master to discipline his slaves as he saw fit.[35]

The following case of an extraordinary slave master illustrates well the type of resistance that "protectors of slaves" and magistrates had to deal with. Seven slaves belonging to Pedro Elejalde sought refuge with judicial authorities and accused their master of untold crimes of cruelty and neglect. Elejalde was not a man to back down. Rather than deny the accusations, he justified his behavior. Condemned by the local court, he was exonerated by the Royal Audiencia, which condemned the court officials for irregular and partial proceedings. Appeal followed appeal and went from the Royal Audiencia to the Consejo Supremo de Indias and back to the Royal Audiencia. Having begun in 1797, the matter ended in 1809 with Elejalde finally paying only the up-keep of the seven slaves during the original trial in 1793.[36] Unlike Elejalde, the ordinary slave master was unable to resist the law and the persuasive arguments of the slave attorneys.

In a number of cases of alleged cruelty, the forcible sale of slaves seems to have been well deserved, and it was certainly a boon to the slaves. In other cases, however, it does not seem that the treatment had been extremely cruel by most standards.[37] For instance, the potential harm of moving with a master to an area of difficult climate was sometimes considered sufficient justification for the court's intervention.[38] In effect, attorneys who argued such cases were gradually amplifying the legal significance of the term "extreme cruelty." Although it continued to mean excessive pain and harm inflicted on a slave, the term was also coming to connote considerable discomfort and inconvenience, and even what modern divorce courts refer to as incompatibility and mental cruelty. Indeed, in one instance it was argued that the sacred institution of marriage allowed for legal separation; all the more so should slavery since it had nothing of the sacredness of marriage.[39] Another effective approach of the proslave attorneys was to insist that the lot of the slave was of its very nature misera-ble, and that the slave's only means of easing or diminishing that misery was to seek a better master.[40]

That many attorneys in New Granada defended the slaves, orated against the masters, and fought for the implementation of protective slave legislation is worthy of note. Even more impor-tant is the fact that these attorneys, working in an official capacity, sought to amplify the interpretation and application of this legis-lation. Indeed they actively, though unconsciously, contributed to a process whereby slavery was slowly evolving in the direction of contractual labor.[41] But proslave attorneys could not have argued as they did, challenging the wealthy and modifying the slave institution, if they had not enjoyed the support of the magistracy, of the Royal Audiencia. The very fact that a few masters were punished for maltreating slaves and quite a few more were obliged to sell maltreated slaves, the fact that masters were obliged to accept slave-redemption money and grant a writ of manumission in exchange—all of this indicates a magistracy that actively favored the implementation of protective slave legislation. They appointed capable men to defend slaves at the Royal Audiencia level. They encouraged the line of argumentation used by proslave attorneys by deciding cases in their favor. To masters who complained of, and wanted to sue, "protectors of slaves" for their supposedly exaggerated and obnoxious zeal in investigating denunciations of cruelty, the Royal Audiencia answered: The protectors are only doing their duty. Restraining them in their efforts to protect the slaves would frustrate the clear intention of the royal lawgiver.[42]

Protecting the rights of slaves in matters pertaining to liberty, ownership, and humane treatment occupied many attorneys and involved a surprising number of slaves. But it would be unrealistic to expect that the majority of African slaves in New Granada had cause and opportunity to avail themselves of this protection. Most of them had no legitimate claim to liberty, no talent or opportunity for acquiring enough property to purchase their writ of manumission, and perhaps insufficient provocation to denounce their masters for excessive cruelty. Admittedly, among those who did have cause some were prevented from doing so by vigilant masters, or they were badly served by *sindicos-procuradores* who forfeited professional integrity rather than lose the friendship of magistrates, slave owners, and relatives. But all things considered, the number of slaves who obtained redress and the number of protectors who fulfilled their obligations seriously remain impressive.

Leaving aside the question of extreme corporal punishment, it remains for us to consider the rights of slaves to the necessities of life, to protection from overwork, to the practice of religion, and to marriage. As we have already seen, there were laws that ordered masters to give their slaves the necessary food, clothing, shelter, and health care and to avoid overworking them. But it is difficult to determine to what extent masters observed these laws, since the court records contain few references to such matters. One can only draw tentative conclusions. There was no doubt considerable, though not necessarily malicious, neglect in some of these areas. But complaints of inadequate food and clothing and of overwork usually accompanied more serious denunciations of extreme cruelty. Indeed, such accusations seem to have been thrown in to buttress and give background to a denunciation of extreme cruelty. In a few cases where an investigation of neglect or overwork was carried out, the investigator was unable to come to any conclusion.[43] Several factors could explain this. Until the promulgation of the Royal Cédula of 1789 there was no objective or precise criterion regarding proper care and reasonable demands of work. And testimony from fellow slaves or from neighbors was often contradictory.[44] On the other hand, external circumstances were such in New Granada that the implementation of these laws possibly did not constitute a great problem. Staple foods were relatively easy to raise or gather, and for both slaves and free men they consisted of maize, plantains, beans, and yucca. Clothing and shelter were not items of prime necessity either, since most plantations and mines were located in tropical regions and the needs of the slaves were very modest. The tendency to overwork slaves does not seem to have been very widespread, judging by the small number of accusations to this effect. As we have seen, masters were under no great pressure from competitors. Evidence on health care is rather skimpy. It is usually mentioned in connection with the nursing care given or not given after a lashing, but there are also references to medical treatment for heart disease, ulcers, and various external wounds. Finally, the only old and infirm slaves mentioned in the documents were either domestic slaves, or field slaves on former Jesuit plantations. No direct evidence was found that old and infirm slaves were turned out or freed to spare the master useless expense, or that the mortality rate was particularly high and old age rare.[45]

The crown promulgated its policy for the Christianization of African slaves several times. These laws stipulated that slaves had to be properly indoctrinated in their new religion.[46] That this was or could be done effectively is doubtful except in the case of beloved domestic slaves. Priests were scarce and preferred urban assignments, whereas most slaves worked in mines and on plantations. Sunday mass attendance by slaves was irregular because of distance or because the slaves preferred to stay home and work on their own account. The parish priest of Santa Ana, near the mine of Mariquita, offered to catechize slaves on weekdays if they would come to the church for an hour each afternoon. The mine director refused to interrupt the slaves' work, and would only consent to let them out from work at three P.M. Even then, he insisted, instruction would have to be given at the entrance of the mine.[47] On the subject of Christian marriage the records investigated reveal less than a handful of instances in which priests defended a slave's right to marry the person of his choice notwithstanding his master's opposition.[48] On the subject of facilitating the conjugal life of slaves owned by different masters, the record is even leaner. No evidence was found to indicate that an effort was made by ecclesiastics to reunite spouses who belonged to different masters living far apart. Furthermore, very little if anything appears to have been done to foster the family life of slaves or to keep family members from being separated.[49]

Colonial legislation governing the behavior of black slaves was quite restrictive. They were not allowed to go about after curfew without carrying written permission;[50] they were forbidden to carry arms,[51] to purchase or sell intoxicating beverages,[52] or to wear clothing reserved for persons of upper classes.[53] Running away was of course a frequent slave offense, and provisions were made in law for its punishment. A worse crime than running away was to join with other runaways or find refuge in a maroon settlement hidden away in the bush. Numerous and very detailed provisions came from the crown indicating how such slaves should be pursued, captured, and punished.[54]

That much of the American legislation for black slaves was restrictive should not surprise us. Wherever slaves were present in any number, neighboring whites felt more secure if they knew that the slaves were being kept under control. Drunken and armed slaves could be destructive, runaway slaves were usually mischievous, and maroons were downright dangerous marauders. From the evidence at hand it seems that the legislation described above was rather poorly implemented. The court records contain hardly any mention of slaves' breaking curfew laws, and on the few occasions when it is mentioned, no particular importance is given to it. More than likely the law enforcement officers were more concerned with the activity that took place while curfew was being broken. Indeed, an extensive reading of the documents leads one to suspect that slaves went about with relative impunity after curfew, at least in the towns and cities. They visited friends and lovers; they gathered in bars to drink and gamble; they indulged in mischief ranging from petty theft to arson and murder.

The laws forbidding black slaves to sell or buy intoxicating beverages seem to have been disregarded. Although reference is sometimes made in court proceedings to the fact that a criminal had been drinking just prior to a murder, or that such and such a bar was a regular haven for idle slaves, no penalties were invoked against the slaves or the bar proprietors for such infractions of the liquor laws.[55]

Notwithstanding the laws regarding clothing, slaves dressed as their masters or they themselves could afford. On special festival occasions slaves borrowed and displayed the fine clothes and jewelry of indulgent masters and mistresses.[56] A more serious matter was the infraction of injunctions against the bearing of arms. At times violence broke out among slaves,[57] between slaves and their masters and overseers,[58] between slaves and townsmen.[59] On all these occasions the slaves were found to have arms. Sporadic efforts were made to implement the laws prohibiting the practice, but they proved ineffectual. It was only when a slave uprising seemed imminent that officials took any kind of concerted action. In 1737 the governor of the Chocó informed his lieutenant of Nóvita that the situation among the slaves of the area was explosive and that a general uprising was feared. Both of them had vivid recollections of an uprising in their province nine years before that had taken the lives of fourteen white miners.[60] Consequently, the lieutenant governor of Nóvita ordered the forcible collection of all arms and munitions in the possession of Negro slaves. He pushed his precautions to the point of ordering that even mining tools be collected every evening on pain of a thousand-peso fine. In this instance the prohibition to sell arms to blacks was of course strongly enforced.[61]

New Granada masters, like masters in many other slaveholding colonies, were plagued with runaways. Admittedly, cruel treatment, or the fear of being cruelly punished, was the usual cause for these flights. Although the laws against flight and the penalties invoked against runaways were very severe,[62] few instances of strict implementation were found. Regarding the capture of these runaways, officials contented themselves with sending out notices to other officers in the area asking them to be on the lookout for slaves fitting a particular description. When it came to maroons, officials were even more reluctant to act, since many expeditions to capture such runaways had cost a great deal in time, money, and human lives but had brought back very few slaves.[63] Regarding penalties, court officials left the punishing of ordinary runaway slaves up to the masters. Rather they tried, and punished, the slaves for crimes committed during their escape. The courts also guarded captured runaways until the master came to fetch them, and adjudged bounties for the capture of runaways and more especially of maroons. These hardened runaways, however, were seldom captured alive. They preferred to die resisting capture.

Altogether, restrictive slave legislation was not rigidly enforced in New Granada. The reasons for this are not very hard to find.

The constables could not enforce the laws with any degree of regularity and efficiency, because the laws and regulations were very numerous, and often contradictory or picayune. Jails were not secure, and prison breaks were a regular occurrence. And law enforcement officers had more pressing things to do than arrest and discipline the impoverished slaves of negligent masters. This was true in the cities and towns, and even more so in the rural areas. Besides, magistrates were overburdened with other kinds of litigation. They could not be bothered dealing with the misdeeds of slaves unless they were criminal.

The nature of the institution of African slavery was the same, in principle, in all of colonial Spanish America. But the circumstances that obtained in different colonies gave the institution a variety of distinctive features. In New Granada these features were formed under the influence of a fragmented topography, the isolation of the sparse population, and the weak and slowly developing economy. But most important among the influences that marked African slavery in New Granada were the slave attorneys and the magistrates, many of whom were dedicated to the implementation of those laws and the observance of those customs that made the slave institution more humane. On the one hand, they did not enforce the more restrictive legislation very strictly. And although the observance of the protective legislation regarding food, clothes, health care, and work is difficult to document, it is very probable that the degree of enforcement depended on the distance from centers of civil authority. The same may be said of the protection of the basic rights of slaves. Notwithstanding these qualifications, the slave attorneys and the magistrates vindicated, in an impressive number of cases, the rights of the slaves as they were put forth in the *Siete Partidas*, and as these rights were amplified in the relatively humane environment of New Granada. Notarized manumissions were recognized, ownership of property and the possibility of self-purchase were vindicated, and badly treated slaves were assisted in obtaining release from cruel masters and sale to another. The men of law fostered the evolution of a system of slavery that was more akin to contractual labor than it was to slavery. Whether they did this exclusively out of a traditional preoccupation with protecting the rights of the oppressed, or whether they were inspired by the ideas of the Enlightenment, is difficult to establish at this time. Given the conservative nature of the legal profession of Spanish society, and of the educated class in the kingdom of New Granada, and given also the cooperation by *oidores* (justices) of the Royal Audiencia itself in many decisions favorable to black slaves, it is more than likely that the features of the slave institution in New Granada resulted from a natural development of traditional legal principles rather than from a secret campaign to bring the institution to an end.

Notes

[1]The precise territorial limits of New Granada changed more than once during the eighteenth century. In this essay New Granada corresponds to modern-day Colombia, especially to the western third of that country. As regards time span, documents dating from 1700 to 1811 have been used. A more extensive study of the subject of this essay may be found in the author's unpublished dissertation, "The Observance of Negro Slave Legislation in Colonial New Granada" (Columbia University, 1968).

[2]Gilberto Freyre, *The Masters and the Slaves* (New York, 1956; first Brazilian edition 1933); Frank Tannenbaum, *Slave and Citizen. The Negro in the Americas* (New York, 1947); Stanley Elkins, *Slavery. A Problem in American Institutional and Intellectual Life* (New York, 1963).

[3]Charles R. Boxer, *The Golden Age in Brazil, 1695-1750: Growing Pains of a Colonial Society* (Berkeley, Cal., 1962), *Race Relations in the Portuguese Colonial Empire, 1415-1825* (Oxford, 1963); Stanley Stein, *Vassouras. A Brazilian Coffee County, 1850-1900* (Cambridge, Mass. 1957); Marvin Harris, *Patterns of Race in the Americas* (New York, 1964).

[4]Emilio Robledo, *Bosquejo biográfico del Señor Oidor Juan Antonio Mon y Velarde, Visitador de Antioquia*, 1785-1788, 2 vols. (Bogotá, 1954), 1: 73; Jesus Maria Hennao and Gerardo Arrubla, *History of Colombia*, trans. and

ed. J. Fred Rippy (Chapel Hill, N.C., 1938), pp. 98-196; Gavriel Giraldo Jaramillo, ed., *Relaciones de Mando de los Virreyes de la Nueva Granada, Memórias economicas* (Bogotá, 1954).

[5] Angel Rosenbladt, *La Población Indígena y el Mestizaje en América*, 2 vols. (Buenos Aires, 1954). According to the author's calculations there were 850,000 Indians in New Granada in 1492 (1: 102); 825,000 people in 1570 of whom 10,000 were white, 15,000 Negro, mestizo or mulatto, and 800,000 Indian; 750,000 people in 1650 of whom 50,000 were white, 80,000 Negro and mulatto, 20,000 mestizo, and 600,000 Indian; and 1,327,000 in 1825 (1: 36a, 59, 88).

[6] Francisco Silvestre, *Descripción del Reyno de Santo Fé de Bogotá* (1789), published in Bogotá, 1950. According to this author the Audiencia of Santa Fé, in 1789, had a population of 826,550, of whom 44,637 were slaves. Suggestive of the sparse population, even at that time, and its distribution are some statistics taken from the same Silvestre: Santa Fé de Bogotá, city, 18,161 (with 762 slaves, 0.04 percent); province of Cartagena, 118,378 (9,622 of 8 percent slaves); province of Santa Marta, 39,942 (3,988 or 9 percent slaves); province of Mariquita, 47,138 (4,083 or 8 percent slaves), province of Antioquia, 48,604 (8,931 or 18 percent slaves); province of the Chocó, 15,286 (5,916 or 38 percent slaves); province of Popayan, 64,463 (12,441 or 19 percent slaves).

[7] For example, during the period 1713-1730, under the British Asiento, only 2,807 2/3 pieces were introduced into the port of Cartagena. Rosenbladt, *La Población Indígena*, 1: 223, where the author cites Torre Revello, *Historia de la Nación Argentina*, 4, Part 1: 515. See also James F. King, "Negro Slavery in New Granada", *Greater America, Essays in Honor of Hubert Eugene Bolton* (Berkeley, Cal., 1945), pp. 295-318, especially pp. 304-307; Jaramillo, *Relaciones de Mando*, pp. 44-61.

[8] "It was those provisions of slave legislation that most nearly coincided with the popular attitude toward slavery which commanded respect and observance.... [c]ustom unobtrusively reigned supreme." King, "Negro Slavery in New Granada," p. 310.

[9] *Las Siete Partidas del Rey Don Alfonso el Sabio cotejadas con vários codices antiguos por la Real Academia de la História*, 3 vols. (Madrid, 1807).

[10] *Siete Partidas*, part. 3, tit. 21, ley 3; part. 4, tit. 21, ley 7; part. 3, tit. 30, ley 16; part. 4, tit. 22, ley 9.

[11] *Siete Partidas*, part. 3, tit. 5, ley 6, "porque todos los derechos del mundo siempre ayudaron a la libertat": tit. 14, ley 5; tit. 33, regla 1; part. 4, tit. 5, prólogo; tit. 21, ley 1; tit. 22, ley 1; tit. 22, ley 13.

[12]*Siete Partidas*, part. 3, tit. 2, ley 8.

[13]*Siete Partidas*, part. 4, tit. 21, ley 6; part. 7, tit. 8, ley 9; part. 4, tit. 22, ley 4.

[14]*Recopilación de leyes de los reinos de las Indias mandadas imprimir y publicar por la Magestad Católica del Rey don Carlos II, nuestro señor, Impresión hecha de orden del Real y Supremo concejo de las Indias* (Madrid, 1791; Consejo de Hispanidad, 1043), 3 vols. A number of royal decrees that were not included in the *Recopilación* may be found in collections such as *Acuerdos de la Real Audiencia del Nuevo Reino de Granada, 1551-1556* (Bogotá, 1947); Richard Konetzke, ed., *Documentos para la historia de la formación social de hispanoamérica. 1493-1810*, 3 vols. (Madrid, 1953-1963) (hereafter referred to as *Acuerdos* and *Documentos*, respectively).

[15]Manuel Josef de Ayala, *Diccionario de gobierno y legislación de Indias, Colección de Documentos inéditos para la historia de Ibero-América*, 4 vols. (Madrid, 1929), 4: 372-373; Archivo Nacional de Historia (hereafter referred to as ANC), *Reales Cédulas y Ordenes* 19 (1771): 61-62; *Recopilación*, ley 5, tit. 5, lib. 7 (1527, 1538, 1541); ANC, *Minas*, Tolima 2 (1790): 839, 842-843.

[16]*Siete Partidas*, part. 4, tit. 21, ley 6; Konetzke, *Documentos*, 1, No. 154; *Disposiciones complementarias de las Leyes de las Indias*, 3 vols. (Madrid, 1935), 1: 263.

[17]*Acuerdos de la Real Audiencia* 1 (1556): 320; Konetzke, *Documentos*, 1, No. 154 (1545); (II, t. 1, No. 19, 1693); *Disposiciones Complementarias*, 1: 263 (1683); Felipe Barreda Laos, ed., "Regimen colonial de la esclavitud de los negros," *Revista de la Biblioteca Nacional* 16, No. 42, 253-393 (1710): 319-320.

[18]Barreda Laos, "Régimen colonial," pp. 351-363; Konetzke, *Documentos*, III, t. 2, No. 308.

[19]David Brion Davis, *The Problem of Slavery in Western Culture* (Ithaca, N.Y., 1966), p. 240.

[20]Magnus Mörner, *Race Mixture in the History of Latin America* (Boston, 1967), pp. 115-116.

[21]There were fifty-four cases involving outright manumission brought to the attention of the courts for reasons other than contest by heirs or executors, and thirty-one cases of manumission contested by heirs and executors. These numbers seem small. However, one must remember that most manumissions never became court cases. No one has yet counted the manumissions registered in the various Colombian notarial archives. Furthermore, in the absence of information on slave mortality,

one is led to conclude that the relatively low slave population in the late eighteenth century was largely the result of manumissions.

[22]The documents for this case are dispersed as follows: ANC, *Negros y Esclavos*, Antioquia, 6: 994-995, 3: 624-839, 4: 260-272, 1: 804-868; Bolívar, 12: 939-1050, 1: 442-643; and ANC, *Minas* (1771-1774): 7, 602-607. Hereafter *Negros y Esclavos* will be referred to as *NE*.

[23]*Siete Partidas*, part. 3, tit. 2, ley 8; part. 5, tit. 5, ley 45.

[24]*Siete Partidas*, part. 3, tit. 29, ley 3; part. 4, tit. 21, ley 7.

[25]The court cases are spread throughout the eighteenth century and represent the various population clusters of Santa Fé de Bogotá, Cartagena, Mopox, Santa Fé de Antioquia, Medellín, Popayán, and the towns of the present-day Santanders. More than sixty cases of self-purchase were encountered. This is relatively few, but one must keep in mind that they were cases of litigation. Unchallenged cases of self-purchase were not brought to the attention of the courts. An example of self-purchase in the mines is the case of crew captain Domingo Mina, who offered 775 castellanos for his freedom and that of his wife and child. He had earned it by working the master's tools during his own free time. The master asked for an additional 345 castellanos, which Domingo promptly paid. ANC, *NE*, Cauca 2 (1749): 665-768.

[26]*Archivo Histórico de Antioquia*, 32, No. 1045 (1792, Antioquia); ANC, *NE*, Boyacá, 2: 246 (1746, Muzo); Cauca, 2: 8-13v (1728, Popayán). Archivo Histórico de Antioquia, hereafter referred to as AHA.

[27]ANC, *NE*, Bolívar, 2: 586v (1749, Cartagena); Boyacá, 2: 602 (1749, Leiva); Santander, 2: 977v (1772, Cúcuta); Santander, 4: 581v-592v (1811, Cúcuta).

[28]ANC, *NE*, Cauca, 3: 849 (1790, Popayán); Cundinamarca, 2: 411 (1750, Popayán); Antioquia, 2: 635v (1748, Simiti); Cauca, 2: 10 (1728 Popayán); Bolívar, 2: 438v-439, 586v (1749, Cartagena); Cundinamarca, 9: 897-902 (1796, Chocó).

[29]ANC, *NE*, Bolívar, 11 (1755): 777v; Bolívar, 9 (1760): 505v; Santander, 2 (1772): 977v; Antioquia, 1 (1805): 97; Santander 4 (1811): 581v-582v.

[30]ANC, *NE*, Cauca, 3 (1790): 848-849, 854v, 876v; Cundinamarca, 6 (1776): 626-702; *Siete Partidas*, part. 5, tit. 5, ley 3.

[31]ANC, *NE*, Cauca, 3: 854v, 876v, 884 (1790, Popayán).

[32]*Siete Partidas*, part. 4, tit. 21, ley 6.

[33]ANC, *NE*, Antioquia, 1: 612-642 (1771); Antioquia, 1: 159-186 (1797); Cundinamarca, 5: 978-981 (1775, Socorro); Magdalena, 1:

460-538 (1808, Valledupar); Tolima, 2: 793-815 (1749, Ibagué); 1: 386-633 (1782, Mariquita); 2: 935-959 (1803, La Plata); AHA, 33 No. 1078 (1799, Antioquia).

[34] ANC, *NE*, Cundinamarca, 1: 321 (1803, Santa Fé de Bogotá); Santander, 3: 947v, 1002 (1803, Cúcuta); 1: 644-646 (1809, Pamplona); Tolima, 3: 397-400, (1764, Neiva).

[35] ANC, *NE*, Cundinamarca, 6: 626-702 (1776, Popayán); Cauca, 3: 847-932 (1790, Popayán).

[36] The Elejalde case papers are strewn about in a number of different tomes: ANC, *NE*, Antioquia, 4: 273-439; Antioquia, 6: 1-197; 1: 950-953; 2: 1-382; 1: 880939; 1070 (1797-1808).

[37] ANC, *NE*, Bolívar, 12: 284, 295, 303 (1788, Barranquilla); AHA, 32, No. 1040 (1790, Medellín).

[38] ANC, *NE*, Cauca, 3 (1790): 995; Cundinamarca, 4 (1799): 63134; Tolima, 1 (1804): 858-877; 2 (1804): 231-236.

[39] ANC, *NE*, Bolívar, 9: 956v (1760, Mompox).

[40] ANC, *NE*, Antioquia, 1 (1777): 703v; Cundinamarca, 4 (1760): 854.

[41] It does not seem that attorneys were trying to terminate the institution of slavery. Rather they were doing all in their power to humanize it.

[42] ANC, *Real Audiencia*, Magdalena, 1: 536 (1809, Valledupar).

[43] ANC, *NE*, Antioquia, 1: 701r, v, 702-708v (1777, Mompox); AHA, 34, No. 1120 (1803), No. 1166 (1803), No. 1441, 1-4r (1804); ANC, *NE*, Cauca, 1: 1000 (1802, Popayán); Cauca, 1: 969 (1804, Nóvita); Cauca, 1: 245-279 (1778, Popayán); Santander, 1: 972-974, 983-988 (1803, Cúcuta); Santander, 1: 1, 4v-5r (1809, Socorro).

[44] Among the court cases examined, the acceptance of Negro slave testimony as valid seemed to be the common practice, and on only one occasion was the testimony preceded by judicial torture as foreseen by the *Siete Partidas*. All slave witnesses had to take an oath to tell the truth, but unbaptized Negro slaves were unable to, since they were not Christian and the oath was a Christian one.

[45] AHA, 33, No. 1103b (1810); indirect evidence of such treatment is found in a decree of 1786 in AHA, 31, No. 1027, in which masters are reminded of their obligations toward old slaves.

[46] José Antonio Saco, *Historia de la esclavitud de la raza africana en el Nuevo Mundo y en especial en los paises américo-hispanos*, 4 vols. (Havana, 1938), 1: 95, 108; ANC, *Reales Cédulas y Ordenes*, 19: 61-62; *Minas*, Bolívar, 1: 1064-1065.

[47]Konetzke, *Documentos*, 3 t. 1, No. 220 (1771); ANC, *Minas*, Tolima, 3 (1799): 1138-1152.

[48]ANC, *NE*, Cundinamarca, 9 (1781): 845-856.

[49]ANC, *NE*, Boyacá, 1: 564-568; AHA, 30, No. 970; 32, No. 1040; 33, No. 1107; 39, No. 1139.

[50]*Recopilación*, ley 12, tit. 5, lib. 7 (1542); *Acuerdos*, 2 (1558): 108-109; Konetzke, *Documentos*, 1, No. 154 (1545).

[51]*Recopilación*, ley 14-18, tit. 5, lib. 7; ley 29, tit. 19, lib. 1; Konetzke, *Documentos*, 1, Nos. 92, 154, 197, 208; and 11, No. 120; *Acuerdos*, 1: 225-226.

[52]José P. Urueta, ed., *Documentos para la historia de Cartagena*, 2 vols. (Cartagena: 1887-1891), 1, No. 65 (1557-1573): 189-198; James J. Parsons, *Antioqueño Colonization in Western Colombia* (Baton Rouge, La., 1952), p. 119.

[53]*Recopilación*, ley 28, tit. 5, lib. 7 (1571); Jorge Juan and Antonio de Ulloa, *A Voyage to South America*, John Adams trans., abridged (New York, 1964), pp. 28-29.

[54]*Recopilación*, ley 24, tit. 5, lib. 7 (1540, 1574); ley 20, tit. 5, lib. 7 (1540, 1574); ley 20, tit. 5, lib. 7 (1540); ley 25, tit. 5, lib. 7 (1578); ley 26, tit. 5, lib. 7 (1610); ley 23, tit. 5, lib. 7 (1540); Konetzke, *Documentos*, 1, No. 154 (1545); *Acuerdos*, 1 (1566): 319-320.

[55]ANC, *NE*, Bolívar, 10 (1611): 1005-1038: Boyacá, 2 (1676): 545-554. From the absence of references to the liquor laws in eighteenth century cases, one is led to conclude that they were in abeyance.

[56]See note 52.

[57]ANC, *NE*, Tolima, 4 (1741): 15v; Cauca, 2 (1803): 573-578.

[58]For example, ANC, *NE*, Bolivar, 2 (1730): 150-152; Cundinamarca, 8 (1744): 853-863; Magdalena, 5 (1768): 910-932.

[59]ANC, *NE*, Cundinamarca, 9 (1758): 566-567.

[60]ANC, *Réales Cédulas y Ordenes*, 9 (1728): 225-227.

[61]ANC, *NE*, Cundinamarca, 9 (1737): 886-889.

[62]See note 51.

[63]ANC, *NE*, Cauca, 3 (1742-1753): 590-809. See also ANC, *NE*, 2 (1785): 203-456.

7

Slavery, Race, and Social Structure in Cuba During the Nineteenth Century

Franklin W. Knight

Franklin W. Knight provides students of slavery with another sharp warning that conditions of Latin American bondage were very much a function of time and place. As Knight demonstrates, until late in the eighteenth century, Cuba was a sleepy society where master and slave attempted tobacco cultivation and livestock raising with modest success. Relationships among blacks, whites, and mixed-bloods, both free and slave, were easygoing and patriarchal. Since Cuba's strategic location made it a prime target for foreign attacks, the island's sense of community was reinforced by this common danger.

With the nineteenth-century sugar boom, this relatively idyllic pattern of race relations drastically changed for the worse. Slaves were imported in enormous quantities, but never enough to satisfy the demand; and planters' opposition to manumission therefore increased. In an effort to augment production, the routine of plantation life was marked by greater regimentation and cruelty, while great increases in the size of both land-holdings and labor force drove a wedge between masters and slaves, disrupting the camaraderie of old. As the system became more rigid and coercive, servile revolts also increased. As slave disturbances grew, planters viewed the black masses around them with greater and greater fear and distrust. The result was more restrictions on the activities of all blacks, whether free or slave, and mounting racism, exacerbated when the

island came under United States control after the Spanish-American War.
In short, the human cost of economic prosperity was very high indeed.

R. B. T.

An enigmatic relationship exists between slavery and racism. In 1944 Eric Williams confidently remarked, after reviewing the American genesis, that "racism was the consequence of slavery."[1] Recently a number of able and respectable scholars have persuasively refuted that assertion, basing their arguments on the historically exclusionary tendencies of color, class, and occupation intrinsic to European cultures and the Christian religion.[2] Slavery, in some guise, manifested itself throughout the history of mankind, until the present day.[3] Race, with disconcerting semantic variety, became one aspect of group identification long before the European expansion in the fifteenth century. The traditions of both slavery and race are part and parcel of the evolution of Western culture. Nevertheless, the narrow correlation of slavery and race is a peculiarly American innovation, the unfortunate by-product of the transatlantic slave trade and the rise of export-oriented economies in the Americas. By the nineteenth century, as the Cuban case study exemplifies, precise group definition —and discrimination—assumed paramount importance in all American societies. Everywhere the position of the slave was legally defined and socially prescribed. In some places, and among some groups, the system of slavery was under attack. By the middle of the century the concept of race, like the concept of nation, was being forged eclectically from the universal body of political and philosophical ideas, and the local circumstances or reality. The impact of slavery on race relations in Cuba, therefore, must be viewed against this confusing and complex panorama.

The conversion of Cuba from a settler to a plantation society resulted from the conscious decisions of the emergent colonial bourgeoisie, along with the active support of the Spanish crown and its local administrators—especially Luis de las Casas y Aragorri (captain general, 1790-1796); Juan Procopio Basse-court y Bryas, Conde de Santa Clara (1796-1799); Salvador de Muro y Salazar, Marques de Someruelos (1799-1812); and José Cienfuegos y Jovellanos (1816-1819).[4] By 1830 the established order of the old settler society had almost completely disap-peared. Small towns and insignificant class and caste distinctions gave way to the massive importation of African slaves and the rapid expansion of the sugar cane plantation socioeconomic complex from Havana eastward to Camaguey. With the African slave trade under increased attack—and illegal since 1820—the Cubans complemented their labor force with Chinese indentured laborers and Mexican Indians after 1847.[5] This sugar revolution of the nineteenth century created new forces and new strains on the conventional structure and institutions of the society. The cleavages of race, color, and occupation were not new. But the plantation expanded, reinforced, and accentuated them—and in so doing, excessively permeated every facet of the society with the implications of slavery and race.[6]

Indeed, slavery and race dominated the social system. Between 1774 and 1860, Cuba experienced a revolution of startling pro-portions. The population increased from 171,620 to more than 1,396,530. The three castes of white, free colored, and slaves experienced rapid growth rates. The most dramatic and signifi-cant increase came among the slaves whose labor was crucial for the expansion of the plantations and the stimulation of the economic sector. Slaves accounted for more than 43 percent of the total island population in 1840—and the additional 15 per-cent of the free persons of color gave the nonwhite element a brief numerical preponderance.[7]

The purpose and rapidity of African slave input during the nineteenth century did not facilitate the slaves' incorporation into the society.[8] Almost all the new arrivals, or *bozales*, and a progressively larger proportion of the Cuban-born, or Creoles, ended up in large segregated work gangs on rural plantations.[9] The exigencies of a crudely efficient sugar production increased coercion and regimentation on the *ingenios* (sugar factories), thereby created unrest among the slaves, and in large measure alienated them further from the society. This economy and efficiency might have dominated racial consideration, but the reality in which the slaves found themselves was harsh and cruel. Revolts and rebellions fostered greater repression and more police measures in an ever-increasing cycle until 1844.[10] But revolts, rebellions, and repression reflected the development of two separate cultures in Cuba, reciprocally affecting each other. Differences of race, occupation, color, and religion promoted centripetal forces among the basic ethnic groups. Meanwhile, the intermediate and overlapping sector of free persons of color further complicated the situation.

Every institution, group, and class responded to the profound changes. The responses, however, were neither uniform nor stable, because the circumstances surrounding slavery and race continually changed. Above all, slavery and race transcended the parochial affairs of the island, merging in the dynamic interplay of imperial and international forces.[11] Even the two most traditional and conservative social institutions, the Spanish Catholic Church and the imperial bureaucracy, succumbed to the new developments.

The Spanish Catholic Church in Cuba during the nineteenth century faced a severe dilemma. On the one hand it had to uphold the principles of equality, humanitarianism, and paternalism that dated from the early sixteenth century. On the other hand, it found itself a much weakened institution, pitted against the royal administration and the local group of planters and merchants.[12] In theory the Church could not and did not abrogate its principles. But it confined its egalitarian view to religious matters and the afterlife. At the same time, it subscribed fully to the hierarchical concept of Spanish colonial society. The Church, therefore, supported, reinforced, and reflected the plantation structure with its methodical subordination and exploitation of the Afro-Cuban population. No evidence exists that the Church treated its own slaves any differently from the general body of slave owners—that is, some treated their slaves well and others badly, according to the diverse personalities of the owners.

The powerful prerogative of intercession that the Church enjoyed in the earlier period of Spanish colonialism no longer prevailed in Cuba, either against the bureaucrats or the planters. Whenever Church and state came into conflict, especially over the issue of interracial marriages, the state view dominated.[13] Spanish officials often disregarded the role of the Church; for example, they did not consult the Church in 1841 on the question of slavery. On the other hand, they bemoaned the decline of its influence in the island's affairs.[14]

The moral position of the Church probably reached its nadir during the nineteenth century. The general increase in anticlericalism in Spain and throughout Europe hardly helped the local Cuban situation, where priests had a reputation for "quite unclerical" behavior, corruption, and indifference.[15] Most important, however, the Church had signally failed to readjust to the novelties of plantation life. Most priests continued to be assigned to the towns, while the vast majority of slaves on the plantations went without the benefit of clergy, or at best had rather inadequate religious instruction. More than 50 percent of all the priests served in Havana province (401 out of 779), where they administered to less than 10 percent of all the slaves (32,808 out 373,000) and approximately 20 percent of the white population (140,261 out of 793,484). In the sugar-producing rural areas the vast majority of slaves, denied the services of the clergy, forged their religions from memories of Africa and grafted practices of the official Catholicism. The prevalence of essentially religious cults, such as the *Santeria* and the *Náñigo* (of the Abakuá secret society), among the slaves and the urban free Afro-Cubans served to reinforce the distinctions between the traditions of Africa and Spain then coexisting in Cuban society.[16] Unfortunately, these distinctions eventually reinforced the cleavages already present in the society and minimized the role of religion as an integrative force.[17]

The influence of slavery and race was equally prominent in the changing attitudes of the metropolitan administration. Unlike the Church, the Spanish crown only considered the reality of politics, devoid of the concerns of the divine and the afterlife. Its model of a corporate hierarchy for the society, although valid for Spain, broke down in the overseas colonies, where differences of race, color, and condition complicated the problems of justice and legality. The various attempts to codify and compile the laws attest to the complexity of the situation.[18] Moreover, the general principles of Spanish law always contrasted with the particular demands of the varied parts of the empire, infusing further contradiction and confusion to the body of laws.

The official attitude toward interracial marriage, a vexing social problem, graphically demonstrated the effect over time of altered circumstances and changing personnel and advice. Legislation on the subject tended to be congruent with the desires of responsible public opinion in the colonies, with the result that the crown subordinated its moral inclination to promote marriage and to augment the local population, in favor of local familial considerations and the strong aversion to interracial marriages that manifested itself at times.[19] The residual effects of the *Reconquista* and the offices of the Inquisition had started the official interest in marriage, especially for the members of the nobility. The Royal Pragmatic, issued for Spain in 1776, and extended to the colonies in 1778, was a reminder of this interest. But the social connotations of slavery and miscegenation led to a royal decree in 1805 (issued in Cuba in 1806) pertaining to "marriages between persons of known nobility with members of the castes of Negroes and mulattoes." Notwithstanding its title, the interpretations of this decree in Cuba—unlike its predecessors—established civil control over all marriages involving whites of any social class and age, and any nonwhite.[20]

According to Verena Martínez Alier, who studied a sample of 199 cases of interracial marriage in Cuba between 1810 and 1882, the decade of the 1830s represented a watershed in race relations. After that decade—which coincided with the maturation of the plantation slave society—the pattern of objections to interracial marriages shifted from parental dissent to individual initiative, while the government assumed full control in such affairs:

> It seems that particularly during the first three decades, the view predominated that mixed marriages could only be prevented through parental dissent, that is to say, that plebeians—I did not find a single case of a nobleman wanting to marry a colored person—had no need to obtain official permission for a marriage across the color line. Whereas from the thirties onward, the impression became increasingly generalized that inequality in color constituted a civil impediment to marriage for which dispensation *must always be obtained* [emphasis added].[21]

Although not absolutely conclusive, the evidence indicates that official sanction closely reflected local opinion becoming less liberal as the century progressed. The crisis of the 1840s punctuated the official generosity in acceding to requests. After 1864 the abolition of slavery in the United States of America, and its apparent demise in Cuba, led to the total rejection of every application for an interracial marriage license. The complete freeze on permission lasted until the abolition of the law restricting interracial marriage in 1881—the year in which the first general slave abolition law passed the Spanish Cortes.

The official attitude on interracial marriage fluctuated with the growing hostility to slavery and the ambiguous middle sector of free persons of color, often producing difficulty and embarrassment for the crown. The attempts to implement a relatively humane slave code, the *Código Negro Español* for all the overseas colonies in 1789, met hostile rebuff in Cuba, Florida, Venezuela, and Santo Domingo. The provisions were never implemented, and the *vecinos* (enfranchised residents) of Havana suggested that they themselves were the best formulators of any such laws dealing with their slaves. The increasing number of slaves called for greater police measures. As early as 1792, the Afro-Cuban *cabildos*, the urban society of slaves and free persons of color for centuries, lost their right to meet within the city walls.[22] At the same time, the authorities restricted their meeting times to Sundays and watch nights. The restrictions increased during the first four decades of the nineteenth century, although some relaxation occurred under the captaincy general of the Marquis de Pezuela during the 1850s.

The Spanish and Cuban authorities used the frequency of slave revolts and the persistent rumors of widespread racial disorder to increase the regulation and restriction of the free colored community and the slaves. In 1832 the crown asked the Cuban captain general whether, in view of the serious racial situation, the free colored population ought to be expelled from the island. The reply was negative, since expulsion would have aggravated the labor shortage on the sugar estates "and inevitably lead to the ruin of the country."[23] The alternative was to restrict the entry of nonwhite persons, and simultaneously increase the white immigration. Both policies were tried without success. In 1837, amid rumors of revolts, and an actual uprising in Manzanillo, the crown issued an order prohibiting the landing of any enslaved or free person of color in the island. Nonwhite sailors were thrown into jail immediately after entering port, and only released when their ship was ready to set sail. Ironically, this order coincided with one of the periods of extremely heavy illegal slave imports—brought in by planters who were voicing misgivings about the racial situation while expanding their sugar production and reorganizing their *ingenios*.[24]

The *Bando de Gobernación y Policia* and the *Reglamento de esclavos* issued in 1842 by Captain General Gerónimo Valdés represented the ultimate erosion of the conventional patriarchal society of masters and slaves, and accentuated the growing fear with which Cuban whites regarded the nonwhites. The *Bando* not only reactivated the former discriminatory laws of the old Spanish empire, it also introduced some new ones. In his introduction, Valdés admitted that the legislation was calculated "to keep the blacks under a severe discipline and an unalterable subordination."[25] Repeated were all the old prohibitions against occupations and property-holding, and membership in the clergy, the police, the military, and the royal bureaucracy. The *Bando* introduced a series of discriminatory laws licensing the free colored population and severely restricting their mobility and that of all slaves. No slave could travel more than three leagues from a cattle ranch, and a league and a half from any other estate, without the written permission of his master, under pain of being declared a runaway and imprisoned. No slave could rent a room, receive lodging, or travel on ship without his master's written permission. Prohibiting the sale of liquor to slaves affected the urban slaves in particular, since they were denied access to the product during manufacture. Slaves could be used no longer in hunting, nor could they carry firearms.

For the first time in Cuban slave laws, the *Reglamento* virtually dictated the daily routine of the slaves and showed little regard for their humanity. Article 24 declared that "the greatest care should be taken to eliminate excessive drink or intercourse with free colored persons." Although no attempt was made to define "excessive," the government's subsequent conduct after the Matanzas affair of 1844 suggested a frightful concept of the word.[26] For on that occasion, free colored persons who had even minimal contact with slaves were arrested for conspiracy to foment rebellion among the slaves. Articles 25 and 26 required the sexual segregation of single slaves and prohibited the slaves from leaving their dwellings at night. It also stipulated that "a light should burn all night to see that no mixing takes place between the sexes." Article 29 declared that masters should "prevent illicit relations which foment marriages," while advocating the principle of marriage among the slaves. Article 36 asserted that children of mothers who were *coartado* did not enjoy the same benefits, but "may be sold like any other slave."[27] Article 41 declared that slaves should "respect all white persons," and listed the range of punishment for violations, which included twenty-five lashes, torture, and imprisonment.

The increased severity and rigidity were most pronounced in the new legal restrictions against free blacks. They were not permitted to bear firearms or to enter farms without a license. Nor could they travel after eleven o'clock at night except in cases of emergency, when they were ordered to report to the local *sereno*, or nightwatchman, and had to travel with a lighted lantern. Occupations such as farm overseers and bookkeepers began to be legally stipulated as the exclusive rights of the white persons on the island. Captain General Leopoldo O'Donnell used the so-called La Escalera conspiracy of 1844 to arrest, imprison, execute, or deport many leaders of the free colored community, including the poet Plácido and Andres Dodge, a doctor of medicine. O'Connell also temporarily abolished the colored militia units, suppressed some of the mutual aid societies, and threatened to expel all the *emancipados* who had landed in the island since 1825.

The internal situation of Cuba changed by 1850 from the fear of Cuba being either "Spanish or African," to the fear of its being absorbed into the United States. In any case, major official attention shifted from concern over the nonwhite population to the filibuster expeditions attempting to annex the island to the United States. The free colored population was still subject to disabilities, suspicion, and harassment, and the attempt to relieve their condition by Pezuela aroused strong opposition.[28] Nevertheless, the captain general reinstated the colored militia units and permitted the regrouping of the mutual aid societies. At the same time, the government began serious effort to eliminate the slave trade. But the Chinese and Mexican Indians, introduced to facilitate the transition from slave to free labor, further complicated the problem of race.

By the 1860s the unacknowledged official position on slavery and race was clear. Slavery was to be eventually abolished—when it was convenient to do so without disrupting the economy of the island. The nonwhite population would remain in the island, although discriminated against and exploited. The government, after all, had used the race issue as a way of blackmailing the white population into subordination by implying that the removal of Spanish military might would open the way for another Haiti. After the Ten Years War (1868-1878), the racial factor became a basic argument for denying political reforms to the island. The shortsightedness and opportunism of the Spanish government's appeal to, and use of, race was undermined by José Martí, who elevated the issue of nationalism above the issue of race and color.

The implications of slavery, race, and color had no consistent or unified position among the white upper stratum in Cuba. Like the official position, the predominantly articulated view varied through time toward greater exclusion and closer circumscription of the nonwhites. The celebrated example of Haiti, and the antislavery conspiracies of Nicolás Morales in 1795 and José Antonio Aponte in 1812 failed to inhibit the enthusiastic expansion of the slave plantation society. The Spanish government's misgivings on the subject—under persistent English urgings—brought strong objections (under the guise of advice) from the Cuban planters and merchants. Francisco de Arango y Parreño's advocacy of more miscegenation, the abolition of slavery, and the extension of full civil rights to all mixed offspring was merely meant for English consumption, and to "achieve a loan of twenty million pesos."[29] His true feelings, and the views of the Havana upper classes, became evident in their opposition to the Spanish-English treaty agreement of 1817 to end the slave trade to Cuba by 1820.

The generation of Cuban whites who succeeded Arango paid more attention to the role of slavery and the social desirability of the Afro-Cuban population. The debate that prevailed within the elite was less directly concerned with slavery and its effects than with the dilemma of whether Cuba should be a "nation or a plantation."[30] Neither view was particularly hospitable to the Afro-Cuban population. Nationalists such as José Antonio Saco, Domingo Del Monte, Francisco Suárez y Romero, and Rafael

Labra y Cadrana thought that the presence of slavery and a large proportion of Afro-Cubans jeopardized the possibility of social and political reform. And their patently antislavery position did not weaken their manifest hostility to the nonwhite population. On the other hand, the proplantation interests led by Vicente Vásquez Queipo, Cristóbal Madan, Antonio de las Barras y Prado, Juan Poey, and Julian Zulueta supported slavery as the indispensable means of economic growth. They shared with the nationalists the general attitude of white superiority—which in the nineteenth century blended easily with those of the positivists and the social Darwinists—and saw no incompatibility between "civilization and progress." Indeed, they reasoned that white civilization in Cuba depended on the slaves, and was in no danger while the institution of slavery was vigorously administered. "We do not believe," wrote Vásquez Queipo in 1844, "that the Real Junta has forgotten . . . the severe lesson of the neighboring island of Santo Domingo, whose loss resulted in great measure from the intimacy in which the white inhabitants of the French part lived with their slaves, and the numerous population of color which resulted from those foreboding relationships."[31]

Cuban whites divided over the institution of slavery. No fundamental disagreement existed on the question of race. In general, persons of African descent were considered to suffer from some permanent disability. "Mankind," wrote the *Guia de forasteros* in 1840, "is divided into three races of different colors and conditions: white, black, and yellow or copper-colored. The blacks . . . are the least numerous and the most ignorant and stupid."[32] Although no elaboration was made concerning the other two races, the positive impression of the Cuban whites emerged quite clearly in the following edition.

The Cuban peasant is not a crude simpleton like the peasants of other nations. . . . The Cuban lower class has nothing in common with those of Spain, France, or England. Here there are no equivalents to the *Manolos*, the Boxers, and the

Canaille of other countries. Of the upper class we need say nothing; they are the equal of Madrid, Paris, or London in education and sophistication [*delicadeza*].[33]

The chauvinism contained in those views does not disguise the fact that they were part of the body of informed opinion relating to the African—views that covered a wide spectrum from the benignly paternalistic to the explicitly racist.[34] And the journalistic accounts by travelers to Cuba during the nineteenth century provide abundant evidence of the strong anti-African stereotypes that prevailed there.[35]

Adverse views of the African, however, did not prevent miscegenation nor cross-racial marriages. But they retarded the process of national integration and contributed significantly to the discrimination against the Afro-Cubans during and after slavery. Slave owners showed some reluctance in manumitting their slaves as the century progressed. Records of manumission are extremely rare. But the scant evidence suggests that *coartación*, or self-purchase, was a mainly urban affair and not very widespread. In 1877, for example, despite the imminent demise of slavery, Cuban statistics showed only 3,531 *coartado* slaves, out of a slave population of 199,094, or approximately 2 percent. More significant was the fact that 2,702 of these *coartados* were in Havana—which had just about 20 percent of the slaves in the island. By contrast, at the same time, nearly one-half of all the Asian indentured laborers (21,890 out 47,120) were free.[36]

The Afro-Cuban population, slave as well as free, found the accumulated prejudices of slavery and race to be inescapable. Indeed, race formed the most fundamental cleavage in the society. And African ancestry imposed an indelible stain that survived the institution of slavery. Prohibited by law from entering the occupations of the elite during the colonial period (and by tradition afterward), denied access to education and wealth, and ostracized socially, the Afro-Cubans turned inward to themselves and their own community, an act that further increased white suspicion and fears and confirmed white stereotypes of the non-whites.

The response of the community of free Afro-Cubans to slavery and race was less extreme than that of the slaves. The reasons were obvious. Free Afro-Cubans detested slavery and participated in every organized effort to overthrow it. But they were, after all, free, and some of them were culturally and phenotypically very close to the whites. With the abolition of the Offices of the Inquisition in 1830, and the subsequent deemphasis of "*limpieza de sangre*," the possibility of upward mobility became a theoretical possibility. Yet the reality did not work out that way. Very few members of the free colored community passed into the white stratum, despite mixed marriages and personal wealth.[37] Some wealthy members of the free colored group objected to interracial marriages, especially since they considered the prospective white mate to be socially below their "class."[38]

Since the Mexican Indians and the indentured Asians were classified as white (though performing tasks of low status), the free colored population represented a minority group—the minority element among the three defined castes. The hierarchical structure of Spanish colonial society undoubtedly discriminated against them, but also offered them some privileges and some recognition. Torn between the Europeanized ideals of the elite (the Creoles and the Spanish) and the Africanized structure of the slaves, they created their synthesis of the two worlds and sought an accommodation within the system. They were not a revolutionary group in the sense that the slaves and the Creoles were: they desired neither their freedom nor their political independence. They were no less Cuban and no less patriotic than any other group. In short, they did not deserve the fate that nineteenth-century nationalism, the technological changes in the sugar industry, and the abolition of slavery, reserved for them.

The slaves clearly signaled their response to slavery, and their demeaning position that resulted from their unfortunate racial heritage. The pattern of slave protest and the mechanisms for resistance and accommodation to the system of slavery reveal the general attitudes of the slaves. Cuban slave owners who thought their slaves were happy, although at the same time they puzzled over the high rate of suicides and desertions from the plantations, failed to understand the psychology of their human property. Desertions, suicides, murder, and the wanton destruction of property were eloquent testimony of basic opposition to slavery. Urban and rural runaways were so frequent that the Cubans had specially trained dogs and slave hunters. The slaves left in groups to form communities of maroons, or as individuals to join their relatives or friends or merely to strike out on their own. Desertions sometimes reached epidemic proportions. Suicides were so frequent in the 1840s and 1850s that it became a serious topic of discussion in the Spanish Cortes. Finally, the Spanish ministers concluded that to stem the tide of suicides the Cuban slaves needed more sex and more religious instruction.[39] And ever since the successful slave revolt in the French colony of St. Domingue, the slave owners throughout the Caribbean lived in growing fear of their lives. Mutual suspicion and fear was part and parcel of the Cuban slave system.

Nevertheless, the slaves in Cuba made the best of adversity; they managed to salvage some of the religious and cultural values and practices of their native Africa and to form the type of society that gave meaning to their lives. Through their societies, such as the *Carabelas*, the *Cabildos*, and the *sociedades de caridad y socorros mutuos de pardos y morenos*, and religious cults such as *Santería* and *Náñigo*, the slaves interacted with the free black and mulatto society, provided continuity to their community, and sometimes facilitated their mobility upward from their state of subservience.[40] The social organizations of the slaves were the eclectic blend of African and Spanish—albeit more African than Spanish—and ultimately influenced the structure of Cuban culture, particularly in cuisine, dance, music, and language. And the vitality of this Afro-Cuban culture probably drew strength from the massive infusion of African slaves during the nineteenth century.

Unfortunately, the very qualities that made for the mental and physical comfort and survival of the Africans served further to distinguish and define them from the accepted norms of white Cubans. The degree of acceptance of the nonwhite into Cuban society was inversely proportional to the degree of indigenous ethnic, social, and cultural traits he retained. Before the twentieth century, the Africanness of the Cuban society was demeaned, despised, and denigrated by white and nonwhite. Afro-Cubans, therefore, remained beyond the pale of full integration into the society. The abolition of slavery augmented the number of Afro-Cubans at the lowest rung of the ladder—and eliminated the gains in social mobility made possible by the former cardinal distinction between slave and free. By the late nineteenth century, when abolition arrived, the conflict between political integration and social integration had become clear.[41] The connotations of slavery and race, the traditions of the society, the prevailing ill-founded, pseudoscientific ideas about race and culture compounded the neglect, subordination, and discrimination against the black population of Cuba.

The inescapable legacy of slavery, and the perpetuation of the plantation socioeconomic structure after independence, accentuated the mutually reinforcing cleavages of race, color, occupation, and culture. The Asians and the Mexican Indians who were imported to work on the plantations were classified as white —doing "black men's work"; the plantation mentality equated all physically demanding tasks with the duties of the black population. The contradictory reality of integrated communities that existed in Oriente until the end of the century fell victim to the inexorable eastward movement of the plantation complex. Nor did war, the great equalizer, really affect the situation. The Ten Years War (1868-1878) and the War of Independence (1895-1898), of course, produced their pantheon of nonwhite heroes. Máximo Gomez, Antonio Maceo, and Modesto Díaz emerged as the most capable of Cuban military leaders. Nevertheless, racism partially undermined the nationalist effort during the Ten Years War, and again during the War of Independence. Cubans who feared a "Negro Republic" during the 1870s were quite reluctant to accept Afro-Cubans as equal citizens in a free and independent state.[42]

The penetration of commercial and military interest from the United States at the end of the century aggravated the situation. The increased capital development of the sugar industry under United States auspices sharpened the exploitation of all the workers, not just the Afro-Cubans.[43] The infusion of men, machines, techniques, and military personnel between 1880 and 1920 introduced the social conduct of the mainland and its more exclusive concept of race and color. The North Americans changed fundamentally the somatic norm image of Cuba and Puerto Rico, replacing the traditionally liberal definition of white—which included Asians, Mexican Indians, as well as all those whose Afro-American ancestry was not too obvious—with a more stringent criterion.[44] The directors of the first census taken by the occupying United States powers in 1907 blatantly admitted that they were reclassifying the Asians, Indians, and half-castes "as colored, where they belong."[45] The rigid definition of white or black, or a curiously defined biological race, removed the former escape valves of "passing" that had characterized the colonial Cuban society. Above all, it meant that Cubans who wanted to be acceptable to the United States had to follow the pattern of color and race of the foreigners. The increased segregation and discrimination against the Afro-Cubans contributed to the formation of the Independent Party of Color by Pedro Ivonet and Evaristo Estenoz. Proscribed by law, the party resorted to force, and in a bloody confrontation with the army in the early summer of 1912, some three thousand black persons were reported killed.[46] It was the most significant racial disturbance after slavery.[47] Although the virulent racism and the obvious segregation of the United States never developed in Cuba, the situation up to the middle of the twentieth century showed a marked exclusion of the nonwhites from the upper echelons of the society.[48] The Chinese entered the medium-sized commercial activity in large numbers, whereas the Afro-Cubans and the immigrants of African descent from the neighboring islands worked on the plantations, in the army, and in the police force.

The relationship between slavery and the genesis of racism is inextricably intertwined in the anomalous situation of Cuba and the Cubans during the nineteenth century. Throwing caution to the winds, Cuba enthusiastically entered the South Atlantic System amid convincing evidence of the anachronism and disintegration of the system. Cuba imported most of its slaves when the majority of the western countries no longer engaged in slavery and the transatlantic slave trade. Cubans adopted slavery and the plantation society although it perverted their traditions, their culture, and their values. When African slaves, whom they considered congenitally inferior, became scarce, they readily imported Mexicans and Chinese, whom they regarded as racial equals, to do work deemed peculiarly African. And Cuba rapidly became the largest and most efficient sugar producer of the nineteenth century by curiously combining massive capitalism, the latest industrial technology, African slaves, and Asian semi-slaves. By the later part of the century, the island had become a wealthy plantation colony—interspersed with highly schismatic nationalists and areas of relatively poor small farmers, artisans, and businessmen of all races and colors. Moreover, thirty years of bitter struggle against Spain culminated in economic subordination to the United States—and no solution of the basic social problems created by slavery and the sugar plantation.

The repercussions of massive slave imports and massive sugar exports went beyond the mere reversal of population proportions and the economy. Sugar and slavery formed the umbilical cord that linked Cuba with the wider world of economic, philosophical, political, and social ideas. The universal body of ideas were refashioned and adapted to describe or explain the domestic Cuban condition.

The Cuban elite showed a cosmopolitanism and a sophistication unusual for their time and place—the more surprising in their colonial situation. Forced to defend slavery, they postulated the rights of property and the security of civilization—accepted euphemisms for racial and economic arguments. African slaves were economic assets. Emancipation threatened economic ruin. They even reasoned in a convoluted way that slavery was a medium for civilizing the Africans. The reasoning and the arguments were neither new nor originally Cuban. Yet the international community (even the opponents of slavery) more or less accepted them, because the prevailing views of man and society supported the inferior status of the African. The nineteenth century, after all, represented the acme of European ethnocentricity and self-confidence. Non-Europeans were "lesser breeds."[49]

Universal ideas of science, society, and race hardly penetrated below the elite. That the lower classes of white and free persons of color came to share the *Zeitgeist* of the elite derived from the reality of plantation life in the Caribbean. For the sugar revolution established a work force that was predominantly African whereas the proprietary and managerial positions were white. The reasons for the use of African slaves on the tropical plantations are varied and complex. But by the nineteenth century, slavery was synonymous with Africa, and sugar was synonymous with slavery. The ultimate consequence was a labor force that was racially, culturally, religiously, and occupationally different from, and opposed to, the upper classes. Law and tradition emphasized the distinctions, and the necessities of plantation life perpetuated them. Nor did miscegenation, industrialization, or the use of Asian and Indian labor alter the situation. Acceptance into the upper classes depended on the phenotypical approximation to the elite norms—as well as wealth and a "decent" occupation. Although mobility undoubtedly existed, the process was retarded by the structure of the society that exerted centripetal tendencies on white and nonwhite. The plantation fostered two separate societies in Cuba. For those whites caught in the penumbra of sociocultural divisions, the only recognition was race, which allowed them to escape from the discrimination, the segregation, and the coercion of the system.

The evolution of slavery and race was not atypical in Cuba during the nineteenth century. The plantation system drastically modified the conventional attitudes of the ruling classes as it radically revolutionized the society. The integration of Cuba into the wider world precluded the possibility of any autonomous resolution of the problems of race. The social order of white over nonwhite seemed to derive support not only from the international ideas of medical science and nationalism, but also from the essentially social engineering views of positivists, Marxists, and Darwinists. The abolition of slavery did not lead to the increased social integration of the Afro-Cubans, the Asians and the Indians.[50] The old order was never challenged. Fundamental change depended on a complete intellectual, political, and social metamorphosis, and that, despite the promises of José Marti, failed to materialize in the first sixty years of independence.

Notes

[1]E. Williams, *Capitalism and Slavery* (Chapel Hill, N.C., 1944), p. 7.

[2]Contrary views are found in Carl Degler, "Slavery and the Genesis of American Race Prejudice," *Comparative Studies in Society and History* 2 (1959): 49-67; Winthrop Jordan, *White over Black: American Attitudes Toward the Negro, 1550-1812* (Chapel Hill, N.C., 1968); Roger Bastide, "Color, Racism and Christianity", in J. H. Franklin, ed., *Color and Race* (Boston, 1969), pp. 34-49; Gordon Allport, *The Nature of Prejudice*, abridged ed. (New York, 1958). David Brion Davis qualifies Williams' economic determinism in *The Problem of Slavery in Western Culture* (Ithaca, N.Y., 1966), pp. 152-154.

[3]See M. I. Findley, ed., *Slavery in Classical Antiquity* (Cambridge, England, 1960), and C. W. W. Greenidge, *Slavery* (London, 1958).

[4]The process is treated at length in Manuel Moreno Fraginals, *El Ingenio: El complejo económico social cubano del azúcar* (Havana, 1964); Franklin W. Knight, *Slave Society in Cuba during the Nineteenth Century* (Madison, Wis., 1970); Robert J. Shafer, *The Economic Societies in the Spanish World 1763-1821* (New York, 1958); Raul Cepero Bonilla, *Obras Históricas* (Havana, 1963); Roland T. Ely, *Cuando reinaba su majestad el*

azúcar (Buenos Aires, 1963); Francisco Pérez de la Riva y Pons, *Origen y régimen de la propiedad territorial en Cuba* (Havana, 1946).

[5]Duvon C. Corbitt, *A Study of the Chinese in Cuba 1847-1947*, new ed. (Wilmore, Ky., 1971); Juan Pérez de la Riva, "Documentos para la historia de las gentes sin historia. El Tráfico de culies chinos," *Revista de la Biblioteca Nacional José Martí*, 6 (1965): 77-90.

[6]Gwendolyn Midlo Hall, *Social Control in Slave Plantation Societies, a Comparison of St. Domingue and Cuba* (Baltimore, Md., 1971); Knight, *Slave Society*, pp. 59-120.

[7]The *Guia de forasteros en la siempre fiel isla de Cuba . . . 1883* (Havana, 1883), p. 515, has a summary of all Cuban census returns between 1774 and 1877.

[8]Philip D. Curtin, *The Atlantic Slave Trade: A Census* (Madison, Wis., 1969), pp. 36-43, 244-247; Rolando Mellafe, *La esclavitud en hispanoamérica* (Buenos Aires, 1964).

[9]Knight, *Slave Society*, p. 134; Verena Martínez Alier, "Marriage, Class and Colour in Nineteenth Century Cuba" (Ph.D. diss., University of Oxford, 1970), p. 61, note 1.

[10]José Antonio Saco, *Historia de la esclavitud de la raza africana en el nuevo mundo. . . ,* 4 vols. (Havana, 1930). See also Elias Entralgo, *La liberación etnica cubana* (Havana, 1953), p. 19; H. Thomas, *Cuba. The Pursuit of Freedom* (New York, 1971), pp. 168-183.

[11]The historical literature is extensive. Some examples: A. F. Corwin, *Spain and the Abolition of Slavery in Cuba, 1817-1886* (Austin, Tex., 1967); J. M. Callahan, *Cuba and International Relations: A Historical Diplomacy* (Baltimore, Md., 1899); R. G. Caldwell, *The Lopez Expeditions to Cuba, 1848-1851* (Princeton, N.J., 1915); P. S. Foner, *A History of Cuba in its relations with the United States*, 2 vols. (New York, 1962-1963); A. Nevins, *Hamilton Fish: The Inner History of the Grant Administration* (New York, 1957); Herminio Portell Vilá, *Historia de Cuba en sus relaciones con los Estados Unidos y España*, 4 vols. (Havana, 1938-1941); *Narciso Lopez y su época*, 3 vols. (Havana, 1930-1958), by the same author; and C. J. Bartlett, "British Reaction to the Cuban Insurrection of 1868-1878," *Hispanic American Historical Review* 37 (1957): 296-312.

[12]See Moreno Fraginals, *El Ingenio*; Martínez Alier, "Marriage, Class and Colour"; Thomas, *Cuba*, pp. 150-151. Contrary views, but not very convincing, are found in H. Klein, *Slavery in the Americas: A Comparative Study of Virginia and Cuba* (Chicago, 1967), pp. 86-105.

[13]Martínez Alier, "Marriage, Class and Colour."

[14]Informe presentado a la junta informativa de ultramar . . . (Madrid, 1869), pp. 11-12; Archivo Histórico Nacional, Madrid, *Sección de Estado Subsección de Esclavitud* leg. 8052 (7), f. 1.

[15]The phrase is from Frederika Bremer, *The Homes of the New World: Impressions of America*, trans. Mary Howitt, 2 vols. (New York, 1853), 2: 271. See also Knight, *Slave Society*, pp. 107-113.

[16]The best works are by Fernando Ortiz, *Hampa afro-Cubana, los negros esclavos* (Havana, 1916), and his "La fiesta afro-cubana del día de reyes," *Revista Bimestre Cubana* 15 (1920): 5-26; and Lydia Cabrera, *El Monte . . .*, 2d ed. (Miami, Fla., 1968); *La sociedad secreta Abakuá narrada por viejos adeptos*, 2d ed. (Miami, Fla., 1970).

[17]Contrast the religious zeal of the sixteenth-century missionaries in L. Hanke, *The Spanish Struggle for Justice in the Conquest of America* (Philadelphia, 1949); John L. Phelan, *The Millennial Kingdom of the Franciscans in the New World*, 2d ed. revised (Berkeley and Los Angeles, 1970); C. Gibson, *The Aztecs under Spanish Rule* (Stanford, Cal., 1964), esp. pp. 98-135; and Robert Ricard, *The Spiritual Conquest of Mexico*, trans. L. B. Simpson (Berkeley and Los Angeles, 1966).

[18]*Recopilación de las leyes de los reynos de las Indias*, 3 vols. (Madrid, 1943); José M. Zamora y Coronado, comp., *Biblioteca de legislación ultramarina*, 7 vols. (Madrid, 1844-1849); and Juan Manzano Manzano, *Historia de las recopilaciones de Indias*, 2 vols. (Madrid, 1950).

[19]M. Mörner, *Race Mixture in the History of Latin America* (Boston, 1967), pp. 35-39; Richard Konetzke, ed., *Colección de documentos para la historia de la formación social de hispanoamérica, 1493-1810*, 4 vols. (Madrid, 1962), 3: 406-413, 438-442, and 463-481; also, Martínez Alier, "Marriage, Class and Colour."

[20]See, for example, "Consulta del consejo de las Indias sobre el expediente de Doña Maria del Carmen Correa y de Don Juan Josef Ximenez, naturales de Caracas, solicitando licencia para casarse, dispensándose a éste la calidad de pardo," Madrid, 26 August 1806. Konetzke, *Documentos*, 3: 829-830.

[21]Martínez Alier, "Marriage, Class and Colour," pp. 19-20.

[22]Fernando Ortiz, "Los cabildos afro-cubanos," *Revista Bimestre Cubana* 16 (1921): 5-39.

[23]Quoted in Hall, *Social Control*, p. 128.

[24]Franklin W. Knight, "Cuba," in David W. Cohen and Jack P. Greene, eds., *Neither Slave nor Free: The Freedman of African Descent in the Slave Societies of the New World* (Baltimore, 1972), pp. 278-308.

²⁵*Bando de gobernación y policía de la isla de Cuba expedido por el Excmo. Sr. D. Gerónimo Valdés, presidente, gobernador y capitan general* (Havana, 1842), p. 4.

²⁶Hall, *Social Control*, pp. 57-60 and 129-130; Francisco Gonzalez del Valle Ramirez, *La conspiración de la escalera* (Havana, 1925).

²⁷*Coartación* was the Cuban and Spanish system of pre-fixing the purchase price of a slave in order to facilitate self-purchase on the installment plan. If the slave were sold during the time of period, the amount paid to the former owner was subtracted from the price paid to the new master. Konetzke, *Documentos*, 3: 565-568; H. H. S. Aimes, "Coartación: A Spanish institution for the Advancement of Slaves into Freedom," *Yale Review* 17 (1909): 412-431.

²⁸Knight, *Slave Society*, pp. 139-143; Martínez Alier, "Marriage, Class and Colour," pp. 51-52. See also Pedro Deschamps Chapeaux, *El negro en la economia havanera del siglo XIX* (Havana, 1971).

²⁹Francisco de Arango y Parreño, *Obras*, 2 vols. (Havana, 1952), 2: 306-307.

³⁰M. Moreno Fraginals, "Nación o plantación. El dilemma político cubano visto a través de José Antonio Saco," in Julio Le Riverend et al., eds., *Estudios Históricos Americanos* (Mexico City, 1953), pp. 241-272.

³¹*Informe fiscal sobre fomento de la población blanca* . . . (Madrid, 1845), p. 33.

³²*Guía de forasteros* . . . *1840* (Havana, 1840), p. 82.

³³*Guía de forasteros* . . . *1841*, pp. 116-117.

³⁴William Stanton, *The Leopards Spots: Scientific Attitudes Toward Race in America, 1815-1859* (Chicago, 1960); P. D. Curtin, *The Image of Africa: British Ideas and Action, 1780-1850* (Madison, Wis., 1964).

³⁵Most notable are Bremer, *Homes of the New World*, pp. 308, 444; Samuel Hazard, *Cuba with Pen and Pencil* (Hartford, Conn., 1871), pp. 95, 98, 168, 197; Antonio Gallenga, *The Pearl of the Antilles* (London, 1873), pp. 77, 82, 98-99, 109, 192; and Richard Dana, *To Cuba and Back* (New York, 1859), pp. 8, 45.

³⁶*Guía* . . . *1883*, p. 518.

³⁷Deschamps Chapeaux, *El negro*, pp. 32-49; Knight, "Cuba"; Hall, *Social Control*, pp. 127-135.

³⁸Martínez Alier, "Marriage, Class and Colour," pp. 33-34.

³⁹*A. H. N. Madrid. Ultramar. Esclavitud*, leg. 3550: "Expediente sobre los medios de evitar los frecuentes suicidios de esclavos."

⁴⁰*Carabelas* were fellow passengers across the Atlantic in slave ships,

who later formed social groups. The name was applied indiscriminately to all members of any social group. Ortiz, "Los cabildos afro-cubanos"; Cabrera, *La sociedad secreta Abakuá*; Thomas, *Cuba*, pp. 515-522.

[41]Carlos de Sedano, *Estudios Politicos* (Madrid, 1872), pp. 348-351. See also Justo Zaragoza, *Las insurrecciones en Cuba. . .* , 2 vols. (Madrid, 1872-1873); [Cristobal Madan] *El trabajo libre y el libre cambio en Cuba* (Paris, 1869); and Rafael Labra, *La reforma política de ultramar, 1868-1900* (Madrid, 1902).

[42]Ramiro Guerra y Sanchez, *Guerra de los diez años 1868-1878* (Havana, 1950); Thomas, *Cuba*, pp. 245-270.

[43]See the report of U.S. Deputy Consul General H. P. Starrett to the Department of Commerce, quoted in *The New York Times*, 16 June 1912, p. 13, col. 1.

[44]On somatic norm image, see H. Hoetink, *The Two Variants in Caribbean Race Relations: A Contribution to the Sociology of Segmented Societies*, trans. Eva Hooykaas (London, 1967), pp. 120-190.

[45]*Censo de la república de Cuba bajo la administración provisional de los Estados Unidos, 1907* (Washington, 1908). See also David F. Healy, *The United States and Cuba, 1898-1902* (Madison, Wis., 1963); Thomas, *Cuba*, pp. 436-493; and the English-language paper edited by A. D. Roberts and Irene A. Wright, which referred to the Cubans as "Coons" and "Niggers": *The Cuba News* 2, No. 9 (29 March 1913): 1, col. 2, and 15, col. 3.

[46]The exact death toll is difficult to ascertain. *Cuba en la Mano*, new ed. (Miami, Fla., 1969), p. 871, refers to "millares de millares de negros." Thomas, *Cuba*, p. 523, gives a figure of 3,000 by General Monteagudo's own admission. *The New York Times*, 27 June 1917, p. 5, col. 4, estimated the rebel strength at between 2,000 and 4,000—not all of whom perished in action.

[47]Afro-Cubans also participated in the general uprisings of 1906.

[48]Lowry Nelson, *Rural Cuba* (Minneapolis, Minn. 1950), pp. 156-157; Wyatt MacGaffey and Clifford Barnett, *Cuba* (New Haven, Conn., 1962), p. 49.

[49]The phrase is from the poem by Rudyard Kipling, *Recessional* (1897).

[50]Had merely economic causes fostered slavery and racism, social mobility would have been considerably lubricated by personal wealth. This did not occur in Cuba.

8

The Abolition of
Slavery in Venezuela:
A Nonevent[1]

John V. Lombardi

In many respects the abolition of slavery in Spanish American countries developed out of the cataclysmic events surrounding the wars for independence. The prolonged, seesawing struggle for military superiority wrought great havoc among the slaveholding societies of Spanish America. While contending armies vied desperately for victory, military leaders worked to undermine the enemy's position of promising liberty to slaves who joined the fight. During the course of the wars, slaves served admirably as soldiers in both the rebel and loyalist forces, and even many of those who remained on the sidelines must have been moved by the spectacle of such a dramatic split among their masters.

More than any other country in Latin America, Venezuela was torn by civil and social disorders relating to the battles for independence. As John V. Lombardi demonstrates, Venezuela's victorious native aristocrats found that the old slavocracy simply could not be restored. The independence struggles damaged the fragile mystique of the master class, economic conditions did not favor the continuance of slavery, and, worse, opposing political factions could not resist appealing to bondsmen for support in their attempts to retain or seize power. Accordingly, in 1854 the liberal Monagas government decreed abolition for fear that the opposition would try to gain political capital by exciting servile revolts. Abolition, however, was little more than a gesture. As Lombardi explains, the real decline of slavery had occurred earlier; the principle of gradual emancipation had already been accepted, and the act of 1854 was practically a "nonevent."

R. B. T.

Venezuela, "Tierra de Gracia" as Columbus called it, has a past marked by variety and complexity. From a poverty-stricken outpost of Spain's empire in the sixteenth century, Venezuela grew to become her most profitable nonmining colony during the eighteenth century. This late flowering came as a result of the energetic commercial operations of the Caracas Company in the export of the valuable cacao seed. The combination of a climate and soil especially suited to cacao with a protected market ably exploited by some of Spain's most capable businessmen proved a sure formula for prosperity. For more than two generations the Caracas Company held a monopoly on most of Venezuela's commerce, and from this privileged position helped stimulate the province's economy while collecting a handsome profit for the company. However, in the 1780s the decline of cacao prices, financial and political problems at home, and increasing Creole restlessness under company domination in Caracas brought this experiment in Enlightenment economics to an end.[2]

As the Caracas Company encouraged increased production of cacao and reaped comfortable profits from its trade, the Creole landlords grew rich as well. But in order to capture the full benefit of the cacao boom, the planters soon realized they would need more workers, and that meant more black slaves. And so they revitalized the languishing slave trade to Venezuela. Between 1730 and 1780 a record number of blacks entered the province. But as the short-lived cacao boom declined after 1780, the volume of the slave trade fell off too. By 1810, as a result of the declining fortunes, of Venezuelan planters and the disruption of the normal trade by the Napoleonic wars, almost no slaves entered the province.[3]

Indeed, the revolutionary Caracas Junta officially ended the slave trade in 1810, but the institution of slavery itself still existed in a reasonably healthy state.[4] For the next thirty years the controlling oligarchies, whether Conservative or Liberal, tried to find a way of eliminating the odious institution from their land. In spite of the almost total unanimity of opinion against slavery, these leaders found no solution to the problem of abolition until 1854.[5]

In abolishing black slavery, Venezuela enjoyed none of the panoply of a crusade, none of the high-flown and heart-stirring rhetoric of popular tribunes, and none of the hard-fought abolitionist campaigns witnessed in Brazil or Cuba. Yet during the generation from the declaration of independence to the abolition of slavery, captive blackmen formed a significant, if not dominant, element of Venezuelan society. This lack of public interest in abolition does not, however, indicate indifference toward the black man's plight. Quite the contrary; early in republican life, Venezuela ratified Bolívar's battlefield promise of freedom with a clumsy and inefficient manumission system. Clearly aware of the service rendered the republic by armed black men drafted and freed to fight Spaniards, the legislators passed into law the noble principle of free birth. After 1821 no person could be born a slave in Venezuela.

Yet no abolition controversy appeared between the free birth law of 1821 and the end of slavery in 1854. To understand how this happened, we need to look at three interrelated topics. Clearly, the wars for independence had a profound effect on the institution of black slavery in Venezuela; and abolition, when it finally came, only completed a process begun in 1810. But the independence crusade only partially explains the peculiar characteristics of Venezuela's abolitionism. The transformation of Venezuela's economy after 1830 proved equally important to the fate of enslaved blackmen. Finally, a clear understanding of the social and political impact of slaves on their society helps explain the manner and timing of their liberation.

Independence

Until April 1810, Venezuelan Negro slaves belonged to a well-defined social group with rights and duties established by almost three centuries of Spanish colonial practice and legislation.[6] Moreover, at the beginning of the nineteenth century Venezuelan slave owners viewed the future with some confidence. To be sure, the Haitian revolution had been quite a shock, and in its wake Spain's series of laws designed to alleviate the lot of the captive blackmen took on new meaning. But local officials, generally sympathetic to the problems of slave control, could be counted on to ignore lenient slave laws.[7]

Nor did the *coup d'état* of 19 April worry the complacent slave owners. The authors of this *golpe*, who were determined to end Spanish rule while preserving their own privileges, came from the best segment of society and many owned slaves themselves. Yet somehow, in spite of the respectability of its instigators, the coup became radicalized. And a decree ending the slave trade symbolized this alarming tendency.[8]

Once the independence movement changed from a seizure of power to a full-scale civil war, slaves found the feuding white aristocrats sympathetic to the notion of freedom. In the beginning the royalists proved much more willing than their opponents to encourage slave participation. By 1812 the Spanish captain Domingo Monteverde had incorporated slaves into his forces with the promise of freedom, and with their help had made amazing progress.[9] The revolutionary leader Miranda proposed to counter this threat by making the same offer to slaves who would join the patriot cause. Unfortunately, this decision came too late to save the shaky republican government. In any case, the aristocrats of Caracas refused to cooperate with the plan. Many had visions of a Haitian holocaust, and when rumors that a destructive slave rebellion had caught fire along the coast reached the republicans, many of them began to repent their revolutionary ardor. These events, culminating a long series of political and military disasters, helped overturn the First Republic and restore Spanish rule.[10]

Despite the collapse of the First Republic, the struggle between royalists and republicans continued. The royalists, with support from rebellious slaves, held Caracas, but the dispersed patriots kept on fighting. During the early years of the war, patriot commanders avoided wholesale induction of slaves into their armies. Indeed, much of the early royalist success rested on a highly pragmatic attitude toward the participation of all the lower classes in the battle, including, of course, slaves.[11] Only after Simón Bolivar's spectacular march to Caracas from Colombia ended in a second patriot defeat in 1814 did republican commanders realize that a more receptive attitude toward slaves might have military consequences. When Bolivar rejoined the battle in 1816, after his educational stay in Haiti, he made the practice of awarding freedom to slaves fighting for the republic official patriot policy.[12]

Slaves, eventually drafted by royalists and republicans alike, entered the war in a number of ways. Some enlisted in response to decrees issued by field commanders offering freedom for service. Runaway slaves found the warring armies a good refuge from their irate masters and a source of quick absolution of all their sins against society. More often, however, the armies picked up slaves found on plantations in the war zone, and this process, which slowly drained slave labor from the countryside, continued until the end of the war.[13] It is hard to estimate how many slaves joined the wars for independence. But slaves generally joined the armies in small groups, rarely in mass, and they deserted frequently. And in spite of a significant slave contribution, slavery survived independence.

The effect of the war on slavery is difficult to measure. It seems certain, however, that these years of devastation, confusion, and disorganization greatly hastened the eventual abolition of slavery. Because the army remained the ultimate refuge for runaway slaves during the war, plantation discipline collapsed. More importantly, black slaves discovered a sense of power during these years as the contending armies wooed their support. The war impressed upon their masters the terror of a massive slave revolt. At the war's end a reaction came, as masters reasserted their authority, but its severity was tempered by fear.[14]

As the threat of a Spanish reconquest of Venezuela grew remote, civilian slaveholders became less tolerant of the military policy of slave conscription. Thus the wartime libertarianism ended in 1819 when the Congress of Angostura began restructuring the institution of slavery, which had been badly damaged, if not totally destroyed, by the disorganization of war and the freedom decrees of various royalist and republican leaders.[15] Although the Angostura delegates reflected slave owners' dissatisfaction with the policy of liberty for blacks, it took the subsequent congress in Cúcuta to reestablish slavery in Venezuela. In 1821 this assembly passed the *Ley de Manumisión*, the most important statement of republican slave philosophy, and a decree that survived relatively unchanged until abolition in 1854. In essence, the law sanctioned slavery, confirmed the abolition of the slave trade, recognized the freedom of slaves who had served in the armies of independence, set up a system for the gradual elimination of slavery through a locally administered manumission scheme financed by various taxes on inheritances, and, most importantly, provided for the free birth of all slave children. The free birth provision doomed slavery to gradual extinction, a process that would have been completed sometime in the 1860s.[16]

At the time, this law was as much of a reaction as was politically and militarily safe. To have reestablished colonial slavery in its entirety would have been resented by newly freed black soldiers as well as by those still enslaved. Nor should it be forgotten that in 1821 the Spanish threat of reconquest, although remote, still continued, and republican armies might need slave recruits. By and large, the 1821 manumission law proved an artful compromise that provided the basis for all subsequent slave legisla-

tion. When the newly independent Venezuelan congress recon-
sidered the measure in 1830, few substantial changes were
made.[17]

The manumission system, established between 1821 and 1830,
survived unchanged until abolition primarily because it effectively balanced the interests of government and slave owner. The
national government, or more precisely the party in power,
naturally concerned itself with survival. Even though all governments worried about the economic health of slave owners, they
worried even more about slave violence; it was not that they
expected a spontaneous uprising of the oppressed blackmen, but
they did fear the political potential of adequately led rebellions
espousing the cause of black freedom. To keep in command,
then, all governments from 1821 to 1854 advocated the policy of
gradual but effective manumission. In practice, however, during
the generation the manumission system operated, it freed a little
over twenty slaves a year, many of these old or injured. Few
Venezuelans thought the system effective, and many urged its
reform.[18]

Planters and slave owners found themselves continually in
conflict with the central government on this question. Nevertheless, regardless of party affiliation, each successive administration
followed identical policies. Each secretary of the interior sent
directives to local officials in the futile effort to make the gradual
abolition of slavery a reality. On the other side, slave owners
showed no intention of sacrificing their property for governmental stability. With admirable consistency they resisted every effort
to organize an efficient manumission program.

As the conflict evolved, it became evident that both sides tacitly
accepted the manumission laws as the rules governing their dispute. The government refrained from changing the system, and
the slaveholders paid the manumission taxes they could not
avoid. But property owners felt free to influence local officials,
avoid or delay paying taxes, appeal all adverse decisions in slave
matters, and complicate manumission through prolonged
litigation.[19] The government, on the other hand, had the power

to settle disputes with local officials, veto changes in the law, and influence local governments.[20] These two interest groups balanced each other so evenly that all attempts to change the rules met defeat until the balance collapsed in 1854.[21]

The Economy

Without some idea of Venezuela's rapidly changing economy, her slave policy is difficult to understand. Each maneuver, tactic, and strategy used had much of its rationale in a financial calculation or its explanation in an economic situation.

Throughout this period Venezuela was a model agricultural export economy. With almost no native manufactures, she produced coffee, cacao, sugar, hides, and indigo for export, along with smaller quantities of other commodities. But coffee, the crucial crop, earned the most money and was the most susceptible to price fluctuations.[22]

With the end of the wars for independence, Venezuela, ruled by the firm hand of General José Antonio Páez, separated from the Colombian confederation, and the economic recovery begun in the late 1820s grew into a full-fledged boom during the 1830s. Planters whose lands, houses, and slaves had been ravaged by war began the task of reconstruction with good prospects for a rapid recovery.

Before 1810 Venezuela had concentrated her exports on cacao to the near exclusion of other crops. But by the late 1820s a tendency to shift from cacao to coffee accelerated as a result of the independence movement.[23] When the planters returned to their fields after the war, they had to devise some way to effect a quick recovery. Those whose cacao plantations were relatively unharmed continued producing, but most found large parts of their holdings beyond hope of salvation. For these men, continued investment in cacao appeared impossible since expensive new cacao trees took about six years to begin producing. Coffee, on the other hand, produced a marketable crop in half the time and could be planted at almost four times the density. Although coffee produced only one harvest a year, each unit of land generated almost twice as much income when planted in coffee as when planted in cacao.[24] With these conditions, plus the expanding world demand, which kept prices high, the decision to plant coffee is not surprising. Moreover, planters found it relatively easy to borrow the capital necessary to establish a plantation and maintain it for a number of years, although at extremely high interest rates.[25]

The coffee boom, which lasted almost unabated until the 1840s, was extraordinary from almost every point of view. Whereas the total quantity of cacao exported grew very slowly between 1830 and 1840, the production of coffee doubled and then almost tripled in the same decade.[26] Naturally, such unprecedented growth had profound effects on all aspects of Venezuelan society. Traditional relationships among capitalists, workers, commercial factors, planters, and government could not withstand both the onslaught of war and the exposure to the dynamics of rapid economic expansion.

Although a detailed examination of the first Venezuelan coffee boom falls outside the limits of this paper, a quick survey of its major characteristics is possible.[27] In general terms, the 1830-1850 period can best be studied by division into two decades. During the first (1830-1840), the Venezuelan economy reached its peak of expansion and speculation. High interest rates discouraged few individuals, since most planters counted on a continuation of strong coffee prices to make good their investments. The economic picture appeared so rosy that the traditional lords of Venezuela, the landholding elite, supported legislative measures to remove all restrictions on money lenders that had been retained in Venezuelan law from the colonial regime. In gratitude for vast sums of fresh capital needed to finance coffee expansion, the planters voted for the famous *10 de abril* law, which allowed creditors to charge any rate of interest under any conditions and denied debtors legal redress.[28] Moreover, in the euphoria of rising coffee prices and easy credit, landowners allowed the new capitalists, mostly foreigners and their agents, to capture General Páez and turn him into the charismatic defender of the mercantile-commercial elite.[29]

During the decade of the 1830s, planters not only had high prices and easy credit, but also an abundant labor supply. The relative stability established and guaranteed by the Páez regime, plus the return of discharged soldiers, encouraged better organization of rural labor. Even more important, workers found planters willing to pay well on the basis of high coffee prices. Rural laborers found it more advantageous to trade their work for the wages offered by planters than to stay in subsistence agriculture. Since coffee production is a seasonal operation, the growers needed large numbers of workers only at harvest time. For the duration of the growing season, only a small maintenance force was needed for the cleaning and pruning operations. With a large floating work force readily available, few planters worried much about labor problems.[30]

This happy picture changed as the decade drew to a close. By the late thirties coffee prices began to sag, disturbing the delicate balance among debt, interest, and income.[31] As prices declined, planters borrowed more money to expand in order to sell more coffee to pay off their loans. But by the first years of the 1840s, coffee prices had sunk so low that many planters found it impossible to pay even the interest on their debts. When this happened the mercantile-commercial elite made full use of their cherished *10 de abril* law and proceeded to auction off the properties of their debtors, usually at prices well below actual value. Planters clamored for some kind of relief, but the federal government, long dominated by the financial sector, showed little interest.[32]

To make things worse, the labor situation deteriorated at about the same time. As coffee production soared and more and more land came under cultivation, a larger percentage of the labor force became occupied with maintenance; there was a corresponding reduction in the men available for seasonal harvest work. But falling coffee prices made it harder for planters to attract any but the most temporary workers, since they could no longer afford to pay more than could be realized in subsistence agriculture.[33]

When the decline of the late 1830s became a full-fledged depression in the early 1840s, the planter class looked for ways to restore their prosperity. They believed that the cause of economic distress could be traced to the dominance of Páez' financial and commercial friends. Without the unfair advantages given capitalists and merchants under Páez' Conservative government, the planters thought they would soon be prosperous.[34] And so they tried defeating the *paecistas* at the polls, first in 1844 and again in 1846.[35] But the central government had no intention of relinquishing power, and in response to the deepening crisis and the futility of political action, some planters turned to rebellion.

Before discussing the role of this violence in the eventual abolition of slavery, we must first consider the place of slaves in the economy. By and large, black slaves were counted twice in a planter's economic calculations. First, slaves were workers subject to servitude, but nonetheless influenced by the same conditions governing free peons; and second, slaves served as financial assets in every planter's calculations.

Black slaves performed only a small and declining role in the labor force.[36] Since slaves were concentrated in the traditional cacao and sugar regions, coffee expansion drew less on slave labor than the proportion of slaves in the labor force would suggest. If the slaves went from an established plantation to a new area, peons would have to be hired to keep up the old plantation, and the additional cost to the planter would remain the same. Over time, the number of healthy slaves available for field work declined as the free birth provision of the manumission laws took effect.

As financial ciphers in Venezuela's elaborate credit structure, slaves played an important role. Each slave, as chattel, could be used as collateral for much-needed loans. Many slaves, of course, were already mortgaged to the Church since long before independence, whereas others had been put up as collateral for secular loans. And a planter's slaves probably represented a high percentage of his total capital. Because land alone was worth relatively little, slaves along with coffee trees were the major capital resources of the planter.[37]

This state of affairs clearly explains the absence of debate over slavery, except as a financial matter. No one worried much about slaves, since their fate was determined by laws and treaties long sanctioned by time, custom, and necessity.[38] Even so, most of the elite, whether Conservative or Liberal, could generate a good deal of steam about the iniquity of abolishing slavery without adequate and prompt compensation. The only thought given to slaves, other than as financial ciphers, concerned their revolutionary potential. As the years progressed and the number of workable slaves declined to insignificance, their political and social importance grew greater, particularly as depression and its attendant discontent grew after 1844. The revolutionary disturbances that began in 1846 and continued throughout the 1850s brought slaves more into prominence until the reigning oligarchy decided that slaves were more of a social and political liability than an economic advantage and ordered the institution abolished.

Slaves in Society

Since slaves formed such a small part of the population, they rarely appeared in the press except in advertisements of one kind or another. Because the elite agreed on the slave question, no one discussed such problems as the evils of servitude or the benefits of abolition. And since everyone viewed slavery in principle as an evil thing that should eventually be abolished, an abolitionist would have had a hard time stirring up any enthusiasm.

So while slaves waited for manumission or death to set them free, they continued to work for their masters. Although the available information does not allow a statistical breakdown of slave jobs, it is possible to divide most bondsmen into four occupational groups: field hands, artisans, domestics, and runaways. The traditional occupation of slaves was field work, but by the time of the 1830 census, common laborers were fast becoming a minority. The job of clearing and harvesting had shifted from owned hands to hired hands. This process helped account for the high concentration of domestics among slaves. Most owners of one, two, or three slaves evidently preferred to keep their property constantly occupied in housework or cooking rather than send them out into the fields. A few masters were privileged to own slave artisans, usually shoemakers or carpenters, and others a stevedore or sailor, who presumably paid their master all or part of their wages.[39]

Although domestic service and field work absorbed most slave energies, a significant group of bondsmen opted for the life of a fugitive. In a country as sparsely populated as Venezuela, with rugged mountains cutting through the areas of highest slave concentrations, it is not surprising that slaves found it easy and tempting to take to the hills.[40]

Slave catching was a rather haphazard operation. Both the police and private citizens could chase runaways, but were singularly ineffective and so poorly motivated that some owners employed hungry peons to hunt slaves in their spare time, a job reputed to be both dangerous and distasteful.[41] Now and then a runaway community or *rochela* became so large and its members so bold as to threaten nearby communities. Panicky public leaders would form an expedition, guns would be distributed, and the defenders of society would sally forth to deal with the threat to their safety. Often the expedition would find an abandoned encampment, sometimes one or two individuals might be caught, and rarely some determined resistance would be encountered. In any case, the *rochela* would be destroyed, and the runaways either captured or dispersed.[42]

In spite of the futility of slave existence, few slaves opted for violent revolt. From the end of the independence wars to abolition, there is no record of any large-scale organized rebellion of slaves. This does not mean that slaves were always peaceful or that they never took up arms for their freedom; only that the enslaved population never found the leadership or the occasion to mount a major rebellion. The outnumbered slaves, dispersed over a large geographic area, found organizational and communication problems insurmountable. Their natural leaders had been killed or freed during independence or had found escape to the hills a more attractive alternative to revolt.[43]

Perhaps the greatest deterrent to slave violence, however, was the periodic violence led by the master class. To be sure, no one admitted recruiting slaves to overthrow a government, but both Liberals and Conservatives indulged in the practice. Although slaves participated in the 1835 Revolución de las Reformas, their action had few consequences, primarily because of the short duration of the revolt. But when the economic crisis of the 1840s continued and the Conservative government refused to help the Liberal planters, another and more serious revolt broke out in the wake of the fraudulent elections of 1846. Horror-struck Conservative oligarchs pronounced lengthy and self-righteous condemnations of the Liberal oligarchs' tacit offer of freedom to all slaves joining the rebellion. Profoundly shaken by the relatively few atrocities attributable to slaves seeking freedom, the government accused their opponents of extraordinary irresponsibility and immorality in unleashing the prohibited weapon.[44]

It is almost impossible to assess the influence and magnitude of slave participation in these uprisings, but there is no question that they did participate and in numbers sufficient to scare the oligarchs concerned. Although Venezuelan Negro slaves were disinclined to revolt on their own, and most slaves opted for passive resistance or flight, slaves served their masters as cannon fodder in civil wars in the hope of liberation.

Abolition

In sum, then, from the wars of independence to abolition, Venezuela never suffered any kind of moral crisis over her slave problem. Although most everyone agreed that slaves should be free, almost no one thought they should be freed immediately. Conventional wisdom decreed that much time would be required to prepare the slave for the awesome responsibility of freedom. Underlying such pious platitudes were a number of unpleasant facts. Even in decline, the institution of slavery represented a considerable amount of money; in 1854, for example, the value of slave property equaled that of the Venezuelan coffee crop for the same year.[45] Since abolition without indemnification was never considered, the government was reluctant to assume the burden of a slaveholder compensation of 3 million pesos. With the unstable political conditions prevalent in Venezuela after 1840 and the severe economic depression that hit about the same time, no governing party could have wanted to add the social disruption and expense of abolition to their difficulties.

Had the Conservative oligarchy been able to maintain its hold on the reins of power for another decade after 1848, or had the newly triumphant Liberal oligarchy dominated the country more securely in 1848, Venezuela probably would have stuck with her ineffectual but philanthropic manumission system until death brought about the abolition of slavery sometime in the 1860s. But this was not to be. The Conservatives lost control of their hand-picked president. General José Tadeo Monagas when, in search of a more stable political base, he defected to the Liberals. In turn, the Liberals, inexperienced in government and racked by internal feuds, failed to gain complete control of the country. Conservative-led bands harassed the government, spreading rumors of impending slave uprisings, as government troops rushed hither and yon looking for nonexistent revolts. Conservative *caudillos* let it be known that freedom would be one of the first orders of business come the restoration of their party.[46] In view of these events, it is clear why the Liberal government began to think seriously about some way of eliminating the possibility of a Conservative-led slave rebellion. As the political situation worsened during the early 1850s, the Liberal dynasty of the Monagas family searched harder and harder for a solution to their political difficulties.[47] Finally, in 1854, President José Gregorio Monagas sent Congress a message asking for the abolition of slavery. With this order on their desks, the legislators quickly came up with an abolition decree. The President signed the bill into law on 24 March 1854.[48]

Although we have little direct evidence, it is not difficult to guess what motivated this demand for abolition. The Conservative rebels were increasing their revolutionary activity, and the continual drain on the treasury caused by sporadic uprising in one province or another was becoming serious.[49] Moreover, the coffee depression continued to hang on, and planters remained in desperate straits. The Liberal Monagas administration undoubtedly knew that the twelve or thirteen thousand slaves liable to be freed by an abolition decree would have a relatively small effect on the economy as a whole. The Liberal ministers most likely calculated that the risk of allowing the Conservatives to capture the banner of abolition was greater than the risk of alienating a small number of slave owners. Conservatives, of course, accused the Monagas government of freeing the slaves to acquire a few loyal soldiers and prevent a general uprising on behalf of the Conservative cause.[50] And, in a sense, they were probably right.

Notes

[1] In the preparation of this paper I was aided by a Fulbright-Hays grant (1965-1966), a Fundación Creole grant (1967), and an Indiana University International Affairs Center grant (1969).

[2] For a provocative analysis of Venezuela's colonial past, see Federico Brito Figueroa, *La estructura económica de Venezuela colonial* (Caracas, 1963). The standard work on the Caracas Company, recently reissued in Spanish, is Roland D. Hussey, *La Compañia de Caracas, 1728-1784* (Caracas, 1962).

[3] Although the exact number of slaves brought into Venezuela during the colonial period is extremely difficult to determine, more slaves entered the province in the half-century after 1730 than in the two preceding centuries. Brito Figueroa's *La estructura económica*, pp. 112-138, has estimates on the slave trade to Venezuela. See also Miguel Acosta Saignes, *La trata de esclavos en Venezuela* (Caracas, 1961).

[4]Venezuela's population in 1810 was composed of four symbolic ethnic groups: whites, Pardos (mulattoes), Negroes, and slaves. The largest group, the Pardos, may have made up 80 percent of the population. Negroes and black slaves equaled about 10 percent at the most. The best information on Venezuelan population in this period is Alexander Von Humboldt, *Viaje a las regiones equinocciales del nuevo continente hecho en 1799, 1800, 1801, 1802, 1803 y 1804 por . . . y A. Bonpland*, 4 vols., 2d ed. (Caracas, 1956). A summary of Venezuela's population after 1830 can be found in my book *The Decline and Abolition of Negro Slavery in Venezuela, 1820-1854* (Westport, Conn., 1971).

[5]For information on the politics and society of Venezuela (1830-1858), the following works are particularly helpful. Federico Brito Figueroa, *Ensayos de historia social Venezolana* (Caracas, 1960); Brito Figueroa, *Ezequiel Zamora: un capítulo de la historia nacional* (Caracas, 1951); Ramón Díaz Sánchez, *Guzmán: elipse de una ambición de poder* (Caracas, 1950); José Antonio Páez, *Autobiografía del general. . .*, 2 vols. (New York, 1867-1869); Caracciolo Parra Pérez, *Mariño y las guerras civiles*, 3 vols. (Madrid, 1958-1960); John G. A. Williamson, *Caracas Diary, 1835-1840: The Journal of . . . First Diplomatic Representative of the United States to Venezuela*, ed. Jane Lucas de Grummond (Baton Rouge, La., 1954); and Robert Ker Porter, *Sir Robert Ker Porter's Caracas Diary, 1825-1842: A British Diplomat in a Newborn Nation*, ed. Walter Dupouy (Caracas, 1966). For some provocative long-range views of Venezuelan history, see Germán Carrera Damas, *Crítica histórica: ensayos y artículos* (Caracas, 1960); Brito Figueroa, *Historia económico-social de Venezuela; una estructura para su estudio*, 2 vols. (Caracas, 1966); Robert L. Gilmore, *Caudillism and Militarism in Venezuela, 1810-1910* (Athens, Ohio, 1964); and Laureano Vallenilla Lanz, *Cesarismo democrático: estudios sobre las bases sociológicas de la constitución efectiva de Venezuela*, 4th ed. (Caracas, 1961).

[6]Richard Konetzke, ed., *Colección de documentos para la historia de la formación social de Hispanoamérica, 1493-1810*, 3 vols. (Madrid, 1953); Rolando Mellafe, *La Esclavitud en Hispanoamérica* (Buenos Aires, 1964); and Acosta Saignes, *Vida de los esclavos negros en Venezuela* (Caracas, 1967).

[7]Konetzke, *Documentos*, 2: 754; 3: 113-114. At one time royal theorists believed a tightening up of the slave system would be useful. See *ibid.*, 3: 553-573. Some years later, however, the royal conscience became considerably liberalized. *Ibid.*, 3: 643-652; 3: 543-544. Also useful is the "Consulta del consejo de las Indias sobre el Reglamento expedido en 31 mayo

de 1789 de los negros esclavos de América," in Konetzke, *Colección*, 3: 726-732; and Humboldt, *Viaje*, 2: 105-106.

[8]*Materiales para el estudio de la cuestión agraria en Venezuela (1800-1830)* (Caracas, 1964), 1: 40-41. Brito Figueroa, *La estructura económica*, p. 112-138. *Libro de actas del supremo Congreso de Venezuela, 1811-1812*, 2 vols. (Sesquicentenario de la Independencia, Nos. 3 and 4 [Caracas, 1959]), 1: 254-262.

[9]Narciso Coll y Prat, *Memoriales sobre la independencia de Venezuela* (Sesquicentenario de la Independencia, No. 23 [Caracas, 1960], pp. 237-239.

[10]The text of a decree authorizing slave enlistments issued in May of 1812 has evidently been lost, and many authors confuse the slave enlistment decree with the more famous *Ley Marcial*, which never mentions slaves. See Feliciano Montenegro y Colón, *Historia de Venezuela*, 2 vols. (Sesquicentenario de la Independencia, Nos. 26 and 27 [Caracas, 1960]), 1: 244: and Héctor Parra Márquez, *Presidentes de Venezuela: El Dr. Francisco Espejo (ensayo biográfico)* (Caracas, 1944), pp. 159-161. For some interesting comment on the slave enlistment decrees, see the following letters to Miranda in the *Archivo del General Miranda* (Havana, 1950), 24: 55-56, 199, 288, 211, 212, and 405-413. Also Parra Pérez, *Historia de la Primera República de Venezuela* (Sesquicentenario de la Independencia, Nos. 19 and 20 [Caracas, 1959]), 2: 299, 308-309, 415-417; Francisco Javier Yanes, *Relación documentada de los principales sucesos ocurridos en Venezuela desde que se declaró estado independiente hasta el año de 1821* (Caracas, 1943) 1: 41; and Vicente Dávila, *Investigaciones históricas* (Quito, 1955), pp. 13-17. See also *Causas de infidencia* (Sesquicentenario de la Independencia, Nos. 31 and 32 [Caracas, 1960]), 2: 92; José de Austria, *Bosquejo de la historia militar de Venezuela* (Sesquicentenario de la Independencia, Nos. 29 and 30 [Caracas, 1960]), 2: 103; and Francisco Miranda, *Textos sobre la independencia* (Sesquicentenario de la Independencia, No. 13 [Caracas, 1959]), pp. 164-165; U.S. Department of State, Consular Despatches, La Guaira, No. 84, Vol. 1 (Robert Smith, La Guaira, 30 November 1810).

[11]*Materiales para*, 1: 134-135, 136-137, 164-170, 171-178; Austria, *Bosquejo*, 2: 210; Juan Vicente González, "Biografía de José Felix Ribas," in *Pensamiento político venezolano del siglo XIX: textos para su estudio* (Caracas, 1960-1962), 2: 203.

[12]*Cartas del Libertador*, 3 vols., 2d ed. (Caracas, 1964), 1: 139-140, 182,

240-244, 292, 309-310, 322-325; *Decretos del Libertador*, 3 vols. (Caracas, 1961), 1: 55-56, 56-57; Austria, *Bosquejo*, 2: 447, 448; Vicente Lecuna, *Crónica razonada de las guerras de Bolívar*, 2 vols., 2d ed. (New York, 1960), 1: 460; *Materiales para*, 1: 297, 314-315.

¹³For various examples of slave enlistment, see the series of *expedientes* in *Archivo General de la Nación (AGN)*, Gran Colombia—Intendencia de Venezuela, 4 (1822), 338; and 9 (1822), 24-229. Also useful is Austria, *Bosquejo*, 2: 448; Arturo Santana, *La Campaña de Carabobo (1821): Relación histórica militar* (Caracas, 1921), pp. 192, 194. For slave enlistment decrees, see Austria, *Bosquejo*, 2: 447; *Decretos del Libertador*, 1: 55-56, 125, 214; *Las fuerzas armadas de Venezuela en el siglo XIX*, 8 vols. (Caracas, 1963-1965), 2: 169. Bolívar's long correspondence with Santander over slave policy in Colombia helps explain Bolivar's abolitionist stance: *Cartas del Libertador*, 2: 223, 273, 305, 307, 309, 323, 328, 344, 348, 351, 361, 369, 379-380, 381. For Santander's side of the exchange, see *Bolívar y Santander, correspondencia, 1819-1820* (Bogotá, 1940), pp. 139-140, 167-169, 180-182, 183-185, 230-231, 238. Bolívar's opinions later on in the war can be found in *Cartas del Libertador* (Caracas, 1929), 5: 11, 349; 6: 33.

¹⁴*AGN*, Gran Col.—Int. de Ven., 32 (1821): 43-46; 63 (1822): 184; 4 (1822): 190-193; Tomás José Hernández de Sanavria, *Fomento de la agricultura: Discurso canónico-legal sobre la necesidad de una ley que reduzca los censos en Venezuela* (Caracas, 1823); *Materiales para*, 1: 297, 314-315; Porter, *Diary*, pp. 608, 609, 699, 756, 1067-1068; Public Record Office (London), Foreign Office, 80, Vol. 26, ff. 51-54 (PRO, FO 80/26, 51-54) (Belford H. Wilson to FO, Caracas, 19 May 1844); PRO, FO 80/32, 117-121 (Belford H. Wilson to FO, Caracas, 31 March 1845); U.S. Department of State, Diplomatic Despatches, Venezuela, No. 79, Vol. 1 (U.S. Dept. State, No. 79, 1) (John G. A. Williamson, Caracas, 25 June 1837); U.S. Dept. State, No. 79, 1 (John G. A. Williamson, Caracas, 7 July 1840); U.S. Dept. State, No. 79, 2 (Allen A. Hall, Caracas, 25 May 1844).

¹⁵*Correo del Orinoco*, No. 51, 5 February 1820.

¹⁶For the text of the 1821 Cúcuta law, see *Cuerpo de leyes de la república de Colombia* (Caracas, 1961), pp. 31-34. See the outstanding pioneer study by Harold A. Bierck, Jr., "The Struggle for Abolition in Gran Colombia," *Hispanic American Historical Review* 33 (August 1953): 365-386.

¹⁷For the text of the 1830 version of the manumission law, see *Colección completa de las leyes, decretos y resoluciones vijentes sobre manumisión, expedidas*

por el Congreso constituyente de la república y gobierno supremo de Venezuela, desde 1830 hasta 1846 (Caracas, 1846), pp. 1-6.

[18]Unfortunately, everyone agreed that manumission was a failure. The best account of this failure is in the annual *Memorias* of the Secretaria del Interior y Justicia between 1831 and 1856. For illustrations of the impossible funding of the manumission program, see *AGN*, Gran Col.—Int. de Ven., 50: 336-362. A variation of the 1830 manumission law was repassed in 1848, *Gaceta de Venezuela*, No. 913, 7 May 1848. For a more detailed analysis of the manumission program, see John V. Lombardi, "*Manumisión* and *Aprendizaje* in Republican Venezuela," *Hispanic American Historical Review* 49, November 1969.

[19]For some pungent comments on the manumission program, see Joaquin Mosquera, *Memoria sobre la necesidad de reformar la ley del congreso constituyente de Colombia, de 21 julio, de 1821, que sancionó la libertad de partos, manumisión, y abolición de tráfico de esclavos y bases que podrían adoptarse para la reforma* (Bogotá, 1825; Caracas, 1829); *Los propietarios de la provincia de Guayana a los propietarios y hombres imparciales del mundo* (Caracas, 1838); and *El Observador Caraqueno*, No. 4, 22 January 1824. See also my article on manumission cited in note 18 above.

[20]Some of the changes proposed by slave owners and vetoed by the government are in *La Bandera Nacional*, No. 89, 9 April 1839; *Correo de Caracas*, No. 19, 14 May 1839; and *El Liberal*, No. 158, 7 May 1839, and No. 201, 3 March 1840. For a good sample of government decisions on manumission and other slave matters, see *Colección completa; AGN*, Int. y Just., 66 (1833): 190-213; 256 (1842): 1-45; 64 (1833): 193-197; 291 (1843): 119-121; 180 (1838): 84-92, 101-112; 195 (1839): 51; 49 (1832): 266-279, 284-295, 307-323, 324-326; 51 (1832): 249-265; 88 (1834): 391-397, 406-506; 161 (1837): 324-333.

[21]Although the manumission system freed only nine hundred slaves, Venezuelans were inordinately proud of their philanthropy. *El Observador Caraqueno*, No. 4, 22 January 1824; *Correo de Caracas*, No. 7, 20 February 1839; U.S. Dept. State, No. 79, 1 (J. G. A. Williamson, Caracas, 12 April 1838); PRO, FO 80/29, 19-22 (Alejo Fortique to FO, London, 9 April 1844).

[22]Economic history has been little cultivated for Venezuela. Particularly helpful for the early, Gran Colombia period are the relevant chapters in David Bushnell's *The Santander Regime in Gran Colombia* (Newark, Del., 1954). Also useful are the interpretive essays by Carrera Damas,

Tres temas de historia (Caracas, 1961), and Brito Figueroa, *Ensayos de historia social Venezolana* (Caracas, 1960). For statistics on the exports of Venezuelan coffee and cacao, see Lombardi, *The Decline and Abolition of Negro Slavery in Venezuela*, Appendices.

²³Humboldt, *Viaje*, 3: 137-139; Hussey, *La compañia de Caracas*, Apéndice II; José Domingo Díaz, *Semanario de Caracas* (Sesquicentenario de la Independencia No. 9 [Caracas, 1959]); Francisco Depons, *Viajes a la parte oriental de Tierra Firme*, 2 vols. (Caracas, 1960), 2: 38-39; Porter, *Caracas Diary*, pp. 141, 354, 432, 434, 596; Robert Ker Porter (Caracas) to Colonel Campbell (Bogotá), 6 February 1829, *Lilly Library* (Indiana University), 1828-1840, Porter Mss., Sir Robert Ker Porter, Autograph Letter Books, 1: 48-50.

²⁴Agustín Codazzi, *Obras escogidas*, 2 vols. (Caracas, 1960), 1: 154-155; Tables 1 and 2; Ramón Veloz, *Economía y finanzas de Venezuela, 1830-1944* (Caracas, 1954).

²⁵For information on interest rates and credit problems, see Brito Figueroa, *La estructura económica*, pp. 285-300; *El Venezolano*, No. 234, 13 April 1844; Nos. 274, 275, 276, 29 March to 26 April 1845; *AGN*, Gran Col.—Int. de Ven., 4 (1822): 190-193; 148 (1823): 31; *Representación dirigida al soberano Congreso sobre que se reduzcan los réditos de los censos constituidos al dos y medio porciento* (1831) in *Sociedad Económica de Amigos del Pais: memorias y estudios, 1829-1839*, 2 vols. (Caracas, 1958), 1: 141-152; *El Patriota Venezolano*, No. 6, 26 January 1832; *La Bandera Nacional*, No. 60, 18 September 1838; *El Promotor*, Nos. 4 to 10, 15 May to 26 June 1843; *El Venezolano*, No. 174, 26 April 1843; No. 177, 9 May 1843; No. 234, 13 April 1844; *Gaceta de Venezuela*, No. 888, 14 November 1847; and *El Liberal*, No. 366, 19 July 1842; No. 367, 22 July 1842; No. 605, 4 July 1846; PRO, FO 80/14, 36 (Daniel F. O'Leary, Caracas, 22 February 1841).

²⁶See Lombardi, *The Decline and Abolition of Negro Slavery in Venezuela*, Appendices.

²⁷For a detailed analysis, see my paper coauthored with James A. Hanson, "The First Venezuelan Coffee Cycle," *Agricultural History*, October 1970.

²⁸The literature on the *10 de abril* is enormous. See for example *El Conciso*, No. 81, 12 April 1834; Fermín Toro, "Reflexiones sobre la ley de 10 de abril de 1834," in *Pensamiento político*, 1: 107-225; *La ley de 10 de abril y el comercio de Venezuela* (Valencia, 1838); Alberto Rojas, *Influencia de la ley de 10 de abril de 1834 sobre la propiedad territorial en Venezuela* (Caracas,

1844); *El Venezolano*, Nos. 194, 197, 199, 202, 206, and 207, 8 August to
24 October 1843, in *Pensamiento politico*, 4: 627-667; *El Agricultor*, No. 4,
13 March 1844.

²⁹For the political history of the 1830-1850 period, see Francisco
Gonzáles Guinán, *Historia contemporanea de Venezuela*, 15 vols. (Caracas,
1954); Parra Pérez, *Mariño y las guerras civiles*; Díaz Sánchez, *Guzmán*;
Williamson, *Caracas Diary*; and Porter, *Diary*.

³⁰It would be too much to expect planters ever to be satisfied with their
workers. However, the complaints registered during boom times were
mainly about behavior rather than excessive cost or shortage. See for
example Caracas, 1833, *Memoria que presenta el gobernador de la provincia de
Caracas a la honorable Diputación de la misma reunida en sus sesiones ordinarias
de 1833* (Caracas, 1833), p. 21; *Memorias de la Sociedad de Amigos del País*,
No. 23, 15 November 1834, in *Sociedad Económica de Amigos del País*, 2:
345-356.

³¹See Lombardi, *The Decline and Abolition of Negro Slavery in Venezuela*,
Appendices.

³²See for example *El Promotor*, Nos. 4 to 10, 15 May to 26 June 1843; *El
Venezolano*, No. 177, 9 May 1843; *El Agricultor*, No. 4, 13 March 1844; *El
Venezolano*, No. 234, 13 April 1844; *El Liberal*, No. 366, 19 July 1842;
Tomás Lander's articles in *El Venezolano*, Nos. 194, 197, 199, 202, 206,
and 207, 8 August to 24 October 1843, in *Pensamiento politico*, 4: 627-667;
Rojas, *Influencia; El Eco de Venezuela*, No. 2, 1 March 1846; *Gaceta de
Venezuela*, No. 890, 28 November 1847; PRO, FO 80/14, 36 (Daniel F.
O'Leary to FO, Caracas, 22 February 1841); PRO, FO 80/22, 46-51
(Daniel F. O'Leary to FO, Puerto Cabello, 30 June 1843); PRO, FO
80/11, 33-35 (Robert Ker Porter to FO, Caracas, 29 March 1840); PRO,
FO 80/25, 84-91 (Belford H. Wilson to FO, Caracas, 13 March 1844);
U.S. Dept. State, No. 79, 1 (John G. A. Williamson, Caracas, 12 April
1838); U.S. Dept. State, No. 79, 2 (Allen A. Hall, Caracas, 1 March 1841).

³³*El Liberal*, No. 75, 17 October 1837; *El Venezolano*, Nos. 50 and 113,
24 May 1841 and 31 May 1842. An accurate reflection of the growing
concern with labor can be obtained from the police codes included in
Fernando Ignacio Parra Aranguren, *Antecedentes del derecho del trabajo en
Venezuela, 1830-1928* (Maracaibo, 1965), pp. 283-351, 465-468. Also
good on the labor problem are *El Venezolano*, No. 104, 12 April 1842; No.
151, 3 January 1843; No. 181, 30 May 1843; *El Liberal*, No. 541, 19 April
1845; *Protesta razonada* (Caracas, 1845); *Gaceta de Venezuela*, No. 826, 15
November 1846; *El Republicano*, No. 57, 11 June 1845.

[34]For some planter pleas, see Rojas, *Influencia*; and the items cited in note 32 above. The hardheaded reaction of Conservatives can be seen in Santos Michelena, "Movilización del crédito territorial," in *Pensamiento político*, 12: 434-444; *Instituto de crédito territorial* (1845); and *Protesta razonada*. Also useful are *El Liberal*, Nos. 366 and 367, 19 July and 22 July 1842; No. 583, 31 January 1846; No. 605, 4 July 1846; *El Venezolano*, Nos. 274, 275, and 276, 29 March to 26 April 1845; *El Nacional*, Nos. 1 to 4, 4 May to 24 May 1848.

[35]González Guinán, *Historia*; Díaz Sánchez, *Guzmán*; Parra Pérez, *Mariño y las guerras civiles*; Rafael Agostini, . . . *a sus conciudadanos* (Caracas, 1845).

[36]By 1810 the slave population could hardly have exceeded 5 percent, and in major agricultural regions perhaps 9 or 10 percent. Humboldt, *Viaje*, 2: 234, and Lombardi, *The Decline and Abolition of Negro Slavery in Venezuela*, Appendices.

[37]*Sociedad Económica de Amigos del País*, 1: 141-152; *El Patriota Venezolano*, No. 6, 26 January 1832; *AGN*, Int. y Just., 169 (1838): 154-159; *Diario de Debates*, Nos. 65, 94, and 98, 28 March to 9 May 1849; Brito Figueroa, *La estructura económica*, pp. 285-300. It is impossible at this time to be precise about the value of slaves in contrast to other forms of agricultural capital. But it is probably safe to say that slaves were second only to cacao or coffee trees in any planter's capital stock. See for example the evaluation in *Archivo Arquidiocesano*, Obras Pías, Carpeta 15, María de la Torre, 1823. Also extremely important is the document collection on the Hacienda Chuao, Eduardo Arcila Farías et al., *La Obra Pía de Chuao, 1568-1825* (Caracas, 1968).

[38]Treaties with Great Britain, for example, made it impossible for the labor-hungry planters to reopen the slave trade, either with Africa or with other Latin American countries. *Correspondence on the Slave Trade with Foreign Powers, Parties to Treaties and Conventions, Under White Captured Vessels Are to be Tried by Tribunals of the Nation to Which They Belong, from January 1 to December 31, 1843, Inclusive. Presented to Both Houses of Parliament by Command of Her Majesty, 1844* (London, 1844) (Belford H. Wilson to F.O., Caracas, 4 August 1843), pp. 302-305.

[39]Information on slave occupations can be found in *AGN*, Int. y Just., 64 (1833): 37-47, 243-252; 66 (1833): 170-189; 67 (1833): 42-68, 199-204; 88 (1834): 83-89, 259-272; 462 (1852): 195-210; 466 (1852): 4-12; 471 (1852): 80-83; 474 (1853): 87-89.

[40]Accounts of runaways are legion. See for example Caracas, 1833,

Memoria, pp. 18-20; *Memorias de la Sociedad de Amigos del País*, No. 23, 15 November 1834, in *Sociedad Económica de Amigos del País*, 2: 345-356; *AGN*, Int. y Just., 117 (1835): 304-308; 166 (1837): 93-94; 169 (1838): 154-159; 176 (1838): 47-56; 56 (1832): 24-29; 108 (1835): 365-369; 158 (1837): 367; 182 (1838): 215-275; 257 (1842): 322-335.

   [41]Caracas, 1832, *Projecto de reglamento general de policia* (Caracas, 1832); Caracas, 1838, *Ordenanza de Policía, expedida por la Disputación Provincial de Caracas en sus reuniones ordinarias de 1838 y 1839, Edición oficial* (Caracas, 1839), p. 60; *El Liberal*, No. 665, 21 August 1847; *AGN*, Int. y Just., 396 (1849): 83-101.

   [42]*AGN*, Int. y Just., 56 (1832): 24-29; 58 (1835): 365-369; 176 (1838): 47-56.

   [43]*AGN*, Int. y Just., 400 (1849): 122-154; 391 (1848): 347-369.

   [44]For information on slave participation in the 1835 Revolución de las Reformas, see Williamson, *Caracas Diary*, p. 72; *AGN*, Int. y Just., 152 (1836): 1-7; 138 (1836): 251-276; PRO, FO 80/3, 189-200 (Robert Ker Porter to FO, Caracas, 21 September 1836); Porter, *Diary*, p. 937; U.S. Dept. State, No. 79, 1 (J. G. A. Williamson, Caracas, 11 November 1835). On slave action during the 1846 uprising, see *El Republicano*, No. 6, 27 June 1844; *El Centinela de la Patria*, No. 8, 9 December 1846; *Diario de la Tarde*, No. 60, 6 August 1846; *El Liberal*, No. 615, 12 September 1846; No. 617, 26 September 1846; No. 622, 24 October 1846; No. 624, 7 November 1846; U.S. Dept. State, No. 79, 3 (Benjamin G. Shields, Caracas, 30 September 1846).

   [45]See the *Memorias* of the Secretaria del Interior y Justicia for 1858 and 1860 and Lombardi, *The Decline and Abolition of Negro Slavery in Venezuela*, Appendices.

   [46]González Guinán, *Historia*; Parra Pérez, *Mariño y las guerras civiles*; U.S. Dept. State, No. 79, 4 (Benjamin G. Shields, Caracas, 7, 29 January, 17, 24, 29 February, 1, 20 May, 21 September 1848, 27 June, 7 July 1849); *AGN*, Int. y Just., 291 (1848): 347-369; 393 (1849): 229-300; 396 (1849): 83-101.

   [47]*El Republicano*, No. 252, 7 November 1849; *Gaceta de Venezuela*, No. 1094, 26 December 1852; No. 1105, 16 April 1853; *Diario de Avisos*, No. 101, 17 May 1850; *El Alerta*, No. 23, 28 February 1850; *El Republicano*, Nos. 236 and 237, 25 August and 3 October 1849; *Diario de Avisos*, No. 4, 22 January 1850; Caracas, 1852, *Ordenanzas, resoluciones y acuerdos de la honorable Diputación Provincial de Caracas en 1852* (Caracas, 1852), pp. 126-127.

[48]*Diario de Debates*, Nos. 7, 8, 10, 16, 17, 19-24, 26, 1, 7-9, 4 March to 25 March 1854; *Diario de Debates* (Senado), Nos. 3, 5, 6, 21 March and 23 March 1854.

[49]*AGN*, Int. y Just., 361 (1848): 1-187, 358-494; 362 (1848): 1-106, 162-252; 511 (1853): 185-358.

[50]*El Eco de los Andes*, No. 8, 28 March 1855.

9

Abolition and the Issue of the Black Freedman's Future in Brazil

*Robert Brent Toplin**

Confrontations over the issue of abolishing slavery in Brazil brought out increasing references to the topic of race. As diverse groups in the dispute struggled with the question of how to handle possible social and economic consequences of emancipation, they offered conflicting interpretations of the black man's prospects for effective participation in civic life. Robert Brent Toplin uncovers considerable evidence of pejorative stereotypes used in the emancipation controversy.

In some ways descriptions of the slave personality given by proslavery groups in Brazil resemble the "Sambo" image that became popularly accepted among the defenders of bondage in the antebellum American South. Many Brazilians, and abolitionists were not lacking among their number, viewed the slaves as docile, indolent individuals who lacked initiative, education, and manners of "civilized" people. But significant differences of opinion developed as leaders related their perception of the slave's personal characteristics to the pressing question of abolition. Whereas proslaveholder groups identified the "problem" as a hindrance to early emancipation, abolitionists argued that liberation and complemen-

*Some sections of this essay, which appear in the author's book, *The Abolition of Slavery in Brazil*, are reprinted by arrangement with Atheneum Publishers.

tary measures to provide opportunities for freedmen would change the attitudes and work habits of the blacks for the better. In short, many abolitionists accepted the Sambo-like description of the bondsman's personality but stressed that these characteristics reflected the slave personality—a product of socialization under the servile institution. In this way, abolitionists could argue that emancipation was an immediate need both for the good of the blacks and of the nation as a whole.

Although abolitionists won the immediate battle, achieving complete emancipation in 1888, they appear to have lost the war for equality, at least in terms of immediate results. The obvious trappings of slavery were gone, but little else had changed. As Magnus Mörner observes, "It was believed by most abolitionists in Brazil and the rest of Latin America that political justice would automatically bring about socioeconomic justice as well. When abolition came, almost no preparations had been made in Brazil and elsewhere to train the new citizens for their functions in order to integrate them with society."* Indeed, the black man's lot, and the prejudice against him, may have been worse after abolition than before.

R. B. T.

The Negro has not fared well in popular descriptions of Brazil's transition from a slave labor economy to a free labor economy in the late nineteenth century. Influential scholars frequently point out that after the abolition of slavery a disproportionately large number of freed blacks became unemployed or underemployed and quickly fell into the ranks of *les misérables* of Brazil. In contrast, these writers notice that many of the European immigrants who arrived in Brazil around the time of abolition (1888) quickly became productive workers in the national economy. For some reason, it seems that employers found the

---

*Magnus Mörner, *Race Mixture in the History of Latin America* (Boston, 1967), p. 129.

labor of white Europeans considerably more attractive than the labor of black freedmen.

A brief glance at the major works of a few prominent Brazilian social scientists reveals the direction of this interpretation. For example, Roberto C. Simonsen, author of many respected publications on the Brazilian economy, wrote in 1938 that "with the introduction of the European settler to coffee production in São Paulo and Minas Gerais, the inferiority of the black work hand was accentuated in relation to the free labor of the white."[1] Similarly, Sérgio Milliet described the competitive disadvantages of blacks. The former director of São Paulo's municipal library discussed the problem in a classic study of demographic changes in the state of São Paulo, published in several editions during the 1930s and 1940s. He observed the blacks' concentration in the most undesirable and unhygienic living areas of the region. Then, somewhat inconsistently, Milliet suggested that the group's high mortality rate might be attributed to its inability to thrive as well as other groups in São Paulo's climatic conditions. On the question of economic survival, Milliet noted that whites not only replaced Negroes and mulattoes in diverse types of economic activities, but through their "elevated proficiency" relegated the colored freedmen to the status of "the most miserable class in society."[2] Even Brazil's famous Marxist historian, Caio Prado Junior, emphasized the immigrants' competitive advantages in his famous survey *História Econômica do Brasil* (Economic History of Brazil), first published in 1945. Prado described the white foreigner's technical aptitudes as "much superior to [those of] the national who recently stepped out of slavery or some similar condition."[3] Another writer, Celso Furtado, assessed the social and economic deficiencies of Brazil's Negro freedmen in greater detail. Furtado, a reform-minded economist and once a high-level planner in the presidential administration of Jango Goulart, studied the response of ex-slaves to the postabolition free labor system in his book *The Economic Growth of Brazil*:

The man raised under slavery is altogether unfit to respond

to economic incentives. Because he has almost no habits of family life, the idea of accumulating wealth is almost entirely alien to him. Moreover, his rudimentary mental development sets narrow limits upon his necessities. Work being a curse for the slaves and leisure an attainable blessing, raising his pay above the cost of his necessities—which are defined by the slave's subsistence level—promptly introduces a strong preference for leisure.

In the old coffee region, where in order to retain the working force it was necessary to pay relatively high wages, there was soon a slackening in working standards. Being able to meet his subsistence expenses on two or three working days a week, the erstwhile slave saw a more attractive proposition in "buying" leisure than in working when he felt he had enough to live on.[4]

How can we assess the low regard for free black labor expressed by these prominent twentieth-century social scientists? Do their descriptions reflect racist attitudes? Actually, a sweeping charge of racism would not be fair or accurate. Some of the writers mentioned have long stressed the need for justice in Brazil —including the specific importance of racial equality. An effort to dismiss their views simply as racist literature would distort an assessment of their perspective on the issues and confuse our understanding of the factors that influence historical interpretation. Especially important, we should remember the context in which their ideas have developed.

Many modern-day interpretations concerning the behavior of freedmen are not new; rather they represent the cumulative result of a thesis constructed in numerous books and essays over several decades. Writers such as Simonsen, Milliet, Prado, and Furtado have been at the mercy of their sources. Not only have older secondary works treated the subject in the same manner, but, indeed, many of the original nineteenth-century documents portray an identical picture of a lethargic response by blacks following the abolition of slavery. Yet this view mirrors the arguments of only *some* groups in a major debate that embroiled political leaders in the abolitionist era. By placing the interpretation in historical perspective—against the full background of ideas expressed in the late nineteenth century—we discover a striking fact. The explanation that has become popular in the twentieth century corresponds closely to the views of nineteenth-century slavocrats and other groups hostile to the blacks.

During the years of the antislavery movement, Brazil's leaders devoted considerable attention to the fate of Afro-Brazilians —perhaps more than at any time in the nation's history. Spokesmen who represented variant political positions—abolitionists, slavocrats, and many who stood between the two extremes —faced the central questions squarely: How well could slaves make the transition to freedom? What new problems would they encounter? What would be the future role of blacks in Brazilian society? How could the condition of freedmen be improved? Unfortunately, many of the abolitionists' viewpoints on these crucial questions have been eclipsed in twentieth-century history books by emphasis on the old antiabolitionist and antiblack arguments.

In the context of developments that preceded the rise of a well-organized abolitionist campaign in the 1880s, it is not surprising that Brazilian slaveholders tried to exploit negative attitudes toward blacks in defending the servile institution. Beginning in the 1860s, significant outcries against human bondage began to put slave proprietors on the defensive. The United States abolished slavery; then Cuba took giant steps toward emancipation, culminating in major reform in 1880 and definitive abolition in 1886. Brazil increasingly appeared isolated as the last great slave power in the Americas. In 1871 the Brazilian government passed a law that many believed would soothe the nation's conscience while showing the world that Dom Pedro's empire was committed to the principle of emancipation. The Rio Branco Law (often called the Free Birth Law) declared free all children of slave mothers born after 28 September 1871 and established a government-sponsored fund to liberate slaves. Reactionary slavocrats vehemently opposed the bill, but as they found ways to circumvent the law and weaken it in practice, they learned to applaud its value and defend it for their own purposes. When a new and more potent antislavery movement gathered force in the 1880s, slaveholders emphasized their endorsement of the Rio Branco Law as the best solution for the emancipation problem. It provided the right mechanism for gradual liberation, they insisted. But impatient abolitionists determined to press for a faster solution, forcing slaveholders to explain the reasons behind their resistance to immediate emancipation. The argument that Negro slaves were unprepared for freedom became one of the most fundamental ideas used by defenders of slavery in their opposition to the abolitionists' timetable for change.

Adamant defenders of slavery, to whom abolitionists gave the epithet of "slavocrat," frequently described the slave in pejorative language, identifying him as typically "lazy," "idle," and "slothful." Bondsmen were unambitious and worked effectively only through coercion, they said.[5] Usually these proslavery critics of black labor missed the irony of their logic. By attributing much of the problem to slavery, they gave a telling condemnation of the very institution they were trying to protect.

Antônio Coelho Rodrigues, a planter-politician from the northeastern province of Piaui, asserted that little could be expected from a man who had spent all of his life as a slave. Freedom could not erase the years of accumulated bad habits. "There are two main problems in the slavery question," Rodrigues explained: "to free the slave from captivity and to incorporate the freedman into civil society." Rodrigues suggested that abolitionists had shown themselves incapable of providing a solution for the second problem. "If they had more prudence in their plans and more probity in their means," he argued, "they would be the party of the future, and not limit their views to simple liberation of the Negroes." Rodrigues questioned the outcome of setting more than a million bondsmen loose upon society, warning, "the police already have enough problems on their hands."[6]

Many other opponents of abolition cautioned against the danger of releasing the slaves, who would only swell the ranks of Brazil's vast population of vagabonds. Already the empire was too heavily burdened with a large class of such aimless "parasites," they said. In 1878 a *fazendeiro* conjectured that the idle element represented 3-1/2 million in the country of 11 million people.[7] A decade later a journalist provided statistics indicating that vagabonds accounted for 42 percent of Brazil's population.[8] It seemed that emancipation would inflate these figures greatly and plague the state with monumental responsibilities.[9]

In the process of developing their unfavorable profile of the Negro, opponents of abolitionism sometimes alluded to concepts of race, slipping into discussions about "instincts" and innate characteristics. Luis Pereira Barreto was direct and frank in expressing his low regard for blacks and their potential role in society. Barreto, a slave owner and enthusiast of Comtian positivism, declared that it was a scientific fact that the "Aryans" were superior to the Negroes, as evidenced by the "Aryans'" greater intelligence and progress in human evolution toward civilization. It was senseless to offer immediate liberty to the Negroes, he declared, because freedom would be useless in their hands and would only increase their impatience. Barreto cautioned the abolitionists against "dumping in the center of the society a horde of semibarbaric men, without direction, without a social goal, without savings, and what is more distressing yet, in an age that does not permit them to reconstruct their education." He believed that liberating thousands of dangerous slaves could bring a conservative reaction that would make the Negroes' condition even worse than under slavery.[10] Arguing in the same vein, the editors of the proslaveholder newspaper *O Cruzeiro* charged that the abolitionists did not understand the unreliable nature of the slave. When not obligated to work, the Negro would turn to crime and vagabondage "like a savage animal of the African deserts." "The animal instinct in them is superior to reason," added the editors.[11] Similarly, a propaganda pamphlet disseminated by the Commercial Association of Rio de Janeiro expressed apprehension about freeing the blacks. The truth is, the Association claimed, "that in Brazil, as all over, the freedman is incompatible with any regime of economy, order, labor, and morality." It described the free blacks as "miserable" individuals who were ignorant of their rights and duties and without a proper notion of morality. Abolition would have to wait until some adequate plan could be arranged to provide for "the adaptation of an inferior and uneducated race to the precepts of the civilization and the social state of the other races."[12]

Antiblack biases also gained currency among some antislavery spokesmen who worried about the consequences of mass liberation. Francisco Antônio Brandão, one of Brazil's first influential positivists, found slavery anachronistic and detrimental to the empire's economic development, but he expressed reservations about the potential of the free black:

What will be the consequences of a premature measure for abolition? Everyone knows that the slave is absolutely lacking in instruction, is still in the infancy of social sentiments, shows no love of labor, and carries it out only by fear of castigation. He is increasingly inhabiting a country in which the material necessities of life can be satisfied with little exertion by hunting game, fishing, and eating fruits. Furthermore, he nurses an antipathy toward whites and mestizos. We repeat, in this state the slave cannot be assimilated into society. . . .[13]

A few statements by writers who were both antislavery and antiblack smacked of outright race prejudice. Most such claims of racial inferiority were offered as personal assessments of black character, unsupported by the supposedly sophisticated evidence of the "scientific" schools of racism emerging at the time in Europe and the United States. Only a few people in the academies and intellectual circles had much exposure to the ideas of Houston Stewart Chamberlain, Joseph Arthur Gobineau, or the Social Darwinists. Louis Couty, a Frenchman and professor in the Polytechnic School in Rio de Janeiro, probably came closest to espousing the new interpretations reaching popularity in other countries. Couty wrote several books and articles on slavery, immigration, and politics in Brazil that attracted considerable attention from all groups—slavocrats, abolitionists, and the many who adopted positions between the two. He described slavery as an inefficient and antiquated system that had to be abandoned, but argued that immediate abolition would be disastrous because the slaves were not ready for freedom. Couty warned Brazilians not to imitate the naive ways of abolitionists in other countries:

> The theoretical partisans of complete equality of the black and white races had believed in the possibility of rapid trans-formation of the slave into a free worker; and in the English parliament and in the French parliament they clearly man-ifested the hope of seeing the freedman immediately become an active and useful worker.[14]

Unfortunately, thought Couty, many Brazilian abolitionists were endorsing the same theory, giving particular emphasis to the historical conditions that had led to the slave's present condition. Abolitionists believed, said Couty, that when the black man came to Brazil on slave ships he was the intellectual and moral equal of the European colonist, but after the conditioning of years or generations in slavery, he became reluctant to carry out serious and sustained work. Give the black man his liberty, said the abolitionists, and he will respect manual labor and work effec-tively.

This interpretation was too simplistic, insisted Couty. The em-phasis on environment and customs diverted attention from im-portant factors related to "biological and social conditions." No rapid transformation in work habits was possible, because the problem involved race as well as environment. To understand the nature of racial differences, Couty suggested study of the shape of the black's cranium and his record of difficulty in learning the ways of "civilized people." Couty believed the evidence would support his contention that the black was less intelligent than the white man and was in a primitive state of evolution—that is, an inferior being. Consequently, he called for mass immigration of Europeans to replace the slave workers, a process that eventually would permit the complete abolition of slavery.[15]

During the 1880s, many Brazilian leaders were preoccupied with attracting white European immigrants who, they believed, offered intelligence and skills superior to those of other groups.[16] This had been a major concern during the days of the African slave trade when some Brazilians opposed the traffic because it only increased the population of "stupid slaves," perpetuating ignorance in the empire. One writer at the time suggested that liberated blacks who did not work should be shipped back to Africa.[17] After the close of the Atlantic slave trade, Francisco Antônio Brandão Junior rejoiced, claiming it would work to the "advantage of the white race, which, being the more intelligent, will eventually triumph over the Negro race by exclusive dominance or by complete fusion, as is now happening."[18] As Brazilians addressed the manpower issue in the last quarter of the nineteenth century, they spoke of the good and poor "blood" in the nation's racial and ethnic stock and the need, as a prominent slaveholder from Rio de Janeiro described it, of "inoculating new blood into our veins."[19] Almost all believed that an increase in white "blood" would improve the national character. The immigration of Italians and Germans would help "to populate this vast land, instituting a new crossing from which will emerge the New Brazilian, much better than the present one," reported the governor of Pernambuco.[20]

Pro-immigration leaders from São Paulo and the deep south showed more reluctance to consider assimilation as an answer. They intended to recruit Europeans, with the expectation that immigrants would work to the exclusion of other groups and avoid racial intermixture. The country was already terribly debilitated from the "impure blood" of Africans, they thought, and there was no need further to "bastardize" the population.[21]

São Paulo was most successful in attracting Europeans. The Paulistas were fortunate in being able to offer more fertile soil, a more attractive climate, higher wages, and better employment opportunities than in other provinces of the empire. Also, they took concerted action to attract foreigners, especially through the leadership of important political figures such as Antônio Prado, Rodrigues Alves, Martinho Prado Junior, and the Baron of Parnaiba. The provincial government of São Paulo aided immigration in the 1880s by taxing slavery to raise funds for recruitment, issuing government grants to private immigration societies, supplying funds for the transportation of Europeans, providing food and lodging for settlers in Brazil, and arranging other forms of subsidy. Consequently, the province received the bulk of the immigrants. Of 55,965 Europeans who settled in Brazil in 1887, 34,306 went to São Paulo.[22]

The immigration fetish also excited leaders in other parts of Brazil. Provinces to the south of São Paulo were successful in attracting Europeans. Numerous Germans moved to Rio Grande do Sul and Santa Catarina, and many Poles settled in Paraná.[23] Leaders in other sections tried to attract immigrants, too, but with less success. Interest in the subject intensified in Bahia, for example, when the abolition of slavery appeared imminent. Citizens formed the Bahian Immigration Society to sponsor subsidized programs similar to those of the Paulistas. They hoped the new efforts would facilitate "the transition from the boorish labor of the slave to the intelligent labor of the European. . . ."[24] *Fazendeiros* in Minas Gerais and Rio de Janeiro also advocated immigration, particularly the recruitment of Portuguese and Germans. They found the Portuguese attractive for the language and customs they shared with Brazilians, whereas Germans appeared to offer the special qualities of the "Anglo-Saxon Race." During the 1880s it became dramatically clear, however, that the region from São Paulo south to Rio Grande do Sul could appeal to foreigners with much greater success than other areas of the empire. The presence of many slaves, weaknesses in the economy, and climatic conditions all operated to the disfavor of other provinces.

Pro-immigration spokesmen frequently referred to "the manpower problem"—a labor shortage that they said could be alleviated by importation of great masses of foreigners. Until enough Europeans could be found to fill the gap, emancipation of the slaves would have to be delayed. Few of those who emphasized the "manpower problem" showed much interest in recruiting ex-slaves, despite the fact that the ranks of the freed blacks could easily supply one of the largest and most immediately available sources of labor after abolition. In an age when many identified manpower shortage as a crucial economic problem, their hesitancy in welcoming the employment of freedmen betrayed their social and racial prejudices.

Leaders who readily acknowledged the title of "abolitionist" and scorned temporizing measures for emancipation denied the existence of a manpower shortage of great dimensions. "Is there a serious shortage of people in this country?" asked Henrique de Beaurepaire Rohan. "No, certainly not. There are millions of men who could devote their labor to plantation agriculture."[25] Similarly, Domingo Maria Gonçalves cast skeptical eyes on the labor deficiency bugaboo, explaining that one could always say there was a lack of work hands as long as *fazendeiros* refused to pay their laborers decent wages.[26]

Abolitionists supported the drive to attract foreigners to Brazil and described slavery as a significant deterrent to immigration, but they also directed their attention to the slaves and the important role they could play in the economy as freedmen. Joaquim Nabuco, the most influential abolitionist spokesman in parliament, expressed this attitude when he discussed the case of the people who already were "Brazilians":

> The recourse to immigration is very important, but it is secondary to . . . another: that of transforming and linking all of our population to labor. If the people do not toil it is because they *cannot* or *do not wish* to do so, and our task is to make sure that they are able and that they desire to work, creating the competitive spirit that they lack if they are short

on initiative, destroying the obstacles—*whatever they are*—that obstruct them, if it is because they are unable to work.[27]

Although problack abolitionists stressed the central role of freedmen in the future labor market, they also indicated awareness of attendant difficulties, acknowledging that the "school of slavery" had done little to prepare its victims for the competitive system. They admitted that slavery provided an undesirable socialization process, nurturing attitudes that compounded the problems. Rohan noted that the prevalence of slave labor in major production activities pushed the freedmen into a life of hunger, crime, and idleness.[28] Gonçalves claimed that slaves were "semibarbarized by the sad institution," and Nabuco referred to the "animal-like" passions of slaves.[29] Another abolitionist, J. Simões, agreed that the blacks had been kept ignorant under slavery, and Luis Anselmo Fonseca believed they had to be carefully protected and guided. "The slave is a little more than a brute and a little less than a child," said Fonseca.[30] But abolitionists saw these conditions as a result of slavery and, therefore, another reason for abolishing it. Moreover, abolitionists differed from most slaveholders in that they proposed to do something about the black's social and economic deficiencies. Throughout the antislavery campaign, abolitionists discussed and presented numerous projects to help the freedmen make new adjustments. Abolitionist literature abounded with recommendations for programs to provide productive opportunities for black freedmen. Particularly salient were programs for education, land reform, and monetary incentives.

Leading abolitionists such as André Rebouças, J. Simões, Francisco Maria Duprat, and Manoel Pinto de Souza Dantas appealed for agricultural schools and apprenticeship programs to assist *libertos* (freedmen) in finding jobs after emancipation.[31] "Liberty without labor cannot save this country from the social bankruptcy of slavery. Labor without technical instruction and without moral education of the worker cannot open horizons for the Brazilian nation," argued Joaquim Nabuco.[32] Domingo Maria Gonçalves voiced the same opinion, proposing that liberation be accompanied by opportunities to attend agricultural schools. "One thing without the other can bring the complete ruin of the nation," he warned. When Gonçalves wrote his book *A instrucção agricola e o trabalho livre* (Agricultural Instruction and Free Labor) in 1880, he had already organized a school in Pernambuco to provide a basic education for 100 Indians and was at work on a new project in Campos where he established a school for 200 youths, mostly black and mulatto orphans. He created the program under great difficulty. The legislature of Rio de Janeiro authorized it, but the provincial president refused to carry out the decision. Gonçalves tried to establish the school on his own initiative but found money lenders in the province reluctant to finance his project. Finally he pulled together a shoestring budget and established a school to teach the poor agronomy, horticulture, mechanical agriculture, animal husbandry, and veterinary science. Gonçalves stressed the problem of inadequate interest in education by noting that Brazil, an agricultural nation, did not sponsor a single agricultural school.[33]

The issue of land reform also attracted the attention of many abolitionists. Joaquim Nabuco stressed the need for an "agrarian law"—legislation that would tax large estates and provide small property for the desperate masses of poor who were increasingly migrating to the cities. Like the education issue, Nabuco linked "democratization of the land" with the abolition of slavery. "One is the complement of the other," Nabuco said. "Finishing with slavery does not complete the job; it is necessary to complete the work of slavery."[34] Manuel Rodrigues Peixoto also asked for levies on land and specifically pointed to the inadequacy of proposals to tax only the land adjacent to railroads. Peixoto called for a general tax that would encourage owners of inefficient large estates to divest some land for more diligent small farmers.[35] The mulatto André Rebouças expressed an especially compassionate concern for the fate of the freedman in his discussion of the land reform issue. On frequent occasions he proposed that the government give small farms to the *libertos*, emphasizing that the blacks deserved this opportunity after 300 years of unpaid toil in slavery. He believed that if blacks could gain a stake in society through individual proprietorship, they would become more industrious workers.[36]

Finally, abolitionists underscored the need to provide incentives. Freedmen who could be rewarded amply for their labor would work well, they said. Slaves would handle their tasks better if planters could promise them liberty in return for an energetic approach to their responsibilities. Abolitionists discussed a variety of examples that attested to the value of incentives. In one situation a planter promised his seventy slaves freedom in five years if they produced a specified amount of sugar in the allotted time. The bondsmen met their quota, then remained on the plantation, working effectively through a partnership arrangement. A Bahian planter made a similar promise, offering freedom in three years if his slaves could meet a production target. The bondsmen worked vigorously, reached their mark, and brought large returns to the proprietor. Also, the Viscount of Silva Figueira (from Rio de Janeiro) gave his 201 slaves liberty on the basis of a term of services and provided food and land for his workers. As a result, the laborers handled their responsibilities with new gusto, and the viscount's crops increased significantly. In other cases cited, *fazendeiros* offered the liberated parcels of land, clothing, medical supplies, and advances in food and money before harvest time.[37] These incentives worked successfully to instill a positive attitude toward labor and to encourage the manumitted to remain on the plantations. In one of the most celebrated cases, which received great publicity, Paula Souza, a wealthy planter from São Paulo and former slavocrat, summoned his five hundred bondsmen and announced unconditional liberty for all of them. In an emotional speech that moved him to tears, he discussed the responsibilities of liberty, then promised a contract equal to that which he had consummated with European immigrants to all those who wished to remain working with him. Only five left permanently. Most of the group took short leaves to celebrate their new freedom, then returned to productive work on the Sousa estate.[38]

Other slaveholders experienced similar situations when abolition came on a national scale. Slaves greeted the news of liberation with profound emotion. When planters gathered them together to make the announcement, some embraced their friends in disbelief and shouted *vivas*, while others stood silent in disbelief. Within a short time, many grabbed their few belongings and ran toward the roads to look for relatives on other plantations or simply to experience freedom of movement for the first time. A large number worked their way into the towns and cities, joining the noisy festivities.[39]

The slaves' first reactions to news of emancipation seemed to confirm the worst fears of old slavocrats. Mass emigrations, which had plagued planters particularly during the last year of the servile institution, continued at an accelerated pace after national liberation, as thousands of freedmen quickly left the estates. Excited by new opportunities of freedom and a chance to escape from authority, they wandered in the countryside and gathered in congested cities. *Fazendeiros* watched in horror, complaining of "anarchy" on the plantations and a "paralyzed" economy. Ripe coffee beans dropped to the ground.[40] Desperate proprietors tried to arrange new contracts with freedmen, only to find that the workers would break agreements and leave the fields at their slightest displeasure. Feeling proud but sensitive about their new status, freedmen resisted subtle pressures on the job, which were designed to increase production or maintain discipline. They balked at mild forms of coercion, charging that such treatment was an offense to their dignity and reminiscent of the old days of control by an overseer. Frequently they quit their jobs, walking off in a huff. Those who remained worked at a leisurely pace, often taking long breaks to eat lunch, talk, smoke, or rest.[41]

Impatient *fazendeiros* viewed the situation as a nightmare turning into reality. They did not care to understand that, generally, the desire to evade work was only a temporary reaction in celebration of liberty. They did not recognize that after a lifetime in slavery it was understandable that freedmen sought a "vacation" from the rigorous plantation routine.[42] Actually, most of the *libertos* terminated their wandering after a few weeks or months and began to seek employment. After sobering to the responsibilities of earning a living and to the need to obtain food and clothing, many signed contracts with *fazendeiros* and returned to work in the rural districts. Those who had fled during the time of slavery tended not to return to their old masters. They preferred to contract with different *fazendeiros* in places that would not provide a constant reminder of the days of slavery. Many never took extended leaves from the plantations. After marking a short time to celebrate liberty, they again fell into the work routine on their former masters' estates.[43]

Some ex-slavocrats were surprised by the behavior of their liberated slaves. After all their gloomy predictions, the results of emancipation proved satisfactory. When Paulino de Souza gathered his workers together to make the important announcement, he asked forgiveness. Immediately, one of the liberated stood up and made a speech, indicating that Paulino did not need to ask forgiveness and that they would stay on the *fazenda*. With *vivas* to the abolitionists, Paulino's ex-slaves began their celebration. The results of abolition also impressed the notorious former police chief, Antônio Coelho Bastos. After all his workers remained on the plantation, he admitted to a friend, "The abolition law only proved advantageous to me."[44] Reports from provincial authorities in diverse points of the empire similarly indicated that many of the old fears had been exaggerated. With the exception of the popular festivities and some minor incidents, provincial leaders in São Paulo, Rio de Janeiro, Minas Gerais, Bahia, and Alagoas announced that the transition had been made without disorders and without need for major intervention by the authorities.[45]

As freedmen prepared to return to work, however, many were shocked to learn that planters no longer wanted them. This situation became especially noticeable in São Paulo, where in 1888 alone, 92,086 immigrants entered the province, a number larger than the Paulista slave population at the beginning of the year.[46] Feeling renewed confidence in a seller's market, many *fazendeiros* turned the freedmen away, declaring that the ex-slaves' temporary absences were examples of "Negro ingratitude" in response to their masters' emancipatory actions. Proprietors in São Paulo announced their preference for foreign labor, viewing the freedmen as "vagabonds"—a group of "irresponsible" or even "useless" people.[47]

Ex-abolitionists expressed considerably more hope about the future of the freedmen and tried to prepare them for a new, constructive role in society. In São Paulo and Bahia, for example, ex-abolitionists established special schools to educate both children and adults, teach them their "rights and duties," and assist them in finding employment.[48] Joaquim Nabuco voiced the concern of his friends a few days before passage of the emancipation law when he said,

> Abolition directed only toward liberating the slaves without bothering to place them in the social and normal conditions of free men would prepare a sad future for the enslaved race. Fortunately, our form of abolitionism bases its cause on the present and the future of the Negro race, in slavery and in liberty, and, therefore, we need union and determination on the eve of the day in which their social state is going to be decided.[49]

Unfortunately, the momentum of abolitionism died out after 13 May. Abolitionists were not entirely to blame for the simplicity of the emancipation law, which was not followed by attendant social legislation to benefit the liberated. The violence of the last years of slavery served as a catalyst to frighten proprietors into action and precipitate the fall of the servile institution. Ironically, though, violence weakened the radical abolitionists' chances of effectuating related goals. The element of fear stimulated political leaders who had shown little interest in the plight of blacks to jump on the antislavery bandwagon and declare themselves "abolitionists." The "Golden Law" was passed by legislators representing multifarious interests; it was not solely the product of hard-core abolitionists. After abolition, political power remained in the hands of the great *fazendeiros*, men who did not wish to bear the costs of the abolitionists' humanitarian programs and who saw serious threats in some of their more radical suggestions, such as the subdivision of large, landed estates. In the months following 13 May, ex-abolitionists became preoccupied with new political battles fomented by the planters, namely, the issues of indemnification and republicanism. The few private benevolent organizations created by the reformers could hardly cope with the monumental task of elevating the condition of the liberated masses. Hence rural proprietors succeeded in snuffing out the flames of agitation and discontent by destroying the most symbolic institution of bondage, while leaving other forms of exploitation intact.[50]

Emancipation did not result in any significant change in the position of free blacks in the Brazilian social structure. In a society of rigid class lines, they were left on the lowest rung of the social ladder. The new, emerging order was a competitive society, and freedmen were ill-prepared to participate in it. The "school of slavery" had hardly developed occupational competence. Some women found urban jobs in the domestic services, and the few freedmen who had special skills acquired positions as artisans. Some well-mannered house servants retained privileged positions, and freedmen who were fortunate in obtaining land outside the cities succeeded in supplying the growing urban centers with fruit, vegetables, and eggs. But, for the majority, particularly those who had been field hands, the opportunities were limited to temporary, insecure, and degrading jobs. As marginal men in the economy, they formed the occupational groups that worked for the lowest wages. Many who joined the exodus to the cities established *favelas* (shanty towns), whereas workers in the rural areas became tenant farmers or sharecroppers.[51]

The position of most blacks in Brazil remained bleak in the decades that followed. Without land, and deficient in education and capital, they were locked in the culture of poverty. This persistent condition tended to reinforce the popular prejudices of the dominant classes that stereotyped blacks as lazy, shiftless vagabonds. As early as 1895, Antônio Guimarães Barroso commented on the sickening examples "of a society full of ruinous prejudices originating from the institution of slavery." The former abolitionist from São Paulo sadly looked back on the shattered hopes of the freedmen, saying, "I never believed, nor did it ever pass through my imagination, that with the extinction of slavery a new class of free slaves would be created."[52]

In modern times many have forgotten the importance of a crucial fact about the abolition of slavery in Brazil—that it was not accompanied by complementary social measures to benefit the liberated. Blacks received juridical freedom and little else. Nothing was done on a large scale to offset the weight of a lifetime in slavery that freedmen carried with them when they suddenly entered the competitive world as "free laborers." The diverse types of opportunities that abolitionists had hoped to create never came to fruition.

Today many of the popular history texts in Brazil contain critical commentary on the economic hardship to the planters brought on by the government's hurried decision in 1888 to pass immediate emancipation without indemnification. But few give much attention to the statement of abolitionist Rui Barbosa, who said during the heat of the debate over compensation: "If someone should be indemnified, it ought to be the slaves for having been in captivity so long."[53]

Notes

[1]Roberto C. Simonsen, *Aspectos da história econômica do café* (Rio de Janeiro, 1938), p. 49.

[2]Sérgio Milliet, *Roteiro do café e outros ensaios* (São Paulo, 1946), pp. 145-155.

[3]Caio Prado Junior, *História Econômica do Brasil* (São Paulo, 1969), p. 257.

[4]Celso Furtado, *The Economic Growth of Brazil: A Survey from Colonial to Modern Times* (Berkeley and Los Angeles, 1965), pp. 153-154.

[5]Peixoto de Brito, *Considerações geraes sôbre a emancipação dos escravos no império do Brasil. Indicação dos meios próprias para realisal-a* (Lisbon, 1870), pp. 20-22; *Brazil*, 4 April 1884, p. 1; *Annaes da Câmara do Parlamento Brasileiro* 1 (1884): 246; *Annaes do Senado do Parlamento Brasileiro* 1 (1888): 42.

[6]Antônio Coelho Rodrigues, *Manual do subdito fiel ou cartas de um lavrador a sua magestade o Imperador sôbre a questão do elemento servil* (Rio de Janeiro, 1884), p. 92.

[7]*Congresso Agricola: Colleção de documentos* (Rio de Janeiro, 1878), p. 58.

[8]*Provincia de São Paulo*, 10 April 1888, p. 1.

[9]*Annaes da Câmara* 2 (1884): 68; 1 (1885): 139; *O Cruzeiro*, 6 November 1880, p. 1; *Associação Commercial do Rio de Janeiro: Elemento Servil* (Rio de Janeiro, 1884), p. 6.

[10]See the *Provincia de São Paulo*, 20 November to 30 November 1880.

[11]*O Cruzeiro*, 20 December 1880, p. 3.

[12]*Associação Commercial do Rio de Janeiro: Elemento servil*, pp. 8-10.

[13]Francisco Antônio Brandão Junior, *A escravatura no Brasil* (Brussels, 1865), pp. 53-54.

[14]Louis Couty, *L'esclavage au Brésil* (Paris, 1881), p. 63.

[15]*Ibid.*, pp. 46, 63-74.

[16]*Congresso Agricola*, p. 70; *1° Centenário do Conselheiro Antônio da Silva Prado* (São Paulo, 1946), p. 169.

[17]Augusto de Carvalho, *O Brasil: Colonização e emigração* (Porto, 1876), pp. 130-134.

[18]Brandão, *A escravatura no Brasil*, p. 155.

[19]See "A nossa lavoura" by Pedro D. G. Paes Leme in *Demonstração das conveniências e vantagens a lavoura ao Brasil pela introducção dos trabalhadores asiaticos (da China)* (Rio de Janeiro, 1877), p. 117.

[20]*Mensagem* of the governor of Pernambuco, Alexandre José Barbosa Lima, 6 March 1893, pp. 28-29.

[21]*Congresso Agricola*, pp. 38-39.

[22]*Jornal do Commércio*, 9 January 1888, p. 1; *Relatório* of the president of São Paulo, Francisco de Paula Rodrigues Alves, 27 April 1888, p. 64; *The Rio News*, 24 January 1884; 15 February 1884; Nazareth Prado, ed., *Antônio Prado no império e na república* (Rio de Janeiro, 1929), pp. 53-57; Simonsen, *Aspectos da história econômica do café*, p. 54; Pierre Monbeig, *Pionniers et Planteurs de l'état de São Paulo* (Paris, 1952), p. 92; *Dados para a história de immigração e da colonização em São Paul* (São Paulo, 1916), p. 8; P.

Pereira dos Reis, "Algumas considerações sôbre a imigração em São Paulo," *Revista Sociologia*, March 1961, p. 83.

[23]Milliet, *Roteiro do café e outros ensaios*, p. 145.

[24]*Falla* of the president of Bahia, João Capistrano Bandeira de Mello, 4 October 1887, pp. 135, 140-154; *Falla* of the president of Bahia, Manuel do Nascimento Machado Portella, 3 April 1888, pp. 12-14, 30-35; *Falla* of the vice-president of Bahia, Aurelio Ferreira Espinheira, 3 April 1889, p. 98.

[25]Quoted in André Rebouças, *Abolição immediata e sem indemnização* (Rio de Janeiro, 1883), pp. 18-19.

[26]Domingo Maria Gonçalves, *A instrucção agricola e o trabalho livre* (Rio de Janeiro, 1880), pp. 58-59.

[27]Joaquim Nabuco, *Conferências e discursos abolicionistas* (São Paulo, n.d.), pp. 253-254.

[28]Rebouças, *Abolição immediata*, pp. 18-19; *Congresso Agricola*, pp. 243-251.

[29]Gonçalves, *A instrucção agricola*, p. iv; Joaquim Nabuco, *O abolicionismo* (São Paulo, 1938), pp. 23-24; *Conferência do Sr. Joaquim Nabuco a 22 de 1884 no Theatro Polytheama* (Rio de Janeiro, 1884), pp. 33, 37-38.

[30]*Gazeta da Tarde*, 11 December 1882, p. 2; Luis Anselmo Fonseca, *A escravidão, o clero e o abolicionismo* (Bahia, 1887), p. 590.

[31]*Gazeta da Tarde*, 1 August 1882, p. 1; 11 December 1882, p. 2; *Annaes do Senado* (1887), 3, 16-18 June; *O Libertador*, 1 January 1881, p. 5; *Brasil Agricola*, 30 August and 31 August 1881; *Falla* of the president of Alagoas, José Moreira Alves da Silva, 15 April 1887, p. 5. Abolitionists carried out some projects by their own initiative. João Clapp, president of the Abolitionist Confederation, and Luiz Gama, a black abolitionist leader in São Paulo, operated night classes for slaves and freedmen. In the city of Maceió in Alagoas, abolitionists in the *Sociedade Libertadora Alagoana* founded a school for *ingenuos* (children conditionally freed by the Rio Branco Law), registering 216 students in the program's first year.

[32]Nabuco, *Conferências e discursos abolicionistas*, p. 296.

[33]Gonçalves, *A instrucção agricola*, pp. iii-viii, 46-62.

[34]Carolina Nabuco, *The Life of Joaquim Nabuco* (Stanford, 1950), p. 55; Nabuco, *Conferências e discursos abolicionistas*, p. 286.

[35]Manuel Rodrigues Peixoto, *A crise do assucar: Os pequenos engenhos centraes, a colonisação e o problema servil* (Rio de Janeiro, 1885), pp. 285-286. When Peixoto discussed these ideas in the Chamber of Deputies in

1885, he was still cautious on some aspects of the emancipation question and was not considered a full-fledged abolitionist.

[36] André Rebouças, *A agricultura national* (Rio de Janeiro, 1883), p. 126; Inácio José Verissimo, *André Rebouças através a sua auto-biografia* (Rio de Janeiro, 1939), p. 214; André Rebouças, *Diário e notas autobiográficas*, ed. Ana Flora and Inácio Verissimo (Rio de Janeiro, 1938), p. 315; *Diário da Bahia*, 18 April 1888, p. 1.

[37] *Congresso Agricola*, pp. 247-248; *Revista Illustrada*, 15 March 1887, p. 3; *The Rio News*, 5 June 1880, p. 1; 15 July 1880, p. 1; 5 February 1881, p. 1; *Brasil Agricola*, 31 January 1881, pp. 74-75; Gonçalves, *A instrucção agricola*, pp. 24-45.

[38] *Provincia de São Paulo*, 8 April 1888, p. 1. Newspapers from diverse points of the empire reported on Paula Souza's experience, and, in some cases, published the text of his letter about it. See *Revista Illustrada*, 14 April 1888, p. 2; *Provincia de Minas*, 14 April 1888, p. 3; *Diário da Bahia*, 20 April 1888, p. 2; *Gazeta Mineira*, 19 April 1888, p. 1.

[39] *Revista Illustrada*, 2 June 1888, p. 2; *Provincia de São Paulo*, 5 April 1888, p. 1.

[40] Paulino José Soares de Sousa Jr. to Visconde de Paranaguá, 4 June 1888, 4.6.888, Arquivo do Museu Imperial; Florestan Fernandes, *A integração do negro na sociedade de classes* 2 vols. (São Paulo, 1965), 1: 49; *Provincia de São Paulo*, 1 May 1888, p. 2; Furtado, *The Economic Growth of Brazil*, pp. 153-154; Roberto C. Simonsen, "As consequências econômicas da abolição," *Revista do Arquivo Municipal de São Paulo*, May 1938, p. 266; *Relatório* of the president of São Paulo province, Francisco de Paula Rodrigues Alves, 10 January 1888, p. 23; Nicia Vilela Luz, "A administração provincial de São Paulo em face do movimento abolicionista," *Revista de Administração*, December 1948, p. 94.

[41] *Provincia de São Paulo*, 9 May 1888, pp. 1-2; Fernandes, *A integração do negro*, 1: 49.

[42] *Gazeta do Povo*, 19 March 1888, p. 1.

[43] *Ibid.*, 16 March 1888, p. 1; *Provincia de São Paulo*, 5 April 1888, p. 1.

[44] *Revista Illustrada*, 2 June 1888, p. 2.

[45] *Relatório* of the president of São Paulo, Pedro Vicente de Azevedo, 11 January 1889, p. 144; *Falla* of the president of Minas Gerais, Luiz Eugenio Horta Barbosa, 1 June 1888, p. 51; *Falla* of the vice-president of Bahia, Aurelio Ferreira Espinheira, 3 April 1889, p. 95; *Falla* of the president of Alagoas, José Cesario de Miranda Monteiro de Barros, 6 October 1888, p. 4. Also, see the *Relatório* of the minister of agriculture,

commerce and public works, Rodrigo Augusto da Silva, 1888, p. 25.

⁴⁶Simonsen, *Aspectos da história econômica do café*, p. 54.

⁴⁷Fernandes, *A integração do negro*, pp. 16-18, 32, 49, 55; *Provincia de São Paulo*, 9 May 1888, p. 1. For descriptions of similar attitudes in other sections of Brazil, see Fernando Henrique Cardoso, *Capitalismo e escravidão: O negro na sociedade do Rio Grande do Sul* (São Paulo, 1962), pp. 269, 276, 316; Octavio Ianni, *As metamorfoses do escravo: Apogeu e crise da escravatura no Brasil meridional* (São Paulo, 1962), pp. 264-265.

⁴⁸*Provincia de São Paulo*, 9 May 1888, pp. 1-2; *Diário da Bahia*, 10 May 1888, 26 May 1888.

⁴⁹*Gazeta do Povo*, 2 May 1888, p. 1.

⁵⁰Cardoso, *Capitalismo e escravidão*, p. 269; Abdias do Nascimento, "80 Anos de abolição," *Cadernos Brasileiros*, May-June 1968, pp. 3-8. Thirty years after abolition Rui Barbosa recalled the way in which the freedmen had been left to themselves, describing the emancipation experience as an "atrocious irony." See the introduction to Rui Barbosa, *Emancipação dos escravos; Obras Completas de Rui Barbosa* (Rio de Janeiro, 1945), 11: xxxvii-xxxviii. Similarly, in 1885 Joaquim Nabuco noticed that slaves could no longer be found in the two freed provinces of Ceará and Amazonas, but "slavery" seemed to continue there in other forms. See Nabuco, *Conferências e discursos abolicionistas*, pp. 291-292. Nilo Odalia believes the planters' post-abolition fight for indemnification was a diversionary tactic to preclude discussion of measures to help the freedmen, particularly consideration of programs to redistribute land. See "A abolição da escravatura," *Anais do Museu Paulista* 18 (1964): 138.

⁵¹Stanley J. Stein, *Vassouras: A Brazilian Coffee County, 1850-1900* (Cambridge, 1957), pp. 271-274; Afonso de Toledo Bandeira, *O trabalho servil no Brasil* (Rio de Janeiro, 1936), p. 83; Fernandes, *A integração do negro*, pp. 3-4, 10, 31-32, 39-43, 49-50; Pierre Denis, *O Brasil no século XX* (Lisbon, n.d.), p. 349; Fernando Henrique Cardoso and Octavio Ianni, *Côr e mobilidade social em Florianópolis: Aspectos das relações êntre negros e brancos numa comunidade do Brasil meridional* (São Paulo, 1960), pp. xxix, 94, 151.

⁵²*A Redempção*, 13 May 1895, p. 1.

⁵³Frank Bennett, *Forty Years in Brazil* (London, 1914), p. 112; Abdias do Nascimento et al., *O negro brasileiro: 80 Anos de abolição* (Rio de Janeiro, 1968), p. 21.

10

Beyond Poverty:
The Negro and the
Mulatto in Brazil*

Florestan Fernandes

Florestan Fernandes' essay further documents the plight of Afro-Brazilians after the abolition of slavery. Fernandes contends that Brazilian racial views were determined over the centuries by the influence of slavery and cannot be considered the products of "external influence" or an "imported cancer," although nineteenth-century European racial thought may have reinforced homegrown ideas and encouraged their frank and open expression. In his view, Brazilian racial attitudes are "an inherited cultural pattern, widespread in Brazilian society as much as slavery was in the past," rituals that mask indifference and oppression with public amicability between whites and blacks.

According to Fernandes, the weight of the past helped to make a mockery of abolition in Brazil. The blacks received little help after emancipation, and, worse, the demise of slavery came concurrently with significant transformations in the national economy, changes that gave semiskilled European immigrants special advantages while leaving black freedmen on the margins of economic activity. Brazilian blacks were lucky if they found positions as subsistence farmers and sharecroppers. The formal

*This paper was first presented in a condensed version at a seminar on Minorities in Latin America and the United States (College of the Finger Lakes, Corning, New York, 5 December 1969).

exploitation under slavery disappeared to be replaced by the anonymous workings of an increasingly rationalized and capitalistic economic system in which the black man found little place. Whites could hardly miss the correlation between poverty and black color and drew regrettable conclusions that ignored the causes of the situation. By their heavy concentration at the bottom of the socioeconomic scale, blacks became the double victims of both class and race prejudice.

R. B. T.

At first glance, the most impressive aspect of the racial situation in Brazil is the adamant denial by most Brazilians of the existence of any "color" or "racial" problem. Racial prejudice and the resulting discrimination (racial segregation, for example) are seen as sinful and dishonorable, and the Brazilian view of their nation as a racial democracy cannot be dismissed out of hand. Rather, what we have in this regard is two different levels of reality perception and behavior connected with "color" and "race": (1) overt perception and behavior in which racial equality and racial democracy are presumed and proclaimed, but also (2) covert perception and behavior in which a complex combination of factors, in part a product of the Brazilian past, move through, below, and beyond the social stratifications to negate the validity of racial democracy.

This overlay is not exclusive to Brazilian race relations; it appears in other levels of social life. In the case of race relations, it is clearly a product of the prevailing racial ideology and concept of racial utopia, both built during the time of slavery by the dominant white stratum—the rural and urban masters. Indeed, the curious quality of Brazilian racial attitudes and practices is of even greater antiquity, antedating the area's discovery by Cabral (1500). As early as the fifteenth century, when African slavery was practiced on a small scale in Lisbon, and (more importantly) attempted in the Azores, the Cape Verdes, Madeira, and São Tomé, pioneering the modern plantation system, tensions began to develop in Portuguese law and cultural tradition. The heritage of Roman law made it a simple matter for the Portuguese crown to frame ordinances that classified the African (and the Indian) as *things*, as movable property, which established the transmission of social position through the mother (according to the principle *partus sequitur ventrem*) and which denied to the slave any human condition (*servus personam non habet*). On the other hand, slavery was in subtle conflict with certain religious principles and mores created by the Catholic conception of the world. In general, the result of this moral conflict was not to give to the slave higher status and more humane treatment, as Frank Tannenbaum believed. Rather, it brought about a tendency to disguise things, separating the formal concept of the slave from the real being.

Nevertheless, Brazil has a good intellectual tradition of penetrating, realistic, and unmaskingly objective observations on the racial situation. First of all, conservative groups sometimes revealed their conceptions of clear racial distinctions; in particular many masters and some nonslaveholding aristocratic white families found the expression of arrogantly self-affirmative statements on matters of racial inequality and race differences hard to resist. Second, some outstanding figures, promoters of the ideals of national emancipation or of abolitionism, such as José Bonifácio de Andrade e Silva, Luiz Gama, Perdigão Malheiro, Joaquim Nabuco, Antonio Bento, and others, tried to point out the nature of the whites' values and behavior regarding Negroes and mulattoes. Third, the "Negro movements" after World War I (especially in São Paulo and Rio de Janeiro during the 1920s, 1930s, and 1940s), as well as conferences on race relations convened by Negro intellectuals, contributed to a new and realistic perception and explanation of the complex Brazilian racial situation.

The findings of modern sociological, anthropological, and psychological investigations have confirmed and deepened the impression gained by earlier writers: Brazilian race relations were not quite what they appeared to be on the surface.[1] In the present discussion, I shall limit myself to three special topics: the roots of competitive social order in Brazil, some objective evidence of racial inequality and its sociological meaning, and the Brazilian pattern of racial prejudice and discrimination.

The Roots of Competitive Social Order in Brazil

In common with all modern countries in which slavery was a part of colonial exploitation and the plantation system, Brazilian society faced great difficulties in spreading and integrating the competitive social order. Literally speaking, this social order emerged with the rupture of the old colonial system, but its evolution was more an urban phenomenon until the last quarter of the nineteenth century. The blunt fact was that slavery represented a great obstacle to the differentiation and universalization of the competitive social order. The reason is very well known. As the contemporary observer Louis Couty pointed out,[2] the devaluation and degradation of work produced by slavery impeded the development of a wage-earning class in both urban and rural Brazil and obstructed the emergence of a small farmer sector. As a result, until the middle of the nineteenth century the market economy did not give rise to typical modern forms of economic relations and labor organization. Only in a few cities could competition perform some basic constructive functions and integrate the roles of some important social agents: the landlords or planters as suppliers of tropical products; the agents of export-import business; native and foreign merchants and traders; some bankers or financial agents; the professionals, teachers, and bureaucrats; the few manufacturers and factory workers; the technicians, artisans, and skilled workers.

With the interruption of the slave traffic and passage of emancipation laws, these sectors began to grow. In the last quarter of the nineteenth century, the crisis of the slavery system—which attained a structural and irreversible decline in the 1860s

—reached its climax. Then the modernization of the urban sector became a strong and autonomous social force, operating simultaneously through the economic and political levels. This was a historical point of inflexion in which the disintegration of the master-slave social order and the integration of the competitive social order appeared as concomitant social phenomena.[3]

In this context the situation of the Negroes and mulattoes was affected significantly. Previously, as slaves or as freedmen, they had a strong and untouchable position in Brazil's economy. Now, with the entire system of production beginning to change, they were menaced on two fronts. With the abolition of slavery, thousands of European immigrants flocked into Brazil's richest and most developed areas to enter both the rural and the urban wage-earning classes. Some found positions as traders, merchants, shopkeepers, and manufacturers. In those areas of the south where foreign colonization was combined with an emphasis on small-scale landholding and in places where cattle ranches controlled by pivotal traditional families predominated, new opportunities were monopolized by Europeans. Furthermore, the economic position of Negroes and mulattoes in southern Brazil was undermined by nationals as well as immigrants. Many other colored workers left the stagnant plantation economy of the north and northeast or were sold as slaves for work on the richer coffee estates in São Paulo, Rio de Janeiro, and Minas Gerais. Their presence made competition keener, and because some of the migrants could offer special skills, they succeeded in wresting many economic opportunities from resident freedmen.[4] Consequently, many Negroes and mulattoes were frozen out of competition by both foreigners and nationals and left in dependent or marginal positions.[5]

Thus we may conclude that the victim of slavery was also victimized by the crisis of the slave system of production. The social revolution of the competitive social order started and finished as a *white revolution*. Because of this, white supremacy was never menaced by abolitionism. On the contrary, it was only reorganized in other terms in which competition had a terrible consequence: the exclusion, partial or total, of the freedmen from the vital flux of economic growth and social development.

As freed Negroes and mulattoes entered the new social order, therefore, they had several choices, all spoliative and deplorable. First, they could return to the regions of their origins (or of their descendants), that is, to some rural area of the northeast or a stagnant and backward community of the interior of São Paulo, Minas Gerais, or Rio de Janeiro. This solution implied submersion into a subsistence economy. Second, they could remain as rural laborers, in general changing from the old masters to new employers. This was not a favorable solution, since the ex-slaves did not possess the education or cultural traditions of the immigrants but had to compete with them for low-paying jobs.[6] Third, they could concentrate in a big city like São Paulo and in the conglomerations in the slums. This solution implied permanent or temporary unemployment for the men, parasitism and overburdening work for the women, and general anomie. Life in the city rarely was the equivalent of sharing the opportunities of the city. Three succeeding generations have known what social disorganization can mean as a style of life. Fourth, they could flee to the smaller cities in which the semiskilled, skilled, or artisan groups could protect themselves from competition with the whites, foreigners, or nationals, and could start a new life. This solution implied voluntary acceptance of a disadvantageous position and could lead to a plight similar to that of freedmen in the northeast, during the period of the disintegration of slavery. The destiny of the agents, then, was a function of the stagnation or progress of the selected community—a matter of blind chance.

From this perspective it is clear that the problem of the Brazilian Negro and mulatto is, above all, a problem created by the incapacity of the national society rapidly to develop a growing capitalistic economy able to absorb them into the labor market. Because of this, they were expelled to the periphery of the competitive social order or to semicolonial and colonial structures inherited from the past. These structures performed important functions in the maintenance of the rural economy, especially where the plantations, cattle ranches, or villages were dependent on semicapitalistic labor systems.[7]

In this respect, one could argue that the ex-slaves and freedmen underwent the destiny common to all "poor people" in Brazil. Poverty developed out of the destitution of the slaves and the elimination of the freedmen by the effects of competition with free European immigrants. As Caio Prado Jr. has pointed out, slavery simply did not prepare its human agents to become free workers, even unskilled or semiskilled laborers.[8] Behind the structure of the master-slave social order, the "slave" and the "Negro" were two parallel elements. When the "slave" was eliminated by social change, the "Negro" became a racial residuum. He lost the onerous social condition acquired under slavery, only to be expelled as "Negro" downward to the bottom of the "poor people" at the exact moment in which some of its sectors were sharing the opportunities opened by a free labor system and the constitution of a wage-earning class. Thus the Negro was victimized by both his position and by his racial condition. Through his own initiative he started the process by which he could be metamorphosed from "Negro" to a new social being.[9] But his attempt to impose the "Second Abolition" upon himself and upon the indifferent whites was refused and condemned as a manifestation of "racism." In other words, he was denied self-affirmation as "Negro" in spite of his social marginality as such.

Evidence of Racial Inequality and Its Sociological Meaning

If the description given above is correct, the changes in social structure that have occurred in Brazilian society since the abolition of slavery have had no profound effects on the racial concentration of wealth, social prestige, and power. The lack of objective indicators does not permit a complete verification of this conclusion. For example, the 1960 census excluded the racial aspects of the Brazilian population. Nevertheless, the census of 1950 offers some useful information.

As is well known, the percentage of the different racial stocks (or color categories) varies in each physiographic region of the country (see Table I), and in consequence, the degree of concentration of each racial group in the different regions also varies (see Table II). Nevertheless, the two basic indicators —occupational position and level of schooling—that can be traced through the census data reveal a near-monopoly of the best opportunities by the whites. I have selected the position of employer and the completed educational levels in some representative states and in the country as the best indicators available. They involved concepts of roles, values, and cultural traditions of prestige, control of power, and upward social mobility.

The basic sociological evidence of the data is not negative, considering that the 1950 census was taken only sixty-two years after the abolition of slavery. Overall, the census data show that the efforts of colored groups to take advantage of opportunities for freedom and progress have resulted in an improvement of their situation. Negroes and mulattoes have gradually acquired new value orientations and cultural traditions; they have enhanced their importance as economic agents (both in the general labor force and as predominantly small entrepreneurs), and they have discovered and used educational opportunities as a ladder to social integration and upward mobility. The importance of these changes is greater than can be realized at first glance because of the cumulative effects of the economic, social, or cultural process involved in the future of new generations.

Nevertheless, the progress has been both deceptive and too moderate. In reality, Negroes and mulattoes were projected into the strata of the poorest people, which shares very little of the benefits of economic development and sociocultural change. Even in the regions where Negroes and mulattoes constitute the majority of the population, as in the northeast and in the east (in which they constitute, conjointly, 53.7 and 47.3 percent, respectively, of the population and in which they are more concentrated—72.8 percent in the northeast and 95.5 percent in the east, by color group), their participation in the best educational opportunities is marginal, and they are severely under-

TABLE I

Brazilian Population: Physiographic Regions and Color (1950)[a]

Physiographic Regions	Color Groups					Total
	Whites	Negroes	Mulattoes	Yellows[b]	No declaration	
North	577,329	90,061	1,171,352	1,446	4,467	1,844,655
	31%	5%	63.5%	0.07%	0.2%	100%
Northeast	5,753,697	1,374,899	5,339,729	216	25,936	12,494,477
	46%	11%	42.7%	0.002%	0.2%	100%
East	9,978,386	2,959,423	6,007,294	5,967	41,937	18,893,007
	52.8%	15.6%	31.7%	0.03%	0.2%	100%
South	14,836,496	1,093,887	696,956	316,641	31,313	16,975,293
	87%	6.5%	4%	2%	0.2%	100%
Central-West	981,753	174,387	571,411	4,812	4,602	1,736,965
	56.5%	10%	32.3%	0.3%	0.3%	100%
BRAZIL	32,027,661	5,692,657	13,786,742	329,082	108,255	51,944,397
	61.6%	11%	26.6%	0.6%	0.2%	100%

a. Census data Instituto Brasileiro de Geográfia e Estatística—Conselho Nacional de Estatística, *Recenseamento Geral do Brasil* (Rio de Janeiro, Servico Gráfico do IBGE, 1956), 1:5.

b. Asiatics, predominantly Japanese.

TABLE II

Brazilian Population: Percentage Distribution by Color Groups, According to the Physiographic Regions (1950)[a]

Regions	Whites	Negroes	Mulattoes	Yellows
North	1.8%	1.6%	8.5%	0.4%
Northeast	17.9%	24.1%	38.7%	0.06%
East	30.8%	52.0%	43.5%	1.8%
South	46.3%	19.2%	5.1%	96.2%
Central-West	3.06%	3.1%	4.0%	1.5%
Brazil	100 %	100 %	100 %	100 %

a. Omitting the cases without declaration of color.

represented in the ranks of employers. In terms of the states selected, the range of inequality relating to employer positions is striking. Whites hold these positions in a proportion of 3, 4, 5, and even 6 or 8 times to 1 of the Negroes. The same is true of the mulatto, whose situation is only slightly better than that of the Negro. We find that whites hold employer positions, on the average, in a proportion that oscillates between 2, 3, or 4 times more than the mulattoes, excepting the case of Rio de Janeiro. The same trends are reproduced in the sharing of educational opportunities. In some states, especially at the secondary school and university level, the situation is shocking (see Tables III and IV). The comparison of the data furnished by these tables with those of Table V shows that the exclusion of Negroes and mulattoes from the best economic and educational opportunities follows the same general pattern in the eight selected states. Whether mulattoes are considered alone or considered together with Negroes makes only a slight difference even in the more "mixed" and more racially "democratic" states.

The meaning of these data is evident. The racial structure of Brazilian society favors the monopoly of wealth, prestige, and power by the whites. White supremacy is a present-day reality in almost the same way as it was in the past. The organization of society impels the Negro and mulatto to poverty, unemployment or underemployment, and to the "Negro's job."[10]

The Brazilian Pattern of Racial Prejudice and Discrimination

Only now are Brazilian social scientists trying to discover the real explanation of this deplorable situation. As Luis de Aguiar Costa Pinto points out, the basic explicative factor is inherent in the persistence of some deep-rooted white attitudes and racial orientations by which the Negroes and mulattoes are both treated as subalterns and, in effect, are subalternized. These attitudes are predominant among the white upper and middle classes, but they appear also in the lower classes and even in the rural areas, especially in the south.

TABLE III

Employers by Color Groups—Brazil and Selected States (1950)[a]

States	Number				Percentage in Each Color Group			
	Whites	Negroes	Mulattoes	Asiatics[b]	Whites	Negroes	Mulattoes	Asiatics[b]
Pará	5,089	208	3,132	88	5.4	0.9	1.4	34.2
Pernambuco	21,121	904	5,836	17	4.0	0.7	1.2	34.6
Bahia	28,178	5,295	20,837	10	6.8	1.6	2.8	15.6
Minas Gerais	85,084	3,910	15,949	107	6.4	1.0	2.5	14.6
Rio de Janeiro	46,477	447	1,283	64	8.2	0.3	0.8	12.5
São Paulo	146,145	2,561	1,396	9,179	5.1	0.8	1.2	10.1
Rio Grande do Sul	49,008	429	576	16	4.2	0.5	0.7	8.8
Mato Grosso	5,171	401	1,330	94	6.6	2.3	2.5	8.9
Brazil	519,197	19,460	78,448	11,018	5.1	0.9	1.8	10.2

a. Census data. Omitting the cases without declaration of position (excepting Pará, in which these cases were included).

b. The Asiatics are nearly all Japanese.

TABLE IV

Educational Levels Completed by Negroes and Mulattoes—Brazil and Selected States (1950)[a]

States		Educational Levels Completed					
Negro Mulatto		Primary		Secondary		University	
		Number	Percent of total[b]	Number	Percent of total[b]	Number	Percent of total[b]
Pará							
	Negroes	1,599	2.2%	85	0.6%	10	0.5%
	Mulattoes	27,536	39.4	2,371	19.2	180	9.5
Pernambuco							
	Negroes	5,899	3.3	192	0.5	7	0.5
	Mulattoes	42,669	24.2	2,889	8.0	189	3.6
Bahia							
	Negroes	17,732	8.3	666	2.1	88	1.5
	Mulattoes	78,742	37.1	44,772	15.2	578	10.1
Minas Gerais							
	Negroes	36,805	5.4	471	0.4	44	0.2
	Mulattoes	103,082	15.3	4,757	4.6	459	2.8

TABLE IV (Continued)

States		Educational Levels Completed					
		Primary		Secondary		University	
	Negro / Mulatto	Number	Percent of total[b]	Number	Percent of total[b]	Number	Percent of total[b]
Rio de Janeiro							
	Negroes	44,541	5.8	2,035	0.8	112	0.2
	Mulattoes	104,315	13.7	9,895	4.1	725	1.6
São Paulo							
	Negroes	76,652	4.3	1,879	0.6	95	0.2
	Mulattoes	31,585	1.8	1,659	0.5	170	0.4
Rio Grande do Sul							
	Negroes	10,091	1.9	310	0.4	14	0.1
	Mulattoes	11,702	2.2	775	1.0	74	0.6
Mato Grosso							
	Negroes	2,543	5.3	59	0.8	3	0.2
	Mulattoes	12,911	27.0	1,148	16.2	89	8.0
Brazil							
	Negroes	228,890	4.2	6,794	0.6	448	0.2
	Mulattoes	551,410	10.2	41,410	4.2	3,568	2.2

a. Census data omitted in the cases without declaration of color and grades (excepting Pará, in which only the cases without declaration of grades were excepted).

b. Total number of persons who have completed the specified level of education for each state.

TABLE V

Population by Color in the Eight Selected States (1950)[a]

States	Color Groups					
	Whites	Negroes	Mulattoes	Yellows	Not Declared	Total
North						
Pará	325,281	59,744	734,574	875	2,799	1,123,273
	28.96	5.32	65.39	0.08	0.25	100
Northeast						
Pernambuco	1,685,028	316,122	1,386,255	83	7,697	3,395,185
	49.63	9.31	40.83	0.00	0.22	100
East						
Bahia	1,428,685	926,075	2,467,108	156	12,551	4,834,575
	29.55	19.16	51.03	0.00	0.26	100
Minas Gerais	4,509,575	1,122,940	2,069,037	2,257	13,983	7,717,792
	58.43	14.55	26.81	0.03	0.18	100
Rio de Janeiro	1,660,834	292,524	415,935	1,032	7,126	2,377,451
	69.86	12.30	17.50	0.04	0.30	100
South						
São Paulo	7,823,111	727,789	292,669	276,851	14,003	9,134,423
	85.64	7.96	3.21	3.03	0.16	100
Rio Grande do Sul	3,712,239	217,520	226,174	495	8,393	4,164,821
	89.14	5.22	5.43	0.01	0.20	100
Central-West						
Mato Grosso	278,378	51,089	187,365	3,649	1,563	522,044
	53.32	9.79	35.89	0.70	0.30	100

a. Information compiled from "Estudos Demográficos No. 145" (Elaborado por Remulo Coelho), Laboratório de Estatística do Instituto Brasileiro de Geografia e Estatística—Conselho Nacional de Estatística (Rio de Janeiro, 1955).

Many Brazilians prefer to believe that these racial orientations are products of "external influence," a negative contribution of immigrants and of the modern mass media of communication. They were and are considered an "imported cancer" to be extirpated by law and formal control.[11] However, the research done by Oracy Nogueira, Roger Bastide, Florestan Fernandes, Luis de Aguiar Costa Pinto, Octávio Ianni, Fernando Henrique Cardoso, and Renato Jardim Moreira has shown that these attitudes and racial orientations are in fact an inherited cultural pattern, as widespread in Brazilian society as slavery was in the past.

Thus at the core of the Brazilian racial problem is the persistence of an asymmetrical pattern of race relations, built to regulate the contact and the social ordination among "master," "slave," and "freedman." As happened in the South of the United States, this type of asymmetrical race relations involves a sort of ritualization of racial behavior.[12] The master's domination and the slave's or freedman's subordination are part of the same ritual, by which emotions and feelings are put under control and masked. In Brazil, this type of ritualization had the same functions, reinforced by Catholic pressure to preserve in some apparent sense the Christian way of life of masters, slaves, and freedmen.

Racial prejudice was inherent in the asymmetrical pattern of race relations because it was a necessary element in basing the slave-master, or freedman-white, relations in the "natural inferiority" of the Negro and in the efficient performance of slavery and subjugation of the slaves and freedmen. At the same time, discrimination was inherent in the slave-master social order in which the proper manner of behavior, the clothing, the language, the occupations, obligations, and rights of the slave and the freedman were rigidly prescribed.[13] The persistence of this pattern after the disintegration of slavery is explained by the fact that the class system did not destroy all structures of the *ancien régime*, especially the structure of race relations.[14]

It is necessary, nevertheless, to take into account that this result is not only part of a process of cultural persistence. Under dependent capitalism, the class system is unable to perform all the destructive or constructive functions assigned to it in developed capitalistic countries.[15] Two processes run together, the modernization of the archaic and the archaization of the modern, as a normal factor of structural integration and of evolution of the society. In reality, as soon as the Negro and the mulatto were put predominantly outside of economic, social, and political reconstruction, they became marginal partners.

The crisis of the asymmetrical pattern of race relations started even before abolition. However, as the Negro and the mulatto lost their importance as historical social agents, they suffered the static effect of their new social position. Only recently, thanks to internal migrations, the economic progress produced by national integration of society, and the weak upward social mobility, have they found disguised and accommodative ways to cope with white supremacy.

In spite of some active white resistance to some outstanding upward-mobile Negro and mulatto personalities, this long period of starvation tended to maintain the ritualistic freezing of racial relations. Even today, the Negro and the mulatto as individuals, but especially as a color minority, are not free to compete aggressively against whites, much less to explore social conflict as a way to fight against racial inequality. In this context, it is very clear that the price of race tolerance and race accommodation is paid by the Negro and the mulatto.

For these reasons, color is not an important element in the racial perception and racial consciousness of the Brazilian white. He has never been menaced, at least until now, by the disintegration of slavery and by competition or conflict with Negroes and mulattoes. The white only perceives, and is conscious of, the Negro or of the mulatto when he faces a concrete, unexpected situation or when his attention is directed to questions related to the "color problem."[16]

For the same reasons the "Brazilian racial dilemma" is also complicated. This is true not so much because whites, Negroes, and mulattoes play their expected roles in disguising or denying "color prejudice" and "color discrimination," but because a change in the racial situation depends on the gradual, slow, and irregular prosperity of Negroes and mulattoes. In this respect, it is unquestionably true that the Brazilian forms of prejudice and discrimination contribute more to maintain the asymmetrical pattern of race relations than to eliminate it.

In sociological terms this means that color prejudice and discrimination are a structural and dynamic source of the "perpetuation of the past in the present." Whites do not victimize Negroes and mulattoes consciously and willfully. The normal and indirect effects of the functions of color prejudice and discrimination do that without racial tensions and social unrest. Because they restrict the economic, educational, social, and political opportunities of the Negro and the mulatto, maintaining them "out of the system" and on the periphery of the competitive social order, color prejudice and discrimination impede the emergence of racial democracy in Brazil.

Conclusions

This general discussion rests on some basic assumptions. Considered sociologically, *the structural element of the Brazilian racial situation* has two distinctive dimensions. One is specifically social. The underdeveloped capitalistic and class societies of Latin America have found it impossible to create a competitive social order able to absorb all sectors of population, even partially, in the occupational and social strata of the system of production. The other, the *"color problem,"* is a complex heritage of the past. It is continuously reinforced by the socioeconomic inequality that has prevailed under dependent capitalism, and preserved through the conjoint manifestation of prejudice and discriminatory behavior on the basis of "color."

These two elements work together to produce cumulative effects dynamically adverse to the change of the racial structure of society inherited from the past. The social order is changing, and with it the patterns of race relations. Nevertheless, the relative position of color groups tends to be stable or to change very slightly.

It is crucial to consider the structure of a class society under dependent capitalism. Extreme concentration of wealth, power, and social prestige severely impedes even the upward social mobility and integration to the competitive social order of white racial stocks. Nevertheless, it is clear that whites very nearly monopolize employer positions and the best educational opportunities. A comparison with the Japanese suggests that, among the whites, there prevails a definite trend to maintain and perhaps strengthen their economic and political privileges and thus preserve present social inequities at the expense of all poor groups regardless of color.

In consequence, the "white poor people" also suffer under the present system. However, the static effects are clearly stronger when we consider the Negroes and the mulattoes. Rather than finding the mulatto in an advantageous position in comparison to the Negro, we learn that he also suffers the economic, social, and political inequities of Brazilian society. Some might argue that "passing"—so easy, especially in the regions where the mulattoes constitute a large part of the population—explains these adverse figures. But the reality is more complex. Each color group, sociologically understood, embraces people who consider themselves and who are accepted under a given color category. Furthermore, my research with Roger Bastide reveals that the overlapping or crossing of color lines is more complicated than had been presumed. Surprisingly, some "light" mulattoes try to "pass for white," but others refuse to do so and even prefer to classify themselves as "Negroes."

The economic, social, and cultural condition of the Negro is the most terrible aspect of the picture given by the census data. In the 1950 census Negroes made up almost 14 million (11 percent of the total population), but they shared fewer than 20,000 opportunities as employers (0.9 percent)—predominantly at modest levels—and only 6,794 (0.6 percent) and 448 (0.2 percent) had completed, respectively, courses in secondary schools and universities. Such a situation involves more than social inequality and insidious poverty. It presupposes that the individuals affected are not included, as a racial stock, in the existing social order—as if they were not human beings or normal citizens.

Notes

[1] In this connection, see the works of Samuel Lowrie; Roger Bastide and Florestan Fernandes; L. A. Costa Pinto; Oracy Nogueira; A. Guerreiro Ramos; Octávio Ianni, Fernando Henrique Cardoso, and Renato Jardom Moreira; Thales de Azevedo; Charles Wagley, Marvin Harris, Henry W. Hutchinson, and Ben Zimmerman; Rene Ribeiro; João Baptista Borges Pereira; Virginia Leone Bicudo; Aniela Ginsberg; Carolina Martuscelli Bori; and Dante Moreira Leite.

[2] *L'esclavage au Brésil* (Paril, 1881); *Le Brésil en 1884* (Rio de Janeiro, 1884).

[3] As a large frame of reference see Florestan Fernandes, *A integração do negro na sociedade de classes* (São Paulo, 1965), Vol. 1, Chapter 1; Roger Bastide and Florestan Fernandes, *Brancos e negros em São Paulo* (São Paulo, 1959), Chapters 1, 2; Octávio Ianni, "O progresso econômico e o trabalhador livre," in Sérgio Buarque de Holanda, eds., *História geral da civilização brasileira*, Vol. 3, *O Brazil monárquico* (São Paulo, 1964), pp. 297-319; Caio Prado Junior, *História econômica do Brasil*, 2d ed. (São Paulo, 1949), Chatper 19.

[4] In general, this sector of the population was racially mixed, and in the south phenotypically and socially "white." The process occurred simultaneously in the cities and in the rural areas.

[5] With reference to the northeast and the emergence of a free labor market, my statements are based on an unpublished study by Barbara Trocoso concerning the freedman in Bahia. With reference to São Paulo, see Bastide and Fernandes, *Brancos e negros*; Fernandes, *A integração do negro*; F. Henrique Cardoso, *Capitalismo e escravidão no Brasil Meridional* (São Paulo, 1962); Octávio Ianni, *As metamorfoses do escravo* (São Paulo, 1962); Octávio Ianni, *Raças e classes sociais no Brasil* (Rio de Janeiro, 1966); Cardoso and Ianni, *Côr e mobilidade social em Florianópolis* (São Paulo, 1960).

[6]Concerning the low wages of the rural free laborer, see Emilia Viotti da Costa, *Da senzala à colônia* (São Paulo, 1966).

[7]See the sources cited in note 5.

[8]Caio Prado Junior, *Formação do Brasil contemporâneo: Colônia* (São Paulo, 1942), pp. 341-342.

[9]Ianni, *As metamorfoses do escravo*; Fernandes, *A integração do negro*, Vol. 1, Chapters 1, 2, 5.

[10]Bastide and Fernandes, *Brancos e negros em São Paulo*, Chapter 5; Fernandes, *A integração do negro*, Vol. 2, Chapter 4.

[11]See especially Bastide and Fernandes, *Brancos e negros em São Paulo*, Chapter 5.

[12]See B. Wilbur Doyle, *The Etiquette of Race Relations in the South: A Study in Social Control* (Chicago, 1937), especially the preface by Robert E. Park, pp. xi-xxiv.

[13]Bastide and Fernandes, *Brancos e negros em São Paulo*, Chapter 2.

[14]See especially Fernandes, *A integração do negro*, Vol. 2, Chapter 6.

[15]Florestan Fernandes, *Sociedade de classes e subdesenvolvimento* (Rio de Janeiro, 1968), Chapter 1, deals with this subject at greater length.

[16]Because of this, some techniques applied by psychologists, social psychologists, anthropologists, and sociologists in the study of personal perception of race, race differences, or race identification are inadequate for the study of the Brazilian situation.

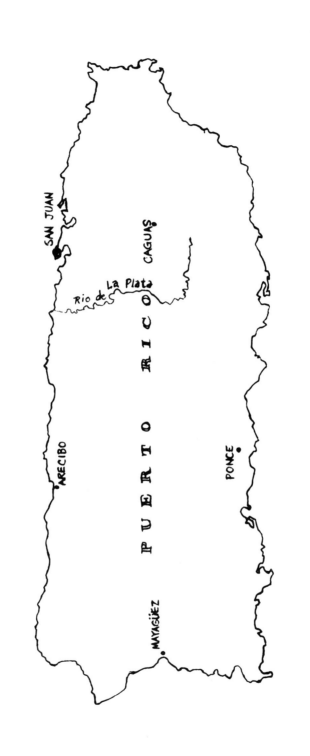

11

The Question of Color in Puerto Rico

Thomas G. Mathews

If one were asked to name an area in the Americas where there has been considerable racial miscegenation and relatively little overt racial discrimination, certainly Puerto Rico would be an appropriate choice. Because Puerto Rico has not experienced much racial tension, many would cite the island society as one of the best examples of amicable race relations that mankind has yet achieved on a large scale. Yet Thomas Mathews points out Puerto Rico's strange irony: its worst prejudice may be the conviction that there is no prejudice. In Mathew's assessment, Puerto Rican society outwardly opposes discrimination but sweeps all but the most flagrant cases of abuse under the rug for fear of harming individual reputations or disrupting the placid course of events. In the long run, Mathews sees two dangers in this ostrichlike approach to the issue of racial prejudice: it serves as an obstacle to redress of present inequities, and it leaves islanders ignorant of their culture's rich African heritage.

R. B. T.

The study of race relations on the small Caribbean island of Puerto Rico would apparently offer all the varied intriguing

299

elements one could hope for in a racially mixed society relatively free from the tensions and violence that have come to mark some of the communities of the Caribbean and North America. We plan to take a new look at some of these varied and intriguing elements that Puerto Rico, in some instances, shares with other societies of the Caribbean and South America, while at the same time emphasizing the unique character of the relations between the races that have come together to form the present-day Puerto Rican. In the process we hope to uncover areas where further study could be carried out, to suggest alternative interpretations of previously accepted data supplemented by newly discovered or recently provided material, and finally to offer some observations about why the current picture contrasts markedly with other communities where black minorities are carrying out significant social revolutions.

Puerto Rico has attracted a number of outside sociologists and historians who have sought to discover an explanation for the apparent racial harmony of this island community. Most of these outsiders have had sufficient professional preparation to become aware of the fact that race relations in Puerto Rico differ notably from the pattern found in the United States or England.[1] Others, using the broader canvas of the Caribbean or Latin America, have lumped, not without justification, Puerto Rico into what Harmannus Hoetink has called the Iberian variant of race relations.[2] In contrast to these studies, one should not perhaps be too surprised to find few local experts offering anything more substantive than a passing comment on the topic.[3] This is in keeping with the low-key approach to the question of race with which the Puerto Rican treats this matter. Whereas Cuba can boast of the multivolume works of José Antonio Saco and Fernando Ortiz, in Puerto Rico the work of Luis Díaz Soler on the history of slavery on the island and the unpretentious but authentic study by the sociologists José C. Rosario and J. Carrión stand as isolated monuments of scholarship. More recent monographs come from Professors Eduardo Seda and Juan Rodríguez Cruz. These works, although impressive, are almost unsupported by any other local scholarly endeavors.[4]

After four hundred years of Spanish colonial rule, Puerto Rico came as a prize of war under the jurisdiction of the United States. A people who, as far as official observance was concerned, were Roman Catholic in religion were abruptly exposed to the principle of religious freedom. An agrarian society that had scarcely developed beyond the family level of enterprise was, not immediately but eventually, transformed into an industrial society with a high mobile social structure and a growing urban middle class. This same society, in the relatively short span of a hundred years, changed its racial composition; having had a majority of 51.24 percent in 1846 classified as "Negro" by the Spanish administration, it had only 23 percent in the same classification in 1950.[5] These are just some of the elements that have intrigued the students of Puerto Rican society, particularly those interested in the study of race relations.

Historical studies of the Spanish colonial period that have dealt with the question of race, either directly as in the cited work of Luis Díaz Soler on the history of slavery or in general works such as that of Antonio Pedreira or Lidio Cruz Monclova, have coincided with the interpretation expounded by the late Frank Tannenbaum in his book *Slave and Citizen: The Negro in the Americas*.[6] The Spanish colonial laws, in contrast to those of the other non-Iberian European powers, contributed to the development of a more lenient treatment of the African slave, thus allowing in the long run a blending rather than a polorization of the black and white races. Díaz Soler writes: "The chroniclers, as well as the slave holders and abolitionists, are in agreement in the opinion that the black slave received better treatment in Puerto Rico than the indentured servants in the French and English colonies of the Caribbean area."

And further on:

In Puerto Rico there were no large contingents of blacks

withdrawn from the general activity of the community. The groups (of blacks) who enjoyed freedom developed an attitude of open congeniality, racial prejudices were eliminated in accord with the conditions which the times allowed. By the time of the suspension of the slave trade in the Spanish Antilles, the slave had adapted to modes and customs of his environment, he had absorbed a feeling of order and had become accustomed to work; he had absorbed a feeling, in accord with his position as a freedman, of moral responsibility to adjust to the way of life of the contemporary society.[7]

It would be erroneous to imply that this well-documented study overlooks the cruelty and inhumanity of the institution of slavery as practiced even in the Spanish colonies, in spite of the above-quoted observations. The research has been too thorough to allow the author to pass over the instances of inhuman treatment, the application of instruments of torture, or the expressions of racial superiority and discrimination by Spaniards in the island aristocracy.[8] Nevertheless the generally accepted impression, backed by worthy opinions of those who fought for abolition, is that the Spanish form of slavery was more benign than any of the others.[9]

There is another point of view, expressed at least by one highly qualified observer, whose opinion has been taken into account by none of the local historians and by very few of the Caribbean specialists. The great emancipator of the slaves of Guadeloupe and Martinique and leading abolitionist of France, Victor Schoelcher, traveled for a year through some of the English-, Spanish-, and French-speaking islands of the Caribbean in 1840 and 1841. His observations were published in two volumes, in 1841 and 1843.[10] In the opinion of one biographer, the immediate result of this voyage was to convert Schoelcher into an ardent abolitionist, whereas hitherto he had limited his defense of the African to agitation for the strict enforcement of the interdiction of the slave trade.[11]

Although he only remained in Puerto Rico three months, Schoelcher gave ample evidence of his remarkable powers of observation and his ability to probe beyond mere appearances. He recognized the leniency and applauded the slave code of Spain, labeling it as undoubtedly the best of all of the slaveholding nations. However, he balanced this evaluation with the basic truth, discovered by all students of the Spanish colonial system but for some strange reason conveniently overlooked by those who wish to stress the leniency of the Spanish slave system: "Unfortunately one does not see that they have ever wished to enforce them." And specifically, "But the laws for the protection of the slaves . . . are an illusion and in fact null."[12] In part, the observations may have been conditioned by the fact that Schoelcher's visit to Puerto Rico came in the months of the *zafra*. As Ballou observed in Cuba, the rules concerning the hours of labor for the slaves during the sugar harvest were universally ignored.[13]

The French visitor did not limit himself to these generalized observations but cited names and cases that had come to his attention during the brief three-month sojourn on the island. Working hours were inhumanely extended; rules and regulations concerning the purchasing of a slave's freedom were a mockery; living conditions of the slaves were judged to be inferior to those accorded the dogs of France; and the punishment of the slaves by the planters was frequently cruelly inhuman. Contrary to the opinion of other observers, Schoelcher felt that the relatively poor state of the plantations in Puerto Rico in comparison with those of Cuba or Jamaica prevented a more benevolent treatment of the slaves.[14] He argued that the *hacendado* had to force his limited slavery resources to the maximum level of production just to stave off bankruptcy. He was careful to point out and cite one exception to the cases he described, that of an Englishman, Mr. Kortwright, who owned and administered a plantation on the north coast of the island.

Admittedly we have here the opinion and observations of a man who, although in no way involved in the Puerto Rican or

Spanish affairs of the time, was preparing a case for the abolition of slavery within the French islands of the Caribbean. Recent research into the question of the treatment of slaves in Puerto Rico has led at least one critical historian, Loida Figueroa, to question also the generally held opinion that the Spaniards treated the slaves with leniency. The problem of enforcing the laws was complicated by the authorities' fear that the encouragement of slave accusations against owners would lead to serious disorders and perhaps general rebellion.[15] Díaz Soler cites the case of one official, whose duty it was to protect the slave, who was accused by thirty-eight planters of false testimony. He was later absolved of any wrongdoing.[16] Much of this historical evidence, coupled with some limited recent research, has led Professor Loida Figueroa to qualify the observation that the Spaniards treated slaves more benevolently than the other Europeans; he affirmed that it often depended on the character of the individual owner. This is perhaps a more accurate conclusion, since it is impossible to ignore the evidence of cruelty, some examples of which could hardly be outdone by the Dutch or English slave owners.

The way is now open for a reevaluation of the day-to-day functioning of the Spanish slave system, which, at least in its first stages, should be free from hasty comparisons with other slave systems in the Caribbean. It would be wise to extend this reevaluation to the remaining quarter of the nineteenth century, if the observations of the British consul in Puerto Rico have any validity at all. The slave was freed in Puerto Rico in 1873 but was forced to serve for three additional years, until 20 April 1876 as a bound servant paid by his master. However, it was not until 22 March 1878 that the emancipated slave received political rights, which certainly were not extensive under the Spanish colonial system. Consul W. B. Pauli wrote in 1875: "Slavery has left its mark on the race, which must take several generations to efface; but this applies equally to those who have long been free, and to their children, and it is not more observable in the 'liberto' of today than in the rest of their colored brothers."[17] It would not be illogical to read into this observation the implication that the effects of slavery on the African in Puerto Rico would be notable for some time to come; exceptional social control would have to be exerted over the recently freed and even those who had not been so recently freed but whose color marked them as unintegrated elements in the society. In effect, as is well known, the control of so-called free labor was tightened, thus in a sense the abolition of the slave system became an excuse for strengthening and broadening the subjection of the working man to his almost feudal *patrón*.

With the advent of American control over the island, the question of color took on much greater importance than it ever had under the Spanish administration. The Americans had difficulty in understanding the society they had acquired. Prominent members of the local government, like José Celso Barbosa, lawyer, doctor, and one of the first black graduates of the University of Michigan, occupied positions of leadership in a society that was not overwhelmingly black to the untrained eye of the casual visitor. The racial mixture of the society, and the fact that it could produce black leaders, undoubtedly became an important factor for consideration in the minds of congressmen who were involved in developing representative government institutions for the island.[18] Some, more prejudiced than others, were bothered by the degree of racial mixture. A Protestant leader and editor of one of the supposedly more liberal journals of the time, Dr. Lyman Abbott, even commented that Puerto Rico's racial hetereogeneity confirmed the wisdom of the U.S. southerner's hostility to racial mixture.[19] An even more conservative visitor felt that it was the "duty" of the United States to impose a strict color line on Puerto Rican society, since without this no regeneration of the islander could be expected. Indeed, he feared that the "horror" of racial mixture had gone too far in Puerto Rico, obliterating forever the color line that "cannot be drawn as yet."[20]

Lyman Abbott and the other Protestant missionaries were extremely active in the first few decades of the twentieth century, having found the island an open field for evangelizing. The

Roman Catholic Church, during Spanish rule and even through most of the first half of the twentieth century, limited its religious activity to the large urban centers. Rarely would one find a rural Catholic church or a parish priest who paid more than a casual visit to the country areas of his parish. Even in the cities, until very recently, the Catholic Church catered to the middle and upper classes and provided expensive private schools for the children of the elite. Tomás Blanco indicates correctly that the elitist nature of the Catholic religious work was furthered by the North American priests and nuns who staffed the facilities; but this did not necessarily imply any abrupt change from the pattern of social and racial discrimination that had already existed under Spanish control. It is just that the Americans were less skilled in practicing their discrimination.

The Protestant missionaries, taking advantage of the nonexistence of religious work among the rural districts and the poorer classes of the towns, naturally found that their clientele were of a dark hue. In effect, the Protestant church membership even today is characteristically darker in color and from poorer economic levels than the professed and practicing Catholics. Some effort was apparently made to educate for the ministry some promising white youths like Dr. José Padín, who was sent on a scholarship to the Quaker college of Haverford, and the Reverend Angel Archilla, who studied in a United States Presbyterian seminary. Although these two examples are exceptions, most of those sent to the Protestants schools in the north returned steeped in fundamentalism which marked the Protestant thought of the 1920s. As a result, the Protestant churches of the island continue to be controlled by those who reflect very conservative social thought. However, in the second half of the twentieth century the Catholic Church is now coming increasingly under the control of a liberal native leadership. It remains to be seen whether this social liberalism will break the subtle color bar that has marked the exclusive private Catholic schools and the wealthier churches.

In its racial composition, Puerto Rico, as some observers have stated, was markedly different from the rest of the islands of the Caribbean and particularly from the Dominican Republic, which had attracted the attention of the previous generation of American expansionists. Congressmen wondered that there were so many whites in Puerto Rico, "supposedly a 'black man's country'."[21] There were several Puerto Ricans who hastened to impress the Americans with the whiteness of the population: "We were coolly informed that white was the prevailing color today, regardless of all 'the hand-me downs.' "[22]

This racial mixture, of which the Puerto Rican was a result, continued through the next few decades to raise doubts and hesitations in the mind of the prejudiced North American. In a history of the island, written by an American benefactor who was connected with the island Red Cross and published in the mid-1920s, we find the comment that the tendency toward racial mixture "produces a degeneration in the quality of the off-spring."[23] Government officials of the same period were not exceptionally discreet in expressing their low opinion of the Puerto Rican. Although some of this attitude was due to cultural and national differences between the two peoples, much of it was based on what we recognize today as racial prejudice. One expert in agricultural sciences argued that "it is partly a matter of race characteristics"[24] that the Puerto Ricans were poor scientists. Even in the 1930s, when a new brand of supposedly liberal government officials came into contact with the Puerto Rican, the same attitudes came to be repeated with perhaps a different vocabulary but with the same general tendency to classify the Puerto Rican as an inferior breed. No less a radical than Rexford Guy Tugwell wrote to Henry Wallace in 1934 deploring the fact that our control of the tropics would produce a migratory flooding of our large cities with "these mulatto, Indian, Spanish people [who] make poor material for social organization."[25]

Even up to and after World War II the U.S. Army (never a very liberal or democratic institution in spite of its much vaunted effect as a social equalizer), when confronted by the Puerto Rican, was stymied as to how to classify him. The Puerto Rican Negro resented his relegation to the segregated units of World War I. Many Puerto Ricans who classified themselves as white would not be acceptable in the white units. The army came up with the classification of "Puerto Rican white" and perhaps solved the problem, at least to its own satisfaction, but such a solution resulted in the resentment of the great body of Puerto Ricans, who considered themselves as white but objected strongly the so-called off-white category into which they had been placed.[26]

During the 1940s in the United States, but to a much lesser degree in Puerto Rico, the darker-colored citizen began to protest the discrimination to which he was subjected. The war undoubtedly had something to do with the spreading of a more aggressive attitude, but politics was also involved. In 1940 a new political party came into power; it was reform-minded and contained important colored leaders in its upper echelon. These people were recognized and accepted as leaders, not because they represented a minority, but rather because of their intrinsic value to the party as lawyers, labor leaders, or political orators. One of the most aggressive of these leaders was the outspoken lawyer Ernesto Ramos Antonini, who for many years, after a fierce internal battle that certainly had racial overtones within his own party, served as speaker of the island House of Representatives. His militant posture did not fit into the mold left by José Celso Barbosa or Pedro Timothee of the previous generation, who were inclined to forego confrontations, particularly in the social sphere, that might be unworthy of their cultural breeding.[27] Indeed, Barbosa had gone so far as to declare (1909) that since the colored people had never attempted to pass over the social barrier to colored participation in social life, there was then no color problem in Puerto Rico! Ramos Antonini did not hesitate to appear and demand attention wherever he felt there might be a reluctance to accept him.

Another less prominent political figure in the new party was Prudencio Rivera Martínez, whose timely switch to the Popular party (his vote was needed to control the lower House) undoubtedly was triggered by frustrated ambitions, perhaps caused by his color, within the Socialist party. As a labor leader who had substantial popular support, he represented a less nationalistic group of the working populace who in previous decades had looked to Barbosa or Timothee for leadership. The bulk of the professional colored middle class followed Leopoldo Figueroa in the minority Republican party.

Under the Popular party, administrative positions once closed to the colored person were slowly opened. Hitherto the officials of the police department were exclusively white, and the supervisors and principals of the public schools mostly white. In 1943 the Popular party also passed a Civil Rights Act that was patterned after the United States measure. There were those who argued that it was unnecessary on the island, but the militancy of Ramos Antonini pressed the issue forward.

Discrimination in public places existed in Puerto Rico in the late thirties and early forties. Tomás Blanco cites one case of the historic restaurant La Mallorquina, which, as he explains it, came for a brief period under "nordic influence" and successfully sought to legally restrict its clientele to the socially white.[28] In the early 1940s Dr. Eric Williams, now Prime Minister of Trinidad, came to visit Puerto Rico on official business for the Anglo-American Commission. The subtle discrimination to which he was subjected in the Hotel Condado is recounted in his recent autobiography.[29] In the article he subsequently published in *Foreign Affairs*, Williams observed that the racial prejudice in the social activities of the community, which antedated the American occupation, continued to exist and in his opinion seemed to be on the increase at that time.[30]

When Puerto Ricans drew up their own constitution in 1952, an extensive Bill of Rights was included that effectively spelled out the illegality of racial discrimination. As in most Latin American countries, the letter of the law was written in the latest style of modern social thought, but it had little effect outside of government on the existing practices of the society for which it was written. Not until 1957, when the United Nations urged national leaders to undertake a study of civil liberties, did the Puerto Rican government take any specific action to implement its constitutional guarantee. Luis Muñoz Marín, then governor of Puerto Rico, in consultation with an old friend and colleague, Roger Baldwin of the American Civil Liberties Union, set up a committee of inquiry into the state of civil liberties in Puerto Rico.

Although the activity of this committee was not limited to the problems of racial discrimination (since it quickly became involved in the more popular inquiry into political persecution), it was, however, advised by a number of academic consultants, one of whom, Professor Eduardo Seda Bonilla, was concerned with the matter of race. The findings of the Committee confirmed the existence of racial discrimination in social organizations such as the private casinos or social clubs, and the fraternities and sororities of the public and private universities. The absence of Negroes in businesses, banks, tourist facilities, and the practice of race discrimination in private schools, according to the findings of the committee, indicated that the constitutional guarantees of equal opportunity irregardless of race or religion were not being observed or enforced.[31]

Unfortunately, even though these findings confirmed that racial discrimination was not limited to the private field of individual or social selection, no governmental action was recommended; such official action, it was argued, would provoke hostile reactions. As Dr. Gordon Lewis has cogently pointed out, this not only goes against the provisions within the Constitution but contradicts the clearly established trend to eliminate in the United States the vague distinction between so-called private and public behavior, since one obviously has direct bearing on the other.[32]

In the complete absence of any militant minority-group pressure for recognition of their rights, the political leaders prefer, since the death of Ramos Antonini, not to stir up more trouble. They hope that the problem will be corrected before it gets out of hand. The legislature in 1963 opened up an inquiry into the hiring practices of the local banks that deprived any Negro of employment. Here again, even with evidence that would have stood up in court, the results of the inquiry closed with the pious hope that the banks, having been shown the error of their ways, would take steps to correct the practice. Steps have been taken to allow a token hiring of darker-skinned tellers, but the insular world of high finance is still hermetically closed to the darker-skinned Puerto Rican.[33,]

As recently as 1969 the same reluctance to enforce constitutional guarantees was evidenced by the conclusions of an island Senate committee of inquiry into discrimination in the hiring of private-school teachers. The inquiry was triggered by a talk delivered to the exclusively white Rotary Club of San Juan by the supervisor of a complex of private schools. In the talk the speaker, who was an American, confessed that recent research by the sociologist Arthur Robert Jensen[34] confirmed what he had always suspected: that the Negro race was inferior to the white. Within twenty-four hours after this was reported to the front page of a leading local newspaper, the speaker's resignation was accepted from his educational post. The subsequent investigation, which turned up plausible indications of discrimination based on race and religion in private and military schools on the island, did not recommend further pursuit of the matter, since the evidence provided would probably not have held up in court.[35]

Thus, while the rest of the world and particularly the United States is experiencing the results of a black revolution, this island with a sizable black minority has preferred to ignore these developments and continue with an unstated policy of slow social transition, which from time to time is moved along with sporadic public disclosures of unresponsive areas where discrimination is too obvious. As early as 1940 Eric Williams noted this phenomenon among the Puerto Rican Negroes when he observed, "The militancy of American Negroes has no counterpart in Puerto Rico. . . ."[36] Pedro Timothee lamented the fact that the black Puerto Rican showed no interest in the history of his race or in the black leaders of the island.[37] An outstanding Puerto Rican poet,

Luis Palés Matos, who did so much to bring public attention to the rich African heritage of the island through his Afro-Puerto Rican poetry, was, however, severely criticized, as Gordon Lewis has shown,[38] by his lesser contemporaries for calling attention to the non-Hispanic heritage of the island's culture.

More recently, as the militancy of the black in the United States has increased, two examples of the lack of Puerto Rican response are significant. The radical intellectuals of the independence movement brought Stokely Carmichael to the island to speak of the common ties binding the black struggle with the struggle for Puerto Rican independence. The visit was a failure, because some leaders of the independence movement made no secret of their reluctance to be identified, or to have their movement tied, closely with black militancy in the United States. Indeed, some argued that such a visit had actually set the movement back and alienated a sizable sector of the population that had been sympathetic. It should be made clear that it was Carmichael's color, and not his militancy, that disturbed these *independentistas*.

The second example, and one which needs no comment, is the visit of Martin Luther King to the island. King himself expressed to the writer his disappointment at the lukewarm response he received. In effect, his fight was not theirs, and they showed little interest in the matter. The Puerto Ricans in the large U.S. metropolitan areas have been reluctant to identify themselves with the black struggle. As Leon Drusine has shown in his doctoral thesis the prevailing attitude of the Puerto Rican is that to identify with the Negro-American is to complicate and retard his own struggle for acceptance.[39] Indeed, there were examples of American Negroes attempting to pass as black Puerto Ricans in order to improve their chance of escaping discrimination.

Efforts to recruit the support of the Puerto Rican for black militancy have had very disappointing results. In 1963 a Black Muslim missionary came to Puerto Rico to live in the slums with the black islanders and specifically to conduct a campaign for black awareness. It was obviously his first visit to a country with Spanish culture, and he was unprepared for his difficult experience. He found that even the colored Puerto Ricans were quick to deny the existence of racial discrimination on the island. He observed with obvious wisdom that the Puerto Ricans "are seeking a white identity and a white image for themselves" and "consequently cannot help but reject or ignore the African roots in favor of those from Spain. . . ."[40]

This self-educated Muslim minister concluded with some irony that "the Latin American system knows more about how to discriminate against the Negroes and make them like it than North Americans."[41] Such circumstances, as observed by this missionary, have led the sociologist Talcott Parsons to comment: "I take the position that the race relations problem has a better prospect of resolution in the United States than in Brazil. . . ."[42] This highly pessimistic observation, which is based on the Marxian premise that things have to get worse before they can improve, has served for some as a rationalization for the acceptance of the black-power philosophy.

Parsons, in effect, is asking for a polarization of the races, but this, as he recognizes, is not in itself a solution to the problem. In the case of Puerto Rico, it would appear to this observer that such a polarization is not an essential prior condition to the desired solution of absolute racial equality and the elimination of discrimination. The black Puerto Rican does not have to discard his identity as a Puerto Rican for a new identity as an Afro-Puerto Rican. One is not incompatible with the other, above all on an island where there already exists such a degree of racial mixture, where overt discrimination is difficult to discover and expose because in fact it is rare, and where there already exist a plethora of open roads for self-expression ready to be taken up by the black islander.

What is necessary, however, is a more aggressive attitude and posture by the black Puerto Rican and, even more important, a realization by this island society that such militancy merits support and sympathy, which will serve to prevent any polarization from developing. The Puerto Rican's awareness and pride in his African roots cannot be looked upon as being divisive or incompatible with a definition of the island character and personality, but in effect it is a more complete and accurate expression of the Puerto Rican's cultural identity.

The isolated example of a maverick like the Puerto Rican engineer who, in his public testimony before one of the commissions of inquiry, urged the government to threaten to withdraw its funds from banks that were guilty of discriminatory hiring practices, provokes little comment and even less action. His appeal for a public boycott of the local branches of Sears or Woolworths falls on deaf ears. The appeal was made in full awareness of its probable result, since the witness acknowledged the lack of response beforehand: "This attitude of withdrawal, of not putting up a fight for themselves, is what I wish to pose here."[43]

This camouflage of the realities of the social circumstances of island society has even worked its way into serious sociological studies. Thus the prestigious Princeton study *Social Class and Social Change in Puerto Rico*, undertaken by Melvin Tumin and his associates, concluded that according to over 80 percent of those interviewed, skin color did not seem to be a significant factor in regard to opportunity in Puerto Rico.[44] More careful analysis of this problem, based on a more sophisticated series of questions put to a much smaller group, produced significantly different answers. Seda's studies conclusively show the importance of color and the resulting social discrimination;[45] and more recently, following the style of Tumin's study, but with greater depth, Hollister has shown significant differences from the percentages reported by the Princeton study. Hollister concluded: "It is abundantly clear that a majority of the respondents believes that skin color *does matter*."[46]

Thus we have a society with a substantial black minority, where discrimination because of race is present but where there is little or no interest, even among blacks themselves, in waging a concerted campaign of social change. It is clear also that such racial discrimination does not appear openly in public places or governmental circles but operates mostly in the social and private spheres of activity, with the obvious resulting effects in business and financial sectors of the community. Having described the racial nuances of the social milieu and having emphasized the absence of militancy (although there is obviously widespread recognition of the problem both by blacks and whites), it remains to try to offer some insight as to why such conditions exist and are apparently bound to prevail since there is an absence of any concerted campaign for change.

Parsons' observation on the lack of polarization, in a sense, is a step toward an explanation. The color spectrum in Puerto Rico is not polarized into black and white as it is in other islands of the Caribbean. In fact, there is reason to believe that, from the very beginning years of the colonization, the population of the island was characterized by its racial mixture. As Pérez Cabral has argued for the Dominican Republic in his *La Comunidad Mulata*,[47] the island of Hispaniola, which was a far greater political center for the Spaniard than Puerto Rico, was undoubtedly populated by offspring of Spanish-Indian mixtures at first and then later, as the Indian was absorbed or disappeared, by mestizo-Negro or mestizo-mulatto offspring. Fray Iñigo Abbad y Lasierra, who wrote one of the first important histories of the island of Puerto Rico after having spent seven years on the island (1771-1778), flatly observed that the mulattoes made up the major part of the population.[48] He also observed that the mulatto and the Negro were treated with open disdain, and in the case of some slave owners, with excessive cruelty.

The French botanist Ledru,[49] who visited the island in 1797, wrote that the number of pure whites was very small, scarcely 10 percent of the population; but Raynal, who had not visited the island, doubled the percentage. Ledru also agrees with Abbad in the fact that the major part of the population was mixed. These observations were made well before the island experienced the influx of capital and agricultural know-how that, despite the prohibition of slave trade, established the large sugar plantations operated by slave labor in the early nineteenth century. It is only then that the census reports begin to show a marked increase in the African element of the population, resulting in black majorities for the first three decades of the nineteenth century. But after midcentury, as noted above, and at an accelerated rate after the abolition of slavery in 1873, the population has whitened. Rather than polarization, the racial mixture continued in Puerto Rico. In the second half of the nineteenth century the Puerto Rican members of the reform commission that recommended to Spain the abolition of slavery on the island observed that such action would not precipitate any drastic social unrest since the population of the island was much more racially mixed, much more homogeneous, than the population of Cuba.[50] This fact has not been lost on the Cuban exile of today, who admittedly comes from the upper levels of the Cuban society and is not accustomed to silencing his own prejudices. As a result, friction has developed between the Cuban exile and his reluctant host, the Puerto Rican, who resents being referred to as a mongrel breed.[51]

At the turn of the century the population figures indicated a white majority on the island, but at least one observer, who visited the island on several occasions both before and after the military occupation, qualified the statistical impression:

> There is a large body of Africans, who constitute according to the census, about three-sevenths of the population. There is little or no race prejudice, and the white or whiter mixtures of the two races pass muster as whites, and not as in the United States as blacks. If all the mulattoes, quadroons, octoroons, quinteros and other mestizos were included with the blacks instead of the whites, the proportions would be changed and the blacks would have a handsome majority upon the island.[52]

There is no way of making an accurate estimate as to what percentage of the population of the island today is of mixed blood, but the impression is that somewhat more than the 23 percent colored according to the 1950 census. One estimate adventures the guess that 70 percent of the population is a result of some degree of racial mixture.[53]

This naturally raises the question of definition of "colored," with all of the socio-psychological implications this problem brings forth. It is well-known that the racial classification of the people in Latin American countries, and of course, Puerto Rico, can change as they move up the social ladder.[54] If the social climber is too dark to move into the white category and be accepted readily, he classifies himself as a mixture of Spanish and Indian.[55] As one wag has suggested, there are perhaps more "Indians" on the island of Puerto Rico now than there were at the time of Columbus.

Since a sizable proportion of the Puerto Rican families contain members who reflect the results of centuries of racial mixture, the question of racial identification is one of extreme sensitivity. Even families with some blond-haired, blue-eyed members can have others whose crisp black hair or full lips or flat nose offer marked contrast to their legitimate blood brothers and sisters. One frequently observes cases of marriages that have been dissolved because the offspring has turned out to be of a darker shade than either of the parents. The husband usually blames the wife for hiding the African strain in her family, but just as often the husband's family has as much or more racial mixture.

In an important article of several decades ago, the sociologist-psychologist Renzo Sereno studied the tendency of the Puerto Rican to deny, hide, or disguise the darker hues of his racial origin. He argued that even the all-white members of the Puerto Rican community share "the inner fear of colored ancestry."[56] Sereno, being concerned primarily with the individual, connected (incorrectly, in my opinion) this phenomenon of race denial with what he identified as a widespread sense of psychological insecurity in Puerto Ricans. There may have been some causal relationship at that time, but currently, after the markedly successful economic development experienced by Puerto Rico, the phenomenon of personal insecurity seems to have been drastically reduced but there has not been a corresponding growth in black racial pride. Quite the contrary, the observations in this area made by Sereno two decades ago are just as valid today.

Although Sereno was more interested in individual behavior, he did observe that this "cryptomelanism" led to a more general social conduct, which would deny or reject any action that might accentuate the racial aspect of a problem, whether this problem be political, economical, or social. Thus the individual, either singly or in a like-minded group, would be reluctant to expose himself by publicly condemning racial discrimination. To do so would bring attention upon himself and/or his group and provoke the question as to why he was concerned. Recently in the press the public has been given an example of this by no less than a university professor who implied that one of the reasons a colleague of his was concerned about racial discrimination was precisely because his family had African blood.[57]

Officials concerned with eradicating racial discrimination have been reluctant to press any particular cases because of the necessity of racially identifying all the persons involved. This task would not only be extremely difficult, but it would be charged with socially explosive traps to which the investigator would be reluctant to expose himself. For example, how is one to line up proof as to whether employment practices are discriminatory when employees of the firm who claim to be white, and may even be white, may have been hired precisely because their more ruddy complexion would counteract possible criticism? When the person is passing as white or even is of mixed ancestry, this "cryptomelanism" is easy to understand; but when the Puerto Rican is clearly a member of the African minority, this reluctance to speak out against discrimination or to express concern for and interest in the African heritage of the island is harder to explain. Yet it exists. Here the black Puerto Rican is quick to point to the examples of the lack of racial barriers or discrimination. With pride they recite the social events they have been invited to, the intimate parties of upper-class whites in which they have been admitted and made to feel at home, the absence of any personal experience of denial because of race, and so on. Such acceptance, such admittance, would disappear if they began to be aggressive or were identified as one who disturbs the social serenity by questioning the order of things. Furthermore, their own chances of advancement, which obviously depend on the whiter elements of the society, would be jeopardized if they contributed to a polarization of the racial issue on the island.

The intellectual element of the population, which would come from the middle or upper-middle class, contrary to the conditions obtaining in the United States, is not concerned with the race problem in Puerto Rico. One might expect a movement of protest to come from this group, but instead there is silence, because any protest might cast doubt on the racial identity of the individual, his family, or his group. Dr. Sidney Mintz, basing his argument on Sereno (with whom he agrees), argues that the middle class is actually the group that practices the most racial discrimination in Puerto Rican society.[58] We see then that the whole gamut of Puerto Rican society (with only a few exceptions),[59] including the all-white group, the middle class, the intellectual elite, the mulatto, and even the blackest sections of the population, refuse to expose themselves by making a concerted public drive and continued vigilance against racial discrimination. In this prevailing negative climate, no black power movement has been developed and the feeble attempts in this direction have soon been abandoned as fruitless. What is further deplorable is that there is no concerted effort, or even interest, in exploring and studying the manifold contribution of the African to Puerto Rican culture.[60]

Thus a society that has drawn richly on the sources of African culture has virtually ignored this facet of its historical development. When and if attention comes to this previously ignored element in Puerto Rico's cultural milieu, it will probably always be subordinated (just as in Cuba), to the primary commitment and dedication to the national culture—since the African elements, even more so than in Cuba, have been fully integrated, in spite of subtle discrimination, into the national scene. There is in fact no subculture of an African nature in Puerto Rico.

Thus, although Puerto Rico could profit from the effects of the surge of interest in black culture that is occurring in other islands of the Caribbean, this surge, when and if it comes, should not disrupt, disturb, or destroy; it should rather contribute positively to round out a more comprehensive appreciation of the richness and depth of the cultural heritage of this island.

Notes

[1] For an evaluation of these studies, see E. Seda Bonilla, "Social Structure and Race Relations" *Social Forces*, Vol. 40, No. 2, December 1961. The most perceptive studies are those of Maxine Gordon, "Race Patterns and Prejudice in Puerto Rico" *American Sociological Review*, Vol. 14, No. 2, p. 294 (although this particular article by Gordon is not cited by Seda another is), and Renzo Sereno, "Cryptomelanism: A Study of Color Relations and Personal Insecurity in Puerto Rico," *Psychiatry*, Vol. 10, No. 3, August 1945.

[2] See for example Eric Williams, "The Contemporary Pattern of Race Relations in the Caribbean," *Phylon*, Vol. 16, No. 4, 1955, and Harmannus Hoetink, *The Two Variants in Caribbean Race Relations: A Contribution to the Sociology of Segmented Societies* (London, 1967).

[3] José Colombán Rosario and Justina Carrión, *El Negro: Haiti, Estados Unidos, Puerto Rico* (San Juan, 1951); E. Seda Bonilla, "Dos modelos de relaciones raciales," *Mundo Nuevo*, 3 (1969): 29; Juan Rodríguez Cruz, "Las Relaciones Raciales en Puerto Rico," *Revista de Ciencias Sociales* 9, No. 4 (1965): 374-386.

[4] See also Tomás Blanco, *El Prejuicio Racial en Puerto Rico* (San Juan, 1948). The study was originally written in 1937 for publication in the *Revista de Estudios Afrocubanos*.

[5] The statistics are taken from Cruz, "Las Relaciones Raciales." The original source is not cited, but it is probably the *Memoria* of Pedro Tomás de Córdova for the earlier date.

[6] Frank Tannenbaum, *Slave and Citizen: The Negro in the Americas* (New York, 1947).

[7] Luis Díaz Soler, *Historia de la Esclavitud Negra en Puerto Rico, 1493-1890* (Madrid, n.d.). See pp. 144-145 and 180.

[8] *Ibid.* Díaz Soler quotes Fray Iñigo Abbad y Lasierra on p. 252.

[9] See the quotation of J. J. Acosta, S. Ruiz Belvis, and F. M. Quiñones,

abolitionists, cited by Blanco, *Prejuicio Racial*, as the basis for his affirmation of Spanish leniency.

[10]Victor Schoelcher, *Colonies Etrangères et Haiti, résultats de L'émancipation anglaise*, 2 vols. (Paris, 1843), Vol. 1. This study, which is not widely known, is not cited by Diaz Soler. The first volume contains the material on the English and Spanish colonies, and the second deals with Haiti and the Virgin Islands. The author also published a volume entitled *Des Colonies Françaises*, which is more widely known.

[11]Andre Midas, "Victor Schoelcher and the Emancipation in the French West Indies," *Caribbean Historical Review* 1, No. 1 (December 1950): 113.

[12]Schoelcher, *Colonies Etrangères*, p. 337.

[13]Maturin M. Ballou, *History of Cuba or Notes of a Traveller in the Tropics* (Boston, 1854), p. 146, note.

[14]Eric Williams has pointed out the marked difference in the Cuban slave codes of two periods, 1789 and 1840, attributing the difference to an economic change in the sugar industry. Eric Williams, "Race Relations in Caribbean Society," in *Caribbean Studies: A Symposium*, ed. Vera Rubin (Seattle, Wash., 1960), p. 54.

[15]Loida Figueroa, *Breve Historia de Puerto Rico*, 2 vols. (Barcelona, 1969), 2: 199.

[16]Díaz Soler, *Historia de la Esclavitud Negra*, p. 187.

[17]Taken from an extract of a report by Consul W. B. Pauli to the Earl of Derby, 12 May 1875. *British Parliamentary Papers, Papers Relating to the Slave Trade* (Shannon, 1969), 92: 210.

[18]J. Hampton Moore, *With Speaker Cannon Through The Tropics* (Philadelphia, 1907). Moore himself was a member of Congress.

[19]Lyman Abbott, "Porto Rico under the American Flag," *Outlook* 92 (1909): 461. This article and the following was called to my attention by M. Hornik.

[20]Eugene P. Lyle, Jr., "Our Experience in Porto Rico," *World's Week*, Vol 11, 1906.

[21]Moore, *With Speaker Cannon*, pp. 47, 52.

[22]Abbott, "Porto Rico under the American Flag."

[23]Knowlton Mixer, *Porto Rico* (New York, 1926), p. 181.

[24]Thomas Mathews, *Puerto Rican Politics and the New Deal* (Gainesville, Fla., 1960), p. 181.

[25]*Ibid.*, p. 159.

[26]Transcripción de declaraciones prestadas en la vista pública celebrada por la Comisión Especial de la Cámara de Representantes para investigar si el sistema de selección de empleados en los bancos de Puerto Rico discrimina por razón de color, raza, o condición social. 22 July 1963, p. 52.

[27]*La Obra de José Celso Barbosa*, ed. Pilar Barbosa, Vol. 3, *Problema de Razas* (San Juan, 1937), p. 31.

[28]Blanco, *El Prejuicio Racial*, p. 76.

[29]Eric Williams, *Inward Hunger: The Education of a Prime Minister* (London, 1969), p. 84.

[30]Eric Williams, "Race Relations in Puerto Rico and the Virgin Islands," *Foreign Affairs* 23, No. 2 (January 1945): 308.

[31]Comité del Gobernador para el Estudio de los Derechos Civiles en Puerto Rico, *Informe al Honorable Gobernador* (San Juan, 1959).

[32]Gordon K. Lewis, *Puerto Rico: Freedom and Power in the Caribbean* (New York, 1963), pp. 287-288.

[33]"Viewpoint," *San Juan Star*, 23 December 1969, p. 34.

[34]See *The New York Times Magazine*, 31 August 1969.

[35]Report of Senator María Arroyo to Senate President Rafael Hernández Colón, 27 January 1970.

[36]Williams, "Race Relations in Puerto Rico."

[37]Letter to *El Mundo*, 16 May 1937, cited by Rosario and Carrión, *El Negro*.

[38]Lewis, *Puerto Rico*.

[39]Leon Drusine, "Some factors in anti-Negro prejudice among Puerto Ricans" (Ph.D. diss., New York University, 1955), p. 108.

[40]*Transcripción*, 23 July 1963, p. 75.

[41]*Ibid*.

[42]Talcott Parsons, "The Problem of Polarization on the Axis of Color," in *Color and Race*, ed. John Hope Franklin (Boston, 1968), pp. 352-353.

[43]*Transcripción*, p. 34.

[44]Melvin Tumin with Arnold Feldman, *Social Class and Social Change in Puerto Rico* (Princeton, N.J., 1961), p. 236 and *passim*.

[45]Seda, *Mundo Nuevo*.

[46]Frederick Hollister, "Skin Color and Life Chances of Puerto Ricans," *Caribbean Studies* 9, No. 3 (October 1969): 93.

[47]José Pérez Cabral, *La Comunidad Mulata* (Caracas, 1967).

[48]Fray Iñigo Abbad y Lasierra, *Historia Geográfica Civil y Natural de San Juan Bautista de Puerto Rico* (Mexico City, 1959), p. 182.

[49]Andres Pierre Ledru, *Viaje a la Isla de Puerto Rico*, trans. Julio L. de Vizcarrondo (Puerto Rico, 1863), p. 165.

[50]Cited by Díaz Soler, *Historia de la Esclavitud*, p. 327.

[51]Juan Rodriguez Cruz and Thomas Mathews, "Race Relations in Puerto Rico," *Newsletter: Institute of Race Relations*, August, September 1968, p. 339.

[52]Margherita Arlina Hamm, *Porto Rico and the West Indies* (New York, 1899), p. 66.

[53]Juan Rodriguez Cruz and Thomas Mathews, "Race Relations in Puerto Rico," *Newsletter: Institute of Race Relations*, January 1965, p. 27.

[54]Sidney Mintz, "Puerto Rico: An Essay in the Definition of a National Culture," *The Status of Puerto Rico*. Selected background studies prepared for the United States-Puerto Rico Commission on the Status of Puerto Rico (Washington, 1966), p. 406.

[55]Julian Steward, *The People of Puerto Rico* (Urbana, Ill., 1957).

[56]Sereno, "Cryptomelanism," p. 266.

[57]*San Juan Star*, Letters to the Editor, 18 September 1969.

[58]Mintz, "Puerto Rico," p. 407.

[59]There is an exception to this blanket statement. The Institute of Puerto Rican Culture has given very modest aid to Sylvia de Villard, a black Puerto Rican performing artist who almost single-handedly has awakened some interest in African music in Puerto Rico. Also see Ricardo Alegría, *La Fiesta de Santiago Apóstol en Loíza Aldea* (Madrid, 1954).

[60]One interesting exception was highlighted on the society page of the *San Juan Star*, 28 September 1969. A Puerto Rican student at Harvard was married in a dashiki wedding gown to a young fellow student from Trinidad.

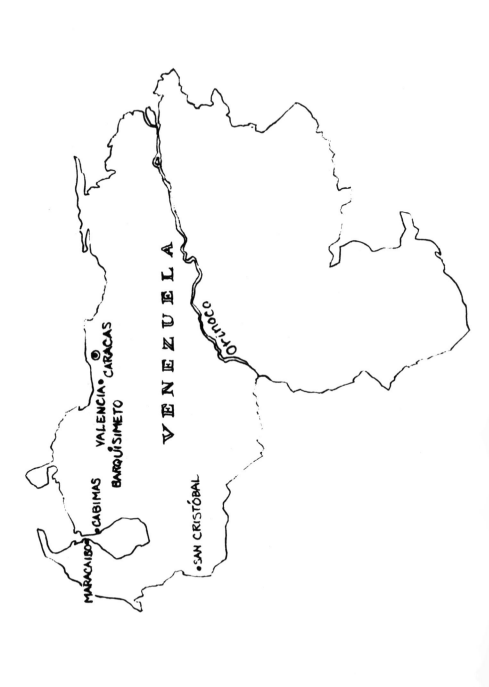

12

Elitist Attitudes Toward Race in Twentieth-Century Venezuela

Winthrop R. Wright

Despite important changes in Latin American intellectual circles in the 1920s and 1930s, when many important figures began to reject racist ideas borrowed from North America and Europe, racism continued to influence social life in the Spanish- and Portuguese-speaking republics. Winthrop R. Wright documents this problem for Venezuela. As Wright indicates, Venezuelan citizens may boast about their black-and-white origins (café con leche), but the thrust of official policy since the nineteenth century, expressed primarily in immigration policies, has been to dilute the café as much as possible. Venezuelans may be proud of their racially mixed past, but those who control the nation's destiny desire a "white" future and, at least until recently, were indifferent to the needs of the black population. In Wright's view, the potential for violence may still be high.

R. B. T.

Venezuelans frequently refer to themselves as a people of *café con leche*. Some have more milk, others more coffee, but all reflect a multiracial society that has resulted from extensive miscegenation. Centuries of racial mixing have created Venezuelans who proudly accept the widely used expression, "I am white, I am Indian, I am black, I am American."

Culturally, as well as physically, Venezuelan society manifests the combining of African, American Indian, and European elements. No definite statistical evidence exists to fix the number of Afro-Venezuelans living today. Most observers agree that at least 10 percent of the population falls into the category of pure black or Afro-Venezuelan.[1] As much as 80 percent of the population are Pardos, a blending of African, Indian, and European. For that reason many Venezuelans rightfully consider themselves members of a hybridized race. Their music, dress, language, foods, tools, and economic and political institutions show the contributions of the three ethnic groups. Venezuelan anthropologists and sociologists may disagree about whether the formation of modern Venezuelan society resulted from the indigenization and Africanization of the Spaniard in Venezuela or from the Hispanization of the Indian and the African but none deny that a long process of transculturation has taken place.[2]

Discussions of prejudice and discrimination usually bog down in semantics, especially when dealing with a complex multiracial society such as Venezuela. As used traditionally in Venezuela, the terms *negro* and *Africano* have applied to obviously black or African people, the so-called pure blacks of Venezuela. Mulattoes are usually not considered as blacks unless their pigmentation is definitely black. For this reason the Venezuelans' visual perception of race differs from that of the white North American. The latter believes that any negroid features makes an individual a black. The Venezuelan considers only those individuals with black skin as being blacks. Color rather than race plays a far more important role in influencing the Venezuelan prejudices. As stated by Juan Pablo Sojo, a student of the Venezuelan blacks, "Here we only have prejudice against the color of the skin."[3] He meant that white Venezuelans do not accept black-skinned people but that they do not react negatively toward other negroid features. By Sojo's definition, to qualify as an Afro-Venezuelan an individual has to have black skin. Thus the mulatto becomes a Pardo, a nonblack. By the same token, Venezuelans do not adhere to the Anglo-Saxon belief that a drop of African blood in the veins makes an individual black. Because they stress the need to whiten their population, white Venezuelans have not condemned individuals for having some African ancestry. Rather they have rewarded the whiter citizens with greater opportunities for social improvement.

In Venezuela, as throughout the New World, the first Afro-Americans arrived as slaves. In the tropics the Africans replaced the Indian as the chief laborers. The Africans' presence was the result of their enslavement. They did the work that the whites refused to do. African slaves worked on plantations to produce cacao, sugar, and later coffee and tobacco. They also supplied the labor for the mines and for the docks of the port cities. Their status as slaves marked the blacks as an identifiable social caste from the outset. Skin color and other basic physical characteristics further identified the black as a separate caste. Race and slavery kept the blacks at the bottom of the social and economic pyramid throughout the colonial era and well into the independence period. After emancipation in 1854, the blacks lived in the shadow of their slave background.[4]

Twentieth-century Venezuelans have continued to hold the prejudices of their colonial ancestors. Although most Venezuelans deny that they have a racial problem like that of the United States, with its virulent segregationist practices, they do place the black in an inferior social position. Rather than attribute their antiblack feelings to the European racial attitudes found in the United States, Venezuelans argue that they do not like blacks because blacks live in poverty. In their own minds contemporary Venezuelans have substituted economic discrimination for racial discrimination. But the result is much the same as North American racism. Like the Yankees, Venezuelans blame economic failure on cultural and physical inferiority. They have developed a circuitous argument that states that they dislike blacks because blacks are poor; the majority of blacks are poor because they are black. Following such logic, the whiter Venezuelans refuse to consider themselves racists. They claim to discriminate for economic reasons alone. For them race remains largely a social concept, for when a black escapes poverty he or she ceases to be socially black. Socially acceptable blacks have adopted the norms of the white society and have broken with their black cultural past.

From a racial point of view, pure definitions become obscured. Until a black man or woman proves his merit he is outwardly judged along a chromatic scale that places positive social values on whiteness and negative social values on blackness. In popular parlance, whiteness describes a state of social and economic achievement as well as racial characteristics. The racial lexicon of Venezuela abounds with phrases that show change toward social whiteness. The most widely used adage, that "money whitens," suggests that Venezuelans do not base their prejudices primarily on racial criteria. In the materialistic and multiracial society of twentieth-century Venezuela an individual's job, education, and wealth determine the opportunities for social mobility. Blacks carry the stigma of their slave heritage and remain the victims of prejudices as long as they remain poor, but they never lose the opportunity to improve their social positions. Financial and political success has socially whitened many black Venezuelans. Others have entered white society through marriage and miscegenation. In the long run, such individuals provide the exceptions that prove the rule. Successful blacks are no longer considered black by the multiracial society. Nor do such individuals identify themselves as blacks. They make no effort to lead black political or cultural movements. Rather they seek to identify themselves with their whiter countrymen. They have proved their ability to operate within the capitalistic society established by successful white Venezuelans. Clothes, education, language, position, and the accumulation of wealth combine to make an individual whiter in the social context. In such a situation the term *blanquear*, to whiten, has tremendous social significance.

The emphasis placed on whitening as a prerequisite for social and political success suggests the antithesis: that black characterizes backwardness, ignorance, poverty, and failure. Only a generation ago, Venezuelan aristocrats considered the blacks as people whose ancestors climbed trees. Blacks, they maintained, spent their lives "like Tarzan of the Apes."[5] Venezuelan aristocrats judged people by their appearances. Accordingly, individuals with "anxious hair" or "hair like springs" lived in the shadow of their black slave ancestors. The elite considered respectable the whiter Venezuelans who had "hair flat as rainwater, of an indefinite light brown color which is neither fair nor dark."[6] "With us," wrote Olga Briceño in the late 1930s, "one of the first things you notice is a person's head. In the long run you will base your judgment on what there is inside, but you will inevitably begin by seeing what you can learn by looking at it. That is why the mulatto and the half-breed find it so much harder than the white man to achieve success and why, when they do, it is due solely to merit."[7]

Miscegenation played an important role in the development of racial attitudes in Venezuela during the nineteenth century. Most visitors to the nation were surprised by the multiracial society they encountered. In a particularly interesting description of Venezuela's racial scene during the late 1830s, John Hawkshaw, an Englishman, noted that the largest portion of the population then represented a mixed race of "every shade of colour from the bronze of the zambo to the lighter shades of the Mulutto and Mistigo [sic]."[8] At the time, Hawkshaw believed that a new race of people would inhabit Venezuela. He even predicted that "this light yellowish-looking race may be the type of the future nations of South America." In Venezuela Hawkshaw found the highest offices of the country open to men of color. "In this country, therefore, the negro is not an object of prejudice; and, if free, immediately takes his stand as high up the scale of society as his capacity and intelligence may entitle him."[9] Not all of the blacks had the means of achieving high goals. Most lacked the education and culture needed to compete with the whites. Although Hawkshaw believed that freedom would work wonders for the blacks because they "possessed . . . greater native vigour and mind than the Indian," he predicted that they would need time and encouragement to remedy years of neglect in order to place themselves on equal footing with those around them. One age of culture would not overcome the intellectual difficulties confronted by blacks, he concluded, who "for generations have had little occasion to exercise their thoughts."[10]

This conclusion fits closely a similar observation made at the beginning of the present century by a North American black, James Weldon Johnson, who served as United States consul at Puerto Cabello between 1906 and 1908. Johnson's observations of Venezuela provide a rare insight into the racial situation of that nation during the first decade of the present century. Late in 1906, Johnson wrote a description of his new post to his friend Booker T. Washington. At Puerto Cabello, an important port city of some 15,000 inhabitants, slightly to the west of Caracas, Johnson discovered a peaceful racial ambience. Few whites of European stock lived in that provincial city. Its upper class included colored men and women, mostly mestizos, in whose veins flowed Spanish, Indian, and African blood. "I see men of Negro blood in all the trades," he reported. "I find them in clerical positions in the large wholesale houses, they are priests, there is one here who is a successful physician, and one of the richest importing and exporting merchants of the city is a colored man—as we use the term."[11]

In spite of a lack of overt prejudice toward colored people at Puerto Cabello, Johnson did not claim to have found a black's paradise in Venezuela. Though individuals of mixed racial backgrounds competed on equal terms with the whites, few pure blacks did. The average black, mulatto, and Indian constituted a definite lower class, as they do now. Even though Johnson did not attribute their inferior condition to reasons of race and color alone, he did note that "the fact is, the great majority of Indians and blacks are poor and ignorant." As for the blacks, he lamented that the pure Negro plays but a small part in life in this country, and there are "very few of him." It seems that his chief work has been to lend a little color to the scene. I judge that soon there will be "none of him." In the course of years the Venezuelans will become a homogeneous race of a Spanish type, in color somewhere between a light brown and a yellow. So, the Negro, in spite of the fact that he has not the great obstacle of prejudice to overcome, will make no name in Venezuela as a Negro.[12]

Unfortunately, any scientific study of the black in twentieth-century Venezuela must overcome a surprising paucity of statistical data. Symptomatic of the racial harmony found in Venezuela, no census taken since the abolition of slavery in 1854 mentions people by race. To all intents and purposes the black disappeared from the official records of modern Venezuela during the second half of the nineteenth century.[13] Since the 1860s national historians have generally overlooked the presence of the black as a separate racial entity. The absence of any clear record of the assimilation of the blacks after emancipation poses a vexing problem for the student of twentieth-century race relations in Venezuela. Further difficulties arise from the fact that during the years between 1854 and the end of the nineteenth century, a number of popular myths concerning the blacks became fixed in the nation's literature. The leading myth maintained that the nation had no racial problem. Yet the degree to which blacks became assimilated into the Venezuelan society and the way the assimilation process took place remain unclear.

The Venezuelans' belief that they had no racial problem sprang from the combination of a long legal tradition of equality, the rhetoric of Simón Bolívar, and the fact that Venezuelan historians, unlike their Brazilian contemporaries, showed little interest in treating the black as a separate element of society after 1854. National historians, including Francisco González Guinán, José Santiago Rodriguez, Lisandro Alvarado, and José Gil Fortoul, treated the period 1810 to 1865 as an epoch of improving race relations. According to their accounts, racial conflicts as such ended in the 1860s during the Federal War (1859-1863). As a result of incessant warfare, two changes took place, the consensus historians stated. First, the old aristocracy disappeared and gave way to a new type of regional *caudillo*. Second, many blacks advanced politically as a result of military careers. The consensus historians whitewashed the nation's racial strife by attributing racial atrocities to the common bloodshed of civil wars. In so doing, the historians attempted to unify a divided populace. Their studies, written mostly from the point of view of the liberal faction that came to power upon the completion of the Federal War, attempted to close the deep rifts that had split the nation.[14]

The consensus historians argued that the struggle for racial equality began during the wars for independence, between 1810 and 1821. In that struggle black slaves fought for and against the Spanish, usually with the promise of obtaining freedom and political rights. To the consensus historians the atrocities committed by the colored *llanero* troops of José Tomás Boves manifested a social conflict. Boves' troops represented part of an egalitarian movement by blacks in their struggle against the white upper class.[15] But historians blended the remaining slave revolts that took place during this period into the struggle for independence. Once independent, Venezuelans dragged their feet. For a number of reasons they postponed the abolition of slavery. The issue of abolition did not arouse much passion, as it did elsewhere in the hemisphere. When proclaimed, it resulted from political and economic rather than humanitarian reasons.[16] With emancipation in 1854 a chapter in Venezuela's racial evolution came to an end. Slavery no longer remained as a cause for racial revolt. Finally, the wars between 1859 and 1863 saw the last examples of racial conflict, according to the consensus historians. Since blacks fought on both sides during that period, it seems difficult to make a clear distinction between racial and political persecution. After 1865, especially, Venezuelan historians failed to treat the black as an identifiable social group, despite evidence that many of the conflicts during those years appear to have had racial overtones.[17]

The assumption that the struggle for political stability brought about racial harmony appealed to the political elites who came to power during the last quarter of the nineteenth century.[18] It has not lost that appeal during the present century. Support came from two other important sources besides the consensus historians. Every constitution since 1830 acknowledged the complete equality of all citizens of Venezuela, although some based the right to vote on minimum property requirements. More important, the words of Simón Bolívar, the nation's political liberator, gave credence to the concept of racial equality. Though he later feared the creation of a "Pardocracy," or a government of the lower colored castes, he encouraged racial harmony when he recruited black troops during the wars of independence. Moreover, in a speech delivered to the Congress of Angostura in 1819, Bolívar reminded his followers of the heterogeneous nature of Venezuelan society:

We must bear in mind that our people are neither European nor North American; they are a mixture of Africa and America rather than an emanation of Europe. . . . While we have all been born of the same mother, our fathers, different in origin and in blood, are foreigners, and all differ visibly as to the color of their skin, a dissimilarity which places upon us an obligation of the greatest importance.[19]

Educated Venezuelans liked to believe that Bolívar's words meant that Venezuela had no racial problem. But in spite of their hopes, several chips appeared in the nation's social veneer by the turn of the century. In particular, Spencerian positivism made a profound impact on a generation of scholars at the Central University of Caracas after 1890. Trained to consider the growth of nations in organic terms, these men increasingly turned their attention to explaining Venezuela's failure to achieve a state of ultimate perfection. The English positivist Herbert Spencer proved a timely prophet of progress. A product of the industrial age many Venezuelans wished to introduce to Venezuela, he gave hope to ambitious politicians and elitists that they could alter the course of their nation's history. In trying to understand the causes of political and economic chaos in Venezuela, the positivists began to question the theory of racial equality. During the first decades of the twentieth century the writings of José Gil Fortoul, Pedro Manuel Arcaya, and Laureano Vallenilla Lanz, all members of a Caracas-based white elite, revealed a growing distrust of the Venezuelan masses.[20] Their studies began to shift the blame for Venezuela's difficulties upon the presence of a racially inferior majority.

This movement culminated in Vallenilla Lanz's classic study, *Cesarismo democrático*, a sophisticated statement in support of dictatorship in Venezuela.[21] Written in part to justify the ironhanded rule of Juan Vicente Gómez, who ran Venezuela like a personal estate between 1909 and 1935, this book also reflected the attitude of Venezuela's elite during those unhappy years. According to Vallenilla Lanz, the unruly Venezuelan race could not govern itself through democratic processes. Without a dictator, he stated, Venezuela had no hope of progressing. Mestizos, mulattoes, blacks, and Indians needed an authoritarian government. Order and progress necessitated the implementation of a "white dictatorship," even if the dictator, like Gómez, was a mestizo.

Men like Arcaya and Vallenilla Lanz seldom criticized the Afro-Venezuelan directly. They disclaimed the simplistic racist theories of Gobineau. But they constantly made disparaging remarks about the Africans who had come to Venezuela as slaves. Arcaya, for instance, considered these Africans uncultured. In his opinion their major contribution to the Venezuelan race amounted to vitality and resistance to disease. With no statistical evidence to support his case, Arcaya argued that most Venezuelans were mestizos, with little African blood. He claimed that the Indian formed the principal element of the nation's tricolored race.[22] Vallenilla Lanz attributed to the African the

Venezuelan's anarchical tendencies. Thus he explained the violent political evolution of the nation during the nineteenth century.[23]

But in spite of their obvious prejudices, these men repeated the fundamental conviction of Bolívar that "we belong to a family resulting from the fusion of three distinct ethnic elements and our national character, our ideals, and in sum, our spirit, are ethnic and social realities."[24] Though clearly antiblack, they accepted the Venezuelan type as a product of the mixing of the three races. The explanation for their seemingly ambivalent concepts of race is probably that when they wrote about blacks and Indians they dealt with abstract beings, not real persons. They held themselves aloof from the Venezuelan masses, whom they feared. They never knew the black intimately and dealt only with his distant African forebears in their works. In such a manner the contemporary black all but disappeared from the pages of the books these influential authors wrote. Even in his book *Disgregación e integración*, published in 1930, Vallenilla Lanz dealt almost exclusively with the colonial black and mulatto. To his credit he showed a keen appreciation and awareness of white supremacy during colonial days, especially in regions in which the blacks predominated. But then, like other Venezuelan intellectuals, he buried the racial conflicts of the colonial epoch in the wars of independence. These he interpreted as a culmination of a racial struggle that had manifested itself in slave revolts during the eighteenth century.[25] For his purposes the black somehow became a Venezuelan during the nineteenth century and disappeared from the scene as a racial type.

When the mestizo Juan Vicente Gómez assumed power in late 1908, he began one of Venezuela's longest and most brutal regimes. With force and cunning he forged a centralized and powerful government that lasted until his death in 1935. Like his predecessor, Cipriano Castro, Gómez came from the Andean state of Táchira. He brought to office with him men from that region who held the black Venezuelan in low regard. Under Gómez the latent antiblack attitude of Venezuela's white elite grew in strength and openness. Pictures of various Gómez cabinets show that he surrounded himself with white officials. No pure black appears in official publications. Few government officials revealed any negroid characteristics. Indeed, one of Gómez' leading English-speaking biographers took pains to point out that Gómez was a mestizo, and thus far above his own brothers, many of whom had black blood.[26] As for the *criollo* aristocracy, they too maintained their claims of *limpieza de sangre* with a fervor matching that of their colonial ancestors.[27] Of course one cannot build a solid case for racism on such frail evidence. But the fact that Gómez turned to the white oligarchy of Caracas for legitimate support reveals much about his lack of concern for the colored masses. For these masses he had contempt. He kept the lower-class Venezuelans uneducated and poor and treated them like children. Ironically, under his rule the masses realized a peace and tranquillity previously unknown to them. They no longer served in endless battles as the cannon fodder of local *caudillos*.

The nation's immigration policies under the Gómez regime provide a clearer example of antiblack practices. During the late nineteenth century, numbers of Antillean blacks came to Venezuela as day laborers, especially from the British islands of Barbados and Trinidad. They worked on railways, in mines, on farms, and as domestics throughout the nation. Few aristocratic families did not boast an Antillean cook or nursemaid. West Indian Negroes worked in the jungles and plains of eastern Venezuela, where most native Venezuelans refused to go.[28] They came in such numbers that in some parts of the interior the Castilian word *ingles* referred to the Antillean black. But toward the end of the century Venezuelan authorities began to express some uneasiness about the presence of the Antillean immigrants.[29] Ostensibly they feared that foreigners would displace native workers. Before the end of the century the national Congress enacted legislation barring the entry of all colored immigrants into Venezuela. With one minor exception, all of the constitutions since the late nineteenth century through 1958 had similar provisions.[30]

When contrasted with Venezuela's open encouragement of white European immigration after 1900, the exclusion of colored people, blacks and Asiatics, appears significant. Venezuela needed people. Its leaders sincerely believed the words of the Argentine Juan B. Alberdi, that "to govern is to populate." They wanted farmers to develop the nation's declining agricultural production. Most believed that hard-working Italian peasants best suited the needs of Venezuela.[31] When referring to white immigrants, they did not express fear that foreigners would take jobs from Venezuelans. Clearly they desired whites, not blacks. They did not want "inferior" races to flock to Venezuela from the Antilles and the Orient. In contrast, not enough whites could come. No doubt exists as to the commitment of the Gómez administration to exclude the influx of Antillean blacks. Even blacks from the United States, whom the Venezuelans acknowledged as superior to those from the Antilles, were not welcomed. When a rumor circulated in Caracas in 1924 that many blacks from the West Indies and the United States might come to Venezuela to pick a large cotton crop, the Gómez government made its position clear. It announced through an official governmental organ that "just the idea of such a thing, even if it might be a rumor, justifies our alarm. The introduction of individuals of this race, under the conditions by which they would come, constitutes a true immigration, and this is not the class of immigrant that Venezuela needs."[32] On numerous occasions during the 1920s and 1930s, Venezuelan officials refused Afro-American and Asiatic seamen permission to spend their shore leaves at Venezuelan ports and did not permit them to leave their ships.[33]

Other evidence of antiblack sentiments during the Gómez period shows up in the popular press and in magazines. Advertising and humor illustrate prevailing racial attitudes. Throughout the twenties and early thirties, advertisements held up the image of the European white as the ideal type. White models encouraged Venezuelans to buy suits, cigarettes, beverages, automobiles, and all the conveniences of modern living. The black, when depicted in an advertisement, either looked like a "black mammy" or a nondescript male with no individual characteristics. The blacks in advertisements had round faces, exaggerated lips, kinky hair, ragged clothes or servant's attire, and no individuality. Their dress revealed poverty or obvious domestic servant status. Much the same held true for humor. A careful study of the humor magazine *Fantoches*, edited by Leoncio Martínez (Leo), a liberal at the time, suggests that the white Venezuelan treated the black as a type, not as an individual. Cartoonists drew stereotyped blacks. Characters looked more or less alike. They had round faces, kinky hair or bald pate, large white lips against black faces, huge ears, and bulging white eyes. Though all of the cartoons depicting blacks did not have antiblack content, the majority did. Cartoonists aimed the bitterest antiblack humor against Antillean blacks. From a racial point of view, some cartoons show that the multiracial Venezuelan society could laugh at itself. Venezuelans took delight in racial situations that would have angered white Southerners of the United States. For that reason any evaluation of Venezuelan humor runs the risk of reading Yankee biases into the Venezuelan mind. Nonetheless, there are clear social implications of a cartoon such as one entitled "The Newly Rich," showing a white house-painter arriving at the door of a black family with four coal-black children. The painter asks, "What do you want done in the house?" To which the father responds fatalistically, "You can start off by whitening it."[34]

Following the death of Gómez, Venezuelans once again attempted to implement the egalitarian principles they had mouthed since the days of Bolívar. Now they inherited an integrated country. In spite of his many faults, Gómez had forged a unified nation. New roads, a professional military, a stable economy, and a national budgetary surplus left Venezuela in an enviable position by 1935. Venezuela remained prosperous by Depression standards. But only the rich enjoyed the prosperity. The democratic rhetoric of most leaders did not lead to any positive social action. Indeed, the dominant group continued Gómez's central authority without him. Conservatives like Eleázar López Contreras, Isaias Medina Angarita, and Estaban

Gil Borges actually feared the uneducated Venezuelan masses. As a result they continued the oppressive government of the elitist Andean group. Men from the state of Táchira controlled the military, and with it the presidency. In conjunction with aristocrats from Caracas, they worked to exclude the masses from participation in the government.

The economic development of the nation concerned the new leaders. Few politicians believed that Venezuela had any industrial potential. In fact, most urged the national government to use its resources to resuscitate the nation's agricultural production. In order to accomplish this goal, they wanted to bring to Venezuela hardy, well-trained agricultural laborers from Europe who would move to the unpopulated interior to establish much-needed agricultural communities. To their way of thinking, the average Venezuelan *campesino* lacked both the education and the technical skills to undertake modern farming on a large scale. As a result, the immigration schemes proposed after 1935 called for attracting European whites, especially from Spain, Italy, and Portugal, but also from the Canary Islands. Proponents of white immigration schemes described the European peasants as industrious and intelligent laborers, whereas the average *campesino* was depicted as an indolent, backward person. European immigrants became symbols of rejuvenation. In the same manner, members of the Venezuelan dominant group advocated the introduction of European blood because they believed the new arrivals would inject a new spirit of energy into the nation.

White immigration became a panacea for the nation's economic difficulties. An editorial in the pages of *La Esfera* of Caracas in early 1937 summed up this optimistic faith in white immigrants. Its author placed the blame for Venezuela's failure to achieve its true destiny upon the lack of an energetic population. Venezuela needed to populate its vast frontier. Tropical diseases, tuberculosis, syphilis, alcoholism, and malnutrition had debilitated Venezuela's present populace. Furthermore, most Venezuelans lacked the spiritual, ethnic, and racial strength required to resolve the nation's many problems. In closing, *La*

Esfera proclaimed: "In order to help our national evolution we need the introduction of other races, the joining of other ideas, the transfusion of blood, the example of creative activity, and the fertile stimulation of the spirit of sacrifice."[35]

The influential liberal oligarch Arturo Uslar Pietri reiterated much the same sentiments in a series of articles he published in *El Universal* in 1937. According to him, Venezuela did not have the capacity to realize its economic potential because of the indolent nature of its mixed race. He singled blacks out particularly as a negative element, writing that "the black, for his part, does not constitute a beneficial part of the race."[36] He also concluded, "That which we may be able to call the Venezuelan race actually is . . . as incapable of a modern and dynamic concept of work and wealth as were its antecedents." Like other white supremacists, he argued that an open-port policy for immigrants would bring disastrous consequences, since work opportunities in agriculture and oil would bring an invasion of black workers from the Antilles and coolies from the Orient. These types, he felt, would only hurt Venezuela's ethnic composition and lower its level of living. In short, the introduction of blacks would delay the general progress of Venezuela's "civilization." On the other hand, he believed that Venezuela had to change its ethnic composition in order to change its course of history and become a modern state. "It is necessary to inject into the country a formidable quantity of new blood with which a new concept of life, with an aggressive economic mentality, will begin the transformation of our ruinous economic and social structure."[37] To accomplish this goal, Venezuela needed to attract European immigrants.

White Venezuelans virulently opposed an open immigration policy that would have allowed blacks to enter Venezuela. Despite the need for agricultural laborers, they did not want more "culturally inferior" persons. Accordingly, the 27 August 1936 issue of *Panorama* wrote a typical editorial entitled "The Negro Danger." Blacks from the British West Indies, it stated, entered the nation at an alarming rate. A large portion of them signed Venezuelan citizenship papers. These job hunters, the paper continued, posed an immediate threat to Venezuelan workers. Their presence endangered the economic well-being of Venezuelans and their nation. Although the same paper had frequently urged the government to encourage European whites to pursue agricultural careers in Venezuela, it vehemently opposed the immigration of blacks for the same purpose. Whites could change their citizenship to improve their lot. But when blacks sought to immigrate to Venezuela, *Panorama* treated them as criminals: "To renounce the country of one's origin and adopt another in order to acquire a job with better conditions . . . is a felony, a betrayal of the hospitality that has been received."[38]

In similar fashion, Alberto Andriani, who framed Venezuela's immigration policy in 1937, also called for an exclusively white immigration program. The son of Italian immigrants, Andriani grew up in the Andean city of Mérida, a region with few blacks. Like other *andinos*, he expressed the prejudices of the region. On the one hand he denied any attempt to treat the Afro-Venezuelan as an inferior race. But on the other hand he wrote, "For many reasons the black has been a factor of deterioration in American countries where the races have mixed or of disorder where they have remained separated." Above all, Andriani desired to alter the racial composition of the nation. "The ideal will be to have a homogeneous white population," he stated, "but that is impossible because our territory còntains a large proportion of Indians and blacks. However, we are able to augment considerably the white element with great success."[39] European immigrants provided a means by which Venezuela could whiten its population. By the same token, the exclusion of the Negro, especially the Antillean black, removed the danger of introducing what men like Andriani considered a retrogressive element into the intellectual, social, and political life of the nation.

The viewpoints just discussed reveal the dichotomy of the Venezuelan racists' attitudes. Outwardly the white attacked the Antillean black as inferior to the Venezuelan black.[40] But in actual practice the Venezuelan black had few friends. Indeed, the Táchira clique that ran the government with the support of the

Caracas-based oligarchy had no sympathy for the poor blacks of Venezuela. If anything, they feared them. The only ray of hope came from the radical Acción Democrática party, which attempted to effect a social revolution of sorts between 1936 and 1948. Purposefully, the leaders of Acción Democrática, which rose to power in 1945 as a result of a military coup, attempted to form a popular political movement with as broad a base as possible. Unlike other parties, it built its power base in the rural parts of the nation, among the colored *campesinos*.[41] Furthermore, its organizers came from the interior, not from Caracas. Its nominal chief, Romulo Betancourt, represented the racially mixed majority of his home state of Miranda. Another founder, the educator Luis Beltrán Prieto Figueroa, a mulatto, also helped to identify Acción Democrática with the colored masses. The same held true for the colored poet Andres Eloy Blanco from Cumaná. Romulo Gallegos, the party's first president, wrote *Pobre negro*, one of Venezuela's best-known novels about blacks. Through hard work and sacrifice, these men and their party became the spokesmen of the tricolored Venezuelan masses. They also became the most outspoken politicians on racial equality.

During a short-lived period of political control between 1945 and 1948, Acción Democrática pressed for basic reforms aimed at improving the lot of the Venezuelan masses. Specifically they worked for agrarian and educational reforms that promised social mobility to the blacks. They also opened up a number of bureaucratic positions to blacks. Throughout its administration the party struggled to abolish vestiges of white racism. Party representatives spoke out on numerous occasions against the exclusionary clauses of existing immigration laws. They wanted an "open port" system whereby all races could enter Venezuela as immigrants. When three Caracas hotels refused to accommodate Todd Duncan, a black North American entertainer, in June 1945, *adeco* (members of the Acción Democrática party) spokesmen led an unprecedented campaign against discrimination. In itself the Duncan case provides a rare example of Venezuelan racial discrimination. The fact that foreigners owned the three hotels that refused to serve Duncan gave many Venezuelans an opportunity to place the blame on Yankees and Europeans. But the incident gave the liberal press ample opportunity to air long-suppressed grievances. Leftist politicians also took advantage of the situation. Though reluctant to admit that Venezuela had a racial problem, critics of the Duncan affair made it clear that the López Contreras and Medina administrations had discriminated against blacks. Romulo Betancourt, then a member of the Consejo Municipal of Caracas, urged immediate action to assure that such discriminatory practices against blacks would never occur again. He did not want racism of the Yankee type to develop in Venezuela, as he felt it had in Cuba and Puerto Rico. In the Congress and the press Acción Democrática joined the Communists and other leftists in condemning the incident.[42]

In the long run, the party's racial policies may have contributed to its eventual undoing in 1948, when a military coup removed President Gallegos from office. Its agrarian reform policy, popular education program, anti-Church position, and attempts to restrict military privileges rank high as causes for its overthrow in late 1948. Evidence also exists to suggest that the upper class and upper-middle class had become extremely apprehensive about Acción Democrática's egalitarian nature. According to José A. Silva Michelena, they especially resented Acción Democrática's encouragement of blacks and "rabble" to occupy high government offices and "to interact with the best families of Caracas."[43] Prior to the advent of the Acción Democrática government, the poor had never held high bureaucratic positions, let alone participated in carequeño social circles. Previous administrations had systematically denied education to the masses. In so doing, they maintained the racial status quo. At the urging of men like Luis Beltrán Prieto Figueroa, the Acción Democrática attempted to implement a massive educational reform aimed at improving the living standards and social opportunities of the colored Venezuelans. Resistance to his plan came from many sectors, but especially from the white conservatives of Táchira and Caracas. Indeed, according to Prieto Figueroa, Dr. Gustavo Herrera, the minister of education in 1942, reputedly said that "if the little Venezuelan blacks are so uppity without knowing how to read or write, where are we going to stop if we educate them?"[44]

Under the leadership of a conservative white elite, Venezuela experienced considerable European immigration between 1948 and 1958. Italians made up the leading group of immigrants, along with Spaniards, Portuguese, and Eastern Europeans. During that decade Caracas changed from a provincial Venezuelan city into an international cosmopolis. Its population grew fantastically, both as a result of European immigrants and from internal migration. The overall impact of the demographic changes in Caracas have not been fully appreciated. If anything, it would seem that the presence of a larger European community would have strengthened the prevailing antiblack sentiments. The governments that have led Venezuela since 1958 have not taken as strong measures to improve the status of the blacks as were taken between 1945 and 1948. The search for technological and agricultural expertise has led some leaders of Acción Democrática and COPEI to encourage Japanese immigration, but while in power both parties have discriminated against the nation's Chinese population and neither party has moved to relax the existing antiblack immigration practices.

Throughout the twentieth century the dominant groups of Venezuela have displayed an obvious preference for less *café* and more *leche*. Although Venezuela has not experienced the tense racial situation found in the United States, the average Afro-Venezuelan has remained forgotten. Few have championed the cause of the black because few have admitted that the black had a problem. Romulo Gallegos immortalized the *llanos* in his *Doña Barbara*, but nobody had written the novel of Barlovento, the predominantly black section along the coast of Miranda state, east of Caracas. As one member of Acción Democrática stated in 1945, "Disgracefully, we have not produced a purely Indian or black writer yet who could write the novel of the Indian or black."[45]

Over the centuries blacks have given much to Venezuelan culture and society, especially in terms of music, art, agriculture, and religion. But from a social and economic vantage point, Venezuelan society has taken much from the Africans, especially their bodies. A representative epitaph for the Afro-Venezuelan appeared in a widely used school textbook, which stated that "the heritage of the black is love for labor, that of the Indian and the Spaniard the love of liberty, valor, and high character."[46] Whether future generations of Venezuelan blacks will continue to accept that description of their role in society depends on whether they begin to identify their low economic and social stations in life with their racial status. How and when that may occur remain questions for future Venezuelans to answer.

Notes

[1] For succinct surveys of the Venezuelan racial picture, see Elizabeth Yabour de Caldera, *La población de Venezuela: un analisis demográfico* (Cumana, 1967); and Magnus Mörner, *Race Mixture in the History of Latin America* (Boston, 1967).

[2] For examples of the conflict, see Miguel Acosta Saignes, "Un mito racista: el indio, el blanco, el negro," *Revista nacional de cultura*, No. 67, March-April 1948; Miguel Acosta Saignes, *Elementos indigenes y africanos en la formación de la cultura venezolana* (Caracas, 1956); Juan Liscano, *Apuntes para la investigación del negro en Venezuela: sus instrumentos de musica* (Caracas, 1947); Carlos Siso, *La formación del pueblo venezolano: estudios sociologicos*, 2 vols. (Madrid, 1953); Juan Pablo Sojo, *Tierras del Estado Miranda: sobre la ruta de los cacahuales* (Caracas, 1938); Juan Pablo Sojo, *Temas y apuntes afro-venezolanos* (Caracas, 1943).

[3] Sojo, *Temas y apuntes afro-venezolanos*, p. 33.

[4] Siso, *La formación del pueblo venezolano*, 2: 432; Mörner, *Race Mixture in the History of Latin America*, pp. 75-138; and Pierre L. van den Berghe, *Race and Racism: a Comparative Perspective* (New York, 1967), p. 57.

[5] Olga Briceño, *Cocks and Bulls in Caracas* (New York, 1939), p. 111.

[6] *Ibid.*, p. 110.

[7] *Ibid.*, pp. 110-111.

[8] John Hawkshaw, *Reminiscences of South America from Two and One Half Years' Residence in Venezuela* (London, 1838), p. 206.

[9] *Ibid.*, p. 208.

[10] *Ibid.*

[11]Johnson to Washington, 30 August 1906, Container 324, Booker T. Washington Papers (BTW), Library of Congress, Washington, D.C.

[12]*Ibid*.

[13]Caldera, *La población de Venezuela*, p. 71; and Mörner, *Race Mixture in the History of Latin America*, p. 2.

[14]See Gillermo Morón, *A History of Venezuela*, ed. and trans. John Street (New York, 1963), pp. 27-28, as a late example of this tradition.

[15]German Carrera Damas has disproved this thesis in his *Boves: aspectos socio-económicos de su acción histórica* (Caracas, 1968).

[16]John V. Lombardi, "The Decline and Abolition of Negro Slavery in Venezuela, 1820-1854" (Ph.D. diss., Columbia University, 1968).

[17]Hudson, "The Status of the Negro in Northern South America," p. 226.

[18]Men of all racial groups held high office during the last decades of the century.

[19]As translated by Mörner, *Race Mixture*, pp. 86-87.

[20]See in particular José Gil Fortoul, *El hombre y la historia* (Madrid, 1916); Pedro Manuel Arcaya, *Estudios de sociológia venezolana* (Madrid, [1917?]); and Laureano Vallenilla Lanz, *Cesarismo democrático: Estudio sobre los bases sociológicas de la constitución efectiva de Venezuela* (Caracas, 1917).

[21]Laureano Vallenilla Lanz, *Cesarismo democrático* (Caracas, 1917).

[22]Arcaya, *Estudios de sociológia venezolana*.

[23]Arcaya, *Estudios de sociológia venezolana*, pp. 10-16; Laureano Vallenilla Lanz, *Disgregación e integración: ensayo sobre la formación de la nacionalidad venezolana* (Caracas, 1930), 1: 139.

[24]Gil Fortoul, *El hombre y la historia*, p. 27.

[25]Vallenilla Lanz, *Disgregación e integración*, 1: 114-118, 129.

[26]Thomas Rourke (pseud.) [Daniel Joseph Clinton], *Gómez, Tyrant of the Andes* (New York, 1936), p. 45.

[27]Aurelio de Vivanco y Villegas and Galvarino de Vivanco y Villegas, *Venezuela al día: Venezuela up to Date* (Caracas, 1928), 1: 36.

[28]State Department Papers, National Archives, Loomis to Hay, 4 March 1901.

[29]Walter E. Wood, *Venezuela: Or Two Years on the Spanish Main* (Middlesborough, England, 1896), pp. 85-87.

[30]In 1948, Article 15 of a proposed immigration law contained a clause stating that no one would be accepted as an immigrant if "his level of living was noticeably inferior to that of the Venezuelan people in gen-

eral." See Congreso Nacional, Senadores, *Diario de debates* (1948), 5 (28 August 1948): 1690.

[31]Based on reading the Gómez press, especially *El Nuevo Mundo*. Also see *Vivanco y Villegas, Venezuela al dia*, pp. 5-6.

[32]*Boletin de la Cámara de Comercio de Caracas*, October 1924, p. 2577.

[33]My thanks to Professor George Schuyler, State University of New York at Stonybrook, for this information.

[34]*Fantoches*, 22 May 1929, p. 8.

[35]*Campaña de "La Esfera": editoriales sobre el problema agro-pecuaria de Venezuela* (Caracas, 1939), pp. 43-46.

[36]*El Universal* (Caracas), 28 July 1937.

[37]*Ibid*.

[38]*Panorama* (Maracaibo), 27 August 1936.

[39]Alberto Andriani, *Labor venezolanista* (Caracas, 1937), p. 56.

[40]For particularly strong statements to this effect by students of the Afro-Venezuelan, see Siso, *La formación del pueblo venezolano*, 2: 509; and Sojo, *Temas y apuntes afro-venezolanos*, pp. 9-23. According to Siso, the Venezuelan black had a potential intellectual superiority to "the Antillean black, the North American black, and even the Brazilian black."

[41]John D. Powell, *Preliminary Report on the Federación Campesina de Venezuela: Origins, Organization, Leadership and Role in the Agrarian Reform Program* (Madison, Wis., 1964).

[42]Although all newspapers mentioned the incident, the best accounts appeared in the following: *Ultimas Noticias* (Caracas), 6 June 1945 and 7 June 1945; *Fantoches*, 8 June 1945; *El Vigilante* (Mérida), 9 June 1945; and *El País* (Caracas), 2 June 1945. Betancourt's speech appears in Concejo Municipal (Caracas), *Actas* (January-June 1945), "Acta de la sesion ordinaria celebrada el dia Martes 29 de Mayo de 1945," pp. 11-12. A widely quoted speech by Senator Manuel Rodríguez Cardenas of Yaracuy, delivered on 4 June 1945, is found in Congreso Nacional, Senadores, *Diario de debates* (1945), 2, No. 19 (9 June 1945): 8-10.

[43]José A. Silva Michelena, "Conflict and Consensus in Venezuela" (Ph.D. diss., MIT, 1966 [mimeographed]), pp. 138-139. My thanks to the author for permission to read the revised edition. See also Laureano Vallenilla Lanz (hijo), *Escrito de memoria* (Mexico City, [1961]), p. 109.

[44]Luis Beltrán Prieto Figueroa, *De una educación de castas a una educación de masas* (Havana, 1951), p. 181.

[45]*Venezuela 1945* (Caracas, 1945), p. 542.

[46]Levi Marrero, *Venezuela y sus recursos: una geografia visualizada* (Madrid, 1964), p. 222.

13

The Gradual Integration of the Black in Cuba: Under the Colony, the Republic, and the Revolution

Marianne Masferrer and Carmelo Mesa-Lago

Attempts to assess changes in Cuba since Castro's takeover frequently become entrapped in polemical arguments over the pros and cons of socialist revolution. Interpretations of race relations in modern-day Cuba often swing in the direction of this larger debate, with conclusions drawn on the basis of whether a writer views Castro's Revolution favorably or unfavorably. Marianne Masferrer and Carmelo Mesa-Lago try to transcend these ideological biases by putting the major trends in Cuban race relations in historical perspective. They examine some of the fundamental aspects of slavery, then turn to the republican period to analyze basic population data and major trends in education, employment, and class relations. Finally, the authors view changes in Castro's Cuba in the light of earlier historical developments to point out that an up-to-date assessment of the status of Afro-Cubans cannot provide simplistic favorable or unfavorble verdicts. As the authors explain, institutional forms of racism in Cuba are gone, but prejudiced attitudes remain.

The implications of this study of Cuba raise questions about the persistence of subtle problems in Latin American race relations raised in earlier essays on Brazil, Venezuela, and Puerto Rico. Modern-day improvements in the Afro-Cuban's situation are tied to general gains for all Cubans from the lower socioeconomic strata. In short, Cuban blacks are benefiting from class gains rather than from attention to their needs as a specific group. Cuban socialism has done much to knock down the old, formal obstacles to integration (exclusive clubs, hotels, and beaches), and its advocates now assert that racism is absent in Cuba. Yet Afro-Cubans remain largely outside the leadership groups, and a disproportionately large number of them continue to labor in menial jobs rather than in professional occupations. Perhaps gains in the high-skill areas will be slow unless recognition is given to the specific injustices done unto blacks historically and to the persistence of prejudiced attitudes that came out of these historical relationships.

R. B. T.

Prejudice within any society is usually a complex phenomenon existing on many levels. On the individual level, the act or state of holding a preconceived and often irrational opinion of another individual or group because of race is common to all societies. When such feelings are reflected in the legal system or in the institutionalized customs of a nation so as to impair the basic rights of citizens, the problem becomes more serious and moves to an institutional level.

In Cuba racial prejudice on the individual and institutional levels has always existed to a lesser degree, both in scope and intensity, than in the United States. At the individual level, the problem itself was somewhat mollified through greater intermarriage and mixing of races. The institution of slavery in Cuba also had structural aspects that distinguished it from its North American counterpart. In addition, the presence of a large number of free Afro-Cubans (that is, blacks or Negroes and mulattoes) dur-

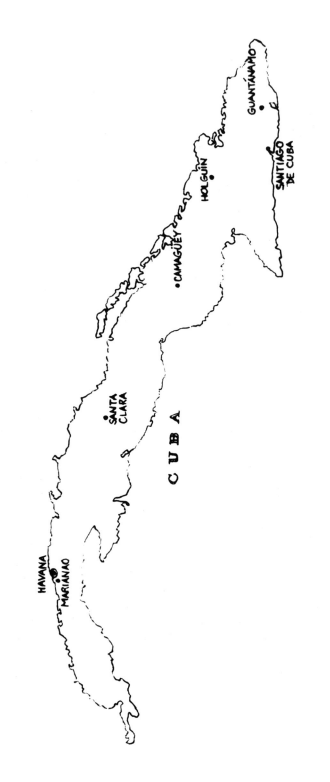

ing the slave period, who were able to live and work with white Cubans of different classes, also aided in assuaging the problem of racial prejudice. The Afro-Cuban also played a relevant role in the wars of independence against Spain, thus becoming a founder of the new Republic. Although slavery in Cuba was completely abolished some twenty-five years later than in the United States, the integration of the black into Cuban society took place at a much faster rate than in the American society, partly because of the preconditions explained above.

The legal system of the Republic banned all institutional forms of racial discrimination at the beginning of the twentieth century. But subtler ways of discrimination customarily exercised against Afro-Cubans, mainly by the upper class, persisted. These racial prejudices and discriminatory practices were incorporated into the policies of social clubs and commercial establishments that catered to the Cuban high stratum and the American tourist. Finally, many of the inequalities endured by the Afro-Cubans were also the result of the economic inequalities of a developing nation.

Cuba offers a unique opportunity to study the integration of the black through three different socioeconomic systems: colonialism, capitalism, and socialism. Therefore this paper will attempt to describe the gradual but steady process of integration of the black in Cuban society and some of the racial conflicts and discriminatory practices that existed during three historical periods: the Colony (1500-1902), the Republic (1902-1958), and the Revolution (1959 to the present). Within the colonial period the institution of slavery will be examined. Whenever data make it possible, various factors focusing on racial composition will be analyzed in the three periods: population trends, education levels and literacy rates, employment and unemployment by occupation, and some specific forms of racial discrimination.

The Colonial Period: 1500-1902

The Slavery System. There were important differences between the origin and development of slavery in Cuba and its growth in the United States. Claude Lightfoot gives an interesting description of these differences: "In Cuba slavery was established against a background of a dying feudal system in Spain, while in North America it arose and developed in the context of rising capitalist society, both in the mother country and in the colonies."[1] Lightfoot points out that the motives of settlers coming to the two areas were also related to this dissimilarity. The Spanish conquistadores came in search of gold to be extracted and brought back to the mother country, whereas the British colonizer, in search of commodities or because of religious reasons, came to work and settle.

Attitudes of the Spanish toward the individual slave produced a somewhat less callous system. The Spanish slave system regarded the slave as a human being with at least some legal rights. This was due partly to protection granted by the *Recopilación de Leyes de los Reynos de Indias: 1680* during the seventeenth century. Under this system the slave was permitted the right to own some property and, if Christian, was allowed to marry and have children considered to be his own. He was offered some protection under the law, which, in 1789, established at least minimal conditions, such as working hours and certain clothing and housing standards. The murder of a slave under the Spanish legal system constituted a crime. In contrast to this, slaves in North America possessed few rights under the law and were regarded as the chattel of their masters. Thus, whereas slaves in most of Spanish America were allowed some institutional protection beyond the power of the master, very few if any institutional recourse existed for slaves in most of North America.[2]

Such structural differences in the institution of slavery did not destroy the dehumanizing treatment of slaves in Cuba, but it did provide a difference in the nature of the system. Although it is very difficult to assess the true enforcement of the laws protecting the minor rights of the slave, it is still important to realize that such laws were at least on the books.

It was also easier for slaves to secure their liberty within Spanish

America. Thus, in 1861, 43 percent of the population was Afro-Cuban and was composed of 26 percent slaves and 17 percent *libertos* (former slaves who bought their liberty or who had been emancipated by their owners).[3] The degree of ethnic mixture reached in colonial Cuba is also important. The Spaniard was more inclined to a union with Negroes or mulattoes than was the Anglo-Saxon. One must remember that the Spanish did not generally bring their wives along as did the English settlers. In addition, the mixed offspring in Cuba were classified and treated differently from in the United States.

Population Trends. Requests for black slaves to be brought into the island began in 1513 and were influenced greatly by the previous requests made in 1501 by the Spanish colonizers on the island of La Española. The population of Cuba in 1550 consisted of a few white families, a few hundred slaves, and fewer than 5,000 Indians. Even by the year 1608, the population continued to be small and totaled around 20,000 inhabitants. By 1662 it had risen to about 30,000 and was divided nearly equally between whites and blacks, although the whites retained a small majority. At the same time, the Indian population shrunk to somewhere between 3,000 and 4,000 individuals, who remained on the eastern end of the island (see Table II).

By the year 1769, the city of Havana had developed into one of the most heavily populated cities in the New World, and the total number of inhabitants in Cuba had risen to 140,000. Part of this increase was caused by the introduction of black slaves for the construction of certain fortification works. In 1789-1791, Spain liberalized to a greater extent the rules for the introduction of African slaves.[4] Whereas in the period 1512-1763, some 60,000 slaves were introduced, a similar number was introduced in 1763-1794 (see Table I). The island also experienced an increase in the white population entering from Haiti; these were French immigrants who had left Haiti because of the rebellion and emancipation of the slaves.

As the plantation economy developed, the slave population

TABLE I

Slave Introduction into Cuba: 1512-1865

Years	Number	Years	Number	Years	Number
1512-1763	60,000	1800	4,145	1812	6,081
1763-1789	30,875	1801	1,659	1813	4,770
1790	2,534	1802	13,832	1814	4,321
1791	8,498	1803	9,671	1815	9,111
1792	8,528	1804	8,923	1816	17,737
1793	3,777	1805	4,999	1817	25,841
1794	4,164	1806	4,395	1818	19,902
1795	5,832	1807	2,565	1819	15,147
1796	5,711	1808	1,607	1820	17,174
1797	4,552	1809	1,162	1821	6,414
1798	2,001	1810	6,672	1822	2,500
1799	4,919	1811	6,349	1823-1831	50,000
				1832-1865	141,439

SOURCE: H. S. Aimes, *A History of Slavery in Cuba* (New York: Octagon Books, 1967; reprint of 1907 edition).

also increased, and many white plantation owners became fearful of the possibility of slave uprisings. In 1795 Nicolás Morales, a *liberto*, led the first conspiracy against the Spanish. Very little, however, is known about this conspiracy. In 1812 José Antonio Aponte, a mulatto, led another conspiracy of which we have some information. Aponte was hanged, but the fear of revolts continued to increase among the Spanish. Gabriel de la Concepción Valdés ("Plácido"), another mulatto, led the conspiracy of *La Escalera* (the ladder) in 1844, which was also aborted by the Spanish governor. Elizabeth Sutherland, discussing the effect of the Aponte and Valdés conspiracies on the Spanish authorities, maintains that their fear produced a "wave of repression which swept through Cuba and hit its high point in 1844 in the 'Year of the Lashings' " when the Spaniards launched a campaign that resulted in the killing of many blacks.[5]

Another indication of this constant fear of the Spanish in Cuba can be seen in a proposal from the minister of the interior, Don Alejandro Ramírez, suggesting that the Cuban economy shift from the plantation economy, with its dependence on increased slave labor, to one with a greater number of small property owners of European origin. Following this proposal, the authorities issued the Royal Decree of October 1817, which was specifically directed toward increasing the immigration of whites to the island. The decree granted foreigners the right to acquire in Cuba any kind of property, either rural or urban estates, under the same conditions as those applicable for Spaniards. It also authorized them to dispose of their properties freely and to take the proceeds with them at any time they might wish to leave the island. Finally, it exempted the new colonizers for five years from payment of taxes and granted a special exemption for fifteen years from the payment of the *diezmos* (special taxes) on the produce of their lands.[6] The colonial government also encouraged white immigration by authorizing local officials to aid in the establishment of new settlements by paying transportation costs and providing a monthly stipend for the first six months. These blatant attempts at increasing the white population of

TABLE II
Population by Race in Cuba: 1774-1899

Years	Total Population	Whites	Percent[a]	Negroes and Mulattoes					
				Total	Percent[a]	Slave	Percent[a]	Free	Percent[a]
1774	171,520	96,340	56.17	75,180	43.83	44,333	25.85	30,847	17.98
1791	272,300	153,599	56.39	118,741	43.61	64,590	23.72	54,154	19.89
1817	630,980	290,021	45.96	339,959	54.05	225,268	35.70	115,691	18.34
1827	704,487	311,051	44.15	393,436	55.85	286,942	40.73	106,494	15.12
1841	1,007,624	418,291	41.51	589,333	58.49	436,495	43.32	152,838	15.17
1861	1,396,530	793,484	56.82	603,046	43.18	370,553	26.53	232,494	16.65
1877	1,521,684	988,624	64.97	489,249	32.15	—	—	—	—
1887	1,631,687	1,102,889	67.59	528,598	32.41	—	—	—	—
1899	1,572,797	1,052,397	66.91	505,543	32.14	—	—	—	—

SOURCE: Oficina del Censo de los Estados Unidos, *Censo de la República de Cuba, bajo la administración provisional de los Estados Unidos, 1907* (Washington, D.C.: The Capitol City Press, 1908).

a. Percentage of total population.

the island did not produce immediate results, and the slave population continued to grow with the expansion of the agricultural sector. Altogether, it is estimated that more than 380,000 slaves were brought to the island during the nineteenth century. This increase can be seen in Table I.

Table II indicates that the black population did not constitute a majority before the nineteenth century; it represented 44 percent in 1774 and about the same proportion in 1791. But by 1817 the percentage of Negroes and mulattoes (54 percent) in the total population surpassed the percentage of whites (46 percent), and the percentage of blacks had risen to 58 percent of the total population by 1841. But in 1861 the percentage of the black population declined to 43 percent, owing mainly to the tremendous increase of the white population, but also because of the sharp decline in the introduction of slaves and the government's repression of slaves in the 1840s.

In 1868 the Ten-Year War began when a white *hacendado* (plantation owner), Carlos Manuel de Céspedes, freed all his slaves, exhorting them to fight with him for the independence of Cuba. One of the heroes of the Ten-Year War and of the War of Independence that followed (1895-1898) was Antonio Maceo, a mulatto and legendary warrior. Maceo was commander of the guerrilla units in Oriente when the Ten-Year War broke out in 1868. The following year slavery was abolished in the rebel-held central part of the island. Blacks began to join the rebel army in large numbers, and it was estimated by some that they represented 85 percent of the fighting force.[7]

Slavery was finally abolished in Cuba in May 1880. Slaves were to remain under the authority of their masters for an additional five years, and ownership was to cease gradually in accordance with the age of the slave. Owners were required to free one-quarter of their slaves beginning five years after the issuance of the decree or in 1885, and an additional one-fourth were to be freed every year afterward, so that all slaveholding was ended by 1888. During the period 1885-1888, owners were obliged to provide food, clothing, housing, medical facilities, instruction,

TABLE III

Education by Race in Cuba: 1827 and 1836

1827	Whites			Blacks		
	Population[a]	Enrollment	Percent	Population[a]	Enrollment	Percent
Havana	35,270	6,293	17.84	9,242	341	3.68
Santiago de Cuba	12,208	1,416	11.51	8,396	145	1.75
Puerto Príncipe (Camagüey)	25,598	751	2.93	7,184	—	—

1836		Enrollment			Enrollment	
Havana	—	6,436	—	—	347	—
Santiago de Cuba	—	1,467	—	—	150	—
Puerto Príncipe (Camagüey)	—	650	—	—	—	—

SOURCE: A. Bachiller y Morales, *Historia de las letras y de la instrucción pública en la Isla de Cuba* (Havana: Cultural S.A., 1936).

a. Segment of the population composed of boys 5-15 years and girls 10-12 years of age.

and a wage of between one and three pesos monthly to be determined by the age and faculties of the slave. The tenure of the slave could be lessened by a mutual understanding between the slave and his master. This did become the process; and by 1884 40 percent of the slaves were free.[8] Independence for the island was finally secured in 1898.

Education. Public education in Cuba up to this point, at least on the primary level, had been considered the responsibility of the religious community in the area or local parish. In 1836 the Royal Patriotic Society conducted a study designed to evaluate the educational facilities on the island (see Table III).

The study in 1836 demonstrated to the Spanish authorities that the educational system of the island needed major reform. Therefore, between 1840 and 1860, various programs were devised to increase the number of schools and teachers and to improve the educational system. On 26 September 1880 the Law of Public Instruction was passed and became the foundation for all regulations concerning primary and secondary education on the island. The law required that each town have one or more public primary schools providing instruction for nonwhite children. This instruction was to concentrate on moral and religious teachings. The instruction to be given to the slaves was not covered by the law, but the government and the respective parish were to inculcate in the masters an obligation to give instruction to their slaves.[9]

Even with all these programs, the census conducted in 1899 demonstrated the existence of widespread illiteracy in the population. It was found that 690,565 inhabitants or 43.8 percent of the population ten years old or older were not able to read or write. Forty-three percent of the illiterates were black or mulatto, a much higher proportion than the percentage of this group in the total population.[10]

Unfortunately no data are available from the colonial period to determine the impact of racial discrimination on the distribution of employment. Nevertheless, the extent of illiteracy among blacks and their former status as slaves suggest that they were forced to occupy the more physically demanding and most menial jobs.

The Republican Period: 1902-1958

Political independence from Spain, the creation of a republican form of government, and the abolition of the institution of slavery did not put a radical end to racial conflicts on the island. Instead, some of the problems persisted into the republican era. In 1912 a racial uprising occurred that became known as the Small War in May. This uprising has been the subject of many varying interpretations concerning its scope and intensity of violence. Many blacks who fought for independence believed that they would be able to gain full political and social equality with the emergence of the Republic. They therefore formed a political party to add pressure to their demands. This party became known as the Black Peoples' Independence party. However, the formation of a political party composed of only one race was prohibited by the Constitution of 1901; therefore the party was outlawed and the blacks turned toward more violent tactics.

John Clytus, an Afro-American militant who lived in Cuba from 1964 to 1967, maintains that the black fighters of the Small War in May were very successful in their first military confrontation with the Cuban authorities and that they would have seized the entire island if the authorities had not called on the United States to intervene. Clytus contends that U.S. soldiers assisted in putting down the black rebels and in doing so participated in a terrible slaughter of innocent black men, women, and children. Clytus also states that the leader of the black rebellion, Evaristo Estenoz, was hanged publicly.[11]

Carlos More, an Afro-Cuban, has also written about the scope of the violence and death in this confrontation. More states that at least 15,000 persons were killed during the uprising and that other authors have placed the number as high as 35,000.[12]

Other Cuban writers, usually whites, have taken a more moderate stand on the degree of racial difficulties on the island at the beginning of the Republic. The members of the Cuban Economic Research Project maintain:

> In the Republican period, the Negro was assimilated and became an efficient and able worker. It is not affirmed that total integration of the black race was accomplished, particularly in the economic field, because the labor opportunities open to colored people were generally in the low wage sectors. Although Cuban laws prohibited the formation of political parties comprising one race, the uprising under the leadership of Ivonet and Estenoz in 1912 did place in jeopardy the cordial relationship that had existed. This matter was, however, successfully settled.[13]

Population Trends. In the early years of the Republic, there was a great influx of white immigrants into the island, which resulted in an increase in the proportion of the white population. But in 1919, during an expansionary process, the sugar industry began to increase its supply of manpower. It therefore pressured the government to change the immigration laws. Consequently the temporary admission of black workers from Haiti and Jamaica was allowed until 1925. Between 1921 and 1925, it is estimated that at least 90,274 black immigrants entered Cuba (Table IV). These statistics should be taken with caution because of the great turnover among the immigrants—many returning to their native countries once the sugar crop had been harvested. The living conditions endured by the immigrants were extremely primitive, especially in the areas of housing and sanitary facilities. The immigrants, though largely illiterate, did provide the sugar industry with the cheap labor supply it had demanded.

In the second half of the 1920s, the economic crisis within the sugar industry produced a halt in the process of immigration. Further deterioration in the economy during the depression of the 1930s resulted in a sharp increase in unemployment. In August 1933 a revolution took place, and the new revolutionary government rapidly adopted measures to protect the native Cuban labor force. In December 1933 the government decreed that 50 percent of all employees on company payrolls were to be native Cubans. These regulations started a process of emigration of Spanish families from the island. The government also ordered the repatriation of all Haitians and Jamaicans. The number of black, mulatto, and Asiatic foreigners declined from 179,000 in 1931 to 70,000 in 1943, while that of the white foreigners declined from 671,000 to 141,000 in the same period. More than three-fourths of the nonwhite foreigners were concentrated in the eastern provinces (Camagüey and Oriente) because of the proximity of these areas to the source of emigration—that is, Jamaica and Haiti.[14]

TABLE IV
Immigration of Workers from Haiti and Jamaica into Cuba: 1921-1925

Year	Haiti	Jamaica	Total
1921	12,483	12,469	24,952
1922	639	4,455	5,094
1923	11,088	4,455	15,543
1924	21,013	5,086	26,099
1925	18,750	4,747	23,497
Totals	63,973	31,212	95,185

SOURCE: Ramiro Guerra, *Azúcar y población en las Antillas* (Havana: Instituto Cubano del Libro, 1970), p. 155.

Table V summarizes the trend in the racial composition of the Cuban population during the Republic. Continuing the trend that began in 1761, the white race was the predominant race in the country in 1907. It represented 69.7 percent of the total population in that year and rose to 72.3 percent in 1919. This was

TABLE V
Population by Race in Cuba: 1907, 1919, 1931, 1943, 1953

Year	Total	Whites		Negroes		Mulattoes		Asiatics	
		Number	Percent	Number	Percent	Number[a]	Percent	Number	Percent
1907	2,048,980	1,428,176	69.7	274,272	13.4	334,695	16.3	11,837	0.6
1919	2,889,004	2,088,047	72.3	323,117	11.2	461,694	16.0	16,146	0.6
1931	3,962,344	2,856,956	72.1	437,769	11.0	641,337	16.2	25,282	0.6
1943	4,778,583	3,553,312	74.4	463,227	9.7	743,115	15.5	18,929	0.4
1953	5,829,029	4,243,959	72.8	725,311	12.4	843,105	14.5	16,657	0.3

SOURCE: Cuba, Oficina Nacional de los Censos Demográfico y Electoral, *Censo de población, viviendas y electoral, 1953* (Havana: P. Fernández y Cía, 1955).

a. Includes mixture of whites and blacks and of these two with Asiatics.

TABLE VI

Black Population by Province in Cuba: 1907, 1919, 1931, 1943, 1953[a]

Provinces	1907 Number	Percent	1919 Number	Percent	1931 Number	Percent	1943 Number	Percent	1953 Number	Percent
Pinar del Rio	59,265	9.7	59,111	7.5	72,933	6.6	77,063	6.5	90,802	5.8
La Habana	122,860	20.2	135,842	17.3	210,982	19.1	263,907	21.8	345,305	22.00
Matanzas	87,987	14.4	92,522	11.8	89,407	8.1	81,849	6.8	87,334	5.6
Santa Clara	122,144	20.0	143,981	18.4	166,143	15.0	168,467	14.0	179,253	11.4
Camagüey	21,381	3.5	40,790	5.2	111,354	10.1	96,812	8.0	133,016	8.5
Oriente	195,360	32.2	312,565	39.8	454,569	41.1	518,244	42.9	732,696	46.7
Totals	608,967	100.0	784,811	100.0	1,105,388	100.0	1,206,380	100.0	1,568,416	100.0

SOURCE: See Table V.

a. Includes blacks and mestizos (i.e., mulattoes and mix of white and black races with Asiatics).

a result of the great increase in white immigration from Spain up to the end of the 1920s. Spanish immigration represented 95 percent of the total number of persons entering the country.[15] Possibly because of the black immigration from Haiti and Jamaica, by 1931 the white proportion of the total population had declined slightly as the proportion of the black population increased slightly. The apparent decline in the proportion of blacks in the 1943 census and their increase in the 1953 census are probably the result of the different methodologies used in both censuses rather than a real change in population trends.[16] Since 1919, therefore, the proportion of whites was stabilized at approximately 73 percent whereas the proportion of blacks remained at 27 percent. No clear trend seems to exist when the black population is separated into mulattoes and Negroes.

The black population was concentrated in the urban areas of the province of Havana, but the greatest proportion of blacks lived in the province of Oriente. In 1907, 32 percent of the black population lived in Oriente, increasing steadily throughout the republican period to reach 47 percent in 1953 (see Table VI). In 1953 approximately two-thirds of the Afro-Cubans lived in urban zones and one-third in rural ones.

Education. The only information available concerning the impact of racial factors on education pertains to literacy rates. But even with respect to this criterion, it is very difficult to assess the extent of any gap in the literacy rates of whites and blacks during the republican period. The categories in the censuses of 1907, 1919, and 1943 are based on different criteria of age and race; and neither the 1931 census nor the 1953 census includes data on this matter. In 1907 only 44 percent of the total white population and 32 percent of the total nonwhite (Negro, mulatto, and Asiatic) population were literate. This had risen to 45 percent of all whites and 38 percent of all nonwhite persons in 1919. According to the 1943 census, the categories had been redefined, making a true comparison difficult. In that year it was found that 72 percent of all whites ten years of age and older were literate and that 67 percent of all blacks in that age category were literate (Table

VII). In spite of these different definitions, it is clear that the rate of literacy among blacks was gradually increasing and the gap between whites and blacks was decreasing slowly.

TABLE VII
Literate Population by Race in Cuba: 1907, 1919, 1943

Year	Literate Whites (Percent)	Literate Blacks (Percent)
1907	44.3	32.9[a]
1919	45.5	38.4[a]
1943	72.2[b]	67.4[b]

SOURCE: See Table V.

a. Total nonwhite population including Asiatics and without age distinction.
b. Population 10 years of age and older.

Employment and Unemployment. It is not possible to make a complete examination of the racial composition of employment and unemployment under the Republic, because no statistics are available. The only census that provided data on this matter was conducted in 1943. There are no statistics in this area in the 1953 census, nor are there any in the study on employment, underemployment, and unemployment conducted by the National Council of Economics in 1956-1957.

The 1943 census provides detailed statistics on the number of nonwhite (Negro, mulatto, and Asiatic) men and women working in various occupations. In that year the nonwhite population represented 25.6 percent of the total population; however, of this percentage, the blacks constituted 25.2 percent of the population and the Asiatics equaled 0.4 percent. Therefore, although the 1943 census referred to the entire nonwhite population of the island, it represented largely the black population.

When examining the labor force, in general, one finds that Afro-Cubans are consistently underrepresented in those occupations requiring very advanced training (see Table VIII). Thus, although blacks constituted 25 percent of the total population, only 15.9 percent of the physicians, 12 percent of the lawyers, and

10.5 percent of the engineers were nonwhite. Black representation decreased more drastically in the banking profession and financial institutions, in which only 8.2 percent of the employees were nonwhite.

This trend continues in industries requiring specialized knowledge. The proportion of nonwhite employees involved in the production of pharmaceutical products was 7.4 percent, and 9.7 percent in the production of chemicals and fertilizers. Although the presence of blacks in the communication field was generally normal or equal to their proportion in the population at large, their representation fell dramatically in the telephone industry, in which only 2.9 percent were nonwhite. Nonwhite representation was also low in those industries catering to tourist trade: 8.4 percent in the hotel industry and guest houses.

In the agricultural sector, nonwhite representation was more equal to the group's general level in the population, equaling 19 percent. Within general manufacturing industries, nonwhite presence was more normal, such as in the production of canned goods (17.3 percent) and candy products (23 percent).

Black workers were greatly overrepresented in domestic and personal services in which the nonwhite percentage equaled 47.3 percent. Within this occupation, the presence of nonwhite women is greatly exaggerated, equaling 37 percent whereas the percentage of white women is 29. The same trend continues within the construction industry, in which the nonwhite percentage is 43.6.

In spite of the clear evidence of discrimination based on race found in the data of the 1943 census, it is fair to conclude that within fifty years, the black in Cuba did make remarkable progress in the area of education and integration into the labor market. The degree of black participation within professional and skilled jobs is an important indication of this trend. A law in 1950 attempted to improve the situation by securing equal employment for Afro-Cubans in those occupations in which a great deal of discrimination was evident, such as clerical positions in banks and department stores. Unfortunately no data are available for

TABLE VIII
Employment and Unemployment by Race and Occupation in Cuba: 1943

Occupation	Employment[a]		Unemployment[b]	
	White	Nonwhite	White	Nonwhite
Agriculture, livestock, fishing	81.0	19.0	24.3	28.0
Agriculture	81.0	19.0	24.4	28.0
Livestock	86.6	13.4	18.0	17.2
Fishing	86.0	14.0	20.8	21.2
Mining	67.3	32.7	9.3	12.7
Construction	56.4	43.6	18.1	23.7
Manufacturing and mechanized industries	65.5	34.5	24.2	24.4
Food and similar products	69.2	30.8	14.3	20.3
Other food industries	61.2	38.8	11.7	14.0
Textiles	78.6	21.4	13.6	19.2
Clothing and similar	57.7	42.3	24.2	26.8
Lumberyards	80.3	19.7	13.0	14.5
Furniture and similar products	62.9	37.1	14.6	21.0
Other wood products	56.7	43.3	18.4	22.0
Paper products	93.0	7.0	9.7	13.7
Printing and similar	75.0	25.0	33.9	17.1
Chemical products and fertilizers	90.3	9.7	10.5	9.7
Pharmaceutical products	92.6	7.4	10.0	15.1
Leather and its products	57.9	42.1	20.2	23.1
Leather processing	86.9	13.1	8.0	23.0
Shoes	57.1	42.9	20.8	23.0
Other leather articles	55.0	45.0	21.0	24.3
Ceramics and products	72.9	27.1	16.2	19.9
Metals and products	61.1	38.9	21.3	23.5
Machinery	72.6	27.4	17.7	20.0
Transportation equipment	81.6	18.4	15.4	11.9
Sugar Industries	73.6	26.4	30.5	40.2

TABLE VIII
(Continued)

Occupation	Employment[a]		Unemployment[a]	
	White	Nonwhite	White	Nonwhite
Tobacco and cigarettes	66.0	34.0	15.1	21.9
Other manufacturing				
industries	81.8	18.2	16.8	25.9
Transportation and				
communications	77.7	22.3	12.4	19.8
Air transport	88.0	12.0	15.6	29.0
Railroads	75.9	24.1	11.5	18.1
Trolleys	87.1	12.9	9.4	9.4
Bus system	89.3	10.7	8.7	13.7
Trucking	82.0	18.0	11.8	12.9
Taxicabs	81.0	19.0	15.2	24.6
Maritime transports	64.4	35.6	16.9	24.6
Other transports	78.3	21.7	13.2	11.9
Telephones	97.1	2.9	8.2	4.0
Telegraphs	81.5	18.5	8.3	15.1
Radio	85.2	14.8	14.1	22.3
Other public services	82.0	18.0	13.3	14.2
Commerce	89.1	10.9	15.1	18.7
Wholesale	83.6	16.4	37.5	34.2
Retail	89.6	10.4	13.1	16.6
Banks and financial				
institutions	91.8	8.2	7.2	13.8
Personal and domestic				
services	58.2	41.8	14.6	15.3
Domestic services	52.7	47.3	13.3	13.7
Hotels and guest houses	91.6	8.4	17.6	12.9
Laundry and cleaners	73.8	26.2	13.6	15.8
Barbers and beauticians	56.4	43.6	17.4	23.5
Miscellaneous	64.2	35.8	15.4	13.9

TABLE VIII
(Continued)

Occupation	Employment[a]		Unemployment[b]	
	White	Nonwhite	White	Nonwhite
Recreational services and similar	61.5	38.5	14.7	21.0
Theaters and movies	80.5	19.5	13.3	21.5
Miscellaneous	46.1	53.9	16.8	20.8
Professional services	86.8	13.2	22.1	23.6
Education	82.0	18.0	25.6	27.7
Medicine	84.1	15.9	15.9	21.7
Lawyers	88.0	12.0	16.2	17.2
Engineering	89.5	10.5	29.6	28.1
Religion and charity institutions	87.5	12.5	13.4	23.9
Government	80.8	19.2	8.3	13.7
Defense	80.4	19.6	4.4	33.5
State, provinces, municipios	81.1	18.9	10.9	20.8
Diverse services (renting, repairs)	73.6	26.4	13.9	17.4
Repairing, renting of automobiles	70.5	29.5	15.3	17.8
Other services	72.7	27.3	10.3	15.1
Not classified	75.6	24.4	19.2	24.0

SOURCE: Cuba, Dirección General del Censo, *Informe general del Censo de 1943* (Havana: P. Fernández y Cía, 1945), pp. 1042 and 1056.

a. Percentage distribution of employment in each occupation between whites and nonwhites (i.e., blacks, Asiatics, and mestizos).

b. Percentages of whites and of nonwhites affected by unemployment in each occupation.

the period 1943-1958 that would allow one to determine the rate of the process of integration within employment.

The 1943 census also reported the incidence of unemployment among white and nonwhite workers in each occupation (see Table VIII). Structural problems in the Cuban economy produced high rates of unemployment among both races in almost every occupational classification. However, the average percentage of unemployed nonwhite workers was three percentage points higher than the average percentage of unemployed white workers.

Black and white unemployment rates were about equal in agriculture, livestock and fishing, manufacturing and mechanized industries, and within some professions such as law and engineering. However, in several diverse areas the percentage of black unemployment was at least twice that of whites. In the leather processing industry, white unemployment was 8 percent, as compared to 23 percent for blacks. In the sugar industry 30.5 percent of the whites were not working, as compared to 40.2 percent of the blacks. Even among government employees on the municipal, provincial, and national levels, the proportion of unemployed blacks was almost twice that of unemployed whites.

It seems reasonable to conclude, therefore, that there was a greater degree of unemployment among blacks in general and particularly within certain occupations, which would be explained by both the low educational level of the black population and the existence of discriminatory practices in employment.

Other Areas of Integration and Discrimination.[17] Racial discrimination existed in a systematic form in exclusive social associations and in those places (i.e., fashionable hotels, restaurants, and night clubs) frequented by persons belonging to the high stratum. The successful Afro-Cuban formed his own associations (the most remarkable of which was the sophisticated Club Atenas), avoiding open conflict by not attempting to enter white associations. On the other hand, the majority of whites were also unable to gain access to the exclusive white associations, lacking either the wealth or social status required or the recommendations of other members.

The majority of the private clubs that partitioned off the beaches in Havana did not admit blacks. But there were some of these beaches, such as La Concha (adjacent to the most exclusive private club, The Yaught Club), to which whites and blacks had access by paying a small admittance fee. The Club of the University of Havana and the Club of the Professionals did not discriminate. During the 1950s, when clubs were expanding to the east of the capital for better beaches, various professional associations (i.e., physicians) organized clubs that admitted black members of these associations. The most beautiful beaches of Cuba, such as Varadero, Guanabo, and Santa María del Mar, had public beaches that were open to all.

In prerevolutionary Cuba, it is difficult to separate discrimination based on race from that based on economic status. For example, blacks were admitted to all public schools on all levels. However, in private institutions, high tuition fees limited or prevented black enrollment. Some of these schools supported separate gratuitous institutions in which there was a more equal distribution of the races. A similar phenomenon could be noted in hospitals. Those of a public nature and thus free were completely integrated, but the so-called *centros regionales* (cooperatives of medical service founded by the Spaniards and later extended to the middle strata) were more exclusive in their policies and for the most part admitted only whites. Blacks were excluded on a financial basis from private hospitals charging high fees; however, other medical cooperatives charging smaller monthly fees (usually about three dollars) were open to blacks.

There were no black ghettos in Cuba similar to those in the United States. In the lower-class urban areas (i.e., Jesús Maria, Atarés, Luyanó, El Cerro) blacks and whites lived together, although there were greater concentrations of blacks in lower-income areas. However, the high-income residential areas, such as Miramar or Biltmore in Havana, were almost completely white.

Access to cinemas, theaters, sports shows, buses, trains, and churches was open to all races. It is important to point out that there were no "black Christian churches" in Cuba, although those practicing African rites were largely black. Black athletes were integrated into the national baseball teams, and many represented Cuba abroad in different international sports competitions.

Black participation in civil, military, and religious associations, trade unions, and political parties varied. Participation was generally high in trade unions and in the army, and low in intellectual associations. From 1939 to 1947, the general secretary of the Cuban Workers' Confederation (CTC) was a Negro, Lázaro Peña. In 1949 two Afro-Cubans, Generals Querejeta and Hernández Nardo, headed the army and police, respectively. During the dictatorial period, prior to the Revolution, President Batista as well as the chief of the armed forces, General Francisco Tabernilla, were mulattoes; and the minister of justice, Céspedes, was black. A large number of congressmen (senators and representatives) as well as members of the judiciary were Afro-Cubans.

Intensity of racial discrimination varied according to geographical region. In the provinces of Oriente and Havana, where black concentration was high, discriminatory practices were lower and blending of races was also greater. Discrimination seems to have been greatest in the central provinces of Las Villas and Camagüey, where Afro-Cubans used separate paths from those of the whites when strolling in public parks.

The Revolutionary Period: 1959 to the Present Day

The racial problem was not dealt with in any revolutionary document before the takeover. In Castro's "History Will Absolve Me" speech not a single paragraph was devoted to this subject. But after the Revolution, a picture of black suffering caused by discrimination was painted that exaggerated the degree of actual prejudice existing on the island.[18]

Just such a description can be found in the writings of Blas Roca, a mulatto, former secretary of the Partido Socialista Popular (prerevolutionary Communist party) and an active propagandist for the Revolution.[19] Roca maintains that the capitalists, *latifundistas*, and imperialists of prerevolutionary Cuba used racist propaganda against blacks in order to divide and thereby weaken proletariat opposition. In this manner the power structure hoped to coalesce white support by depicting the revolution as a racial fight. Roca also contends that the discriminatory hiring practices of white Cubans at this time attempted to create a black labor reserve so that Afro-Cubans could be used for the most physical and poorest-paid jobs. Roca also maintains that the capitalist system continued to enslave the black in a concealed fashion and that capitalists justified their exploitation in the same theoretical terms of inferiority used by the slave owner. The entire racist system was aggravated by the economic and political ties with imperialistic Americans who prohibited the presence of blacks in banks, retail stores, and even in American-owned sugar mills. However, the Revolution, Roca declares, has changed all of this by ending all relations with the United States; and through the establishment of a socialist system, Cuba has eliminated all racism.

What has been the true impact of the Revolution on race relations? It is impossible to use quantitative data to answer this question, because no census was conducted between 1953 and 1970. The complete results of the census taken in September 1970 had not been published at the time this paper was completed. The Cuban statistical yearbook also does not include data on race relations on the island. Thus one is forced to rely on qualitative information such as direct observations of visitors to Cuba.

The magazine *Cuba Socialista* is perhaps the only journal that has published an extensive treatment of the subject of race relations.[20] In this article it is stated that numerous revolutionary measures have contributed to the elimination of cases of open discrimination that existed in Cuba. Some of these measures have been the nationalization of private schools and universities, as well as *centros regionales* and private clinics; the suppression of the exclusive associations of whites; and the opening of private beaches, luxury nightclubs, and hotels to people of low income. At the same time, the standard of living of the black as well as of the lower-class whites has been improved through such measures as urban reform (which reduced rents and thus made acquisition of new dwellings possible), agrarian reform (which supplied jobs to the seasonally unemployed in rural areas), the increase in wages and minimum pensions, and the reduction of the cost of certain public services (i.e., electricity, transportation) or the offering of services free of charge (i.e., medical services, education, public telephones, burials).

The campaign against illiteracy proved to be particularly beneficial to blacks, because they constituted the largest illiterate group. The establishment of compulsory elementary education; the expansion of elementary, secondary, and boarding school facilities; the increased number of scholarships granted to black children—all aided in improving noticeably the educational level of this group. Although it is true that, prior to the Revolution, public education, including the university level, was practically free and was open to blacks, many black families just could not afford to have their children studying in secondary schools or in colleges instead of working.

The "Urban Reform" measures (reducing rent, allowing lower classes to own their own homes, and providing for the construction of low-rent housing) have profited all low-income groups, but they have not changed, to a great extent, the racial composition of urban or residential neighborhoods. Nevertheless, the nationalization of the homes of higher-income groups that have emigrated and the conversion of these homes into schools and dormitories for scholarship students have produced a change in the racial composition of certain areas that were exclusively white.

Medical cooperatives continue to require of their members a modest monthly contribution. The medical services available in rural areas have been greatly expanded, and open access to private clinics for blacks has been assured.

Despite these social improvements, there are four aspects of the problem of race relations that do not seem to have been substantially improved: job distribution, aesthetics, the preservation of an Afro-Cuban culture, and relations between sexes. Many enthusiastic supporters of the ideals of the Revolution have overlooked these problem areas that remain.

Many American social scientists who have spent short periods of time in Cuba have been carried away by their enthusiasm for the Revolution and have therefore misjudged the present situation and actual prerevolutionary condition. The following statement made by sociologist Joseph A. Kahl, who visited Cuba for less than one month in the beginning of 1969, is typical: "*For the first time* Cuba's Negroes share *equally* in the goods and services and civic respect of their society. *They have been fully* integrated in the schools and on the job [emphasis added]."[21] Another sympathizer, Gil Green, former member of the National Committee of the U.S. Communist party, who stayed in Cuba for three weeks in 1969, did point out that there are some racial problems, but he did not explain their nature and underestimated their significance. Green quotes from an interview with a Negro who is presented as typical: ". . . sometimes we bump into individual cases of prejudice, but these are the exception. . . . When it comes to our rights and opportunities we now have them *in full.* . . . Also *we are now leaders in the party, militia and in industry* [emphasis added]."[22]

In sharp contrast with these attitudes there are those of some U.S. black militants who spent several years in Cuba and then became disillusioned and bitterly critical of the "racial prejudices of the Revolution." The most significant case is that of Robert F. Williams, the well-known American leader of the U.S. civil rights movement and one of the founders of the Fair Play for Cuba Committee. Under persecution by the FBI, Williams escaped to Cuba in 1961 and stayed there until 1966, when he went to China. On 28 August 1966 Williams sent from Peking a letter to Fidel Castro complaining about the "ignominious experiences" that he encountered while living in Cuba. He stated in this letter that: (*a*) not only did the Cuban government not give him support for the

Afro-American struggle in the United States, but it deliberately sabotaged his efforts, contributing to the protection of U.S. racism; (b) the Cuban Ministry of Foreign Relations systematically denied visas to all Afro-American journalists who had expressed a desire to visit Cuba; (c) the Tri-Continental Conference held in Havana in January 1966 was manipulated by the Cuban government to keep Afro-Americans out, including Williams himself; (d) the Cuban ambassador in Dar es Salaam, a black, had to take orders from a white Cuban who was the first secretary of the embassy there; and (e) the Cuban government permitted a group of Afro-Cuban soldiers to be slaughtered and massacred in the Congo while having information that this was going to occur. All these facts, asserted Williams, "proved the Cubans to be racists who did not believe in equality of the black man."[23] In the March 1967 issue of his journal, *Crusader*, Williams added: "The negro [in Cuba] is becoming again a pathetic victim to race prejudice and discrimination. . . . Afro-Cubans are beginning to feel the punch of subtle but returning racism."

During 1969, Raymond Johnson and Earl Farrell, who claimed to be members of the Black Panther party, condemned discrimination they had experienced in Cuba; the former hinted and the latter stated openly that Panther idol Eldridge Cleaver, then living in Cuba, was himself disgusted with the "racist" treatment he had encountered. The American writer Lee Lockwood, in Havana at the time, heard the story privately from the Panther leader. According to Lockwood, Cleaver had found that "blacks were under-represented in the upper echelons of leadership and administration, suffered a certain amount of discrimination in job advancement," and were restrained in many ways from "expressing their 'black identity.' " From this, Lockwood wrote: "Eldridge concluded that Cuba's leaders, in giving public support to the black liberation struggle abroad while failing to complete that aspect of their revolution at home, were guilty of a certain hypocrisy."[24]

One of the most detailed reports of the current state of racial relations in Cuba has been given by John Clytus. A sympathetic follower of the Revolution who went to Cuba in mid-1964 and worked there until 1967, he was an English teacher at the University of Havana and the Ministry of Foreign Trade, and a translator for the newspaper *Granma*. Clytus denounced racial discrimination in employment on the basis of his own observations. Describing the racial composition of employment, he said: ". . . For every black face I saw there were at least fifty white faces." Then he added: ". . . Of the seventeen or more Ministries in the country, the top two jobs in each were held by whites." He went further, stating that practically all supervisors in public offices were whites and that ". . . none of the hotels or stores or restaurants had a black supervisor. In fact, blacks were conspicuously absent from these places in any capacity."[25]

Commenting on the "white supremacy in the Cuban power structure," Clytus referred to the almost unique case of Juan Almeida, a black who is one of the three vice-ministers of the army: "He was a piece of window dressing so that the revolution could claim that his high position belied any accusation of racial prejudice. . . ."[26] Clytus also reported other discriminatory practices outside of jobs: "I looked at magazine covers and saw whites. I looked at newspapers and books and saw whites. . . . The 'queen' and her 'court' in the carnival were whites. . . . Ninety per cent of the students in my English class at the University of Havana were whites. . . . I constantly saw black women strolling with white men, but I saw no white women with black men."[27] He also reported the case of a black intellectual, writing on the role of the blacks in Cuban history, who was told not to write about this theme by the government, because his writing could cause division among the people: "There were no white Cubans or black Cubans, just Cubans, they told him."[28] Even when relating the story of the racial uprising of 1912, the new history of Cuba maintains that Estenoz was correct in demanding equality for blacks but that he was incorrect in basing the cause for discrimination on color. The correct analysis identified discrimination of blacks as based on one's economic condition.

Apparently, Clytus' negative impressions of race relations were shared by black students from Guinea, Sudan, Kenya, Rhodesia, South Africa, the Congo, and Angola who were in Cuba at the same time. According to Clytus, in 1967, ninety Congolese students had demanded to be sent back to their country after some members of their group had fought with Cuban soldiers over some racist remark that the latter had made to the African students.[29] Clytus has been attacked as an unsophisticated black racist incapable of understanding some of the difficulties that have impeded a rapid and total abolition of racial discrimination even within a revolutionary process.

Another analytical view of the problem has been presented by Elizabeth Sutherland, a Mexican-American writer and editor with the Black Liberation Movement who spent the summer of 1967 in Cuba. After warning against outsiders and short-term visitors who easily make mistakes by generalizing from their partial experience and their own prejudices on this complex problem, she concludes that all traces of overt racism as they once existed in Cuba have been wiped out, but that certain forms of cultural racism still exist.[30] Sutherland acknowledges that the top leadership of the government and the party is white and that a disproportionately large number of blacks are still performing menial jobs as maids, street cleaners, and ditch diggers. In posters, magazines, television programs, movies, and the theater, white faces are overwhelmingly predominant, she says. (Sutherland tells of the paradoxical case of a black actress who was denied a role in a Spanish play because such roles were supposed to be performed by white females, and of a play involving black characters that was performed by white actors in black painted faces, because of the alleged lack of black actors. This has led to the staging of a play with a "black cast" and a "black plot.") Interracial marriage, particularly of a black man with a white woman, is still rare and often evokes a negative reaction.[31]

Sutherland agrees with Clytus and More on the existence of a revolutionary taboo on talking about racism: ". . . Officially it doesn't exist any more." One of the blacks she interviewed asserts that the Revolution has assumed a paternalistic attitude because it has given blacks "the right to enter the white society." Officials quoted by her forecasted that the economic position of blacks as well as their participation in leadership will improve gradually and that time will eliminate whatever vestiges of racism remain. But a group of black Cuban militants believe that this is not true, but rather that a conscious effort to correct this problem must be made, led by black intellectuals.[32]

Roca called in the early 1960s for the establishment of an institute sponsored by the state that would provide a mass educational program open to all classes that would destroy all stereotypes and myths that depict the Afro-Cuban as inferior. The state should also enact laws designed to ensure equal black representation in all economic and cultural activities in Cuba.[33]

Carlos More, an Afro-Cuban militant who left the island because of the radical viewpoints he held, has referred to the problem of the systematic elimination of the Afro-Cuban culture through various methods: (a) the use of history handbooks that underestimate the role of the black in the independence of Cuba; (b) the alteration of statistical figures regarding the ethnic composition of the population; (c) the systematic exclusion of Afro-Cubans from leading positions; and (d) the mocking of rites (songs, dance, ceremonies) of the African religion by transforming them into folklore. More explains that the Afro-Cubans are subjected to strong propaganda that constantly shows them the many advantages they have received from the Revolution in contrast to the difficult situation of the blacks in the United States and South Africa. It might thus seem that the Afro-Cubans accept their situation and have been integrated into the white value system.[34]

Conclusions

From what has been said, some tentative conclusions can be drawn. From 1919 until the present, the black proportion of the total population of Cuba has been quite stable at approximately 27 percent. The greatest portion of Afro-Cubans live in two provinces—Oriente and Havana. The institutional discrimination that existed under the system of slavery disappeared, to a large extent, with the destruction of that system.

Discriminatory practices did continue on the more personal-individual level in private institutions and exclusive associations during the republican period. Structural problems in the Cuban economy produced high rates of unemployment in all areas of the population, but the rate was greater for Afro-Cubans. In 1943 blacks were consistently overrepresented in menial, unskilled, low-paying occupations and underrepresented in better-paying, skilled, and professional occupations. Much of this dichotomy in the employment field was a product of the general economic status and educational level of blacks. In general terms, black Cubans were less educated and were also poorer than whites and could not afford the advantages of private education or even advanced public educational facilities. All public facilities were open to blacks during the republican period; however, use of these facilities by blacks was limited, again, because of their lower economic position.

The vestiges of institutional discriminatory practices specifically found in exclusive associations or private institutions disappeared with the new revolutionary period. They vanished together with the minority of high-income whites who maintained them. These reforms were largely the result of structural changes undertaken by the government that forced the emigration of this dominant group and consequently destroyed many of the discriminating institutions they supported. However, these improvements have not resulted from direct governmental measures aimed at substantially altering the prevailing ethnic relations. The reforms experienced by blacks under the Revolution (i.e., in education, medical services, and full employment) are the result of social measures of an economic rather than ethnic nature—that have benefited all low-income Cubans. Because blacks were a large proportion of this group, they have also profited greatly from these measures. But racial discrimination still exists in the fields of employment, aesthetics, culture, and relations between the sexes. The Revolution has apparently eliminated most vestiges of institutional discrimination that were present in the republican period, but it has not been able to change the prejudiced opinions of individuals.

Notes

[1]Claude Lightfoot, *Ghetto Rebellion to Black Liberation* (New York, 1968), p. 154.

[2]This is the standard view maintained by most historians. A recently published book, however, proves that the situation of slaves in Brazil and the United States was not so different. See Carl N. Degler, *Neither Black nor White: Slavery and Race Relations in Brazil and the United States* (New York, 1971).

[3]Cuban Economic Research Project, *Study on Cuba* (Coral Gables, Fla., 1965), pp. 6-7.

[4]Cuban Economic Research Project, *Study on Cuba*, p. 7.

[5]Elizabeth Sutherland, *The Youngest Revolution* (New York, 1969), p. 143.

[6]Cuban Economic Research Project, *Study on Cuba*, p. 8.

[7]Sutherland, *The Youngest Revolution*, pp. 143-144. Rumors were spread, Sutherland maintains, against Maceo, saying that he favored black soldiers over whites and that he was attempting to rule the entire island. Spain was attempting to break the unity between whites and blacks by calling it a race war. Sutherland also points out that one Cuban historian in Spain tried further to encourage disunity on racial grounds by spreading the rumor, after Maceo died in battle, that he had actually been murdered by a white compatriot. See also the interpretation given by the Haitian exile living in Cuba, René Depestre, "Carta de Cuba, sobre el imperialismo de mala fe," *Por la Revolución por la poesía* (Havana, 1969), pp. 83-87.

[8]Victor S. Clark, Bulletin of the U.S. Department of Labor, No. 14, July 1902.

[9]Cuban Economic Research Project, *Study on Cuba*, p. 21.

[10]*Ibid.*, p. 22.

[11]John Clytus, *Black Man in Red Cuba* (Coral Gables, Fla., 1970), p. 78.

[12]Carlos More, "Le peuple noir a-t-il sa place dans la révolution

cubaine?", *Presence Africaine*, 4th trimester 1964, p. 198. For a rebuttal to More, see Depestre, pp. 75-135.

[13]Cuban Economic Research Project, *Study on Cuba*, p. 204.

[14]*Ibid.*, pp. 203-205.

[15]*Ibid.*, p. 205.

[16]In 1943 the person answering the census taker defined himself as white or black, whereas in 1953 it was the census taker who made the decision as to the race of the person whom he interviewed.

[17]A major source for the data in this section has been Nelson Amaro and Carmelo Mesa-Lago, "Inequality and Classes," *Revolutionary Change in Cuba*, ed. Carmelo Mesa-Lago (Pittsburgh, 1971), pp. 341-374.

[18]*Ibid.* The first reference to the racial issue under the Revolution was Fidel Castro's speech of 22 March 1959.

[19]Blas Roca, *Los fundamentos del socialismo en Cuba* (Havana, 1961), pp. 97-99.

[20]J. F. Carneado, "La discriminación racial en Cuba no volverá jamás," *Cuba Socialista* 2 (January 1963): 54-56. See also Depestre, pp. 110 ff.

[21]Joseph A. Kahl, "The Moral Economy of a Revolutionary Society," *Trans-action* 6 (April 1969): 33.

[22]Gil Green, *Revolution Cuban Style* (New York, 1970), p. 93.

[23]The entire version of Robert Williams' letter to Castro has never been published. We have used a mimeographed copy of it. Excerpts of the letter were published by Michael Banda in *The Newsletter* of the British Socialist Labour League, on 25 February 1967. We gratefully acknowledge the invaluable help of William E. Ratliff, Hoover Institution, in obtaining these materials.

[24]As reported by Lewis Stearns, "White Man's Revolution in Cuba," *National Review*, 12 January 1971, pp. 43-44.

[25]Clytus, *Black Man*, pp. 23-24.

[26]*Ibid.*, pp. 41-42. See also More, "Le peuple noir," pp. 211-212.

[27]Clytus, *Black Man*, pp. 24, 49, 133.

[28]*Ibid.*, p. 76. More, "Le peuple noir," pp. 182, 185, 208, also reports the case of another Afro-Cuban writer who was accused of being "counterrevolutionary and an agent of imperialism" because he wrote on racial issues.

[29]Clytus, *Black Man*, pp. 42, 152. A similar confrontation that occurred in 1963 between Che Guevara and a group of Afro-Americans is reported by More, pp. 216-217.

[30]Sutherland, *The Youngest*, pp. 138-139.

[31] *Ibid.*, pp. 141-142, 148-149, 153.
[32] *Ibid.*, pp. 146-149, 159.
[33] Roca, *Los fundamentos*, p. 105.
[34] More, "Le peuple noir," pp. 210-220.

The authors gratefully acknowledge Eduardo Masferrer's aid in the computation of statistical tables.

14

Afro-Brazilians: Myths and Realities

Arthur F. Corwin

Arthur F. Corwin brings the study of Afro-Brazilians up to modern times by examining some connections between class and race. He points out a striking socioeconomic fact that prompts questions about Brazil's cele-brated racial paradise—namely, that Afro-Brazilians are disproportion-ately concentrated among the society's lowest classes. Despite more tolerant attitudes about color in comparison to many other countries, millions of Afro-Brazilians find themselves trapped in problems of underemployment and overpopulation. Living in crowded shanty communities where famine and violence are always near, they try to maintain confidence and drive in the face of formidable obstacles. Maria Carolina de Jesus, a former favela dweller, offers a dramatic description of this struggle in her diary, Child of the Dark. Maria gives numerous examples of disturbing racism, but the more fundamental problem that preoccupies her is the difficulty of getting along as a poor person, as one trying to improve her position when there are so few opportunities for the many who are locked in the culture of poverty.

As Professor Corwin notes, the lack of strong racial consciousness in Brazilian society has placed the problems of people like Maria primarily in a class context rather than a racial context. Modernization and the infusion of imported political ideologies may change this situation, how-ever. If a significant movement of protest against poverty should gain momentum in Brazil, the extraordinary concentration of Afro-Brazilians among the have-nots may force attention to the very sensitive issue of racism.

R. B. T.

1.   *Racial Democracy—A Misleading Concept?*

According to Brazilian writers like anthropologist Gilberto Freyre, a leading interpreter of New World civilizations, Brazil has no color line. In a series of remarkable studies beginning with *Casa Grande e Senzala*, first published in 1933, and *Sobrados e Mucambos*, first published in 1936, and in subsequent, widely circulated works, Freyre developed, almost singlehandedly, the rationale for Brazil's national ideology of race relations.[1] According to Freyre and his followers, a unique tropical civilization had its beginnings in the plantations of colonial Brazil. Here, particularly in the coastal zones of the northeast, the familial institutions brought from Portugal, such as the patriarchical family, the *compadre* system, and the patrimonial organization of the fazenda, acquired a special and enduring character. Here also one found the genesis of national customs and the future personification of the Brazilian people: the mestizo. More important, Freyre taught racially mixed Brazilians not to hide their past but to take pride in it, for this is the essence of his thesis: Brazil since the early plantation era has been moving toward a racial democracy and a Brazilian national type unique in the Western world, in which Afro blood or Afro influences have been thoroughly mixed in. Freyre's explanation of this phenomenon is that since the founding of Brazil a constant process of racial miscegenation among white, red, and black, combined with certain Luso-Brazilian cultural factors, has virtually obliterated the color line and opened the way for an egalitarian, racially mixed society.[2]

It is hardly surprising that Brazilian leaders readily accepted the Freyre thesis. One rather obvious explanation is that self-conscious Brazilians, many of them of mixed racial origins, were anxious to justify and dignify the pervasive influence of Indo and Afro elements in a national character that suffered from a slight inferiority complex, perhaps accentuated by massive European immigration to the southern cities. Another and more important reason is that Brazilian leaders have consciously and intelligently sought to establish a humane national tradition, or goal, of racial harmony and assimilation. In this sense, the Freyre vision of evolving racial democracy, its acceptance as a national goal, and its influence on the public conscience, must be considered a major contribution to national unity in a society composed of diverse races.[3]

Brazil's vision of a dynamic process of racial and cultural mixture is essentially the same vision of Latin American historical development and social direction first elaborated by one of the leading philosophers of the Mexican Revolution, José Vasconcelos, in his *La Raza Cósmica* (1925), and in his *Indología* (1926). Such works were intended as much for Latin America as Mexico. Vasconcelos, incidentally, was Mexico's special ambassador to Brazil in 1922 on the occasion of the centenary of Brazilian independence, and at that time he unveiled a statue of Cuauhtemoc, Indian symbol of Mexico's national policy of *mestizaje*.[4]

Whether or not a cosmic race mix is actually emerging in Brazil, Mexico, Cuba, or elsewhere in Latin America may be a moot point. (Vasconcelos himself had second thoughts on the matter.) More important is that such a belief has become an ingredient in Brazil's racial ideology, in Brazil's national pride, and in the Brazilian etiquette about race relations. Carl Degler even suggests, in *Neither Black nor White*, that this facet of the national image has led to an inflexible attitude on the part of many Brazilians that might be paraphrased in these words: "It is un-Brazilian even to consider that Brazil could have a race problem."[5]

Sociologist Costa Pinto has offered another explanation of how the national image of racial integration arose and how it was projected abroad. When certain proud Brazilians hastened to explain to visitors from presumably more advanced Western nations that there was no color prejudice in Brazil, they were sometimes invoking a compensatory mechanism: "True, we are a backward country, but, on the other hand, we have solved our racial question, something you have not done."[6] Probably the growing political and economic dominance of an egocentric North American colossus has helped provoke such defensive attitudes about race throughout Latin America. Noted intellectuals like Francisco Bilbao of Chile, José Martí of Cuba, Enrique Rodó of Uruguay, and many others, have emphasized that however poor and underdeveloped Latin American republics may be, they, at least, have incorporated the Indian and the black into national society.

Also, certain North American writers have helped popularize the Freyre thesis. In particular, historians of the liberal reformist tradition have played an important role. For example, the late Frank Tannenbaum, who first aroused interest in comparative studies of slaveholding societies in the New World, and who introduced his own thesis on the benignity of Latin American forms of slavery, and, later, Stanley Elkins, who elaborated on Tannenbaum's interpretations, were both inclined to appraise uncritically Brazilian and other Latin American systems of slavery.[7] This they did, in part, because they wished to throw into bold relief the Anglo-American failure to solve the race problem.[8] Although the Tannenbaum-Elkins genre of studies said relatively little on the present-day racial situation in contemporary Latin American countries, it somehow seemed to follow in the minds of many of their readers that Latin American cultural traditions and miscegenation had virtually absorbed race problems.

Furthermore, the favorable impression of race relations in Brazil was reinforced by visiting writers, some of them North American anthropologists, who were struck by the virtual absence of a color line in Brazil. In this respect, Donald Pierson's pioneer study of race contact in the Bahia region, where Negroes are more socially integrated than in southern Brazil, has probably been as significant as the Tannenbaum-Elkins school in diffusing a favorable image of racial tolerance in Brazil. Pierson's work, *Negroes in Brazil: A Study of Race Contact at Bahia*, was published by the University of Chicago in 1942. Therein the author noted that racial stereotypes had indeed survived in the traditional communities of the northeast, but his principal conclusion was that discrimination there was class rather than race discrimination. He pointed out that this pattern contrasted sharply with the survival of a caste dichotomy in the United States. Other U.S. anthropologists have made favorable comparative observations that, in turn, have served to give Brazilians reasons to be grateful for a more fortunate heritage of race relations.

Yet the question arises: Have not certain race studies, primarily regional in character, such as Freyre's accounts of the old northeast, inadvertently given rise in the reader's mind, Brazilian and Anglo-American, to an oversimplified or outdated understanding of contemporary race relations in Brazil, but particularly in Brazil's modern cities? In recent years a growing number of Brazilians, including social scientists, journalists, intellectuals, and political militants, have been attacking what some of them call "the great national illusion." In fact, even as the "Freyre thesis" and the "Tannenbaum thesis" were being popularized in the Western world in the 1940s and 1950s through translated works and paperback editions, a new generation of sociologists and historians began to test the hypothesis of racial democracy in a number of community and class-value studies, and to develop a scientific framework for the critical study of ethnology and race relations.[9] In this respect, the "new school of social studies" founded at the University of São Paulo has made outstanding contributions since the early 1950s. The São Paulo school has included such leaders as Roger Bastide, a French sociologist who spent many years in Brazil, and such noted colleagues as Florestan Fernandes, Octávio Ianni, Oracy Nogueira, and Fernando H.

Cardoso.[10] The empirical studies of this group, together with the findings of other notable sociologists and anthropologists such as Luis A. Costa Pinto, Emilio Willems, Thales de Azevedo, and Alberto Guerreiro Ramos, have laid the groundwork for a revisionist view not only of ethnic relations but of the national self-image.[11] North American writers, especially social anthropologists like Donald Pierson, Harry W. Hutchinson, Charley Wagley, Marvin Harris, and Ben Zimmerman, have also contributed to this revisionist school.[12]

Today Brazilian intellectuals are engaged in a growing debate about the validity of the nation's "racial democracy." Some revisionists even seek to establish a countermythology of "national illusions about race" and are often inclined toward a "political sociology" that employs a modified Marxist interpretation of the interplay of race, color, and class privilege. Some revisionist conclusions seem as sweeping and oversimplified as those defended by the followers of Freyre and Tannenbaum. For example, Florestan Fernandes, author of several studies on the problem of integrating the Negro and mulatto groups into urban society, has bluntly affirmed: "The idea of Brazilian racial democracy is nothing more than a myth."[13] Abdias do Nascimento, a founder of the Experimental Black Theater in Rio, and for many years a militant advocate of racial equality, insists that a national mythology about race, racial integration, and conformist pressures on successful mulattoes, prevent Brazil's upper classes from facing up to insidious racist practices, and also work against Brazil's appreciating negritude for its own sake. Using a concept first developed by Guerreiro Ramos, Abdias holds that Brazil's so-called racial democracy suffers from a *patologia de normalidade*.[14] French sociologist Bastide tends to agree.[15]

Likewise, some colored visitors to Brazil have been inclined to share critical assessments of racial tolerance. E. Franklin Frazier, one of the founders of black studies in the United States, spent an academic year in Brazil, 1940-1941, studying race relations, and observed that although there was no race problem in Brazil, the upper classes are conscious of color differences "that are maintained by a subtle system of etiquette." He also observed that there was a more marked color line in southern Brazil, where Negroes suffered from immigrant competition.[16] Another black visitor, Anani Dzidzienyo from Ghana, who studied minority problems in Brazil, stated in 1971: "The popular view of Brazil as a land of racial harmony and opportunity is definitely a misleading, if not completely inaccurate description of the Brazilian racial situation." This African observer goes on to say that Brazil's Euro-plutocrats are the chief beneficiaries of an inegalitarian exploitive structure. As part of their status quo behavior they naturally wish to present to the world a favorable image of race relations: "Brazil is a racial democracy and the subject is not open for discussion."[17]

Fernandes, in an article published in 1971, exemplifies, like the Ghanaian writer, a political interpretation of social realities: Brazil's "racial utopia" is an invention of the ruling classes and a rationale for defending an exploitive social structure characterized by "dependent capitalism" and "internal colonialism."[18]

All of the foregoing suggests that there is a growing cynicism about racial democracy that has serious political implications, for this cynicism seems to feed on Brazil's failure to establish political democracy. Since 1964, when the conservative military regime was established, Brazilian reformers and academicians have more deeply resented an alleged reactionary government that rules in favor of the white upper classes and foreign investors at the expense of Brazil's poverty-stricken masses, including poor blacks. Thus it is hardly surprising that a recent writer has voiced a warning that Brazil's race question "contains the seeds of a potential social crisis."[19]

2.   The Extent of Color Prejudice

At this point a brief reconnaissance of alleged racial discrimination seems in order. As the noted Brazilianist Charles Wagley has said, the claims of Brazil's racial democracy must be judged against a widely documented color prejudice in almost every part of the nation.[20] Pierson's early study, and subsequent studies of rural and urban communities by Hutchinson, Harris, and others, have confirmed the widespread survival of color bias in the coastal regions where plantation slavery once flourished, and in the mining regions of Minas Gerais, where people also cling to "pure family lineage." Such writers have provided a veritable catalogue of Negro stereotypes, such as "Negro doesn't marry, he gets together," "Negro doesn't hear mass, he spies on it," and the like.[21] But these same writers are usually quick to point out that provincial Brazilians are at ease with racial stereotypes, some of which are circulated in a humorous fashion by Afro-Brazilians themselves. Nevertheless, these studies make it quite clear that color discrimination, mild as it may be, plays a part in determining class identification even in those areas where Afro-Brazilians are most at ease and where they often constitute the majority of the population.

It is hardly astonishing that Negro stereotypes and some overt discrimination continue to flourish in rustic Brazilian towns and villages. From this viewpoint, Brazil is perhaps little different from most Latin American and Caribbean countries. Still, for the revisionists of the new political sociology the question of racial democracy in the recessive cultures of "Old Brazil," or the isolated interior, is not as significant as the question of racial democracy in the new "Immigrant Brazil," which, for better or worse, seems to contain the dominant genes of national development. Here we return to the studies on social mobility in the European-style southern cities by Bastide, Fernandes, and others. Investigations by this group have focused less on the persistence of racial stereotypes and more on the urban class structures that, like those in the U.S. north, serve to discourage or block the upward mobility of mulatto and Negro groups, who, otherwise, have had most of the political and civil rights under a republican form of government. For example, Bastide and Fernandes, in several outstanding revisionist studies, have sought to verify the structural discrimination that takes the more subtle form of private clubs and business associations, and, of course, more cautious marriages.[22] Such analysts conclude that it is difficult for mulattoes, and more so for *prêtos*, even if they have all the educational, professional, and financial qualifications, to gain admission to the intimate upper-class circles of Brazil's modern cities.

In Brazil, as in the United States (so American Negro writers have bitterly observed), the Negro is also a yardstick for measuring the relative advancement of the middle and upper classes, and the dignity of a professional position, especially, it would seem, in a society of status-conscious immigrant groups. Such groups appear to follow the old Brazilian rule of thumb: "The darker the skin the lower the class," and vice versa.

In a congress of prominent writers, journalists, historians, and social scientists sponsored by Brazil's Latin American Institute of International Relations, and held in Rio on 4 March 1968, to commemorate the eightieth anniversary of abolition, a surprising amount of testimony was presented to show that color prejudice is a formidable obstacle to Afro-Brazilian vertical mobility. For instance, the frequent observation that first- and second-generation immigrant Brazilians are commonly found in the professions, in the universities, and in the upper echelons of the government bureaucracy, as well as in the officer class of the army and navy, is taken as an unmistakable sign of discrimination by some Brazilians; for the blacks, who have been in Brazil for nearly four and a half centuries, are rarely found in such high-status positions. Mulattoes disguised as whites don't count, says Abdias do Nascimento, and he asks pointedly: "Where are the Negroes?"[23]

Like any group who have made social gains, successful Afro-Brazilians are caught up in the defensive mechanisms of status. Sociologist Guerreiro Ramos, who did an extensive study of public employees, found that of the *prêtos* admitted to the lower levels of the bureaucracy, few would admit being mulatto or Negro. Many said they would not marry someone who was "*muita prêta*," or very dark.[24] Obviously these are the attitudes of Afro-Brazilians who have penetrated the "white establishment," and they do not wish to regress. Such replies also reflect Brazilian feeling that with social advancement a colored person is no longer thought of as belonging to a colored class.[25] "He used to be a *mulatto* but today he is a *branco* practicing law" could be a prototype of countless stories illustrating flexible color attitudes in Brazil. Nevertheless, it seems that nearly all objective students of Brazilian society are in accord with what Pierson said of Bahia around 1940. As he underlined the words, "it is *class* rather than *race* prejudice."[26] Light-skinned mulattoes may affect an air of superiority toward dark-skinned persons but, affirmed Thales de Azevedo, "this is not caste but class rivalry."[27] This basic distinction is supported by Charles Wagley, Jacques Lambert, Costa Pinto, Freyre, and other professional observers of Brazilian behavior, even though it is sometimes impossible, in the words of Oracy Nogueira, to distinguish between class prejudice and color prejudice.[28] Or as Wagley put it: "Brazil is accurately described as a racial and political democracy, but by no stretch of the imagination is it yet a social democracy."[29]

And yet, members of a mixed society from the beginning, Brazilians are predisposed toward racial tolerance. One known drop of African blood, as Pierson noted a generation ago, does not, as in the American South, make a Brazilian a mulatto or a Negro.[30] On the contrary, if an Afro-Brazilian has an education, and especially superior economic status, then one drop of white blood may be enough to make him white. "Money whitens the skin," is a common aphorism. This is most true of "Old Brazil," of the northeast, where African blood tends to run through the whole class structure from top to bottom, but even in Euro-Brazil of the south many Afro-Brazilians have taken advantage of industrial and educational opportunities, including vocational training, to move up socially and disappear into upper-class, *café-au-lait* groups, or occasionally into elite white groups. To some degree this percolating process was accelerated by the populist Vargas regime and a period of rapid economic expansion beginning with World War II.[31]

What has been said thus far about racial etiquette and social mobility applies mostly to the affluent and educated Afro-

Brazilians; but the real problem, from the viewpoint of those who want instant social democracy, is to start millions of depressed Afro-Brazilians (who constitute the majority of the urban poor) on an upward path of social progress in face of the fact that poverty cultures are proliferating far beyond metropolitan Brazil's capacity to absorb them. The exodus of poverty-stricken folk of Afro-Brazilian descent to the slums of the major cities relentlessly continues, so that today Brazil appears to be farther than ever, and even regressing rapidly, from racial integration or social democracy. And all this despite the continuous social advancement of many colored people.

Unskilled labor in oversupply not only depresses wages but human dignity. Job-hunting women, the breadwinners for most of the lower-class Afro-Brazilian families, often resort to any of the hundreds of private employment agencies that have sprung up in the cities of Brazil. Abuses are commonly reported.[32] Want ads often contain the phrase: "No colored need apply." The President of the Association of Employment Agencies of Guanabara State has stated: "In spite of all that is said about liberty and equality, more than 90 percent of the firms that hire through agencies give notice that they don't want colored people."[33] Complaints are common that in spite of the Afonso Arinas law of 1951 prohibiting job discrimination, employers still use such tip-off expressions as "light or white," "of good appearance," or "Portuguese preferred," in job notices, especially when recruiting salesmen, shop assistants, secretaries, airline stewardesses, and other positions that involve contact with the public.[34]

Discrimination against colored persons in all types of employment was one of the most common complaints voiced in the conference of 1968 marking the eightieth anniversary of abolition. But the heart of the problem—and this bears repeating—lies not in the relatively few grievances, real or imagined, of the Afro-Brazilian bourgeoisie but rather in the miserable conditions at the bottom of the socioeconomic heap. To attribute these conditions to racial discrimination is a false conception of the problem. As Wagley has said of Brazil, so one could say of most Latin American and Caribbean countries: The masses cannot afford the basic essentials of life; "under such conditions the issue of racial discrimination is scarcely a vital one." And he adds: "Lower-class whites and lower-class coloured are both segregated and discriminated against."[35]

3. Impact of European Immigration

After the abolition of slavery in 1888, and the founding of a republic in 1889, Brazil's new national leaders, more so than the deposed Dom Pedro, promoted mass immigration and foreign investment as the most rapid methods for modernizing the country. What happened thereafter is in some ways similar to developments in the United States, if we substitute "Brazilian south" for "U.S. north." In the period 1870-1963 about 5 million immigrants sailed for Brazil, including approximately 1.6 million Portuguese, 1.5 million Italians, 700,000 Spaniards, 243,000 Japanese, 200,000 Germans, 110,000 Russians (many of Jewish descent), and 675,000 from other countries.[36] Nearly all of these immigrants entered after abolition and settled in Brazil's south.

In 1940 European immigrants and their descendants constituted about one-third of the population of southern Brazil.[37] These were the people, who, in conjunction with foreign investors, principally British and North American, created the industrial dynamism of São Paulo, Rio de Janeiro, Belo Horizonte, Curitiba, Florianopolis, Pôrto Alegre, and many lesser cities. These cities in turn have acted like magnets for several million migrants from rural areas and from the depressed cities of the northeast, a region similar to the Deep South of the United States following the Civil War.[38] Many of the northeastern migrants, especially since 1940, have been illiterate, poverty-stricken Afro-Brazilians.

Massive immigration followed by massive internal migration helps account for the fact that today more than 60 percent of Brazil's people and more than 80 percent of the national income are found in one-sixth of the national territory, chiefly in the states of Minas Gerais (southern part), Guanabara, Rio de Janeiro, and São Paulo. São Paulo state, with but 3 percent of the national territory, had in 1970 some 18 million residents, or about 19 percent of Brazil's population; and it employed more than half of Brazil's industrial workers.[39] By 1973 the metropolitan area of São Paulo had over 8 million inhabitants. Rio, the next-largest city in the south, had over 5 million inhabitants in the metropolitan area, and Belo Horizonte nearly 1.5 million.[40]

As Bastide, Ianni, Fernandes, Cardoso, and others have made clear, European immigrants, for the most part organized in cohesive, conjugal units, or nuclear families, created a competitive urban superstructure, Mediterranean-style, in the southern metropolises, and in doing so they served to reinforce and whiten the preexisting Portuguese social establishment and semicapitalist structure.[41]

During the formative period of national transformation, approximately 1890-1930, nearly 80 percent of European immigrants settled in the state of São Paulo.[42] A mulatto and Negro population that once constituted a majority was simply overwhelmed. In the laissez-faire economic conditions that followed, poor and illiterate Afro-Brazilians were ill-prepared to compete in a surplus labor market, which, according to Octávio Ianni, was deliberately fostered by official and private immigration promoters.[43] Blacks recently emancipated or not, had no industrial skills. They were either accustomed to economic paternalism or to a permissive migratory life, and had little understanding of contractual responsibilities in the new laissez-faire labor market, or in family life.[44]

According to the São Paulo school of race relations, abolition came before the slave had been prepared for liberty and self-employment. Many freedmen preferred the anonymity of the cities. This migration not only destroyed the old paternalism between white proprietor and black laborer, but also set an urban slum pattern. The migrant Negro passed not into an urban labor proletariat like the peasant immigrants from Europe but into a casual-labor *lumpenproletariat*, the women working as servants, odd-jobbers, and prostitutes, for the most part, and the men becoming common laborers, porters, scavengers, or social parasites. Later migrations of rural blacks to the cities, down to the present, continued to reinforce the miserable *lumpenproletariat*, for, according to Ianni, the rural Negroes after abolition occupied, at best, the preproletarian condition of disorganized, casual laborers.[45]

Fernandes believes that "things had moved too fast" after 1890. The Negro's maladjustment, which could have been a passing phenomenon, became a structural maladjustment by the 1920s. Instead of being absorbed by the urban labor organization and the competitive social system, noncompetitive blacks found themselves displaced by struggling immigrants to the outer fringes of urban society, where they subsisted as before on menial or seasonal employment. Many immigrants, who were of humble peasant origins themselves, at first shared a subproletarian condition with poor mulattoes and Negroes, but as the immigrants rose on the socioeconomic scale they naturally sought to dissociate themselves from Brazil's lowest classes, and to imitate the attitudes of upper-class Brazilians who associated color with lower-class status.[46]

In spite of the foregoing, mass European immigration and laissez-faire conditions were not entirely negative in their effects on Brazil's poverty folk, white and black. With special reference to Afro-Brazilians, Fernandes has said that emulation of the immigrant has, in many cases, created a "new type of Negro with a new mentality, a new behavior, and new social aspirations." It was from the immigrant that the "New Negro" learned the "value of an integrated family, domestic cooperation, systematic savings, owning a home, and putting an end to man's sexual irresponsibility and the cult of the 'Negro mother.' "[47]

It follows that in the southern industrial cities that constitute the "New Brazil," many mulattoes and Negroes, who emulated the immigrants, were made to feel keenly, in the words of Arthur Ramos, a minority condition, an unwritten color line, and job discrimination, especially in the more competitive, immigrant city of São Paulo.[48] According to the 1950 census (and the proportions are probably much the same today), the state of São Paulo was 86 percent white, or nearly-white. Mulattoes then constituted but 3 percent of the population, Negroes 8 percent, and Orientals 3 percent. These rough approximations should be contrasted with the state of Bahia, where blacks, by all accounts, feel much more comfortable. In 1950, according to census estimates, there were in that state 30 percent white, or nearly-white, 51 percent mulatto, and 19 percent Negro.[49]

Given his minority condition in São Paulo state and city, the "New Mulatto" and the "New Negro" have tended to form associations, especially in the city, and to initiate cultural movements that seek to achieve equality with whites, such as the Frente Negro Brasiliera, founded in 1931. It is indeed significant that the most noted Negro leaders of contemporary Brazil have come from São Paulo city, and the example has spread elsewhere through "New Brazil."[50]

Self-conscious associations of middle-class colored peoples, and special newspapers such as *Clarim do Alvarado*, founded in São Paulo, and *Quilombo*, founded in Rio, apparently have not been necessary in the old colonial cities of the northeast, where easygoing, less competitive Brazilian folkways are still an integral part of a more traditional way of life, and where Afro-Brazilians feel more accepted because they are mixed into every social stratum, including many elite families. A number of studies (for example, that of Thales de Azevedo) reaffirm that there is relatively little color discrimination in large northeastern cities such as Salvador.[51] In this sense, Old Brazil, or better said, preindustrial Brazil, about which Freyre wrote so much, is still the Garden of Innocence.

From what has been said thus far, the reader should not conclude that the ethnic sensitivities of New Brazil are principally the result of massive European settlement there, for as Fernandes has made clear, the immigrants simply absorbed attitudes and behavior patterns already incorporated into an historic system of race relations.[52] Most European settlers, especially those from Portugal, where African blood is thoroughly mixed in, accepted established norms of Brazilian racial tolerance. Yet they also accepted a social pattern that slows down the process of Afro-Brazilian assimilation, namely, the closed kinship system. "The nucleus of Brazilian institutions for most of our history," said Thales de Azevedo, "has been the large and closely knit familial unit formed around the big house of the sugar plantations, headed by a rich, powerful, and authoritarian father who added to his role of paterfamilias of Roman tradition the functions of political boss, business entrepreneur, and feudal lord."[53]

Today metropolitan families, especially in the south, are more open, more exogamous, less paternalist than the landed gentry described in the works of Freyre, yet patriarchialism and a condescending view of negroid peoples have survived in the modern cities.[54] According to Emilio Willems, many successful European immigrants have worked their way into Brazil's native social elite by adopting precisely the same patterns of familism and nepotism that characterized the old Portuguese power structure in Brazil.[55] Heavy immigration from Portugal and Italy reinforced a Latin family pattern and preoccupation with purity of lineage because, as Antonio Candido explained, "they themselves were carriers of analogous traits."[56]

Like members of the Luso-Brazilian patriarchy, the immigrant family has generated nearly as many children as the lower classes and tends to function within the extended family, or *parentela*. Wagley found that individuals of the middle and upper classes of Rio and other cities often have 100 to 200 kinsmen with whom they maintain contact, "while people related to wealthy and traditional families often have many more."[57] Thus, as T. Lynn Smith has pointed out on several occasions, there is little or no room for upward social mobility. Middle- and upper-class families have primary obligations to clan members, or to their *compadres*. To say the least, there is very little room in the family enterprise for aspiring outsiders, and less so if they are dark-skinned.

4.   Bleaching Brazil?

A second ingredient in the national ideology of race relations is that the population of Brazil is being gradually bleached through such factors as European immigration, high fertility among white Brazilians, and perennial miscegenation that tended to absorb the Negro into mulatto ranks, and the mulatto into the white ranks. Many writers, Brazilian and foreign, have commented on the gradual disappearance of the Negro. Past census reports have certainly supported such observations. Thus the *Statistical Yearbook of Brazil* for 1956 showed the following percentages of racial composition:[58]

Racial Composition (Percentages)

Year	White	Mixed[a]	Negro	Yellow	Unknown
1872	38.14	42.18	19.68	—	—
1890	43.97	41.40	14.63	—	—
1940	63.47	21.20	14.64	0.50	0.10
1950	61.66	26.54	10.96	0.63	0.21

a. Mixed—mulatto and Indo-mestizo.

Official figures on racial composition for the decennial periods 1960 and 1970 are still not available, but government publications continue to use the 1950 percentages as if they were nearly correct for present-day Brazil. However, all Brazilian statistics on race should be taken with a grain of salt, according to Jacques Lambert,[59] the late Hubert Herring,[60] Charles Wagley,[61] and others. Aside from incomplete data, widespread miscegenation and Brazilian social etiquette complicate any sorting-out of racial categories. Brazilians prefer to call a dark-skinned person *moreno*, that is, brown-skinned. Or they use terms like *prêto*, or *pessoa da côr*, which can be loosely translated as "colored." The term

"Negro" is not always considered polite because it has lower-class connotations in Brazil and the Caribbean. Also, a light-skinned mulatto is usually called *branco*, or sometimes *branco de Bahia* (where mulattoes are commonly found in the upper classes). Garcia-Zamor maintains that if some Negro blood were a criterion for ethnic classification, as it is in Anglo-Saxon America, then half of the Brazilians classified as white in the 1950 census "would have been easily considered Negro."[62]

In the nature of things, Brazilians are inclined to be generous in their definition of white or nearly-white. In South Africa, noted Andrew Marshall, "white" Brazilians have been told there must be a mistake in the hotel reservations.[63] Such stories, true or not, are still told about certain hotels in southern Brazil. In any case, it would probably be closer to the ethnic facts to say that presently about 50 percent of Brazil's population is of European descent and culture, and that many families have some mixture of Indian and African blood; that 40 percent is predominantly of Afro-Brazilian descent, perhaps 25 percent mulatto and 15 percent Negro, the remainder being mostly an Indian, or *caboclo*, ethnic mixture.

Before 1950 the white elite of New Brazil could believe seriously in the eventual absorption of the African strain. In fact, this was the unstated population policy of metropolitan Brazil. After the establishment of the Republic the highest national priority was given to European immigration, and African immigration was prohibited.[64] This policy of "Europeanization" did not mean that Afro-Brazilians, or Indo-Brazilians, were to be eliminated, as some writers charge, but acculturated. Aside from providing a cheap labor supply, immigration was intended to reinforce European culture in Brazil, complete the conquest and settlement of half a continent, introduce industrial capital and technology, and promote a progressive form of *mestiçagem*, or race mixture. Actually, Brazil's immigration policy did not differ much in purpose, or expectations, from other New World countries up to World War II.

In southern Brazil, at least, it seemed that mass immigration had Europeanized the social structure. Many visitors in the 1930s and 1940s, who took New Brazil for all of Brazil, were impressed with the absorption or assimilation of the colored peoples. They noted considerable social mobility and intermarriage between *brancos* and successful mulattoes or *morenos*, who sometimes were taken for Negroes by the outside observer. In his fundamental work on Brazil, first published in 1946, sociologist T. Lynn Smith voiced a common observation of the time: "There can be little doubt that the Brazilian population is steadily becoming whiter in color."[65]

Until recent times, with the exception of Rio, the percentage of subproletarian mulattoes and *prêtos* in the immigrant cities remained small, and, generally speaking, these were accepted as a convenient and cheap source of domestic service for Brazil's *nouveaux riches*. The colored population, which made up about 60 percent of the population in the states of São Paulo and Rio de Janeiro at the time of abolition, had dropped to around 30 percent in Rio by 1950 and around 11 percent in São Paulo.[66] Indeed, New Brazil, if not all Brazil, appeared to be progressively whitening the population.

At this point one might ask if Mendelian laws of color dominance hold not only for sweet peas, but, all in all, for the human race (as geneticists say they do); and if Afro-Brazilian mothers are noted for high fertility, then how does one explain the "bleaching process" of the past? Was this process due primarily to Brazil's "racial democracy," that is, to *brancos* who readily married *caboclos*, mulattoes, and *prêtos*? Or was it more the result of those historic factors listed by Smith, namely, white upper-class mothers who reproduced as rapidly as their dark-skinned counterparts, but this coupled with an extremely high rate of infant mortality among the dark-skinned infants; massive European immigration to the temperate zones of the south; and the fact that upper-class white men, and near-white (as always since the discovery of Brazil), continued to sire illegitimate children with dark-skinned servant girls or mistresses?[67] Was the urge to marry whiter than oneself a hypergamous factor in bleaching the population, as Bastide suggested?[68] Again, was whitening, in part, a false impression from census reports reflecting racial etiquette more than the facts?

One thing seems certain in the present generation: some of the aforementioned factors in the bleaching process have been rapidly changing. For one thing, public health programs have reduced the differential survival rate that for over four centuries favored the relative increase of white and quasi-white Brazilians over the dark-skinned, lower classes. For another, immigration in recent years has been of small proportion compared to the great flow of dark-skinned peasants to the urban areas. During the decade 1940-1950 foreign immigration averaged less than 12,000 per year. In the decade 1951-1960 immigration rose sharply to an annual average of around 59,000, but then dropped to less than 18,000 per annum in the decade 1961-1970.[69]

In the meantime, waves of rural migrants were moving into the southern cities, where the standard of living was decidedly higher. Internal migration helps explain the remarkable growth of the city of São Paulo from 2.2 million inhabitants in 1950 to well over 7 million by 1970. In the same period Rio's population rose from about 2.4 million to 5.2 million; Belo Horizonte from 353,000 to about 1.3 million; and Pôrto Alegre from 350,000 to 1 million.[70] A high proportion of the new urban settlers was of Afro-Brazilian origins. It is likely that since 1950 an average of 150,000 poor blacks and mulattoes have been moving annually to southern industrial, commercial, and coffee-growing regions.

Because of the low social and economic status of the Afro migrants, there is virtually no intermarriage between them and the immigrant society of the south. Even more significant, according to students of race relations in Brazil, is that, in spite of popular beliefs, formal marriage between black and white at any level has always been rare.[71] Brazil, it is true, acquired a heritage of racial fusionism from colonial times—a fusionism that has become, in the words of Thales de Azevedo, "a national creed." Today Brazilian tradition strongly supports racial miscegenation but "not necessarily intermarriage."[72] In reality, the fusionist tradition of Brazil's upper classes is much the same now as when the first Iberian adventurers waded onto American shores and divided up the land and the native women. Nearly everywhere in Latin America, so in Brazil, the males of the dominant class heartily breed with Indian, Negro, and mestizo women but shy away from formal marriage.

As in Spanish America (and most of the Western world) marriage among the upper classes is a planned contract to be used for "whitening" (if need be) or improving the family lineage, as well as maintaining socioeconomic status.[73] Therefore a black Brazilian today must bear special gifts in order to marry into an elite white family. Of course, since late colonial times a small number of *prêtos*, along with countless mulattoes, have been admitted into select social groups with the tacit understanding that for purposes of marriage alliances and fraternal organizations they are "white" in the cultural sense.[74]

The nature of race relations is further illustrated by the *mulata*. This striking symbol of racial fusionism is celebrated in Brazilian song and legend. Not only is the *mulata* a national type, and a token of racial democracy, but as Bastide, Costa Pinto, René Ribeira, and others would have it, a national myth. Brazilian writers, for example, Freyre in his studies of plantation society, or Jorge Amado in his best-selling romance, *Gabriela, Clove and Cinnammon*, have written absorbing accounts of how the dark Venus has made herself irresistible to the erotic European proprietors of Brazil.[75] Bastide calls this "compensatory behavior." In a society of unequals the Dusky Venus quite naturally prefers the white man because it is usually he who can advance her interests.[76] The Ghanaian writer, Dzidzienyo, has asked whether the *mulata* is more a sign of Brazilian sexuality and permissiveness.[77] Costa Pinto believes that the praise lavished on the *mulata* is simply a rationalization for sexual accessibility rather than marriage.[78] Brazilian *machos* generally regard the *mulata* as the ideal beauty, but, typically, one hears complaints that no dark *mulata* but only a *branca*, or a *café-au-lait*, candidate could ever hope to be selected as "Miss Brazil."[79] Degler uses a nineteenth-century refrain to sum up a vital historical heritage:

> White women are for marrying
> Mulatto women are for fornicating
> Black women are for service.[80]

In Indo-American countries like Mexico, Peru, and Colombia, the historical formula would vary only slightly:

> White women are for marrying
> Mestizo women for fornicating
> Indian women for service.[81]

But then Smith in his classic *Brazil* can quote such common folklore as follows:

> If white women were for sale,
> Either for gold or for silver,
> I should buy one of them
> for a servant for my *mulata*.[82]

Taken literally, the foregoing aphorisms would be a gross oversimplification of race relations in Latin American countries, but they do suggest, particularly in the case of Brazil, that race mixture is not due to any conscious practice of "racial democracy," nor to Luso-Brazilian customs of racial tolerance (as suggested by Freyre), but rather, as Azevedo has said, to "concubinage" practiced by the upper classes, and, more important, to the "free unions" practiced by the lower classes.[83]

Although no data are available, it would appear that much less sexual contact takes place between the immigrant population of New Brazil and the colored people compared to the old plantation era when whites and blacks lived in a symbiotic relationship. As always, upper-class *brancos* still have offspring by colored mistresses, but this seems to be of little demographic importance compared to the inbreeding that takes place in slum cultures and isolated villages where often the colored population is the majority. Today the children of the underprivileged are surviving in unprecedented numbers.

After 1940 the sweeping health campaigns of the Pan American Sanitary Bureau, U.S. technical aid programs, and the Vargas populist administration, combined with the loose mating habits of the landless peasantry and the slum dwellers, had revolutionary effects on the survival rate of the Afro-Brazilian poverty groups just at the time when European immigration was slowing down to a trickle. Moreover, if one can believe the 1970 census, there may be a declining fertility in Brazil's middle and upper classes. The social impact of such factors is seen in the flood of *lumpenproletarians* to cities that fail to civilize them. People who knew Brazil in 1940 and know Brazil today, like T. Lynn Smith, have been impressed with the increasing visibility of Afro migrants.[84]

It seems indisputable that the migrant flow to the southern metropolis has caused a sharper definition of the pecking order, mainly along socioeconomic lines. At the very bottom, concentrated in shanties, much like the *mucambos* of slave days, one finds Brazil's teeming Afro poverty culture. Naturally, the new political sociology has not failed to include the "bleaching thesis" in its general attack on the mythology of race relations in Brazil. Bastide regards the policy of *blanchiment*, or the "aryanization of Brazil," not only an implicit statement of white superiority but, like the racial democracy thesis, an instrument of white domination, for it presumes that colored people must become like whites to advance socially or economically.[85] The belief that the Negro race will be transformed through absorption stems from racial prejudice, according to Garcia-Zamor. The whites who advocate it are merely justifying a passive attitude toward the Negro's social condition.[86] Others allege that the policy of *branqueamento* seeks to extinguish the Negro race, or at least suppress the values of negritude, or that it is simply a rationale for doing nothing to help the Negro advance as a Negro.[87] Mushrooming slums filled with miserably poor Afro-Brazilians seem to encourage such allegations. All the while, the migrants are on the move.

5.   *The Migrant Problem*

The major source of the Afro-migrant problem is Old Brazil, sometimes referred to as "Afro-Brazil." For our purposes Old Brazil is roughly everything north and northeast from Rio including most of the state of Minas Gerais, and nearly all of Espirito Santo, Bahia, Alagôas, Sergipe, Pernambuco, Paraiba, Rio Grande do Norte, Ceará, and Maranhão. In the semitropical coastal area of Old Brazil was first founded the free-breeding, cane-sugar plantation society of colonial times. Here were born out of wedlock the whole gamut of mixed breeds: *mamelucos, caboclos, mestiços, cafusos, cabras, pardos, mulatos, prêtos*, and a dozen other gradations of color and caste.[88] Here Portuguese masters and adventurers, who rarely brought women from Portugal, mixed easily with Indian slaves and servants, and then, as the Indian tribes melted away, they mixed in much greater numbers with African servile labor. In fact, African women were imported as select concubines.

In his careful evaluation of a controversial subject, Rollie Poppino calculated that during the three centuries from approximately 1550 to 1850, Brazil must have received a minimum of 3,750,000 African slaves, a figure that is close to agreement with the tentative estimate of 3,646,800 proposed by Philip Curtin.[89] Perhaps as many as 3 million Africans were imported into Old Brazil alone. In any event, a vast infrastructure of negroid peoples was thriving by the beginning of the nineteenth century. According to the census of 1817-1818, the total population of ten years of age or older included 1,930,000 Negro and mulatto slaves; 585,000 free Negroes and mulattoes; 259,400 civilized or baptized Indians; and 1,043,000 whites, most of them of mixed Euro-Afro-Indo ancestry. An unknown number of African runaways lived in the backlands, often mixed in with uncounted

Indo-nomads. At that time most of the population was still found in Minas Gerais and in the semitropical coastal region of the northeast.

In colonial times, Afro-Brazilians, free, slave, or runaway, began migrating into the semiarid *sertão*, or back country of the northeast, and into the mining regions of Minas Gerais, and later in the nineteenth and twentieth centuries to the coffee plantations farther south in the Paraiba, São Paulo, and Guanabara regions. Creole slave owners, entrepreneurs, and capitalists moved also, eventually merging with the flood of European immigrants that followed the abolition of slavery in 1888. In the twentieth century Old Brazil's inefficient plantation economy continued to decline, until today some 60 percent of its people live as a landless or village peasantry, often loosely attached to a landowner, employer, or boss man (*patrão*), much in the manner of the Negro sharecroppers and the "poor whites" of the post-abolition United States South.[90] To a lesser extent economic decline and social abandonment also characterize the old mining economy of Minas Gerais.

In the meantime, as Smith has emphasized, the rural landless Brazilian of the peasant class, probably half of which is mulatto or Negro, acquired a notorious reputation for his tendency to shift about from place to place. "In few nations are such large proportions of the rural people, who in turn are over half of the total population, so constantly on the move."[91] In the northeast this residential instability is accentuated by periodic *secas* or droughts, and by population pressures on the monopolistic proprietory system.

Today the situation in the greater part of Old Brazil may be starkly summed up: 2 or 3 percent of the population own the land and urban property, whereas most of some 27 million fertile peasant folk live and breed on the edge of starvation, either as peons in a quasi-feudal agrarian structure, or as rootless squatters in northeastern cities and in the drought-stricken *sertão*. It was in the *sertão* that Francisco Julião, now exiled, raised the "Marxist specter" of Peasant Land Leagues in the decade 1955-1964. More details of this disaster area can be found in Josue de Castro's angry Marxist denunciations of *Death in the Northeast: Poverty and Revolution in the Northeast of Brazil* (New York, 1966).[92]

Growing industries in such coastal cities as Salvador or Recife, each with more than a million inhabitants, have absorbed some of the Afro peasantry. Furthermore, government development programs such as SUDENE, inaugurated in 1959, have promoted industrial growth in the northeastern cities and settled some migrants in agrarian colonies. The trans-Amazonian highway system now under development supplements these efforts. Unfortunately, such efforts simply have not kept pace with the same government's widespread vaccination, sanitation, and potable water programs, accelerated by the Alliance for Progress and itinerant health missionaries. As a consequence, it seems that Afro-Brazil, where 65 percent of the adult population is illiterate, still exports more disinherited peasants than it does cotton, sugar, or consumer goods.

Many Brazilian "civilizers," who loved the mulatto and *prêto* abstractly but urged little more than health measures for these neglected people in far-off Recife or Belem, now are disturbed at the sight of "peasant hordes," of all shades, camped inside the glittering cities of the south. In the European cities the migrants hope to find—and often do—better employment, educational, recreational, and health facilities, and perhaps low-cost public housing. Some, perhaps, seek to escape the rigid class structure and traditional stereotypes of the feudal northeast.[93]

Unfortunately, most migrants remain "dispossessed peasants" even in the most dynamic metropolis, either by choice, or because the economy cannot absorb them. In Brazil, merely to keep up with population growth, over 920,000 steady jobs would have to be created annually for men, women, and youth age fourteen or over, a rate probably twice the capacity of Brazil's erratic economy.[94] As a result, the destiny of many Afro-Brazilian migrants to the south and to the coastal cities of the northeast has been subemployment and the promiscuous *favela*, possibly the worst type of peasant slum in the Western world, and certainly one of the most malodorous. Perhaps its equal can be found only in certain Afro-Caribbean areas like Haiti, or coastal Venezuela.

6. Favelas

In the southern metropolises shanty towns are called *favelas*, in northeastern cities, *invasões* (literally, "invasions"), and sometimes *favelas* are lumped with more permanent slums and called *bairros pobres*, that is, "poor districts." Whatever they are called, shanty clusters of every conceivable size are found in all large cities of Brazil.

Tourists are, perhaps, more familiar with the gay side of the *favela* dwellers in southern cities, especially Rio. More settled generations of *favelados* maintain the splendid traditions of Mardi Gras or Carnaval, and, at appointed times, send brilliantly attired *samba* troops into the main avenues of the metropolis. Brazil would not be Brazil without them. But here we are concerned with the other side of Carnaval. As seen by metropolitan governments, the spreading slums are an increasing threat to social and political stability, and a growing source of criminal problems.[95]

Family life in newly established *favelas* can be on a near-animal level. Typically, a government survey found that a family group exists, but "it is fragile, precarious, open, variable, people come and go, to a point that family is reduced to blood ties between mother and children."[96] As previously indicated, most of the *favelados* of the southern cities originally migrated from primitive rural and urban areas of the Afro-northeast. Their rudimentary consensual family organization, characteristic of the landless peasantry, tends to disintegrate in a large urban economy where social and employment alternatives act as centrifugal forces.[97]

Most *favela* men, unable to find steady employment for lack of skills, and vagrant habits, enter the ranks of the street-corner leisure class, or they find low-paid transient employment as it suits their needs. If a man's growing family makes demands on his time or earnings, he may move on and shack up somewhere else. For a peasant man the city often means liberation. But for a peasant woman it usually means that she assumes the support of her children without help from the extended family. Much has been written by sociologists about the "mother cult" in these circumstances, for it is the mother, defenseless against pregnancy, who struggles heroically, or masochistically, to raise her brood.[98]

A raw description of degraded life in a São Paulo *favela* is found in the celebrated diary of the Negro woman Maria Carolina de Jesus, *Quarto de Despejo* (1960).[99] Since paternal help is rarely available, women, as exemplified by Carolina, become remarkably self-sufficient as in a perverted version of the Amazon myth, and look with relative indifference on formal marriage with roving, worthless males (from time to time, the government promotes mass marriage of couples living in free unions). An estimated 70 percent of *favela* births are out of wedlock. To quote Carolina, mother of three illegitimate children born of different fathers: "August 10. Father's Day. What a ridiculous day!"[100]

To meet the demands of a cash economy, a *favela* mother forages for work such as domestic service. Young children are frequently left unguarded or abandoned. Older children are sent into the streets as hustlers. Teen-age boys fall into a delinquent pattern and soon imitate their "absent fathers." Teen-age girls are easily seduced, and the pattern is repeated in the next generation.[101]

Favela clusters may be found anywhere on unwanted ground, usually on steep hillsides, on tidal flats, or at the bottom of ravines. In Rio in 1969 nearly one million Cariocas, or about 20 percent of the population, were living in some 300 *favelas*, big and small. The largest *favela* complex then contained an estimated 300,000 people. At that date anywhere from 25 to 30 percent of Rio's population was mulatto or *prêto* by Brazilian census standards, but in the *favelas* probably 70 percent of the people were colored. In São Paulo about 10 percent of the population was colored in 1969, and probably the shanty-town population was then about 800,000 with approximately the same proportions of coloreds.[102]

It is possible to remove a *favela*, but to transform *favela* culture is another matter. In 1963, to give but one illustration, a fleet of bulldozers flattened a Rio slum and forced 22,000 furious inhabitants to reside in a new housing project called Villa Kennedy in honor of the founder of the Alliance for Progress. The results, on the whole, were disastrous. The former *favelados* had received no training in how to live in housing with running water and inside toilets, and Villa Kennedy became "*Favela* Kennedy."[103] Nevertheless, with support from the Conservative Revolution, progressive municipal governments in New Brazil, particularly in Rio, less so in São Paulo, have succeeded during the past few years in replacing the more conspicuous slum shacks with low-cost public housing, sometimes in the shape of huge "satellite cities" containing up to 200,000 transplanted *favelados*. But the problem of shanty towns is far from solved. As Brazilian officials see it, public housing can rapidly become superslums and new *favelas* "pop out of the ground like mushrooms."[104]

In Old Brazil the government has funded an impressive number of programs for public housing, public works, road building, and industrialization. But abject poverty is as visible as ever. The back country continues to discharge surplus peasants into the coastal cities, and traditional society there has yet to be shocked or frightened into an energetic response, other than to call for the expulsion of Communist agitators and the leftist clergy. The government has silenced most radical agitators, with some exceptions such as the outspoken archbishop of Recife, Dom Helder Câmara.

Jacques Wilson, who toured the northeast, has reported that the affluent of Recife, Natal, Fortaleza and other cities in the land of despair continue to live like the sugar barons of former years in elegant villas or plush apartments overlooking the beach, while nearby the self-perpetuating *favela*, "gut-gripping, nauseating, and squalid," is still as much a part of the urban picture as a new skyline of high-rise buildings that reflect a new surge of economic life.[105] The statistical dimensions of Recife's slum problem are revealed by the 1970 census. Of some 195,000 dwellings, over 100,000 were classified as *mucambos*, or patchwork shacks, in spite of impressive advances in public-housing construction.[106] It seems that nothing can quite match the fertility rates of people living on the borderline of starvation. Under the circumstances, it is hardly a surprise that many frustrated missionaries and social workers, who have done virtually nothing for birth control, have sought to join forces with Brazilian leftists. Both groups now advocate more revolution and less religion if the poor and meek are ever to inherit the earth.[107]

7.   Marginality and the Christian Mission

Favela man just happens to be the most visible expression of a national problem in social marginality. From the viewpoint of modern urban civilization, probably half of Brazil's population, urban and rural, could be classified as marginal to some degree. Marginal peoples are a mixture of several races, but possibly half of this group would be poor mulattoes and Negroes. As used here, the concept of social marginality is that employed by social anthropologists to analyze family disintegration, social tensions, or social statistics among subcultural groups caught between two or more conflicting cultural forces.[108] Marginal groups at best enter into a transitional relationship with an urban civilization developed and controlled by corporate groups. Unfortunately, as we have seen, urban marginality can become a self-perpetuating, *lumpenproletarian* way of life.

To be sure, in Brazil, as elsewhere in Latin America and the world, since the first cities many marginal people have become functional urbanites through employment opportunities, civic education, paternal adoption (godparentage for the servant class, for example), military service, missionary efforts, and the like. But swamped with migrant invasions, and lacking an open-employment, industrialized economy, most metropolitan cities in

Latin America are not prepared today to reach out and transform marginal folk into functional citizens.[109]

Most Brazilian and Latin American social scientists attribute urban problems more to social marginality than to ethnic cleavages, racial discrimination, or the heritage of slavery or serfdom. This focus also includes not only structural obstacles that serve to maintain a high degree of urban marginality, but also the regressive mores of displaced peasant cultures that seem to have little functional utility for penetrating socioeconomic institutions dominated by European-style, or better, Mediterranean-style, upper classes. In other words, urban integration of poverty folk, Afro-Brazilian or other, requires that they give up vestigial folkways and somehow acquire the social values and motivations of the dominant groups, including their stable conjugal-family organization. Otherwise, as Bastide and Fernandes have shown in two outstanding studies, the poor cannot compete for the social, economic, and educational opportunities offered by the industrial cities of Brazil.[110]

The persistence of vestigial folkways might best be illustrated by a consideration of religious behavior. Afro-fetish cults dating back to the colonial slave trade have always flourished in the poverty-stricken but picturesque cities of Old Brazil such as Salvador, Belem, and Recife, but now, because of internal migration, they also thrive in the peripheral slums of New Brazil, including the new federal capital of Brasilia. In Old Brazil Afro-fetichism is known as *candomble*. In Rio and São Paulo it is commonly called *macumba*, which can be traced to the Bantu tribes of the Congo and Angola, but a more general name throughout Brazil is *umbanda*. These cults occasionally sacrifice domestic animals in order to gain the favor of the gods. Spiritualism, mixed Catholic and African imagery, and hysterical, hypnotic, or ecstatic seizures, is the essence of this religious behavior. To a lesser extent the *caboclo* cults, a mixture of Indian with Catholic, and some African symbolism, are found also in the southern metropolises. Almost all the practitioners of these cults consider themselves to be *Catolicos*.[111] Here one would have another intriguing chapter in Brazilian "mythology."

Brazil, whose population is over 90 percent Catholic, in the nominal sense, has presently about one priest for every 8,000 people, compared to one for every 5,000 in Spanish America, and one to every 800 or 900 in the United States and Europe. As in the past, about half of Brazil's clergy are presently non-Brazilians.[112] It seems true that priests and Protestant evangelists, together with social workers, Peace Corpsmen, and sundry volunteers laboring in urban slums and rural villages, have improved living standards and health conditions for some people, but, give or take a few million converts over the years, Christian evangelism after four hundred years is still fighting a losing battle against aboriginal customs, reinforced by the population boom in marginal Brazil. In recent years Afro-Brazilian cults have gone public in New Brazil, and they now seem as accepted as Mardi Gras. Leonard Greenwood, staff writer for the *Los Angeles Times* (4 January 1970), described the bizarre New Year's scene in the world's largest Catholic country:

> Along the beaches of sophisticated Rio de Janeiro, the night is lit by the flow from thousands of sacrificial candles. Seven hundred miles inland, the country around the world's most modern capital, Brasilia, throbs with the beat of the ceremonial drums of Africa. Throughout the vastness of Brazil, people sometimes so poor their children's stomach are distended from hunger offer feasts of chickens, goats, or hearts, and wine. It is the last night of the old year, the beginning of the new. It is time to propitiate the gods. . . .
>
> Millions go down to the beach. . . . Richly dressed old ladies, laden with jewelry, and young blonde jetsetters kneel in the sand before their candles, rubbing shoulders with the poor people of the favelas. . . . Young white men in hand-tailored suits join in the circles around the sand-sculptured altars and chant, sway and clap their hands in rhythm with the old black women who are the direct descendants of Brazil's African slaves. . . .

Today, although *umbanda* still has its strongest roots among the poor and the black, it has thousands of adherents among the white and wealthy. . . . Estimates put the number of true believers as high as 20 million.

The above estimate may be an exaggeration of what is in part a fashion, like astrology; nevertheless, according to Roger Bastide and others, fetichism and occultism brought in fragmented form from Africa have, together with other syncretic beliefs, the therapeutic function of aiding the disinherited in their struggle against disease, spiritual poverty, and lack of cultural identity.[113] Perhaps. But the question arises: Does the vigorous spread of Afro-spiritualism also pose a significant obstacle to metropolitan assimilation of poverty cultures? Concerning a similar phenomenon in Indo-Mexico, one anthropologist suggested that perhaps folk religion can retard the spread of formal education, encourage male physical superiority and independence, female docility and fertility, and prevent the growth of civil and institutional bonds to replace the decaying village mores and the rudimentary kinship systems of child care.[114]

Who these days blames folkways for sustaining poverty cultures? And for the frustration of "social democracy"? Finding that most mulattoes and blacks are at the bottom of the social ladder and the Euro-Brazilians are the top dogs, especially in the metropolises, Florestan Fernandes reached the rather expected conclusion that a competitive socioeconomic system does not guarantee a democratic society, especially if a little racial prejudice serves to harden class lines.[115] Other writers, like Octávio Ianni, Fernando A. Cardoso, Caio Prado, Jr., and Ruy Faco, blame either feudal Brazil or capitalist Brazil for the immobility and exploitation of marginal folk.

8.   *Government Action*

Brazil has made an impressive beginning on a national system of social insurance that provides various medical, retirement, and disability benefits for the employee and his family. Thus far, however, only government and company employees have been uniformly covered. In 1968 the system reached but 27 million out of some 90 million people.[116]

As in several Latin American countries, Uruguay and Argentina, for example, social insurance in Brazil includes some pronatalist family allowances. The first such law, passed in 1941, provided that the federal government would pay a small subsidy, *abono familiar*, to low-income employees who had six or more legally recognized children under the age of eighteen.[117] Later an income surtax was levied on single employees and childless couples. The purpose of such laws was to help populate Brazil, then considered the highest national duty, and also to encourage regular employment and stable family life.[118] In January 1969 the monthly allowance was scarcely equal to one dollar per child.[119] Even so the large-family subsidy does not cover the agricultural workers, especially the peasantry, nor workers in thousands of small shops and industries in the interior. The semiemployed or unemployed *lumpenproletariat* of the *favelas* are automatically disqualified as transient workers living in common-law relationships, and only rarely are domestics covered.[120] And if one excepts services given gratis, such as immunization, handouts, and vocational training, then most of Brazil's marginal population is outside the family-protection program initiated by Vargas in the 1930s.

It is evident that Brazil has nothing like the Aid to Dependent Children program of the United States, which provides family allowances, medicare, food stamps or surplus food commodities, and day-care centers, for precisely those groups who lack or shun steady employment and tend to ignore contract marriage. The North American ADC program, which was serving over 11 million children in January 1973, more than two-thirds of them from Negro, Puerto Rican, Chicano, and Indian folk cultures, would appear fantastically generous to Afro-Brazilian poverty groups. Where else in the New World could a peasant woman receive $150 to $800 a month (depending on the state) in cash, health, and food services for producing six or seven "abandoned" children?

In view of Brazil's slum problems, Dr. Mario Altenfelder, president of Brazil's National Foundation of Child Welfare, has recommended family allowances in order to keep poverty mothers at home with their offspring, in the belief that a subsidy would fortify the decaying slum family and relieve pressure on Brazil's few child-care institutions, which are overloaded with Afro-Brazilian children.[121] It is characteristic that the National Foundation must seek help from UNICEF and other outside sources to start a fund for this purpose. If Brazil were to initiate, by grace of international philanthropy, or by some new tax revenue, a mass program of home aid, mainly for Afro-Brazilian marginal groups, the question then becomes: Would such a program repeat the sad experience of the ADC system of the United States whereby slum mothers, instead of being moved into the main current of national society, would be subsidized to stay at home in the depths of a displaced peasant culture, and breed promiscuously with roving menfolk, their children repeating the cycle?

Given the fact that many Afro-Brazilians are poor, disorganized, and outside a social insurance system that is linked to steady employment in corporate entities, it is understandable that many kinds of exploitation or discrimination cannot be remedied by laws. The imperial Constitution of 1824 established the principle that all citizens were eligible for employment in the public service. The first republican Constitution of 1891 declared that "all shall be equal in the eyes of the law." The Constitution of 1934 stated that "there shall be no privilege, or distinction in respect of birth, sex, race, occupation . . . social class, religious belief, or political views." Article 121 provided that "labor legislation shall comply with the principles of social equality." The constitutions of 1937 and 1946 omitted reference to race and class but repeated other egalitarian provisions.[122]

However, abstract guarantees of equality have not reduced the day-to-day problems of racial discrimination. The First National Congress of Brazilian Negroes, held in São Paulo in 1945, recommended laws against color prejudice, especially in hiring practices.[123] In July 1951 the Brazilian parliament, which then had no Negro members, passed the Afonso Arinas law, which made acts of racial discrimination in employment and education a penal offense.[124] Since that date some types of government employment have been more fully opened to educated Afro-Brazilians. As we have seen, there are still complaints of discrimination against qualified blacks.[125] But, again, it bears repeating that the more urgent question is how to protect the civil rights of the *lumpenproletariat*.

It is the familiar story of unskilled labor exceeding demand. The national minimum wage of about $25 a month and child-protection codes are rarely enforced.[126] Afro-Brazilian children, and others, are seen throughout Brazil employed in menial tasks, and apprentices find protection only in larger firms. Since child labor is often needed to support female-headed families, nowhere can this form of labor exploitation be rigidly suppressed.

The present conservative regime has expressed serious concern about the victims of poverty and family disorganization. Speaking before the Brazilian Chamber of Deputies on 14 September 1967, the head of the Brazilian Legion of Assistance, Yolanda Costa e Silva, wife of then-President of Brazil, made the frank admission: "Article 167 of the Constitution declares that the law will establish assistance for mothers, children, and adolescents, but such assistance is yet to be organized in this country."[127] How much needs to be done is also suggested by a survey of Afro-Brazilian slum poverty that bears the significant title: "The Unwed Mother: An Old Brazilian Problem." The authoress, Teresa Barros, made this harsh assessment: "Help for the unwed mothers in Brazil is almost a myth . . . and there are no statistics available."[128]

By any statistical estimates available, the Conservative Revolution faces dismal problems in underdevelopment. According to one estimate, in 1968 some 45 percent of the population received a per capita annual income of around $100 whereas the United Nations considers that a family with a per capita income under $500 is living in a "precarious situation."[129] The Brazilian Legion of Assistance estimated that of the 3 million or more babies added annually to the national population, more than two-thirds will suffer malnutrition.[130] *Favela* children with swollen bellies have, in fact, been compared to "starving Biafrans."

Brazil, as a "developing country," receives some financial and technical aid for social programs from international agencies, most of them U.S.-funded. These include UNICEF, UNESCO, FAO, PAHO/WHO, Alliance for Progress, the U.N. Special Fund, the World Bank, the Inter-American Development Bank, the Peace Corps, and the Partners of the Americas Program. Brazil also receives help from over eighty American philanthropies, including the Rockefeller, Ford, Guggenheim, and Kellogg foundations, U.S. Catholic Relief via *Caritas Brasileira*, and from many medical missionary groups such as the Seventh Day Adventists. European philanthropies are also deeply involved.[131] The truth is, said Senhora Costa e Silva, that Brazil has to accept help from friendly countries, but "we should not overlook the possible collapse of this kind of help on which, sad to say, so many of our programs depend." Must we believe, she asked, that this immense territory of Brazil with its inexhaustible resources and great people cannot find the solution to her own problems?[132]

All things considered, probably Brazil has never had a more efficient government than the Conservative Revolution inaugurated in 1964. Generals have ruled Brazil for nearly a decade, but, as Lewis Beman pointed out, the generals have brushed aside inept and nepotistic politicians and given important government agencies to a band of young, innovative, and dedicated technocrats who enjoy unusual autonomy in promoting national development. They are adept at pulling off a *jeito*, a clever way of getting around an obstacle.[133] The ultimate goal of this technocratic government is to solve Brazil's social and political problems, first, by creating general economic prosperity leading to full and remunerative employment, and second, by creating the taxing, funding, and organizational power to carry economic development and social services to all Brazilians.[134]

As indicated earlier, the government is seeking to draw off the northeastern poverty migration into expanded industrial projects and into areas adjacent to the trans-Amazonian highway and colonization program.[135] Not since the Vargas regime has the federative government established such an alphabet soup of planning agencies, most of which have strong technical direction and solid funding, and most of which are designed to benefit marginal Brazilians. Some examples are FUNRURAL, a social insurance plan for rural laborers; MOBRAL, a frontal attack on some 15 to 20 million illiterate adults started in 1970 that has already established thousands of teaching units;[136] and COHAB, a program that builds cheap prefabricated housing costing about $10 per month on a 20-to-30-year payment plan. This slum-clearance program has had considerable success, although many *lumpenproletarians* resist formal commitments of any kind, and others cannot scrape up $10 a month.

Efforts made in behalf of public education and vocational training are a special matter of pride to Brazil's politico-military leaders. President Medici has stated that "never in our history has so much been invested in education with so many progressive results."[137] For the first time a serious start has been made on a universal, free public education program (as provided by a major reform law of December 1961). The percentage of children, ages seven through eleven, starting primary school has been raised from 79 percent in 1960 to about 90 percent in 1970. The percentage of students, ages fifteen to eighteen starting secondary school was raised from about 10 percent in 1960 to 30 percent in 1970. The number of university students has been increased from only 93,000 in 1960 to 417,000 in 1971, with a goal of 650,000 by 1973.[138]

The fact is, however, that few children from poverty cultures, including Afro-Brazilians, rarely finish primary school. Some may later attend vocational schools or apprenticeship programs. In the past marginal blacks have made little use of vocational schools, and few ever finished secondary school, or sought a university fellowship.[139] Today, it would seem, there are more opportunities for marginal Brazilians than ever before.

If the Conservative Revolution's attempts to reduce marginal-

ity are to succeed, the planners must somehow avoid the investment patterns of other New World welfare states: limited resources spread humanely but thinly in all directions at once;
much rhetoric about preventive measures but, in fact, preoccupation with remedial measures; and always priority given to health
measures. For nearly forty years Brazilian governments, beginning with Getulio, have been pursuing the illusion that medical
care and a dash of literacy carried to the urban slums and rural
areas would somehow fortify the family, slow the peasant exodus,
increase economic productivity, and spark the magic "multiplier
effects" of bourgeois civilization.[140] Actually, Brazil's "rural
slums" have run parallel to such superficial efforts.

It is not, of course, that Brazil lacks people. In 1940 the nation
had a population of 41 million; in 1960 the count was 72 million.
In 1970 Brazil reached a population of nearly 94 million. The
number of births per thousand is about 43, compared to 18 per
thousand in the United States, and 23 per thousand in Argentina.
The 1970 census suggests a slight decline in fertility, but whether
census figures can be trusted or not, it seems likely that the
population will double in 25 years or less. At present about 52
percent of the population is under twenty years of age.[141]
Moreover, about half of the children are the offspring of consensual unions Child-welfare agencies are overloaded with abandoned children.[142] This "sloughing off" of unwanted children is
a primitive form of birth control, and adoption agencies are at a
loss to place them, especially if they are black.

Meanwhile, the present conservative government is still acting
on pronatalist premises: Brazil is not overpopulated; it is simply
that population is badly distributed over an immensely rich territory. Such assumptions seem to be another variation of "national mythology." The government, however, does not oppose
private birth-control efforts.[143]

9.   *Political Activism?*

Some reformers and some students of race relations in Brazil believe that the poor blacks need special help. They point out that the Brazilian government never established anything like a Freedman's Bureau to help former slaves, and that corporate philanthropies have never made a special cause of the Negro in Brazil as they have in the United States.[144] On the other hand, Brazil's black leaders have initiated, from time to time, in the southern cities various self-help organizations. But the organizers of these mutual-aid fraternities and civil rights associations are usually middle- and upper-class mulattoes, and some *prêtos*, who already consider themselves assimilated, perhaps for several generations, into the dominant culture. What they want is to remove the last obstructions to complete social equality and to full acceptance by the upper classes.[145] Most of these movements have been sporadic, nonmilitant, and short-lived. Maybe this is because Brazil's racial democracy really works.

Whether needed or not, Brazil has nothing like the North American Negro's National Association for the Advancement of Colored Peoples, or the Urban Coalition. The Frente Negra Brasileira founded in São Paulo in 1931 as a nationwide movement is now defunct. More recently, some Afro-Brazilian leaders have actually called for a national service to protect the Negro like Brazil's National Indian Service. Others have demanded militant black organizations on the model of those in the United States. But as Degler has said, the Conservative Revolution is not about to allow a Brazilian version of the Panteras Negras, or Black Liberation, for that matter.[146]

Moreover, as Degler noted, miscegenation has practically erased the color line and, in effect, created a "mulatto escape hatch" that works both for and against the advancement of Brazil's colored population.[147] Persons of Afro-Brazilian descent accepted as *brancos* are not forced to identify with the problems of the lower-class blacks, as in the United States where caste rules still prevail. Yet this also means that Brazil's poor blacks and mulattoes lack effective ethnic leadership.

According to Dzidzienyo, one cannot expect people of color who have been accepted into Brazil's middle and upper classes as "honorary whites" to upset the established pattern of race relations. Rather they are expected to testify to the efficacy of racial democracy.[148] But perhaps successful Afro-Brazilians are simply good Brazilians who strive to uphold the national traditions of racial harmony and racial integration. Besides, most Brazilians seem to realize that racial discrimination is not the basic cause of Brazil's social problems.

Nevertheless, there are signs of ferment. In May of 1968 a small group of Negro students at the University of São Paulo organized a movement to promote the advancement of poverty-stricken Afro-Brazilians. This organization, the first of its kind, is patterned after black organizations in U.S. universities.[149] The outlook is that as the government rapidly increases university enrollment, the universities will become increasingly radicalized, and the problems of Afro-Brazilians will become more of a political issue.

Thus far Brazil's poor blacks have not been organized politically (for one thing, only literate people over eighteen are allowed to vote), nor have political agitators openly appealed to racism or color consciousness; but Brazilian Marxists can, as in Cuba, easily identify the protean elements of a class struggle, namely, dark-skinned proletariat versus exploiting white-skinned "establishment" and allied foreign investors.

Since 1964 the conservatives have been running a race against the incubus of a radical revolution. On the one hand, the government has strived to moralize society, unify the country, uplift the *lumpenproletariat* through planned development, and, on the other hand, it has outlawed dissenting political parties, expelled Marxist revolutionaries, and radical priests, and silenced leftist college professors.[150] In the meantime, it is likely that urbanization and industrialization will accentuate feelings of racial sensitivity and self-consciousness among Afro-Brazilians. Formerly the lower classes who lived on rural estates, or as backland squatters, or as picturesque urban poverty folk, accepted as inevitable paternalism and low social status, as similar groups did in the Old South of the United States. But for the ambitious migrant or for the middle-class types who seek new opportunities in industrial cities, urbanization can intensify, as Bastide has warned, feelings of inferiority, prejudice, and discrimination, especially when Negroes first become competitors with the whites, or with mulatto middle groups.[151]

Similarly, Wagley has observed that if easygoing, traditional Brazil continues to modernize, then social values must change, and Brazil cannot then escape Western racial and class concepts that "are entering Brazil along with industrial . . . improvements."[152] Metall and Paranhos de Silva expressed concern that social grievances may become fused with imported political ideologies and the demands of poor blacks, and thereby threaten the presumed unity of Brazilian society. Such are some perspectives on racial innocence in Brazil.[153]

Perhaps Andrew Marshall has offered the proper perspective. When Brazil is held up as a shining example of a nation that has solved her racial problem, this British observer replies: "She has done no such thing for the simple reason that the problem has never arisen," If it does arise, said Marshall, writing in 1966, then it will be part of a much broader conflict, namely, the revolt of the miserable "have-nots," in which Negro elements just happen to be the most numerous.[154]

Notes

[1] The English editions are, respectively, *The Masters and the Slaves: A Study in the Development of Brazilian Civilization* (New York, 1946, and later editions); and *The Mansions and the Shanties: The Making of Modern Brazil* (New York, 1963). Other relevant works by Freyre are *Brazil: An Interpretation* (New York, 1945), republished as *New World in the Tropics: The Culture of Modern Brazil* (New York, 1959); "The Brazilian Melting Pot," *The Atlantic Monthly*, February, 1946, pp. 104-108; *Nordeste* (Rio de Janeiro, 1937); *Ordem e Progresso*, 2 vols. (Rio de Janeiro, 1959), and by Freyre and others, *Novos estudos Afro-Brasileiros* (Rio de Janeiro, 1937).

[2] For example, Freyre states that "Negroes are rapidly disappearing in

Brazil, merging into the white stock. . . . The position of ethnic minorities in terms of color or race has never been a major problem." *New World in the Tropics*, pp. 119, 157.

³The German scientist Karl Friedrich Philipp von Martius was the first to suggest racial amalgamation as a major theme in Brazilian history, in an essay published in 1844 by the Brazilian Institute of History and Geography under the title "Como se deve escrever a historia do Brasil." Martius also suggested that history should be used to promote love of country and civic virtues. According to E. Bradford Burns, a century would pass before a Brazilian, namely Freyre, would take up Martius' grand plan. See Burns, *Nationalism in Brazil: A Historical Survey* (New York, 1968), pp. 41-43; and Martius' essay in English translation in Burns, ed., *Perspectives on Brazilian History* (New York, 1967), pp. 21-42.

⁴Gabriela de Beer, *José Vasconcelos and His World* (New York, 1966), pp. 90-125.

⁵Degler, *Neither Black nor White: Slavery and Race Relations in Brazil and the United States* (New York, 1971), pp. 96-97.

⁶Luis A. Costa Pinto, *O Negro no Rio de Janeiro: Relacôes de raças numa sociedade em mudança* (São Paulo, 1953), pp. 330-331. The author also suggests in this work that behind defensive attitudes about color is a fear of admitting the importance of color in Brazilian society.

⁷Tannenbaum, *Slave and Citizen: The Negro in the Americas* (New York, 1946, and later editions); and Elkins, *Slavery, A Problem in American Institutional and Intellectual Life* (Chicago, 1959). Here one might note that in a chapter on "Race" in *Ten Keys to Latin America* (New York, 1960), Tannenbaum reflects on contemporary race relations and qualifies somewhat the optimistic tone of *Slave and Citizen*.

⁸See Degler's brief discussion of Tannenbaum-Elkins interpretations and their acceptance or rejection by other writers such as Daniel P. Moynihan, Arnold Sio, David B. Davis, and Herbert Klein, in *Neither Black nor White*, pp. 19-21.

⁹For example, Oracy Nogueira was carrying on empirical research on discrimination in employment practices in São Paulo as early as 1941, according to Richard M. Morse, "The Negro in São Paulo, Brazil," *Journal of Negro History* 38 (July 1953): 302-303. Also Emilio Willems, another contributor to modern sociology in Brazil, was questioning defensive behavior about racial equality in the 1940s; see "Race Attitudes in Brazil," *American Journal of Sociology* 54 (March 1949): 402-408. In this

article Willems described several studies based on questionnaire techniques.

[10]A major research project on racial prejudice in São Paulo headed by Bastide and Fernandes produced or inspired a series of important studies such as Bastide and Fernandes, *Brancos e Negros em São Paulo* (São Paulo, 1955); Fernandes, *A integração do Negro na sociedade de classes*, 2 vols. (São Paulo, 1964); Octávio Ianni, *As metamorfoses do escravo* (São Paulo, 1962); Fernando H. Cardoso, *Capitalismo e escravidão: O Negro na sociedade escravocrata do Rio Grande do Sul* (São Paulo, 1962); Cardoso and Ianni, *Côr e mobilidade em Florianopolis* (São Paulo, 1960); and Oracy Nogueira, "Skin Color and Social Class," in Vera Rubin, ed., *Plantation Systems in the New World* (Washington, 1959), pp. 164-179. As Ianni pointed out, this series owes much to UNESCO, which originally initiated special research projects on race relations in several parts of the world. See Ianni, "Research and Race Relations in Brazil," in Magnus Mörner, *Race and Class in Latin America* (New York, 1970), pp. 256-278.

[11]Some works by this group are Costa Pinto, *O Negro no Rio de Janeiro* (São Paulo, 1952); Willems, *Cunha: Tradição e transição em uma cultura rural do Brasil* (São Paulo, 1947); Azevedo, *As elites de côr: um estudo de ascensão social* (São Paulo, 1955), a study also inspired by the São Paulo research project on race relations in Brazil; also by Azevedo, *Cultura e situação racial no Brasil* (Rio de Janeiro, 1966); and Guerreiro Ramos, *Introdução crítica a sociologia brasileira* (Rio de Janeiro, 1967).

[12]Wagley, Harris, Hutchinson, and Zimmerman were the principal contributors to a UNESCO-sponsored study on *Race and Class in Rural Brazil* (Paris, 1952). Other significant works by these social anthropologists are Wagley, *An Introduction to Brazil* (New York, 1963; rev. ed., 1971); Harris, *Town and Country in Brazil* (New York, 1956); and Hutchinson, *Village and Plantation Life in Northeastern Brazil* (Seattle, Wash., 1957).

[13]"O Brazileiro e racista," *O Cruzeiro* 30 November 1968, p. 101.

[14]"80 anos de abolição," special edition (175 pp.) of *Cadernos Brasileiros*, Instituto Latino Americano de Relacões Internacionais, Rio de Janeiro, 10 (May-June 1968): 4.

[15]Bastide, "The Development of Race Relations in Brazil," in Guy Hunter, ed., *Industrialization and Race Relations: A Symposium* (London, 1965), pp. 23-24.

[16]Frazier, "A Comparison of Negro-White Relations in Brazil and in the United States" (1944), in *On Race Relations: Selected Writings*, edited

with introduction by G. Franklin Edwards (Chicago, 1968), pp. 82-102. See also Frazier, "The Negro Family in Bahia, Brazil," *American Sociological Review* 7 (August 1942): 465-478.

[17]Dzidzienyo, *The Position of Blacks in Brazilian Society*, published by the Minority Rights Group (London, 1971), pp. 5-6. The author was a research fellow at the Institute of Race Relations in London.

[18]Fernandes, "Mas alla de la pobreza; el negro y el mulato en Brasil," *Revista Mexicana de Sociologia* 33 (April-June 1971): 253-270.

[19]Garcia-Zamor, "Social Mobility of Negroes in Brazil," *Journal of Inter-American Studies and World Affairs* 12 (April 1970): 242.

[20]Wagley, *An Introduction to Brazil* (1971), p. 125.

[21]See note 12 and Pierson, *Negroes in Brazil* (1942).

[22]Especially *Brancos e Negros em São Paulo* (1955) by Bastide and Fernandes; and *A integração do Negro na sociedade de classes* (1964) by Fernandes. See also note 10.

[23]"80 anos de abolição," p. 6; also, Nascimento, et al., *O Negro revoltado* (Rio de Janeiro, 1968).

[24]"O Brasileiro e racista," *O Cruzeiro*, 30 November 1968, p. 102.

[25]R. A. Metall and M. Paranhos de Silva, "Equality of Opportunity in a Multiracial Society: Brazil," *International Labour Review* 93 (January-June 1966): 483.

[26]Pierson, *Negroes in Brazil*, pp. 349-350.

[27]Azevedo, *As elites de côr*, pp. 38-44.

[28]Nogueira, "Preconceito racial de marca e preconceito racial de origem," *Anais do XXXI Congreso International de Americanistas* (São Paulo, 1955), 1: 430-431; cited by Metall and Paranhos de Silva, "Equality of Opportunity," p. 500. Willems reached the same conclusion, "Race Attitudes in Brazil," p. 408.

[29]Wagley, *An Introduction to Brazil* (1971), p. 133.

[30]Pierson, *Negroes in Brazil*, p. 349.

[31]For a discussion of upward mobility in Brazil since World War I, see Rollie E. Poppino, *Brazil: The Land and the People* (New York, 1968), pp. 303-317.

[32]Claudio Kuck, "A industria de emprego," *O Cruzeiro* 40 (28 December 1968): 60-61.

[33]*Ibid.*, p. 61.

[34]For example, Nice Rissone, "Quem libertou a mulher negra," in "80 anos de abolição," pp. 139-146; or Garcia-Zamor, "Social Mobility of Negroes in Brazil," pp. 249-250.

[35]Wagley, *An Introduction to Brazil* (1971), p. 133.

[36]Poppino, *Brazil*, pp. 90-93.

[37]For a summary view of immigration to Brazil and its contribution to economic development, see T. Lynn Smith, *Brazil: People and Institutions*, rev. ed. (Baton Rouge, La., 1963, and 1972), Chapter 8.

[38]On internal migration, see Smith, *ibid.*, Chapter 9.

[39]Kathleen Burke, "And the Boom Goes On," *Brazilian Business* 52 (September 1972): 69.

[40]Estimates provided by Brazilian Embassy, Washington, D.C., 9 January 1973.

[41]See note 11.

[42]Burke, "And the Boom Goes On," pp. 69-70.

[43]Ianni, "Research on Race Relations," p. 270.

[44]F. Fernandes, "Immigration and Race Relations in São Paulo," in Mörner, ed., *Race and Class in Latin America*, pp. 125-127; and Frazier on the weaknesses of "The Negro Family in Bahia," pp. 465-478.

[45]Ianni, "La formación del proletariado rural en el Brasil," *Revista Mexicana de Sociología* 33 (April-June 1971): 475-488. See also Ianni, *As metamorfoses do escravo*; and Cardoso, *Capitalismo e escravidão*.

[46]Fernandes, "Immigration and Race Relations," pp. 134-135.

[47]*Ibid.*

[48]Ramos, *The Negro in Brazil*, trans. Richard Pattee, originally published in 1939 (Washington, 1959), pp. 91-103.

[49]Fernandes, "Mobilidade social e relações sociais," in "80 anos de abolição," p. 55.

[50]Ramos, *The Negro in Brazil*, pp. 91-103.

[51]Azevedo, *As elites de côr*, pp. 38 ff. But Hutchinson in the provincial town of Villa Recôncavo found a marked concern among upper-class *fazendeiros* and sugar-mill owners to maintain their "Portuguese purity" through endogamic marriage, *Village and Plantation Life in Northeastern Brazil*, p. 100.

[52]Fernandes, "Immigration and Race Relations," p. 141.

[53]Azevedo, *Social Change in Brazil* (Gainesville, Fla., 1963), pp. 1, 56.

[54]*Ibid.*, pp. xiii-ix.

[55]Willems, "The Structure of the Brazilian Family," *Social Forces* 30 (1953): 339-345. "The Brazilian system, as that of Latin America, is largely family-ridden" is the conclusion of this article.

[56]Candido, "The Brazilian Family," in *Brazil: Portrait of Half a*

Continent, ed. T. L. Smith and Alexander Marchant (New York, 1951), p. 306.

[57] Wagley, *An Introduction to Brazil* (1971), p. 181.

[58] According to Public Information Office, Brazilian Embassy, Washington, D.C., 9 January 1973.

[59] Lambert, *Os dois Brasis* (Rio de Janeiro, 1959), pp. 86-88.

[60] Herring, *A History of Latin America*, rev. ed. (New York, 1968), pp. 825-826.

[61] Wagley, *An Introduction to Brazil* (1963), p. 143.

[62] Garcia-Zamor, "Social Mobility of Negroes," p. 244.

[63] Marshall, *Brazil* (New York, 1966), p. 121.

[64] For a discussion of some objectives of immigration policy as expressed in legislation, see J. Fernando Carneiro, *Imigração e colonização no Brasil* (Rio de Janeiro, 1950).

[65] Smith, *Brazil* (1972), p. 73. And on p. 187 of the 1946 edition.

[66] For various estimates, see Costa Pinto, *Negro no Rio de Janeiro*, Chapter 4; *Jornal do Brasil*, 12 May 1968; and Degler, *Neither Black nor White*, pp. 144-147, 194.

[67] Smith, *Brazil* (1972), pp. 73-74. As for color dominance, geneticists generally concur that the complexities of human reproduction obscure the genetic origins of physical and mental traits, but that, nevertheless, Mendel's laws still hold for humans. If there were but one unmixed black and one unmixed white to start the human race, and all progeny survived, the emergence of a dominant and a recessive color characteristic would be as visible as Mendel's experiments with sweet peas. Successive generations would show, if crossbreeding were balanced, a gradual and geometric dominance of dark pigment over light, according to Dr. A. Chovnick, geneticist, and Joseph Speyer, cell biologist, at the University of Connecticut. See also E. W. Sinnott, L. C. Dunn, and T. Dobzhansky, *Principles of Genetics*, 4th ed. (New York, 1950).

[68] Bastide, "Dusky Venus, Black Apollo," *Race* 3 (November 1968): 10-18.

[69] Smith, *Brazil* (1972), pp. 213, 634; and *Brazil*, a handbook published by Ministerio das Relações Exteriores (Brasilia, 1969), pp. 222-227.

[70] *Tabulações avançadas do censo demografico VIII recenseamento geral—1970. Resultados prelinares.* Published by Fundação IBGE (Rio de Janeiro, 1971).

[71] Garcia-Zamor, "Social Mobility of Negroes," p. 246.

[72] Azevedo, *Social Change in Brazil*, p. 56; Hutchinson, *Village and Plantation Life*, p. 100.

[73] Azevedo, *Cultura e situação racial no Brasil*, p. 5. It is acceptable, said René Ribeiro, for a dark-skinned man of superior social or economic status to marry a light-skinned woman of lower status, *Religião e relações raciais* (Rio de Janeiro, 1956), pp. 108-110.

[74] See note 23.

[75] Amado's *Gabriela, cravo e canela*, which has gone through several editions, was first published in 1958.

[76] Bastide, "Dusky Venus," p. 18.

[77] Dzidzienyo, *The Position of Blacks in Brazilian Society*, p. 9.

[78] Costa Pinto, *Negro no Rio de Janeiro*, p. 214.

[79] Dzidzienyo, *The Position of Blacks*, pp. 9-10.

[80] Degler, *Neither Black nor White*, p. 188.

[81] See Mörner's essay on *Race Mixture in Latin America* (Boston, 1967).

[82] Smith, *Brazil* (1946), p. 64.

[83] Azevedo, *Cultura e situação racial no Brasil*.

[84] Smith, *Brazil* (1972), p. 639.

[85] Bastide, "The Development of Race Relations," pp. 19-20.

[86] Garcia-Zamor, "Social Mobility of Negroes," pp. 253-254.

[87] See "80 anos de abolição."

[88] See Freyre's works in note 1.

[89] Poppino, *Brazil*, p. 171; and Curtin, *The Atlantic Slave Trade: A Census* (Madison, Wis., 1969), pp. 47-49.

[90] João Batista de Vasconcelos Torres, *Movimentos migratorios das populações rurais brasileiras* (Rio de Janeiro, 1957).

[91] Smith, *Brazil*, Chapters 9 and 13; José Francisco de Camargo, *Exodo rural no Brasil: formas, causas e conseqencias economicos principais* (Rio de Janeiro, 1960); and Manuel Diegues Jr., "Internal Migration in Brazil," *World Population Conference*, 1965, Vol. 4 (New York, 1967).

[92] See also Castro, *Documento do Nordeste*, 3d ed. (São Paulo, 1965); and *Geografia da fome* (Rio de Janeiro, 1946).

[93] Irving L. Horowitz, *Revolution in Brazil: Politics and Society in a Developing Nation* (New York, 1964), p. 289.

[94] *First National Development Plan 1972/74*, IBGE Foundation (November 1971), p. 61.

[95] "El escuadrón de la muerte," *Visión*, 14 February 1969, pp. 50-51.

[96] "Familia e menor internada no estado da Guanabara, estudo de

4,000 cases" (mimeograph, 83 pp.), Centro de Planejamento Social (CEPS) - PUC - R. J. (Rio de Janeiro, 1966), pp. 4-24.

[97]Poppino, *Brazil*, p. 302.

[98]See for example J. Mayone Stycos, *Family and Fertility in Puerto Rico: A Study of the Lower Income Groups* (New York, 1955); or Arthur F. Corwin, *Contemporary Mexican Attitudes Toward Population, Poverty, and Public Opinion* (Gainesville, Fla., 1963).

[99]An English edition of Carolina's book is entitled *Child of the Dark* (New York, 1962).

[100]*Ibid.*, p. 96.

[101]*Informe nacional do Brasil*. Anexo I. "Teses presentadas no seminario sobre o problema do menor abandonado," Minas Gerais, 1959 (typewritten report), 46 pp. Anexo 2. "A criança abandonada," . . . contribucao ao XI Congreso Pan Americano da Criança, Bogota, Novembre 1959 (typed), 9 pp., firmado, Mariana Agostini de Villalba Alvin, et al.

[102]According to questionnaire replies from officials of the Fundação Nacional do Bem-Estar do Menor, 2 June 1969.

[103]Interview with Dr. Mario Altenfelder, Fundação Nacional do Bem-Estar do Menor, 22 December 1968.

[104]According to interviews with Edson Seda de Moraes, 18-19 December 1968, Planejamento, Fundação Nacional do Bem-Estar do Menor, and with public information officers, Brazilian Embassy, Washington, D.C., 6 January 1973.

[105]Wilson, "Recife, Land of Despair," *Pensacola Journal* 14 September 1972.

[106]Wilson, "Recife, Land of Despair."

[107]For example, the political action proposals of French priest Paul Gallet (pseudonym), *Freedom to Starve* (Baltimore, Md., 1973).

[108]Some of the landmark literature on the concept of marginal man is as follows: Robert E. Park, "Human Migration and the Marginal Man," *American Journal of Sociology* 33 (1928): 881-893; Everett V. Stonequist, "The Problem of the Marginal Man," *American Journal of Sociology* 41 (1935): 1-12, and his *The Marginal Man* (New York, 1937). Some later refinements and critiques are Arnold W. Green, "A Reexamination of the Marginal Man Concept," *Social Forces* 25 (1947): 167-171; David I. Golovensky, "The Marginal Man Concept: An Analysis and Critique," *Social Forces* 30 (1952): 333-339; and Aaron Antovsky, "Towards a Refinement of the 'Marginal Man' Concept," *Social Forces* 36 (1956): 57-62.

[109]For broad historical perspectives on the civilizing role of the metropolis in Latin America, see Richard M. Morse, "Latin American Cities: Aspects of Function and Structure," *Comparative Studies in Society and History* 4 (1962): 473-493.

[110]Bastide and Fernandes, *Brancos e Negros em São Paulo*; Fernandes, *A integração do negro na sociedade de clases* (1964). Also, competitive advantages and disadvantages of ethnic and immigrant groups in a New World metropolis are described by Nathan Glazer and Daniel P. Moynihan, *Beyond the Melting Pot: The Negroes, Puerto Ricans, Jews, Italians, and Irish of New York City* (Cambridge, Mass., 1963).

[111]See Bastide's exhaustive study, *Les religions africaines au Brésil* (Paris, 1956); and introductory accounts by Arthur Ramos, *The Negro in Brazil*, pp. 91-103; and Wagley, *An Introduction to Brazil*, pp. 232-251.

[112]Azevedo, *Social Change in Brazil*, pp. 61-62; and A. G. Gustavo Perez and Francois Lepargneur, *O problema sacerdotal no Brazil* (Brussels, 1965).

[113]Bastide, *Les religiones africaines*; and Candido Procopio de Camargo, *Aspectos sociologicos do espiritismo em São Paulo* (Friburgo, 1961).

[114]For example, Norman D. Humphrey, "The Generic Folk Culture of Mexico," *Rural Sociology* 7 (1943): 364-377.

[115]Florestan Fernandes, "La persistencia del pasado," *Revista Mexicana de Sociología* 28 (1966): 787-811.

[116]Interview with Jaime de Moura e Silva, Legião Brasileira, 19, 23 December 1968.

[117]United States Department of Health, Education and Welfare, *Social Security Programs Throughout the World 1964* (Washington, 1964), pp. 16-17.

[118]Rubens Vaz de Costa, "Population and Development: The Brazilian Case," *Population Bulletin*, Population Reference Bureau, Washington, D.C., 25 (1969): 96. The author noted that Brazil's population policies have always been expansionist.

[119]Replies to questionnaire by Tomiko Tanaami, Planejamento, Fundação Nacional do Bem-Estar do Menor, 2 June 1969.

[120]Interviews with Brazilian Welfare employees in Rio and São Paulo, 18-23 December 1968.

[121]Interview with Dr. Altenfelder, Fundação Nacional do Bem-Estar do Menor, 22 December 1968.

[122]United Nations, *Yearbook on Human Rights for 1951* (1953), cited by Metall and Paranhos de Silva, "Equality of Opportunity," p. 494.

[123]Bastide and Fernandes, *Brancos e Negros em São Paulo*, p. 301.

[124]Metall and Paranhos de Silva, "Equality of Opportunity," p. 494.

[125]Claudio Kuck, "A industria de emprego," pp. 60-61.

[126]Information supplied by Jayme de Moura e Silva, Legião Brasileira da Assistencia, 19-20 December 1968.

[127]Legião Brasileira, *O problema da maternidade da infancia e da adolescencia no Brasil*, Relatorio de excelentissima Senhora Yolanda Barbosa da Costa e Silva, Presidente de Legião Brasileira da Assistência, a Commissão de Saude, da Camara dos deputados, 14 de setembro de 1967 (Brasilia, D.F.), pp. 17-21.

[128]Teresa Barros, "Mae solteira, um velho problema brasileiro," *O Cruzeiro*, 28 December 1968, pp. 102-103.

[129]*O problema de maternidade*, pp. 16-17.

[130]*Ibid.*, p. 17.

[131]Fundação Nacional do Bem-Estar do Menor, "Aspectos da politica do bem-estar no Brasil," ASPLAN (Rio de Janeiro, 1968), pp. 101-105.

[132]Legião Brasileira, *O problema da maternidade*, pp. 4, 6, 47. And *EQUIPE FNBEM*, Jornal Interno da Fundação do Bem-Estar do Menor, Rio de Janeiro, Ano 2, 2 December 1968.

[133]Beman, "How Brazilians Manage Their Boom," *Fortune*, December 1972, pp. 110-119.

[134]*First National Development Plan 1972/74*; and Public Information Office, Brazilian Embassy, Washington, D.C., 9 January 1973.

[135]Trans-Amazonian Highway, a report presented by the Ministry of Transportation to the VI World Meeting of the International Road Federation (Montreal, October 1970), p. 4; and H. J. Rosenbaum and W. G. Tyler, "Policy-Making for the Brazilian Amazon," *Journal of Inter-American Affairs and World Affairs* 13 (July-October 1971): 416-433.

[136]*Educação*, Revista do Ministerio de Educação e Cultura, Brasilia, 1 (July, September 1971): 119, 127.

[137]Editorial, *Cidades e Municipios* 5, No. 9 (1971): 38-39.

[138]Education statistics are from *Brasil*, Handbook of Ministerio das Relacoes Exteriores (1969), pp. 233-235; and Smith, *Brazil* (1972), pp. 714-715.

[139]Fernándes, "Mas alla de la pobreza," p. 262.

[140]See Hernan di Carvalho, *Sociologia da vida rural brasileira*.

[141]Smith, *Brazil* (1972), pp. 635-639; and Andrew Collver, *Birth Rates in Latin America: New Estimates of Historical Trends and Fluctuations* (Berkeley, Cal., 1965), pp. 26-28. *The Demographic Yearbook 1965* (New York: United Nations Statistical Office, 1966) gives a figure of 51 percent

for illiteracy in Brazil and 44 percent for illegitimacy. As to the latter figures, Brazilian welfare workers are generally inclined to think they are too low.

[142]"Familia e menor internado no estado da Guanabara," pp. 10-17, 38-40; also "Analise do problema do menor e diretrizes," Special Report prepared for Fundação Nacional do Bem-Estar do Menor, 1967.

[143]Subsidized by the International Planned Parenthood Federation, BEMFAM (Sociedade do Bem-Estar Familiar), a private group founded in 1965, operates birth control clinics and provides training in family planning. As of mid-1970, BEMFAM had established sixty clinics in Brazil's major cities. For a brief summary of private population control activities and demographic research in Brazil funded by U.S. private and public agencies, see Agency for International Development, *Population Program Assistance* (Washington: Office of Population, December 1971), pp. 143-144. See also, Walter Rodrigues, "Progress and Problems of Family Planning in Brazil," *Demography* 5, No. 2 (1968): 800-810.

[144]Degler, *Neither Black nor White*, pp. 272-273; Fernándes, *A integração do negro*, 1: 6; 2: 172-173; Garcia-Zamor, "Social Mobility of Negroes," pp. 252-253.

[145]Richard M. Morse pointed out that Negro associations have no interest in preserving Afro-Brazilian folkways since Negro leaders are already culturally assimilated but rather assail attitudes that make their members racially self-conscious, *From Community to Metropolis: A Biography of São Paulo* (Gainesville, Fla., 1958), p. 255.

It might also be noted that, except for a brief flirtation during the short-lived Quadros Administration in 1961, Brazilians have not looked to intimate relations with African countries.

[146]Degler, *Neither Black nor White*, pp. 174-185.

[147]*Ibid.*, pp. 178-182, 219-232, 271-281.

[148]Dzidzienyo, *The Position of Blacks*, p. 9.

[149]Garcia-Zamor, "Social Mobility of Negroes," p. 250.

[150]Michael Sieniawiski summarized the regime's war on smugglers, tax-evaders, immoral films, and corrupt government, "A New Puritanical Brazil," *San Francisco Chronicle*, 8 February 1969, p. 7.

[151]Bastide, "The Development of Race Relations," p. 25. Also, Harley R. Hammond, "Race, Social Mobility and Politics in Brazil," *Race* 4 (1963): 3-16.

[152]Wagley, ed., *Race and Class in Rural Brazil*, p. 165.

[153]Metall and Paranhos de Silva, "Equality of Opportunity," p. 504. Costa Pinto has made a similar observation: "There is a racial question in process of aggravation that will tend toward a crisis in the future," *O negro no Rio de Janeiro*, pp. 344-345.

[154]Marshall, *Brazil*, p. 120.

Index